THE CLASSICAL TRADITION IN SOCIOLOGY
THE AMERICAN TRADITION

THE CLASSICAL TRADITION IN SOCIOLOGY

THE AMERICAN TRADITION

VOLUME III

Edited by
JEFFREY ALEXANDER
RAYMOND BOUDON
MOHAMED CHERKAOUI

SAGE Publications
London • Thousand Oaks • New Delhi

Editorial arrangement © Jeffrey Alexander, Raymond Boudon, Mohamed Cherkaoui, 1997

First published 1997

All rights reserved. No part of this publication may be reproduced, stored in a retrieval system, transmitted or utilized in any form or by any means, electronic, mechanical, photocopying, recording or otherwise, without permission in writing from the Publishers.

Every effort has been made to trace all the copyright holders of the material reprinted herein, but if any have been inadvertently overlooked the publishers will be pleased to make the necessary arrangements at the first opportunity.

SAGE Publications Ltd
6 Bonhill Street
London EC2A 4PU

SAGE Publications Inc
2455 Teller Road
Thousand Oaks, California 91320

SAGE Publications India Pvt Ltd
32, M-Block Market
Greater Kailash
New Delhi 110 048

HM
22
.U5
C53
1997
v.3

British Library Cataloguing in Publication Data

A catalogue record for this book is available from the British Library

ISBN 0-7619-5325-6 (set of four volumes)

Library of Congress Cataloging in Publication data has been applied for

Typeset in Berthold Baskerville by The Bardwell Press, Oxford, England
Printed in Great Britain at the Cambridge University Press, Cambridge, England

CONTENTS

VOLUME III

AMERICAN SOCIOLOGY IN THE TWENTIETH CENTURY: FROM PRAGMATISM TO FUNCTIONALISM AND QUANTITATIVE SOCIOLOGY
(continued)

49. Small-Group Theory and Research *Robert F. Bales* 1
50. Bringing Men Back In *George C. Homans* 11
51. The Oversocialized Conception of Man in Modern Sociology *Dennis H. Wrong* 25
52. Deviant Behavior and Social Structure: Continuities in Social Theory *Robert Dubin* 40
53. The Curious Importance of Small Groups in American Sociology *Allan Silver* 66
54. The Authoritarian Personality *T. W. Adorno, Else Frankel-Brunswik, Daniel J. Levinson and R. Nevitt Sanford* 78
55. Some Types of Character and Society *David Riesman* 104
56. Contributions to the Theory of Reference Group Behavior *Robert K. Merton and Alice S. Kitt* 129
57. TVA and the Grassroots *Philip Selznick* 154
58. Democracy and Oligarchy in Trade Unions *Seymour Martin Lipset, Martin A. Trow and James S. Coleman* 176
59. The Dynamics of Bureaucracy *Peter Blau* 189
60. The Organization Man *William H. Whyte* 213
61. The Power Elite *C. Wright Mills* 248
62. C. Wright Mills *Ralph Miliband* 272
63. The Sociology of C. Wright Mills *Eugene V. Schneider* 278
64. The End of Ideology in the West *Daniel Bell* 285
65. Two Views of Mass Society *William Kornhauser* 298

AMERICAN SOCIOLOGY IN THE TWENTIETH CENTURY: RECENT TRENDS IN SOCIOLOGICAL THEORY

66. Social Differentiation and Organic Solidarity: *The Division of Labor* Revisited *Hans-Peter Müller* 313

67. Social Theory and Talcott Parsons in the 1980s
    David Sciulli and Dean Gerstein   326
68. The Role of Efficiency and Power in Explanations of
    Division of Labour   *Dietrich Rueschemeyer*   345
69. Evaluating the Model of Structural Differentiation in
    Relation to Educational Change in the Nineteenth Century
    Neil J. Smelser   363
70. Against Nostalgia: Talcott Parsons and a Sociology for the
    Modern World   *Robert J. Holton and Bryan S. Turner*   377

AMERICAN SOCIOLOGY IN THE TWENTIETH CENTURY

FROM PRAGMATISM TO FUNCTIONALISM AND QUANTITATIVE SOCIOLOGY
(continued)

49

Small-Group Theory and Research

Robert F. Bales

Certainly one of the important problems of any field of research is that of gathering together and keeping accessible to researchers the main body of relevant literature. The field of small-group research is currently in good condition in this respect – so good, happily, that I need not undertake any survey of the literature in this paper, except to indicate the main sources in which surveys can be found. It is interesting to note, however, that none of these main sources is more than five years old.

Cartwright and Zander[1] edited the first major compilation of articles, under the title *Group Dynamics: Research and Theory*, in 1953. A year later, Lindzey's *Handbook of Social Psychology*,[2] appeared. Among several relevant chapters in this book, those by H. H. Kelley and J. W. Thibault, on "Experimental Studies of Group Problem Solving and Process," and by H. W. Riecken and G. C. Homans, on "Psychological Aspects of Social Structure," are especially notable on substantive aspects. The Lindzey volume also contains two excellent surveys of the literature on methodology: a chapter on "Systematic Observational Techniques," by R. W. Heyns and Ronald Lippitt, and one on "Sociometric Measurement," by Lindzey and E. F. Borgatta. In 1954, Strodtbeck and Hare published an exhaustive bibliography of small-group research from 1900 through 1953[3] which helped to provide historical perspective on the field. Building on this groundwork, Hare, Borgatta, and Bales published a compilation of papers and a large annotated bibliography in 1955.[4] The bibliography of this work, in turn, formed the basis for a chapter in Gittler's *Review of Sociology*, by the same authors.[5] The latest extension of this work is a book, not yet published, by Hare, which will probably be entitled *Social Interaction, An Analysis of Behavior in Small Groups*. This book, I believe, represents the first attempt to write a rounded treatise on small groups based entirely on empirical studies. One should not review a book before it is published, of course, but it seems to me an encouraging sign of the maturation of the field that empirical studies exist in sufficient variety and depth to make such a venture possible.

Source: Leonard Broom, Leonard S. Cottrell and Robert K. Merton, *Sociology Today: Problems and Prospects*, (New York: Basic Books, 1959).

If I may make one further remark without trespassing on the territory of a reviewer, I am impressed by the number of studies that build on the work of earlier investigators. I sometimes have the feeling that complaints about the so-called "non-cumulative character of knowledge" in our field refer not so much to the character of knowledge as to our failure to accumulate it. In an important sense, of course, every scientific worker must gather for himself the facts from which he works. But the researcher in small groups today can begin his study immeasurably further along than his colleagues of even five years ago. It may turn out that the distinguishing mark of the last five years of development in this field is the degree of accumulation and consolidation that the literature has undergone.

Nevertheless, as I explore the maze of available studies relevant in one way or another to our present scientific needs, the most insistent need I feel is for synthesis. The very respectable body of studies that we now have has raised my level of aspiration; I am no longer content merely to discover that "X makes a difference significant at the .05 level if everything else is carefully controlled." I am not even satisfied with an occasional feeling that I "understand," in a general way, most of the things that go on in the groups I happen to know. As scientists, most of us have aspirations that go beyond this feeling of "understanding." What we would really like to be able to do is *predict*. This, of course, is what the layman also expects us to be able to do.

Generally, when the layman thinks of prediction he means prediction about the course of natural events, not about a highly controlled laboratory event. Some laymen, indeed, seem to feel that the scientist should be able to predict without any special information – in other words, to foretell the natural future by a kind of clairvoyance. The scientist, on the other hand, knows that prediction of complex natural events – for example, of the weather – requires access to a very large amount of information which usually must be gathered in very small bits, more or less continuously, from many scattered sources, and compiled and reduced to compact empirical generalizations – all of this before the more abstract part of the scientific theory can be brought to bear. In the case of weather prediction, we can form some idea of the process by thinking of all the scattered weather stations and the many readings of temperature, humidity, wind, and so on summarized in the weather maps that form the factual base for the weather forecaster.

The nearest thing to this kind of publicly exposed, practical, naturalistic prediction I can think of in the social sciences is the prediction of elections by poll. Some aspects of demographic theory perhaps also come close, although the predictions are generally less specific and apply to a longer time span than prediction of elections. In neither of these instances, however, is the theory very complex in the sense that it specifies the relations of a large number of qualitatively different factors in interaction with one another. Sampling theory and straight extrapolation of present trends into the future more or less take the place of behavior theory. The difficulty in making these predictions stems not from the variety of factors involved in the theory but from the large number of geographically separated persons from whom information must be obtained. The measurement made on each person or unit is relatively simple, and the combining process requires little more than simple addition.

But the sort of prediction that would actually make a difference in the practice of the "interpersonal arts" is quite different. (By the "interpersonal arts" I mean the arts of changing motivation and behavior through person-to-person communication – for example, the arts of developing an appropriate and binding group decision, of teaching and learning, of individual psychotherapy, of leading a training group in human relations, of fostering cooperation and morale in a crew or work group.) In such situations, what the therapist, leader, or any other interested participant wants to be able to do is to read the signs that appear in the behavior (his own as well as others) – to diagnose accurately what is going on, predict where it is going, and how it will change if he takes a given action – all of this soon enough for him to intervene and try to change the course of events if he deems it desirable.

It is hardly thinkable that the participant in complex interpersonal situations like these could obtain all the information he would need, or, if he could obtain it, that he could process it fast enough to be able to predict with absolute accuracy. This would be omnipotence, or something very close to it. But much less than absolute accuracy would answer very well. What my values specify as desirable and what I think is probably attainable is some enhancement of the ability to read the signs better than most people now can, and some increase in the ability to do something intelligently experimental about it.

A social participant in a course of events who is in a position to take remedial action can get along with middling-to-poor prediction, as we do at present. But the scientist who can arrange matters so that he can obtain more information on more relevant factors must hope for a corresponding improvement in prediction. To obtain the improvement in prediction, he must be able to calculate the weights of various factors relative to one another under given conditions. It is this sort of synthesis that one misses in the literature. An accumulation of studies does not solve the problem, although it is a necessary step.

I assume that most of my colleagues will agree with the foregoing. But the next point is one on which I must be prepared to lose some friends. It is simply this: I do not believe that the ordinary English language, or any of the special versions of it that we devise for theoretical purposes, will be nearly adequate to the demands of the sort of prediction we are talking about. In fact, from what I can find out, it does not appear that any existing body of mathematics is suited to the task either.

Yet I do not despair entirely. Quite the contrary. I believe that science has recently come into possession of the ideal method of representing the kind of theory we require. The method is computer simulation, and I shall describe it briefly later. But before talking further about this method, let us examine some of the characteristics of the phenomenon to be represented in an attempt to form a more concrete conception of the problem of synthesis that must be solved if naturalistic prediction in interpersonal situations is to be much improved over predictions based purely on common sense

Some Factors in Naturalistic Prediction

In order to obtain a perspective from which we can view a number of factors in behavior, let us suppose that we as scientific theorizers can explore the mind of each member of a group of, say, five persons, engaged in some task. We shall suppose that we have the power to examine in detail everything that goes on in a very small interval of time, or to wait and look back over a long interval. In other words, we shall permit ourselves to substitute hindsight for foresight. We shall also suppose that we have the power to examine the characteristics of the environment from a longer distance in time than that available to the participants. As scientific theorizers, in other words, we should like an omniscient perspective, far beyond that available to any of the group members in their moment-to-moment behavior decisions. They may attempt to maintain such a perspective, but they must do it by symbolic representation of facts that are not available to them.

And now we must admit, of course, that the scientific theorizer does not escape this problem when he tries to predict. As a predictor, the scientific theorizer, like the practical human being he is theorizing about, has to reduce his demands for an omniscient information-gathering apparatus if he wants to predict forward in real time from real information. The trick in improving prediction, since omniscience is so hard to come by, must lie in learning how to get more information, or how to make more and better inferences from what we have, or both, and to do either or both before something else happens. These are the requirements of naturalistic prediction, and all good theory must eventually face up to them. But as a theorizer, the scientific predictor, like the theorizing human being he is predicting about, has to be prepared to think and talk about states of affairs to which he has had no empirical access, as he struggles by symbolic means to construct an omniscient perspective.

For our theorizing, then, let us adopt the omniscient perspective and go ahead without embarrassment. Our problem is to try to form some concrete idea of the various influences that we would have to synthesize in order to predict interpersonal behavior naturalistically in real time. Let us begin with the perspective of a given member at a point in time. Another member has just completed a remark, and the member who is our point of reference is in the process of thinking about an act which we propose to predict. Let us imagine at least part of the process he might go through, basing our construction on experimental findings in so far as possible.

Somewhere early in the process of thinking about the new act, there must be some analysis of the character of the act that has just occurred. A social act has a large number of possible stimulus properties, depending on the kind of analysis the responder gives it. Suppose that the act were an assertion about some object that forms a part of the task environment of the group. What is asserted about the object may be called the task content of the remark. One very relevant property of a stimulus act is the history of its task content. An assertion made for the first time has a meaning different from that of one made after the content has acquired a history. As we all know, and as Sherif[6] and others have demonstrated, groups tend to develop norms. Individual differences in perceptions – or, at any rate, in verbal statements – tend to moderate over time. Most group members tend to converge toward a group norm as they interact and become aware of one another's judgments.

In attempting to predict the reaction of our hypothetical group member, it is important for us to know whether the statement of task content to which he is reacting is occurring for the first time, or whether it has been made and agreed with (or disagreed with) earlier, and, if so, by how many group members, and of what status. Perhaps the content in question has been prohibited, in effect, by consensus of some sufficiently large portion of the group, or perhaps it has been authorized, in effect, by favorable consensus. Still further distinctions might be drawn, of a similar kind, but perhaps I have already suggested enough to demonstrate that the task content of an act has definition (or lack of it) relative to the norms of the group which strongly affects the probability that our subject will agree (or disagree) with it.

But which way will the effect go? Asch's experiments[7] have dramatized the power of tendencies toward conformity. As he has shown, an individual may testify against a strikingly obvious sensory experience if all other group members testify against it and the individual believes that he alone has had the experience. On the other hand, not all individuals give in, even under extreme pressure. What kinds do not give in? We know little about this question at present from empirical studies. Perhaps some of these intransigents are persons who feel generally compelled to be in opposition to group norms or authority figures. At any rate, it seems clear in principle that we must know more than how the assertion of task content fits into group norms. We must take into account the fact that our particular subject may have an attitude toward conformity or deviance that will affect the probability of his agreement or disagreement.

Thus far we have not considered whether it makes any difference who made the remark and to whom it was addressed. But presumably these matters make a difference to our subject. Whyte[8] pointed out that the corner boys as well as members of formal organizations observe channels; that is, the same suggestion that will be rejected or ignored if made by a low-status member may be acted upon if made by a high-status member. Many earlier experiments have been devoted to showing that subjects perceive and judge content differently according to their assumptions about the character of the source. A series of studies now in process by Bauer[9] and others is showing that perceptions of and reactions to content are similarly influenced by the expectation of communicating them to a particular audience. We must, in other words, take into account our subject's perception of who made the remark, to whom it was addressed, who he himself is in the socially relevant sense, and to whom he addresses his reply.

We are here faced with the problem of characterizing in some relevant way the various kinds of "who" that the subject may consider, and the grounds on which he identifies them. Surely he must look at their behavior up to the present point and the kind of behavior that others have addressed to them. To some degree, there has been a process of learning, or "object-adaptive cognition," going on. To some degree, each social object is unique, a class of one, an object characterized operationally in terms of the individual's past experience with it. But there are no social objects that are simply this. Any social object, including the self, is to some degree treated as a member of a class, and characteristics of the class are attributed to it. We recognize various types or aspects of this process by such terms as "projection," "displacement," "transference," "identification," "internalization," "taking the role of the other," the "generalized other," "reference groups," "marginality," and "ego involvement." One of the most difficult aspects of our predictive problem will surely be to take into account the fact that the subject has been trained from his earliest childhood in a repertoire of social roles – some which he identifies with the self, others which he treats as ego-alien – and that in varying degrees he imposes this stereotyped repertoire on any current social situation.

Among other factors which predispose the subject to identify a present participant with some particularly important figure from the past are presumably the kind, direction, and amount of emotion the subject has to handle at the time. As the amount rises, the tendency to cast present characters in past roles presumably increases. Overdetermined interpersonal dramas tend to arise under stress, as Redl[10] has described so effectively. But in general we get into very difficult problems of prediction as we try to take strong affect into account. The reasons are well known. Psychoanalysis has emphasized the resourcefulness of the psyche in dealing with strong affect. It will inhibit the affect, repress it, reverse it, counteract it, find indirect outlets for it, and generally transform it and disguise it until the subject himself, to say nothing of our hopeful scientific predictor, has no conscious idea of what is going on.

But there are still other factors. We should not forget that the subject is generally capable of looking twice at the object of cognition, and that, in spite of all obstacles, he may form a judgment of it that will stand the test of time. The characteristics of cognition as a problem-solving process have been receiving renewed attention in the past few years, particularly in the work of Bruner and his associates.[11] And, with the development of large-scale computers, a number of computor experts and behavior theorists have been working furiously to program machines to solve more and more difficult problems in ways that seem to resemble human cognition. These two developments, one from cognitive experimentation as such and one from computor programing show considerable similarity and in all likelihood will grow together rapidly. They will surely be involved in future attempts to build predictive models of human behavior and interaction.

The result of cognitive analysis depends on cognitive abilities. These, in turn, can hardly be defined except in relation to the task requirements. If we are to predict successfully, we will have to be able to measure task abilities in relation to task requirements. But task requirements are not easy to describe. Every task is complex to some extent. In spite of something like fifty years of research on individual *versus* group problem-solving, in which many concretely different kinds of task have been used, there is still no very good classification of tasks. Probably one of the most important characteristics of a task object is the degree to which assertions about it can be checked by reference to the physical environment. Festinger[12] and his associates have called this property "physical reality" as opposed to "social reality." A long list of studies could be cited in support of the generalization that as the degree of physical reality of the task object decreases, individuals tend to differ more widely in their initial perceptions or judgments of it, and have more difficulty in coming to consensus about it. However, any such generalization needs to be considerably qualified by other factors – for example, the degree to which major values are involved, the commitment of members to the task, the commitment of members to group solidarity, the urgency of the task, the specificity of the decisions required, and the degree to which the decision will have ulterior consequences.

Let us pause for a moment to consider the factors that have been mentioned as relevant to our prediction problem – the degree to which the assertion of task content conforms or deviates from group norms; the attitude of the subject toward the group norms; the subject's identification of "who" is asserting the content, and "who," in a psychologically relevant sense, he himself is; his attitudes toward the figures in this repertoire of roles; the degree to which emotion aroused in the present situation increases his tendency to construe the present situation in terms of the past; his mechanisms of defense; his cognitive abilities; and the nature of the task in several respects. The list is certainly not complete, though it touches a good many factors that can be certified as important from experimental or good observational studies. In fact, the most common conclusion of the most common type of study is that factor X is "important" – that is, that it makes a difference significant at the .05 level if everything else is carefully controlled.

But what are the relative weights of the various factors, and in what circumstances? In what time order do they interact, and how complex is this interaction? How can the predictor obtain information about their probable state? Is there any dependable device, test, observation that he can use to obtain the needed information in a naturalistic setting? Unfortunately, in my opinion, researchers have given far too little attention to the building of usable instruments. But even if the predictor had a good instrument with which to obtain information on every factor he believed to be important and had floods of information available from moment to moment, how, in fact, could he put all the data together and come out with a prediction? Especially, how could he do it in time to do any good? These are problems of synthesis.

Thus far we have hardly considered the fact that there is more than one person in any group. If we really wished to predict, we should have to perform a similar analysis for each member in the group. Each of them presumably prepares to react to the assertion of task content with which we began. But only a few are likely to react openly. Someone will be ready to reply before the others, or there may be a brief struggle for the floor which someone wins. Once a member of the group has spoken, many things may change. Is his probability of speaking again increased by practice, decreased by catharsis, or both, or neither? If he says the same thing another member wanted to say, will that other be vicariously satisfied or competitively frustrated? If the person who made the original assertion of task content receives agreement, is he encouraged to go ahead or satisfied to stop? If he receives disagreement, is he discouraged into stopping or provoked to battle? Presumably, if we could synthesize what goes on inside the member we dealt with above, we could proceed similarly with this one. The questions that I have just raised might then appear to be false and unanswerable, except by "It depends."

But on what does "it depend"? One cannot simply say, "It depends on the individual personality of the person reacting." Why not? Because part of the process that goes on in that individual personality is based upon the external state of affairs – *e.g.*, whether the last act has made it clear that a majority is in favor of the task content in question; whether the last act has changed the present member's conception of "who" the other is, and who he himself is; whether he has been building up frustration for some time and now encounters the final straw; whether the remark of the other has changed his cognitive picture of the object; and so on. None of these circumstantial factors can be predicted solely from a knowledge of his personality. But none can be predicted without a knowledge of his personality either. "Who" member 1 thinks member 2 is depends (partly) on how member 2 has behaved up to that time. But how member 2 has behaved up to that time depends (partly) on "who" he thinks member 1 is. And so on. In situations of this kind, one small event may make a large difference, by starting in motion a given circular reaction rather than some other. To predict the circular reaction, then, one would have to predict the small event, and that, in turn, is the product of a very large number of factors.

What chance does human intuition have to make a synthesis of this sort? The mere thought of trying to use the English language, or any other natural human language, as the instrument for describing and predicting a process like this tires us out before we begin. People do about as well as they can with natural language in the actual process of interacting, and the result is not good enough. Even with more time, I do not think it would be good enough, because nobody would be able to force himself through the brutal repetition that would be necessary.

Computor Simulation as a Means of Synthesis

There are those who believe that more strenuous attempts to apply mathematical methods of formulation will give the desired results. This is a possibility that is only beginning to be explored. For representing the interrelations of a few variables, existing mathematical methods may be appropriate. The sort of synthesis we need, however, calls for large numbers of variables in highly complex conditional relationships to one another. So far as I know, analogue computers are the most appropriate means of representing systems of this sort. There are many kinds of analogue computers; a scale model of an airplane in a wind tunnel is a good example. But if the nature of the variables is well known, it is not necessary to have a physical model. The analogue of the real system can be constructed by arranging (that is, programing) a general-purpose computer so that its parts are related to one another as they are supposed to be in the real system.

One may know enough about a system to construct such a model as a jigsaw puzzle is constructed – bit by bit, in terms of the fit of one small piece to another. One may know enough to do that and still not know how the whole thing will operate when all pieces are in place. That is what the analogue computor will tell him about his model. The computor is capable of any amount of tiresome canvassing of factors, readjustment of one in terms of the other, and so on.

Newell, Simon, and Shaw[13] have already constructed a highly complex computer program that goes about problem-solving in a way that seems similar in many respects to a behaving organism. Subparts of the program investigate the characteristics of the task objects and describe them in such a way that other subparts of the program can deal with the task objects symbolically, as we deal with cognitive descriptions of objects rather than the objects. Various attempted solutions are produced, tried, and rejected or accepted according to success. The program operating at present is a particular example of the more general class which the authors call "complex information-processing systems." In their words:

> We may identify certain characteristics of a system that make it complex:
>
> 1. There is a large number of different kinds of processes, all of which are important, although not necessarily essential, to the performance of the total system;
> 2. The uses of the processes are not fixed and invariable, but are highly contingent upon the outcomes of previous processes and on information received from the environment;

3. The same processes are used in many different contexts to accomplish similar functions toward different ends, and this often results in organizations of processes that are hierarchical, iterative, and recursive in nature.

The processes that go on in social interaction certainly answer this description. A small group is, in the exact sense of Newell and Simon's definition, an empirical example of a "complex information-processing system." I can see no reason in principle for believing that their tactics of synthesizing models of such systems, using the modern large computor as the medium, and of studying empirically the behavior of the operating total system cannot be applied to our problem of synthesis with the aim of naturalistic prediction.

Of course, the goal that I have here called naturalistic prediction is a very ambitious and idealistic one. But we need a vantage point from which we can successfully put into perspective the problems of theory and research of a whole scientific field. The goal we need to visualize should serve not only as an immediately appealing stimulus to the beginning of work but also as an exacting criterion of scientific progress and an indicator of critical problems for further work. To my mind, nothing less than the goal of naturalistic prediction really answers these needs.

Notes

1. D. Cartwright and A. F. Zander (eds.), *Group Dynamics: Research and Theory*, Row, Peterson, 1953.
2. G. Lindzey (ed.), *Handbook of Social Psychology*, Addison-Wesley, 1954.
3. F. L. Strodtbeck and A. P. Hare, "Bibliography of Small Group Research (from 1900 through 1953)," *Sociometry*, 17 (1954), 107–78.
4. A. P. Hare, E. F. Borgatta, and R. F. Bales, *Small Groups, Studies in Social Interaction*, Knopf, 1955.
5. R. F. Bales, A. P. Hare, and E. F. Borgatta, "Structure and Dynamics of Small Groups: A Review of Four Variables," in J. Gittler (ed.), *Review of Sociology, Analysis of a Decade*, John Wiley, 1957.
6. M. Sherif, *The Psychology of Social Norms*, Harper, 1936.
7. S. E. Asch, *Social Psychology*, Prentice-Hall, 1952.
8. W. F. Whyte, *Street Corner Society*, University of Chicago Press, 1943.
9. R. A. Bauer, personal communication to the author.
10. F. Redl, "Group Emotion and Leadership," *Psychiatry*, 5 (1942), 573–96.
11. J. S. Bruner, J. J. Goodnow, and G. A. Austin, *A Study of Thinking*, John Wiley, 1956.
12. L. Festinger, "Theory of Social Comparison Processes," *Hum. Relat.* 7 (1954), 117–40.
13. Allen Newell and Herbert A. Simon, "The Logic Theory Machine, A Complex Information Processing System," *IRE Transactions on Information Theory*, Vol. IT-2, No. 3, 1956.

50

Bringing Men Back In

George C. Homans

I am going to talk about an issue we have worried over many times. I have worried over it myself. But I make no excuses for taking it up again. Although it is an old issue, it is still not a settled one, and I think it is the most general intellectual issue in sociology. If I have only one chance to speak *ex cathedra*, I cannot afford to say something innocuous. On the contrary, now if ever is the time to be nocuous.

In the early thirties a distinct school of sociological thought was beginning to form. Its chief, though certainly not its only, intellectual parents were Durkheim and Radcliffe-Brown. I call it a school, though not all its adherents accepted just the same tenets; and many sociologists went ahead and made great progress without giving a thought to it. The school is usually called that of structural-functionalism, or functionalism for short. For a whole generation it has been the dominant, indeed the only distinct, school of sociological thought. I think it has run its course, done its work, and now positively gets in the way of our understanding social phenomena. And I propose to ask, Why?

The Interests of Functionalism

I begin by reminding you of the chief interests and assumptions of functionalism, especially as contrasted with what it was not interested in and took for granted, for the questions it did not ask have returned to plague it. If what I say seems a caricature, remember that a caricature emphasizes a person's most characteristic features.

First, the school took its start from the study of norms, the statements the members of a group make about how they ought to behave, and indeed often do behave, in various circumstances. It was especially interested in the cluster of norms called a role and in the cluster of roles called an institution. It never tired of asserting that its concern was with institutionalized behavior, and that the unit of social analysis was not the acting individual but the role. The school did not ask why there should be roles at all.

Second, the school was empirically interested in the interrelations of roles, the interrelations of institutions: this was the structural side of its work. It was the sort of thing the social anthropologists had been doing, showing how the institutions of a primitive society fitted together; and the sociologists extended the effort to advanced societies. They would point out, for instance, that the nuclear family rather than some form of extended kinship was characteristic of industrialized societies. But they were more interested in establishing *what* the interrelations of institutions were than in *why* they were so. In the beginning the analyses tended to be static, as it is more convincing to speak of a social structure in a society conceived to be stable than in one undergoing rapid change. Recently the school has turned to the study of social change, but in so doing it has had to take up the question it disregarded earlier. If an institution is changing, one can hardly avoid asking why it is changing in one direction rather than another.

Third, the school was, to put it crudely, more interested in the consequences than in the causes of an institution, particularly in the consequences for a social system considered as a whole. These consequences were the *functions* of the institution. Thus the members of the school never tired of pointing out the functions and dysfunctions of a status system, without asking why a status system should exist in the first place, why it was there to have functions. They were especially interested in showing how its institutions helped maintain a society in equilibrium, as a going concern. The model for research was Durkheim's effort to show, in *The Elementary Forms of the Religious Life*, how the religion of a primitive tribe helped hold the tribe together.

Such were the empirical interests of functionalism. As empirically I have been a functionalist myself, I shall be the last to quarrel with them. It is certainly one of the jobs of a sociologist to discover what the norms of a society are. Though a role is not actual behavior, it is for some purposes a useful simplification. Institutions *are* interrelated, and it is certainly one of the jobs of a sociologist to show what the interrelations are. Institutions do have consequences, in the sense that, if one institution may be taken as given, the other kinds of institution that may exist in the society are probably not infinite in number. It is certainly one of the jobs of a sociologist to search out these consequences and even, though this is more difficult, to determine whether their consequences are good or bad for the society as a whole. At any rate, the empirical interests of functionalism have led to an enormous amount of good work. Think only of the studies made by Murdock[1] and others on the cross-cultural interrelations of institutions.

As it began to crystallize, the functional school developed theoretical interests as well as empirical ones. There was no necessity for the two to go together, and the British social anthropologists remained relatively untheoretical. Not so the American sociologists, particularly Talcott Parsons, who claimed that they were not only theorists but something called general theorists, and strongly emphasized the importance of theory.

Theirs was to be, moreover, a certain kind of theory. They were students of Durkheim and took seriously his famous definition of *social facts*: "Since their essential characteristic consists in the power they possess of exerting, from outside, a pressure on individual consciousnesses, they do not derive from individual consciousnesses, and in consequence sociology is not a corollary of psychology."[2] Since Durkheim was a great man, one can find statements in his writings that have quite other implications, but this caricature of himself was the one that made the difference. If not in what they said, then surely in what they did, the functionalists took Durkheim seriously. Their fundamental unit, the role, was a social fact in Durkheim's sense. And their theoretical program assumed, as he did, that sociology should be an independent science, in the sense that its propositions should not be derivable from some other social science, such as psychology. This meant, in effect, that the general propositions of sociology were not to be propositions about the behavior of "individual consciousnesses" – or, as I should say, about men – but propositions about the characteristics of societies or other social groups as such.

Where functionalism failed was not in its empirical interests but, curiously, in what it most prided itself on, its general theory. Let me be very careful here. In a recent Presidential Address, Kingsley Davis asserted that we are all functionalists now,[3] and there is a sense in which he was quite right. But note that he was talking about functional *analysis*. One carries out functional analysis when, starting from the existence of a particular institution, one tries to find out what difference the institution makes to the other aspects of social structure. That is, one carries out the empirical program of functionalism. Since we have all learned to carry out functional analyses, we are in this sense all functionalists now. But functional analysis, as a method, is not the same thing as functional theory. And if we are all functional analysts, we are certainly not all functional theorists. Count me out, for one.

The only inescapable office of theory is to explain. The theory of evolution is an explanation why and how evolution occurs. To look for the consequences of institutions, to show the interrelationships of institutions is not the same thing as explaining why the interrelationships are what they are. The question is a practical and not a philosophical one – not whether it is legitimate to take the role as the fundamental unit, nor whether institutions are really real, but whether the theoretical program of functionalism has in fact led to explanations of social phenomena, including the findings of functional analysis itself. Nor is the question whether functionalism might not do so, but whether it has done so as of today. I think it has not.

The Nature of Theory

With all their talk about theory, the functionalists never – and I speak advisedly – succeeded in making clear what a theory was. It must be allowed in their excuse that, in the early days, the philosophers of science had not given as clear an answer to the question as they have now.[4] But even then, the functionalists could have done better than they did, and certainly the excuse is valid no longer. Today we should stop talking to our students about sociological theory until we have taught them what a theory is.

A theory of a phenomenon consists of a series of propositions, each stating a relationship between properties of nature. But not every kind of sentence qualifies as such a proposition. The propositions do not consist of definitions of the properties: the construction of a conceptual scheme is an indispensable part of theoretical work but is not itself theory. Nor may a proposition simply say that there is some relationship between the properties. Instead, if there is some change in one of the properties, it must at least begin to specify what the change in the other property will be. If one of the properties is absent, the other will also be absent; or if one of the properties increases in value, the other will too. The properties, the variables, may be probabilities.

Accordingly, to take a famous example, Marx's statement that the economic organization of a society determines the nature of its other institutions is an immensely useful guide to research. For it says: "Look for the social consequences of economic change, and if you look, you will surely find them!" But it is not the sort of proposition that can enter a theory. For by itself it says only that, if the economic infrastructure changes, there will be some change in the social superstructure, without beginning to suggest what the latter change will be. Most of the sentences of sociology, alleged to be theoretical, resemble this one of Marx's, yet few of our theorists realize it. And while we are always asking that theory guide research, we forget that many statements like Marx's are good guides to research without being good theory.

To constitute a theory, the propositions must take the form of a deductive system. One of them, usually called the lowest-order proposition, is the proposition to be explained, for example, the proposition that the more thoroughly a society is industrialized, the more fully its kinship organization tends towards the nuclear family. The other propositions are either general propositions or statements of particular given conditions. The general propositions are so called because they enter into other, perhaps many other, deductive systems besides the one in question. Indeed, what we often call a theory is a cluster of deductive systems, sharing the same general propositions but having different *explicanda*. The crucial requirement is that each system shall be deductive. That is, the lowest-order proposition follows as a logical conclusion from the general propositions under the specified given conditions. The reason why statements like Marx's may not enter theories is that no definite conclusions may in logic be drawn from them. When the lowest-order proposition does follow logically, it is said to be explained. The explanation of a phenomenon is the theory of the phenomenon. A theory is nothing – it is not a theory – unless it is an explanation.

One may define properties and categories, and one still has no theory. One may state that there *are* relations between the properties, and one still has no theory. One may state that a change in one property will produce a definite change in another property, and one still has no theory. Not until one has properties, and propositions stating the relations between them, and the propositions form a deductive system – not until one has all three does one have a theory. Most of our arguments about theory would fall to the ground, if we first asked whether we had a theory to argue about.

Functional Theories

As a theoretical effort, functionalism never came near meeting these conditions. Even if the functionalists had seriously tried to meet them, which they did not, I think they would still have failed. The difficulty lay in the characteristic general propositions of functionalism. A proposition is not functional just because it uses the word *function*. To say that a certain institution is functional for individual men in the sense of meeting their needs is not a characteristic proposition of functionalism. Instead it belongs to the class of psychological propositions. Nor is the statement that one institution is a function of another, in the quasi-mathematical sense of function, characteristic. Though many functional theorists make such statements, non-functionalists like myself may also make them without a qualm. The characteristic general propositions of functional theory in sociology take the form: "If it is to survive, or remain in equilibrium, a social system – any social system – must possess institutions of Type X." For instance, if it is to survive or remain in equilibrium, society must possess conflict-resolving institutions. By general propositions of this sort the functionalists sought to meet Durkheim's demand for a truly independent sociological theory.

The problem was, and is, to construct deductive systems headed by such propositions. Take first the terms *equilibrium* and *survival*. If the theorist chose equilibrium, he was able to provide no criterion of social equilibrium, especially "dynamic" or "moving" equilibrium, definite enough to allow anything specific to be deduced in logic from a proposition employing the term. I shall give an example later. When indeed was a society not in equilibrium? If the theorist chose *survival*, he found this, too, surprisingly hard to define. Did Scotland, for instance, survive as a society? Though it had long been united with England, it still possessed distinctive institutions, legal and religious. If the theorist took *survival* in the strong sense, and said that a society had not survived if all its members had died without issue, he was still in trouble. As far as the records went, the very few societies of this sort had possessed institution of all the types the functionalists said were necessary for survival. The evidence put in question, to say the least, the empirical truth of the functionalist propositions. Of course the functionalists were at liberty to say: "If a society is to survive, its members must not all be shot dead," which was true as true could be but allowed little to be deduced about the social characteristics of surviving societies.

Indeed the same was true of the other functional propositions. Even if a statement like: "If it is to survive, a society must possess conflict-resolving institutions," were accepted as testable and true, it possessed little explanatory power. From the proposition the fact could be deduced that, given a certain society did survive, it did possess conflict-resolving institutions of some kind and the fact was thus explained. What remained unexplained was why the society had conflict-resolving institutions of a particular kind, why, for instance, the jury was an ancient feature of Anglo-Saxon legal institutions. I take it that what sociology has to explain are the actual features of actual societies and not just the generalized features of a generalized society.

I do not think that members of the functional school could have set up, starting with general propositions of their distinctive type, theories that were also deductive systems. More important, they did not. Recognizing, perhaps, that they were blocked in one direction, some of them elaborated what they called theory in another. They used what they asserted were a limited and exhaustive number of functional problems faced by any society to generate a complex set of categories in terms of which social structure could be analyzed. That is, they set up a conceptual scheme. But analysis is not explanation, and a conceptual scheme is not a theory. They did not fail to make statements about the relations between the categories, but most of the statements resembled the one of Marx's I cited earlier: they were not of the type that enter deductive systems. From their lower-order propositions, as from their higher-order ones, no definite conclusions in logic could be drawn. Under these conditions, there was no way of telling whether their choice of functional problems and categories was not wholly arbitrary. What the functionalists actually produced was not a theory but a new language for describing social structure, one among many possible languages; and much of the work they called theoretical consisted in showing how the words in other languages, including that of everyday life, could be translated into theirs. They would say, for instance, that what other people called making a living was called in their language goal-attainment. But what makes a theory is deduction, not translation.

I have said that the question is not whether, in general, functional theories can be real theories, for there are sciences that possess real functional theories. The question is rather whether this particular effort was successful. If a theory is an explanation, the functionalists in sociology were, on the evidence, not successful. Perhaps they could not have been successful; at any rate they were not. The trouble with their theory was not that it was wrong, but that it was not a theory.

An Alternative Theory

Here endeth the destructive part of the lesson. I shall now try to show that a more successful effort to explain social phenomena entails the construction of theories different from functional ones, in the sense that their general propositions are of a different kind, precisely the kind, indeed, that the functionalists tried to get away from. I shall try to show this for the very phenomena the functionalists took for granted and the very relations they discovered empirically. I shall even try to show that, when functionalists took the job of explanation seriously, which they sometimes did, this other kind of theory would appear unacknowledged in their own work.

The functionalists insisted over and over again that the minimum unit of social analysis was the role, which is a cluster of norms. In a recent article, James Coleman has written: ". . . sociologists have characteristically taken as their starting-point a social system in which norms exist, and individuals are largely governed by these norms. Such a strategy views norms as the governors of social behavior, and thus neatly bypasses the difficult problem that Hobbes posed."[5] Hobbes' problem is, of course, why there is not a war of all against all.

Why, in short, should there be norms at all? The answer Coleman gives is that in the kind of case he considers, norms arise through the actions of men rationally calculating to further their own self-interest in a context of other men acting in the same way. He writes: "The central postulate about behavior is this: each actor will attempt to extend his power over those actions in which he has most interest." Starting from this postulate, Coleman constructs a deductive system explaining why the actors adopt a particular sort of norm in the given circumstances.

I do not want to argue the vexed question of rationality I do want to point out what sort of general proposition Coleman starts with. As he recognizes, it is much like the central assumption of economics, though self-interest is not limited to the material interests usually considered by economists. It also resembles a proposition of psychology, though here it might take the form: the more valuable the reward of an activity, the more likely a man is to perform the activity. But it certainly is not a characteristic functional proposition in sociology: it is not a statement about the conditions of equilibrium for a society, but a statement about the behavior of individual men.

Again, if there are norms, why do men conform to them? Let us lay aside the fact that many men do not conform or conform very indifferently, and assume that they all do so. Why do they do so? So far as the functionalists gave any answer to the question, it was that men have "internalized" the values embodied in the norm. But "internalization" is a word and not an explanation. So far as their own theory was concerned, the functionalists took conformity to norms for granted. They made the mistake Malinowski pointed out long ago in a book now too little read by sociologists, the mistake made by early writers on primitive societies, the mistake of assuming that conformity to norms is a matter of ". . . this automatic acquiescence, this instinctive submission of every member of the tribe to its laws. . . ."[6] The alternative answer Malinowski gave was that obedience to norms "is usually rewarded according to the measure of its perfection, while noncompliance is visited upon the remiss agent."[7]

In short, the answer he gave is much like that of Coleman and the psychologists. Later he added the suggestive remark: "The true problem is not to study how human life submits to rules – it simply does not; the real problem is how the rules become adapted to life."[8]

The question remains why members of a particular society find certain of the results of their actions rewarding and not others, especially when some of the results seem far from "naturally" rewarding. This is the real problem of the "internalization" of values. The explanation is given not by any distinctively sociological propositions but by the propositions of learning theory in psychology.

The functionalists were much interested in the interrelations of institutions, and it was one of the glories of the school to have pointed out many such interrelations. But the job of a science does not end with pointing out interrelations; it must try to explain why they are what they are. Take the statement that the kinship organization of industrialized societies tends to be that of the nuclear family. I cannot give anything like the full explanation, but I can, and you can too, suggest the beginning of one. Some men organized factories because by so doing they thought they could get greater material rewards than they could get otherwise. Other men entered factories for reasons of the same sort. In so doing they worked away from home and so had to forgo, if only for lack of time, the cultivation of the extended kinship ties that were a source of reward, because a source of help, in many traditional argricultural societies, where work lay closer to home. Accordingly the nuclear family tended to become associated with factory organization; and the explanation for the association is provided by propositions about the behavior of men as such. Not the needs of society explain the relationship, but the needs of men.

Again, functionalists were interested in the consequences of institutions, especially their consequences for a social system as a whole. For instance, they were endlessly concerned with the functions and dysfunctions of status systems. Seldom did they ask why there should be status systems in the first place. Some theorists have taken the emergence of phenomena like status systems as evidence for Durkheim's contention that sociology was not reducible to psychology. What is important is not the fact of emergence but the question how the emergence is to be explained. One of the accomplishments of small-group research is to explain how a status system, of course on a small scale, emerges in the course of interaction between the members of a group.[9] The explanation is provided by psychological propositions. Certainly no functional propositions are needed. Indeed the theoretical contribution of small-group research has consisted "in showing how the kinds of microscopic variables usually ignored by sociologists can explain the kinds of social situations usually ignored by psychologists."[10]

What is the lesson of all this? If the very things functionalists take for granted, like norms, if the very interrelationships they empirically discover can be explained by deductive systems that employ psychological propositions, then it must be that the general explanatory principles even of sociology are not sociological, as the functionalists would have them be, but psychological, propositions about the behavior of men, not about the behavior of societies. On the analogy with other sciences, this argument by itself would not undermine the validity of a functional theory. Thermodynamics, for instance, states propositions about aggregates, which are themselves true and general, even though they can be explained in turn, in statistical mechanics, by propositions about members of the aggregates. The question is whether this kind of situation actually obtains in sociology. So far as functional propositions are concerned, which are propositions about social aggregates, the situation does not obtain, for they have not been shown to be true and general.

Explaining Social Change

My next contention is that even confessed functionalists, when they seriously try to explain certain kinds of social phenomena, in fact use non-functional explanations without recognizing that they do so. This is particularly clear in their studies of social change.

Social change provides a searching test for theory, since historical records are a prerequisite for its study. Without history the social scientist can establish the contemporaneous interrelations of institutions, but may be hard put to it to explain why the interrelations should be what they are. With historical records he may have the information needed to support an explanation. One of the commonest charges against the functionalist school was that it could not deal with social change, that its analysis was static. In recent years some functionalists have undertaken to show that the charge was unjustified. They have chosen for their demonstration the process of differentiation in society, the process, for instance, of the increasing specialization of occupations. In question as usual is not the fact of differentiation – there is no doubt that the over-all trend of social history has been in this direction – but how the process is to be explained.

A particularly good example of this new development in functionalism is Neil Smelser's book, *Social Change in the Industrial Revolution: An Application of Theory to the British Cotton Industry 1770–1840*.[11] The book is not just good for my purposes: it is good, very good, in itself. It provides an enormous amount of well organized information, and it goes far to explain the changes that occurred. The amusing thing about it is that the explanation Smelser actually uses, good scientist that he is, to account for the changes is not the functional theory he starts out with, which is as usual a non-theory, but a different kind of theory and a better one.

Smelser begins like any true functionalist. For him a social system is one kind of system of action, characterized as follows: "A social system ... is composed of a set of interrelated roles, collectivities, etc. ... It is important to remember that the roles, collectivities, etc., not individuals, are the units in this last case." Moreover, "all systems of action are governed by the principle of equilibrium. According to the dominant type of equilibrium, the adjustments proceed in a certain direction: if the equilibrium is stable, the units tend to return to their original position; if the equilibrium is partial, only some of the units need to adjust; if the equilibrium is unstable, the tendency is to change, through mutual adjustment, to a new equilibrium or to disintegrate altogether." Finally, "all social systems are subject to four functional exigencies which must be met more or less satisfactorily if the system is to remain in equilibrium."[12] Note that by this argument all social systems are in equilibrium, even systems in process of disintegration. Though the latter are in unstable equilibrium, they are still in equilibrium. Accordingly they are meeting more or less satisfactorily the four functional exigencies. You see how useful a deductive system can be in social science? More seriously you will see that definitions of equilibrium are so broad that you may draw any conclusion you like from them.

But for all the explanatory use Smelser makes of it, this theory and its subsequent elaboration is so much window-dressing. When he really gets down to explaining the innovations in the British cotton textile industry, especially the introduction of spinning and weaving machinery, he forgets his functionalism. The guts of his actual explanation lie in the seven steps through which he says the process proceeds:

> Industrial differentiation proceeds, therefore, by the following steps:
> (1) Dissatisfaction with the productive achievements of the industry or its relevant sub-sectors and a sense of opportunity in terms of the potential availability of adequate facilities to reach a higher level of productivity.
> (2) Appropriate symptoms of disturbance in the form of "unjustified" negative emotional reactions and "unrealistic" aspirations on the part of various elements of the population.[13]

I shall not give the other five steps, as I should make the same criticism of them as I now make of the first two. I think they provide by implication a good explanation of the innovations of the Industrial Revolution in cotton manufacturing. But what kind of an explanation is it? Whatever it is, it is not a functional one. Where here do roles appear as the fundamental units of a social system? Where are the four functional exigencies? Not a word do we hear of them. Instead, what do we hear of? We hear of dissatisfaction, a sense of opportunity, emotional reactions, and aspirations. And what feels these things? Is a role dissatisfied or emotional? No; Smelser himself says it is "various elements of the population" that do so. Under relentless pressure let us finally confess that "various elements of the population" means men. And what men? For the most part men engaged in making and selling cotton cloth. And what were they dissatisfied with? Not with "the productive achievements of the industry." Though some statesmen were certainly concerned about the contribution made by the industry as a whole to the wealth of Great Britain, let us, again under relentless pressure, confess that most of the men in question were concerned with their own profits. Let us get men back in, and let us put some blood in them. Smelser himself makes the crucial statement: "In Lancashire in the early 1760's there was excited speculation about instantaneous fortunes for the man lucky enough to stumble on the right invention."[14] In short, the men in question were activated by self-interest. Yet not all self-interests are selfish interests, and certainly not all the innovations of the Industrial Revolution can be attributed to selfishness.

Smelser's actual explanation of technical innovation in cotton manufacturing might be sketched in the following deductive system. I have left out the most obvious steps.

1. Men are more likely to perform an activity, the more valuable they perceive the reward of that activity to be.
2. Men are more likely to perform an activity, the more successful they perceive the activity is likely to be in getting that reward.
3. The high demand for cotton textiles and the low productivity of labor led men concerned with cotton manufacturing to perceive the development of labor-saving machinery as rewarding in increased profits.
4. The existing state of technology led them to perceive the effort to develop labor-saving machinery as likely to be successful.
5. Therefore, by both (1) and (2) such men were highly likely to try to develop labor-saving machinery.
6. Since their perceptions of the technology were accurate, their efforts were likely to meet with success, and some of them did meet with success.

From these first steps, others such as the organization of factories and an increasing specialization of jobs followed. But no different kind of explanation is needed for these further developments: propositions like (1) and (2), which I call the *value* and the *success* propositions, would occur in them too. We should need a further proposition to describe the effect of frustration, which certainly attended some of the efforts at innovation, in creating the "negative emotional reactions" of Smelser's step 2.

I must insist again on the kind of explanation this is. It is an explanation using psychological propositions (1 and 2 above), psychological in that they are commonly stated and tested by psychologists and that they refer to the behavior of men and not to the conditions of equilibrium of societies or other social groups as such. They are general in that they appear in many, and I think in all, of the deductive systems that will even begin to explain social behavior. There is no assumption that the men in question are all alike in their concrete behavior. They may well have been conditioned to find different things rewarding, but the way conditioning takes place is itself explained by psychological propositions. There is no assumption that their values are all materialistic, but only that their pursuit of non-material values follows the same laws as their pursuit of material ones. There is no assumption that they are isolated or unsocial, but only that the laws of human behavior do not change just because another person rather than the physical environment provides the rewards for behavior. Nor is there any assumption that psychological propositions will explain everything social. We shall certainly not be able to explain everything, but our failures will be attributable to lack of factual information or the intellectual machinery for dealing with complexity – though the computers will help us here – and not to the propositions themselves. Nor is there any assumption here of psychological reductionism, though I used to think there was. For reduction implies that there are general sociological propositions that can then be reduced to psychological ones. I now suspect that there are no general sociological propositions, propositions that hold good of all societies or social groups as such, and that the only general propositions of sociology are in fact psychological.

What I do claim is that, no matter what we say our theories are, when we seriously try to explain social phenomena by constructing even the veriest sketches of deductive systems, we find ourselves in fact and whether we admit it or not, using what I have called psychological explanations. I need hardly add that our actual explanations are our actual theories.

I am being a little unfair to functionalists like Smelser and Parsons if I imply that they did not realize there were people around. The so-called theory of action made a very good start indeed by taking as its paradigm for social behavior two persons, the actions of each of whom sanctioned, that is, rewarded or punished, the actions of the other.[15] But as soon as the start was made, its authors disregarded it. As the theory of action was applied to society, it appeared to have no actors and mighty little action. The reason was that it separated the personality system from the social system and proposed to deal with the latter alone. It was the personality system that had "needs, drives, skills, etc."[16] It was not part of the social system, but only conducted exchanges with it, by providing it, for instance, with disembodied motivation.[17] This is the kind of box you get into when you think of theory as a set of boxes. For this reason, no one should hold their style of writing against the functionalists. The best of writers must write clumsily when he has set up his intellectual problem in a clumsy way. If the theorist will only envisage his problem from the outset as one of constructing explanatory propositions and not a set of categories, he will come to see that the personal and the social are not to be kept separate. The actions of a man that we take to be evidence of his personality are not different from his actions that, together with the actions of others, make up a social system. They are the same identical actions. The theorist will realize this when he finds that the same set of general propositions, including the success and the value proposition mentioned above, are needed for explaining the phenomena of both personality and society.

Conclusion

If sociology is a science, it must take seriously one of the jobs of any science, which is that of providing explanations for the empirical relations it discovers. An explanation is a theory, and it takes the form of a deductive system. With all its talk about theory, the functionalist school did not take the job of theory seriously enough. It did not ask itself what a theory was, and it never produced a functional theory that was in fact an explanation. I am not sure that it could have done so, starting as it did with propositions about the conditions of social equilibrium, propositions from which no definite conclusions could be drawn in a deductive system. If a serious effort is made to construct theories that will even begin to explain social phenomena, it turns out that their general propositions are not about the equilibrium of societies but about the behavior of men. This is true even of some good functionalists, though they will not admit it. They keep psychological explanations under the table and bring them out furtively like a bottle of whiskey, for use when they really need help. What I ask is that we bring what we say about theory into line with what we actually do, and so put an end to our intellectual hypocrisy. It would unite us with the other social sciences, whose actual theories are much like our actual ones, and so strengthen us all. Let us do so also for the sake of our students. I sometimes think that they begin with more understanding of the real nature of social phenomena than we leave them with, and that our double-talk kills their mother-wit. Finally, I must acknowledge freely that everything I have said seems to me obvious. But why cannot we take the obvious seriously?

Notes

Presidential Address delivered at the annual meeting of the American Sociological Association in Montreal, September 2, 1964.

1. George P. Murdock, *Social Structure,* New York: Macmillan, 1949.
2. Émile Durkheim, *Les règles de la méthode sociologique* (8th ed.), Paris: Alcan, 1927, pp. 124–125.
3. "The Myth of Functional Analysis as a Special Method in Sociology and Anthropology," *American Sociological Review,* 24 (December, 1959), pp. 757–773.
4. See especially R. B. Braithwaite, *Scientific explanation,* Cambridge: Cambridge University Press, 1953.
5. James S. Coleman, "Collective Decisions," *Sociological Inquiry,* 34 (1964), pp. 166–181.
6. Bronislaw Malinowski, *Crime and Custom in Savage Society,* Paterson, N.J.: Littlefield, Adams, 1959, p. 11.
7. *Ibid.,* p. 12.
8. *Ibid.,* p. 127.
9. See George C. Homans, *Social Behavior: Its Elementary Forms,* New York: Harcourt, Brace & World, 1961, esp. Ch. 8.

10. C. N. Alexander, Jr and R. L. Simpson, "Balance Theory and Distributive Justice," *Sociological Inquiry*, 34 (1964), pp. 182–192.
11. Chicago: University of Chicago Press, 1959.
12. *Ibid.*, pp. 10–11.
13. *Ibid.*, p. 29.
14. *Ibid.*, p. 80.
15. Talcott Parsons and Edward Shils (eds.) *Toward a General Theory of Action*, Cambridge, Mass.: Harvard University Press, 1951, pp. 14–16.
16. Smelser, *op. cit.*, p. 10.
17. *Ibid.*, p. 33.

51

The Oversocialized Conception of Man in Modern Sociology

Dennis H. Wrong

Gertrude Stein, bed-ridden with a fatal illness, is reported to have suddenly muttered, "What, then, is the answer?" Pausing, she raised her head, murmured, "But what is the question?" and died. Miss Stein presumably was pondering the ultimate meaning of human life, but her brief final soliloquy has a broader and humbler relevance. Its point is that answers are meaningless apart from questions. If we forget the questions, even while remembering the answers, our knowledge of them will subtly deteriorate, becoming rigid, formal, and catechistic as the sense of indeterminacy, of rival possibilities, implied by the very putting of a question, is lost.

Social theory must be seen primarily as a set of answers to questions we ask of social reality. If the initiating questions are forgotten, we readily misconstrue the task of theory and the answers previous thinkers have given become narrowly confining conceptual prisons, degenerating into little more than a special, professional vocabulary applied to situations and events that can be described with equal or greater precision in ordinary language. Forgetfulness of the questions that are the starting points of inquiry leads us to ignore the substantive assumptions "buried" in our concepts and commits us to a one-sided view of reality.

Perhaps this is simply an elaborate way of saying that sociological theory can never afford to lose what is usually called a "sense of significance;" or, as it is sometimes put, that sociological theory must be "problem-conscious." I choose instead to speak of theory as a set of answers to questions because reference to "problems" may seem to suggest too close a linkage with social criticism or reform. My primary reason for insisting on the necessity of holding constantly in mind the questions that our concepts and theories are designed to answer is to preclude defining the goal of sociological theory as the creation of a formal body of knowledge satisfying the logical criteria of scientific theory set up by philosophers and methodologists of natural science.

Source: *American Sociological Review*, 1961, vol. 26, 184–193.

Needless to say, this is the way theory is often defined by contemporary sociologists.

Yet to speak of theory as interrogatory may suggest too self-sufficiently intellectual an enterprise. Cannot questions be satisfactorily answered and then forgotten, the answers becoming the assumptions from which we start in framing new questions. It may convey my view of theory more adequately to say that sociological theory concerns itself with questions arising out of problems that are inherent in the very existence of human societies and that cannot therefore be finally "solved" in the way that particular social problems perhaps can be. The "problems" theory concerns itself with are problems *for* human societies which, because of their universality, become intellectually problematic for sociological theorists. Essentially, the historicist conception of sociological knowledge that is central to the thought of Max Weber and has recently been ably restated by Barrington Moore, Jr. and C. Wright Mills[1] is a sound one. The most fruitful questions for sociology are always questions referring to the realities of a particular historical situation. Yet both of these writers, especially Mills, have a tendency to underemphasize the degree to which we genuinely wish and seek answers to trans-historical and universal questions about the nature of man and society. I do not, let it be clear, have in mind the formalistic quest for social "laws" or "universal propositions," nor the even more formalistic effort to construct all-encompassing "conceptual schemes." Moore and Mills are rightly critical of such efforts. I am thinking of such questions as, "How are men capable of uniting to form enduring societies in the first place?"; "Why and to what degree is change inherent in human societies and what are the sources of change?"; "How is man's animal nature domesticated by society?"

Such questions – and they are existential as well as intellectual questions – are the *raison d'être* of social theory. They were asked by men long before the rise of sociology. Sociology itself is an effort, under new and unprecedented historical conditions, to find novel answers to them. They are not questions which lend themselves to successively more precise answers as a result of cumulative empirical research, for they remain eternally problematic. Social theory is necessarily an interminable dialogue. "True understanding," Hannah Arendt has written, "does not tire of interminable dialogue and 'vicious circles' because it trusts that imagination will eventually catch at least a glimpse of the always frightening light of truth."[2]

I wish briefly to review the answers modern sociological theory offers to one such question, or rather to one aspect of one question. The question may be variously phrased as, "What are the sources of social cohesion?"; or, "How is social order possible?"; or, stated in social-psychological terms, "How is it that man becomes tractable to social discipline?" I shall call this question in its social-psychological aspect the "Hobbesian question" and in its more strictly sociological aspect the "Marxist question." The Hobbesian question asks how men are capable of the guidance by social norms and goals that makes possible an enduring society, while the Marxist question asks how, assuming this capability, complex societies manage to regulate and restrain destructive conflicts between groups. Much of our current theory offers an oversocialized view of man in answering the Hobbesian question and an overintegrated view of society in answering the Marxist question.

A number of writers have recently challenged the overintegrated view of society in contemporary theory. In addition to Moore and Mills, the names of Bendix, Coser, Dahrendorf, and Lockwood come to mind.[3] My intention, therefore, is to concentrate on the answers to the Hobbesian question in an effort to disclose the oversocialized view of man which they seem to imply.

Since my view of theory is obviously very different from that of Talcott Parsons and has, in fact, been developed in opposition to his, let me pay tribute to his recognition of the importance of the Hobbesian question – the "problem of order," as he calls it – at the very beginning of his first book, *The Structure of Social Action*.[4] Parsons correctly credits Hobbes with being the first thinker to see the necessity of explaining why human society is not a "war of all against all;" why, if man is simply a gifted animal, men refrain from unlimited resort to fraud and violence in pursuit of their ends and maintain a stable society at all. There is even a sense in which, as Coser and Mills have both noted,[5] Parsons' entire work represents an effort to solve the Hobbesian problem of order. His solution, however, has tended to become precisely the kind of elaboration of a set of answers in abstraction from questions that is so characteristic of contemporary sociological theory.

We need not be greatly concerned with Hobbes' own solution to the problem of order he saw with such unsurpassed clarity. Whatever interest his famous theory of the origin of the state may still hold for political scientists, it is clearly inadequate as an explanation of the origin of society. Yet the pattern as opposed to the details of Hobbes' thought bears closer examination.

The polar terms in Hobbes' theory are the state of nature, where the war of all against all prevails, and the authority of Leviathan, created by social contract. But the war of all against all is not simply effaced with the creation of political authority: it remains an ever-present potentiality in human society, at times quiescent, at times erupting into open violence. Whether Hobbes believed that the state of nature and the social contract were ever historical realities – and there is evidence that he was not that simple-minded and unsociological, even in the seventeenth century – is unimportant; the whole tenor of his thought is to see the war of all against all and Leviathan dialectically, as coexisting and interacting opposites.[6] As R. G. Collingwood has observed, "According to Hobbes ... *a body politic is a dialectical thing*, a Heraclitean world in which at any given time there is a negative element."[7] The first secular social theorist in the history of Western thought, and one of the first clearly to discern and define the problem of order in human society long before Darwinism made awareness of it a commonplace, Hobbes was a dialectical thinker who refused to separate answers from questions, solutions to society's enduring problems from the conditions creating the problems.

What is the answer of contemporary sociological theory to the Hobbesian question? There are two main answers, each of which has come to be understood in a way that denies the reality and meaningfulness of the question. Together they constitute a model of human nature, sometimes clearly stated, more often implicit in accepted concepts, that pervades modern sociology. The first answer is summed up in the notion of the "internalization of social norms." The second, more commonly employed or assumed in empirical research, is the view that man is essentially motivated by the desire to achieve a positive image of self by winning acceptance or status in the eyes of others.

The following statement represents, briefly and broadly, what is probably the most influential contemporary sociological conception – and dismissal – of the Hobbesian problem: "To a modern sociologist imbued with the conception that action follows institutionalized patterns, opposition of individual and common interests has only a very limited relevance or is thoroughly unsound."[8] From this writer's perspective, the problem is an unreal one: human conduct is totally shaped by common norms or "institutionalized patterns." Sheer ignorance must have led people who were unfortunate enough not to be modern sociologists to ask, "How is order possible?" A thoughtful bee or ant would never inquire, "How is the social order of the hive or ant-hill possible?" for the opposite of that order is unimaginable when the instinctive endowment of the insects ensures its stability and built-in harmony between "individual and common interests." Human society, we are assured, is not essentially different, although conformity and stability are there maintained by non-instinctive processes. Modern sociologists believe that they have understood these processes and that they have not merely answered but disposed of the Hobbesian question, showing that, far from expressing a valid intimation of the tensions and possibilities of social life, it can only be asked out of ignorance.

It would be hard to find a better illustration of what Collingwood, following Plato, calls *eristical* as opposed to dialectical thinking:[9] the answer destroys the question, or rather destroys the awareness of rival possibilities suggested by the question which accounts for its having been asked in the first place. A reversal of perspective now takes place and we are moved to ask the opposite question: "How is it that violence, conflict, revolution, and the individual's sense of coercion by society manage to exist at all, if this view is correct?"[10] Whenever a one-sided answer to a question compels us to raise the opposite question, we are caught up in a dialectic of concepts which reflects a dialectic in things But let us examine the particular processes sociologists appeal to in order to account for the elimination from human society of the war of all against all.

The Changing Meaning of Internalization

A well-known section of *The Structure of Social Action*, devoted to the interpretation of Durkheim's thought, is entitled "The Changing Meaning of

Constraint."[11] Parsons argues that Durkheim originally conceived of society as controlling the individual from the outside by imposing constraints on him through sanctions, best illustrated by codes of law But in Durkheim's later work he began to see that social rules do not "merely regulate 'externally' they enter directly into the constitution of the actors' ends themselves."[12] Constraint, therefore, is more than an environmental obstacle which the actor must take into account in pursuit of his goals in the same way that he takes into account physical laws: it becomes internal, psychological, and self-imposed as well. Parsons developed this view that social norms are constitutive rather than merely regulative of human nature before he was influenced by psychoanalytic theory, but Freud's theory of the superego has become the source and model for the conception of the internalization of social norms that today plays so important a part in sociological thinking. The use some sociologists have made of Freud's idea, however, might well inspire an essay entitled, "The Changing Meaning of Internalization," although, in contrast to the shift in Durkheim's view of constraint, this change has been a change for the worse.

What has happened is that internalization has imperceptibly been equated with "learning," or even with "habit-formation" in the simplest sense. Thus when a norm is said to have been "internalized" by an individual, what is frequently meant is that he habitually both affirms it and conforms to it in his conduct. The whole stress on inner conflict, on the tension between powerful impulses and superego controls the behavioral outcome of which cannot be prejudged, drops out of the picture. And it is this that is central to Freud's view, for in psychoanalytic terms to say that a norm has been internalized, or introjected to become part of the superego, is to say no more than that a person will suffer guilt-feelings if he fails to live up to it, not that he will in fact live up to it in his behavior.

The relation between internalization and conformity assumed by most sociologists is suggested by the following passage from a recent, highly-praised advanced textbook: "Conformity to institutionalized norms is, of course, 'normal.' The actor, having internalized the norms, feels something like a need to conform. His conscience would bother him if he did not."[13] What is overlooked here is that the person who conforms may be even more "bothered," that is, subject to guilt and neurosis, than the person who violates what are not only society's norms but his own as well. To Freud, it is precisely the man with the strictest superego, he who has most thoroughly internalized and conformed to the norms of his society, who is most wracked with guilt and anxiety.[14]

Paul Kecskemeti, to whose discussion I owe initial recognition of the erroneous view of internalization held by sociologists, argues that the relations between social norms, the individual's selection from them, his conduct, and his feelings about his conduct are far from self-evident. "It is by no means true," he writes, "to say that acting counter to one's own norms always or almost always leads to neurosis. One might assume that neurosis develops even more easily in persons who *never* violate the moral code they recognize as valid but repress and frustrate some strong instinctual motive. A person who 'succumbs to temptation,' feels guilt, and then 'purges himself' of his guilt in some reliable way (e.g., by confession) may achieve in this way a better balance, and be less neurotic, than a person who never violates his 'norms' and never feels conscious guilt."[15]

Recent discussions of "deviant behavior" have been compelled to recognize these distinctions between social demands, personal attitudes towards them, and actual conduct, although they have done so in a laboriously taxonomic fashion.[16] They represent, however, largely the rediscovery of what was always central to the Freudian concept of the superego. The main explanatory function of the concept is to show how people repress themselves, imposing checks on their own desires and thus turning the inner life into a battlefield of conflicting motives, no matter which side "wins," by successfully dictating overt action. So far as behavior is concerned, the psychoanalytic view of man is less deterministic than the sociological. For psychoanalysis is primarily concerned with the inner life, not with overt behavior, and its most fundamental insight is that the wish, the emotion, and the fantasy are as important as the act in man's experience.

Sociologists have appropriated the superego concept, but have separated it from any equivalent of the Freudian id. So long as most individuals are "socialized," that is, internalize the norms and conform to them in conduct, the Hobbesian problem is not even perceived as a latent reality. Deviant behavior is accounted for by special circumstances: ambiguous norms, anomie, role conflict, or greater cultural stress on valued goals than on the approved means for attaining them. Tendencies to deviant behavior are not seen as dialectically related to conformity. The presence in man of motivational forces bucking against the hold social discipline has over him is denied.

Nor does the assumption that internalization of norms and roles is the essence of socialization allow for a sufficient range of motives underlying conformity. It fails to allow for variable "tonicity of the superego," in Kardiner's phrase.[17] The degree to which conformity is frequently the result of coercion rather than conviction is minimized.[18] Either someone has internalized the norms, or he is "unsocialized," a feral or socially isolated child, or a psychopath. Yet Freud recognized that many people, conceivably a majority, fail to acquire superegos. "Such people," he wrote, "habitually permit themselves to do any bad deed that procures them something they want, if only they are sure that no authority will discover it or make them suffer for it; their anxiety relates only to the possibility of detection. Present-day society has to take into account the prevalence of this state of mind."[19] The last sentence suggests that Freud was aware of the decline of "inner-direction," of the Protestant conscience, about which we have heard so much lately. So let us turn to the other elements of human nature that sociologists appeal to in order to explain, or rather explain away, the Hobbesian problem.

Man the Acceptance-Seeker[20]

The superego concept is too inflexible, too bound to the past and to individual biography, to be of service in relating conduct to the pressures of the immediate situation in which it takes place. Sociologists rely more heavily therefore on an alternative notion, here stated – or, to be fair, overstated – in its baldest form: "People are so profoundly sensitive to the expectations of others that all action is inevitably guided by these expectations."[21]

Parsons' model of the "complementarity of expectations," the view that in social interaction men mutually seek approval from one another by conforming to shared norms, is a formalized version of what has tended to become a distinctive sociological perspective on human motivation. Ralph Linton states it in explicit psychological terms: "The need for eliciting favorable responses from others is an almost constant component of [personality]. Indeed, it is not too much to say that there is very little organized human behavior which is not directed toward its satisfaction in at least some degree."[22]

The insistence of sociologists on the importance of "social factors" easily leads them to stress the priority of such socialized or socializing motives in human behavior.[23] It is frequently the task of the sociologist to call attention to the intensity with which men desire and strive for the good opinion of their immediate associates in a variety of situations, particularly those where received theories or ideologies have unduly emphasized other motives such as financial gain, commitment to ideals, or the effects on energies and aspirations of arduous physical conditions. Thus sociologists have shown that factory workers are more sensitive to the attitudes of their fellow-workers than to purely economic incentives; that voters are more influenced by the preferences of their relatives and friends than by campaign debates on the "issues;" that soldiers, whatever their ideological commitment to their nation's cause, fight more bravely when their platoons are intact and they stand side by side with their "buddies."

It is certainly not my intention to criticize the findings of such studies. My objection is that their particular selective emphasis is generalized – explicitly or, more often, implicitly – to provide apparent empirical support for an extremely one-sided view of human nature. Although sociologists have criticized past efforts to single out one fundamental motive in human conduct, the desire to achieve a favorable self-image by winning approval from others frequently occupies such a position in their own thinking. The following "theorem" has been, in fact, openly put forward by Hans Zetterberg as "a strong contender for the position as the major Motivational Theorem in sociology":[24]

> An actor's actions have a tendency to become dispositions that are related to the occurrence [*sic*] of favored uniform evaluations of the actor and-or his actions in his action system.[25]

Now Zetterberg is not necessarily maintaining that this theorem is an accurate factual statement of the basic psychological roots of social behavior. He is, characteristically, far too self-conscious about the logic of theorizing and "concept formation" for that. He goes on to remark that "the maximization of favorable attitudes from others would thus be the counterpart in sociological theory to the maximization of profit in economic theory."[26] If by this it is meant that the theorem is to be understood as a heuristic rather than an empirical assumption, that sociology has a selective point of view which is just as abstract and partial as that of economics and the other social sciences, and if his view of theory as a set of logically connected formal propositions is granted provisional acceptance, I am in agreement. (Actually, the view of theory suggested at the beginning of this paper is a quite different one.)

But there is a further point to be made. Ralf Dahrendorf has observed that structural-functional theorists do not "claim that order *is based on* a general consensus of values, but that it *can be conceived of in terms of* such consensus and that, if it is conceived of in these terms, certain propositions follow which are subject to the test of specific observations."[27] The same may be said of the assumption that people seek to maximize favorable evaluations by others; indeed this assumption has already fathered such additional concepts as "reference group" and "circle of significant others." Yet the question must be raised as to whether we really wish to, in effect, define sociology by such partial perspectives. The assumption of the maximization of approval from others is the psychological complement to the sociological assumption of a general value consensus. And the former is as selective and one-sided a way of looking at motivation as Dahrendorf and others have argued the latter to be when it determines our way of looking at social structure. The oversocialized view of man of the one is a counterpart to the overintegrated view of society of the other.

Modern sociology, after all, originated as a protest against the partial views of man contained in such doctrines as utilitarianism, classical economics, social Darwinism, and vulgar Marxism. All of the great nineteenth and early twentieth century sociologists[28] saw it as one of their major tasks to expose the unreality of such abstractions as economic man, the gain-seeker of the classical economists; political man, the power-seeker of the Machiavellian tradition in political science; self-preserving man, the security-seeker of Hobbes and Darwin; sexual or libidinal man, the pleasure-seeker of doctrinaire Freudianism; and even religious man, the God-seeker of the theologians. It would be ironical if it should turn out that they have merely contributed to the creation of yet another reified abstraction in socialized man, the status-seeker of our contemporary sociologists.

Of course, such an image of man is, like all the others mentioned, valuable for limited purposes so long as it is not taken for the whole truth. What are some of its deficiencies? To begin with, it neglects the other half of the model of human nature presupposed by current theory: moral man, guided by his built-in superego and beckoning ego-ideal.[29] In recent years sociologists have been less interested than they once were in culture and national character as backgrounds to conduct, partly because stress on the concept of "role" as the crucial link between the individual and the social structure has directed their attention to the immediate situation in which social interaction takes place. Man is increasingly seen as a "role-playing" creature, responding eagerly or anxiously to the expectations of other role-players in the multiple group settings in which he finds himself. Such an approach, while valuable in helping us grasp the complexity of a highly differentiated social structure such as our own, is far too often generalized to serve as a kind of *ad hoc* social psychology, easily adaptable to particular sociological purposes. But it is not enough to concede that men often pursue "internalized values" remaining indifferent to what others think of them, particularly when, as I have previously argued, the idea of internalization has been "hollowed out" to make it more useful as an explanation of conformity. What of desire for material and sensual satisfactions? Can we really dispense with the venerable notion of material "interests" and invariably replace it with the blander, more integrative "social values"? And what of striving for power, not necessarily for its own sake – that may be rare and pathological – but as a means by which men are able to *impose* a normative definition of reality on others? That material interests, sexual drives, and the quest for power have often been over-estimated as human motives is no reason to deny their reality. To do so is to suppress one term of the dialectic between conformity and rebellion, social norms and their violation, man and social order, as completely as the other term is suppressed by those who deny the reality of man's "normative orientation" or reduce it to the effect of coercion, rational calculation, or mechanical conditioning.

The view that man is invariably pushed by internalized norms or pulled by the lure of self-validation by others ignores – to speak archaically for a moment – both the highest and the lowest, both beast and angel, in his nature. Durkheim, from whom so much of the modern sociological point of view derives, recognized that the very existence of a social norm implies and even creates the possibility of its violation. This is the meaning of his famous dictum that crime is a "normal phenomenon." He maintained that "for the originality of the idealist whose dreams transcend his century to find expression, it is necessary that the originality of the criminal, who is below the level of his time, shall also be possible. One does not occur without the other."[30] Yet Durkheim lacked an adequate psychology and formulated his insight in terms of the actor's cognitive awareness rather than in motivational terms. We do not have Durkheim's excuse for falling back on what Homans has called a "social mold theory" of human nature.[31]

Social But Not Entirely Socialized

I have referred to forces in man that are resistant to socialization. It is not my purpose to explore the nature of these forces or to suggest how we ought best conceive of them as sociologists – that would be a most ambitious undertaking. A few remarks will have to suffice. I think we must start with the recognition that *in the beginning there is the body*. As soon as the body is mentioned the specter of "biological determinism" raises its head and sociologists draw back in fright. And certainly their view of man is sufficiently disembodied and non-materialistic to satisfy Bishop Berkeley, as well as being de-sexualized enough to please Mrs. Grundy.

Am I, then, urging us to return to the older view of a human nature divided between a "social man" and a "natural man" who is either benevolent, Rousseau's Noble Savage, or sinister and destructive, as Hobbes regarded him? Freud is usually represented, or misrepresented, as the chief modern proponent of this dualistic conception which assigns to the social order the purely negative role of blocking and re-directing man's "imperious biological drives."[32] I say "misrepresented" because, although Freud often said things supporting such an interpretation, other and more fundamental strains in his thinking suggest a different conclusion. John Dollard, certainly not a writer who is oblivious to social and cultural "factors," saw this twenty-five years ago: "It is quite clear," he wrote, ". . . that he [Freud] does not regard the instincts as having a fixed social goal; rather, indeed, in the case of the sexual instinct he has stressed the vague but powerful and impulsive nature of the drive and has emphasized that its proper social object is not picked out in advance. His seems to be a drive concept which is not at variance with our knowledge from comparative cultural studies, since his theory does not demand that the 'instinct' work itself out with mechanical certainty alike in every varying culture."[33]

So much for Freud's "imperious biological drives!" When Freud defined psychoanalysis as the study of the "vicissitudes of the instincts," he was confirming, not denying, the "plasticity" of human nature insisted on by social scientists. The drives or "instincts" of psychoanalysis, far from being fixed dispositions to behave in a particular way, are utterly subject to social channelling and transformation and could not even reveal themselves in behavior without social molding any more than our vocal chords can produce articulate speech if we have not learned a language. To psychoanalysis man is indeed a social animal; his social nature is profoundly reflected in his bodily structure.[34]

But there is a difference between the Freudian view on the one hand and both sociological and neo-Freudian conceptions of man on the other. To Freud man is a *social* animal without being entirely a *socialized* animal. His very social nature is the source of conflicts and antagonisms that create resistance to socialization by the norms of any of the societies which have existed in the course of human history. "Socialization" may mean two quite distinct things; when they are confused an oversocialized view of man is the result. On the one hand socialization means the "transmission of the culture," the particular culture of the society an individual enters at to mean the "process of becoming human," of acquiring uniquely human attributes from interaction with others.[35] All men are socialized in the latter sense, but this does not mean that they have been completely molded by the particular norms and values of their culture. All cultures, as Freud contended, do violence to man's socialized bodily drives, but this in no sense means that men could possibly exist without culture or independently of society.[36] From such a standpoint, man may properly be called as Norman Brown has called him, the "neurotic" or the "discontented" animal and repression may be seen as the main characteristic of human nature as we have known it in history.[37]

But isn't this psychology and haven't sociologists been taught to forswear psychology, to look with suspicion on what are called "psychological variables" in contradistinction to the institutional and historical forces with which they are properly concerned? There is, indeed, as recent critics have complained, too much "psychologism" in contemporary sociology, largely, I think, because of the bias inherent in our favored research techniques. But I do not see how, at the level of theory, sociologists can fail to make assumptions about human nature.[38] If our assumptions are left implicit, we will inevitably presuppose of a view of man that is tailor-made to our special needs; when our sociological theory over-stresses the stability and integration of society we will end up imagining that man is the disembodied, conscience-driven, status-seeking phantom of current theory. We must do better if we really wish to win credit outside of our ranks for special understanding of man, that plausible creature[39] whose wagging tongue so often hides the despair and darkness in his heart.

Notes

This is a slightly revised version of a paper read at the meetings of the American Sociological Association in New York City, August 30, 1960.

1. Barrington Moore, Jr., *Political Power and Social Theory*, Cambridge: Harvard University Press, 1958; C. Wright Mills, *The Sociological Imagination*, New York: Oxford University Press. 1959.

2. Hannah Arendt, "Understanding and Politics," *Partisan Review*, 20 (July–August, 1953), p. 392 . For a view of social theory close to the one adumbrated in the present paper, see Theodore Abel, "The Present Status of Social Theory," *American Sociological Review*, 17 (April, 1952), pp. 156–164.

3. Reinhard Bendix and Bennett Berger, "Images of Society and Problems of Concept Formation in Sociology," in Llewellyn Gross, editor, *Symposium on Sociological Theory*, Evanston, Ill: Row, Petersen & Co., 1959, pp. 92–118; Lewis A. Coser, *The Functions of Social Conflict*, Glencoe, Ill.: The Free Press, 1956; Ralf Dahrendorf, "Out of Utopia: Towards a Re-Orientation of Sociological Analysis," *American Journal of Sociology*, 64 (September, 1958), pp. 115–127; and *Class and Class Conflict in Industrial Society*, Stanford, Calif.: Stanford University Press, 1959; David Lockwood, "Some Remarks on 'The Social System'," *British Journal of Sociology*, 7 (June, 1976), pp. 134–146.

4. Talcott Parsons, *The Structure of Social Action*, New York: McGraw-Hill Book Co., 1937, pp. 89–94.

5. Coser, *op. cit.*, p. 21; Mills, *op. cit.*, p. 44.

6. A recent critic of Parsons follows Hobbes in seeing the relation between the normative order in society and what he calls "the sub-stratum of social action" and other sociologists have called the "factual order" as similar to the relation between the war of all against all and the authority of the state. David Lockwood writes: "The existence of the normative order . . . is in one very important sense inextricably bound up with potential conflicts of interest over scarce resources . . .; the very existence of a normative order mirrors the continual potentiality of conflict." Lockwood, *op. cit.*, p. 137.

7. R. G. Collingwood, *The New Leviathan*, Oxford: The Clarendon Press, 1942, p. 183.

8. Francis X. Sutton and others, *The American Business Creed*, Cambridge: Harvard University Press, 1976, p. 304. I have cited this study and, on several occasions, textbooks and fugitive articles rather than better-known and directly theoretical writings because I am just as concerned with what sociological concepts and theories are taken to mean when they are actually used in research, teaching and introductory exposition as with their elaboration in more self-conscious and explicitly theoretical discourse. Since the model of human nature I am criticizing is partially implicit and "buried" in our concepts, cruder and less qualified illustrations are as relevant as the formulations of leading theorists. I am also aware that some older theorists, notably Cooley and MacIver, were shrewd and worldly-wise enough to reject the implication that man is ever fully socialized. Yet they failed to develop competing images of man which were concise and systematic enough to counter the appeal of the oversocialized models.

9. Collingwood, *op. cit.*, pp. 151–152.

10. *Cf.* Mills, *op. cit.*, pp. 32–33, 42. While Mills does not discuss the use of the concept of internalization by Parsonian theorists, I have argued elsewhere that his view of the relation between power and values is insufficiently dialectical. See Dennis H. Wrong, "The Failure of American Sociology," *Commentary*, 28 (November, 1959), p. 378.

11. Parsons, *op. cit.*, pp. 378–390.

12. *Ibid.*, p. 382

13. Harry M. Johnson, *Sociology: A Systematic Introduction*, New York: Harcourt, Brace and Co., 1960, p. 22.

14. Sigmund Freud, *Civilization and Its Discontents*, New York Doubleday Anchor Books, 1958, pp. 80–81.

15. Paul Kecskemeti, *Meaning, Communication and Value*, Chicago: University of Chicago Press, 1952, pp. 244–245

16. Robert Dubin, "Deviant Behavior and Social Structure: Continuities in Social Theory," *American Sociological Review*, 24 (April, 1959), pp. 147–164; Robert K. Merton, "Social Conformity, Deviation, and Opportunity Structures: A Comment on the Contributions of Dubin and Cloward," *ibid.*, pp. 178–189.

17. Abram Kardiner, *The Individual and his Society*, New York: Columbia University Press, 1939, pp. 65, 72–75.

18. Mills, *op. cit.*, pp. 39–41; Dahrendorf, *Class and Class Conflict in Industrial Society*, pp. 157–165.

19. Freud, *op. cit.*, pp. 78–79.

20. In many ways I should prefer to use the neater, more alliterative phrase "status-seeker." However, it has acquired a narrower meaning than I intend, particularly since Vance Packard appropriated it, suggesting primarily efforts, which are often consciously deceptive, to give the appearance of personal achievements or qualities worthy of deference. "Status seeking" in this sense is, as Veblen perceived, necessarily confined to

relatively impersonal and segmental social relationships. "Acceptance" or "approval" convey more adequately what all men are held to seek in both intimate and impersonal relations according to the conception of the self and of motivation dominating contemporary sociology and social psychology. I have, nevertheless, been unable to resist the occasional temptation to use the term "status" in this broader sense.

21. Sutton and others, *op. cit.*, p. 264. Robert Cooley Angell, in *Free Society and Moral Crisis*, Ann Arbor: University of Michigan Press, 1958, p. 34, points out the ambiguity of the term "expectations." It is used, he notes, to mean both a factual prediction and a moral imperative, e.g. "England expects every man to do his duty." But this very ambiguity is instructive, for it suggests the process by which behavior that is non-normative and perhaps even "deviant" but nevertheless "expected" in the sense of being predictable, acquires over time a normative aura and becomes "expected" in the second sense of being socially approved or demanded. Thus Parsons' "interaction paradigm" provides leads to the understanding of social change and need not be confined, as in his use of it, to the explanation of conformity and stability. But this is the subject of another paper I hope to complete shortly.

22. Ralph Linton, *The Cultural Background of Personality*, New York: Appleton-Century Co., 1945, p. 91.

23. When values are "inferred" from this emphasis and then popularized, it becomes the basis of the ideology of "groupism" extolling the virtues of "togetherness" and "belongingness" that have been attacked and satirized so savagely in recent social criticism. David Riesman and W. H. Whyte, the pioneers of this current of criticism in its contemporary guise, are both aware, as their imitators and epigoni usually are not, of the extent to which the social phenomenon they have described is the result of the diffusion and popularization of sociology itself. See on this point Robert Gutman and Dennis H. Wrong, "Riesman's Typology of Character" (forthcoming in a symposium on Riesman's work to be edited by Leo Lowenthal and Seymour Martin Lipset), and William H. Whyte, *The Organization Man*, New York: Simon and Schuster, 1956, Chapters 3–5. As a matter of fact, Riesman's "inner-direction" and "other-direction" correspond rather closely to the notions of "internalization" and "acceptance-seeking" in contemporary sociology as I have described them. Riesman even refers to his concepts initially as characterizations of "modes of conformity," although he then makes the mistake, as Robert Gutman and I have argued, of calling them character types. But his view that all men are to some degree both inner-directed and other-directed, a qualification that has been somewhat neglected by critics who have understandably concentrated on his empirical and historical use of his typology, suggests the more generalized conception of forces making for conformity found in current theory. See David Riesman, Nathan Glazer, and Reuel Denny, *The Lonely Crowd*, New York: Doubleday Anchor Books, 1953, pp. 17ff. However, as Gutman and I have observed: "In some respects Riesman's conception of character is Freudian rather than neoFreudian: character is defined by superego mechanisms and, like Freud in *Civilization and Its Discontents*, the socialized individual is defined by what is forbidden him rather than by what society stimulates him to do. Thus in spite of Riesman's generally sanguine attitude towards modern America, implicit in his typology is a view of society as the enemy both of individuality and of basic drive gratification, a view that contrasts with the at least potentially benign role assigned it by neo-Freudian thinkers like Fromm and Horney." Gutman and Wrong, "Riesman's Typology of Character," p. 4 (typescript).

24. Hans L. Zetterberg, "Compliant Actions," *Acta Sociologica*, 2 (1957) p. 189.

25. *Ibid.*, p. 188.
26. *Ibid.*, p. 189.
27. Dahrendorf, *Class and Class Conflict in Industrial Society*, p. 158.
28. Much of the work of Thorstein Veblen, now generally regarded as a sociologist (perhaps the greatest America has yet produced), was, of course, a polemic against the rational, calculating *homo economicus* of classical economics and a documentation of the importance in economic life of the quest for status measured by conformity to arbitrary and shifting conventional standards. Early in his first and most famous book Veblen made an observation on human nature resembling that which looms so large in contemporary sociological thinking: "The usual basis of self-respect," he wrote, "is the respect accorded by one's neighbors. Only individuals with an aberrant temperament can in the long run retain their self-esteem in the face of the disesteem of their fellows," *The Theory of the Leisure Class,* New York: Mentor Books, 1953, p. 38. Whatever the inadequacies of his psychological assumptions, Veblen did not, however, overlook other motivations to which he frequently equal or greater weight.
29. Robin M. Williams, Jr. writes: "At the present time, the literature of sociology and social psychology contains many references to 'Conformity' – conforming to norms, 'yielding to social pressure,' or 'adjusting to the requirements of the reference group.' . . .; the implication is easily drawn that the actors in question are motivated solely in terms of conformity or non-conformity, rather than in terms of 'expressing' or 'affirming' internalized values . . ." (his italics). "Continuity and Change in Sociological Study," *American Sociological Review*, 23 (December, 1958), p. 630.
30. Emile Durkheim, *The Rules of Sociological Method,* Chicago: University of Chicago Press, 1938, p. 71.
31. George C. Homans, *The Human Group*, New York: Harcourt, Brace and Company, 1950, pp. 317–319.
32. Robert K. Merton, *Social Theory and Social Structure*, Revised and Enlarged Edition, Glencoe, Ill.: The Free Press, 1957, p. 131. Merton's view is representative of that of most contemporary sociologists. See also Hans Gerth and C. Wright Mills, *Character and Social Structure*, New York: Harcourt, Brace and Company, 1953, pp. 112–113. For a similar view by a "neo-Freudian," see Erich Fromm, *The Sane Society*, New York: Rinehart and Company, 195;, pp. 74–77.
33. John Dollard, *Criteria for the Life History*, New Haven: Yale University Press, 1935, p. 120. This valuable book has been neglected, presumably because it appears to be a purely methodological effort to set up standards for judging the adequacy of biographical and autobiographical data. Actually, the standards serve as well to evaluate the adequacy of general theories of personality or human nature and even to prescribe in part what a sound theory ought to include.
34. One of the few attempts by a social scientist to relate systematically man's anatomical structure and biological history to his social nature and his unique cultural creativity is Weston La Barre's *The Human Animal,* Chicago: University of Chicago Press, 1954. See especially Chapters 4–6, but the entire book is relevant. It is one of the few exceptions to Paul Goodman's observation that anthropologists nowadays "commence with a chapter on Physical Anthropology and then forget the whole topic and go on to Culture." See his "Growing up Absurd," *Dissent,* 7 (Spring, 1960), p. 121.
35. Paul Goodman has developed a similar distinction. *Op. cit.*, pp. 123–125.
36. Whether it might be possible to create a society that does not repress the bodily drives is a separate question. See Herbert Marcuse, *Eros and Civilization,* Boston:

The Beacon Press, 1955; and Norman O. Brown, *Life Against Death*, New York: Random House, Modern Library Paperbacks, 1960. Neither Marcuse nor Brown are guilty in their brilliant, provocative, and visionary books of assuming a "natural man" who awaits liberation from social bonds. They differ from such sociological Utopians as Fromm, *op. cit.*, in their lack of sympathy for the de-sexualized man of the neo-Freudians. For the more traditional Freudian view, see Walter A. Weisskopf, "The 'Socialization' of Psychoanalysis in Contemporary America," in Benjamin Nelson, editor *Psychoanalysis and the Future*, New York: National Psychological Association For Psychoanalysis, 1957, pp. 51–56; Hans Meyerhoff, "Freud and the Ambiguity of Culture," *Partisan Review*, 24 (Winter, 1957), pp. 117–130.

37. Brown, *op. cit.*, pp. 3–19.

38. "I would assert that very little sociological analysis is ever done without using at least an implicit psychological theory," Alex Inkeles, "Personality and Social Structure," in Robert K. Merton and others, editors, *Sociology Today*, New York: Basic Books, 1959, p. 250.

39. Harry Stack Sullivan once remarked that the most outstanding characteristic of human beings was their "plausibility."

52

Deviant Behavior and Social Structure: Continuities in Social Theory

Robert Dubin

A theoretical typology of behavior can be tested for its internal logic. It can also be tested for its ability to model that portion of reality for which it stands. On both of these grounds Merton's model of deviant behavior is subjected to tests in this paper. We conclude that his typology provides a magnificent basis for moving forward to a sociologically relevant extension, which includes ten additional types of deviant behavior supplementing the four depicted by Merton. Here, this typology is developed step-by-step, starting with Merton's original paradigm. In successive stages, a substantive modification based on his own discussion of the model is presented, followed by the logical extension of the model to a typology consisting of fourteen distinctive categories of deviant behavior.

Extension of Merton's Typology

In "Social Structure and Anomie,"[1] Merton's typology of deviant behavior includes four modes of adaptation: innovation, ritualism, retreatism, and rebellion. His fifth category, conformity, is of no interest in examining the range of deviant behavior.

It is clear that an important distinction is substantively made in Merton's presentation which is not recognized however in his formal typology. The discussion of innovation together with the examples Merton cites, demonstrates that the innovator is actively seeking alternatives for the institutionalized means he rejects.[2] This is to be sharply distinguished, as Merton himself does, from simple rejection as displayed in the ritualism and retreatism modes of individual adaptation.

This interpretation of Merton's paradigm requires that for innovation the simple rejection of institutionalized means be replaced by an active rejection (rejection and substitution). Thus, Table 1 presents the substantive revision of

Source: *American Sociological Review*, 1959, vol. 24, pp. 147–164.

Merton's model, with the entry in parenthesis representing his original formulation. This initial revision simply modifies the formal Merton typology so as to conform with the actual meaning he gives to innovation in his illustrated discussion of it.[3]

Table 1. Substantive Revision of Merton's Model Based on his Own Discussion of It

Mode of Adaptation	Cultural Goals	Institutionalized Means
Innovation	+	± (−)*
Ritualism	−	+
Retreatism	−	−
Rebellion	±	±

+ = acceptance
− = rejection
± = rejection and substitution (active rejection)
*Merton's entry in his original table.

The next logical step in modifying the Merton typology is afforded by the common distinction, made in both sociology and normal discourse, between the actual behavior of the actor and the values guiding his selection of particular behaviors. This distinction introduces two additional modes of adaptation in the model: we can now subdivide innovation and ritualism into two categories. Behavioral innovation differs from value innovation, and behavioral ritualism is a type of adaptation distinct from value ritualism. Furthermore, it is clear that retreatism and rebellion are not subject to further subdivision from the standpoint of the difference between behavior and value, since both categories, by definition, always involve identical response to both behaviors and values (rejection for retreatism, and active rejection for rebellion).

Table 2 exhibits the first extension of the Merton typology. Examination of the table reveals that the condition of innovation (an acceptance coupled with an active rejection) is met in both behavioral and value innovation. Similarly, the condition of ritualism (a simple rejection coupled with an acceptance) can be met and we can still logically distinguish between behavioral ritualism and value ritualism. We now have six modes of deviant adaptation where Merton originally proposed four.

We further extend the typology by differentiating between institutionalized norms and institutionalized means. Here attention is limited to the institutional setting. Institutional norms become the cultural goals of the larger society translated into guides for *behavior* in the single institution. Thus Parsons, in his analysis of the motivation of economic activity, shows how the success goal of a capitalistic society is defined quite differently in the business institution and the profession.[4] Merton himself makes the distinction now being drawn in the following statement about "retreatists": "They have relinquished culturally prescribed goals and their behavior does not accord with institutional norms."[5] This is precisely the sort of reality we are trying to catch up in differentiating between cultural goals, institutional norms, and institutional means. Such reality has clear-cut consequences in delineating modes of deviant behavior.[6]

Table 2. First Extension of the Merton Typology of Deviant Behavior

Mode of Adaptation	Cultural Goals	Institutionalized Means
Behavioral Innovation (Merton)	+	±
Value Innovation (new)	±	+
Behavioral Ritualism (Merton)	−	+
Value Ritualism (new)	+	−
Retreatism	−	−
Rebellion	±	±

+ = acceptance
− = rejection
± = rejection and substitution (active rejection)

We can define institutional norms as the boundaries between *pre*scribed behaviors and *pro*scribed behaviors in a particular institutional setting. Institutional norms set the limits between which the institutional means are prescribed — the limits of legitimate behaviors in a particular institution. Beyond the norms lie illegitimate behaviors. Institutional means, in contrast, are the specific behaviors, prescribed or potential, that lie within the limits established by institutional norms. Institutional means are actual behaviors of people, the things they do in carrying out functions in the institutional setting in which they are acting. This distinction is incorporated in the typology of modes of deviant adaptations in social action, displayed in Table 3.

Table 3 is an extension of Table 2. The two tables are logically congruent in the following respects: In the column headed Cultural Goals the entries for all of the major categories are identical with those in Table 2. For example, the three types of behavioral innovation exhibit acceptance of cultural goals as demanded by the first line of Table 2. Similarly, all the entries in the last two columns of Table 3 are consistent with their parent entries in Table 2: the entry in the parent category of Table 2 is replicated under either institutional norms or institutional means, or both.[7]

Table 3. A typology of Deviant Adaptations in Social Action

Type of Deviant Adaptation	Mode of attachment to –		
	Cultural Goals	Institutional Norms	Institutional Means
Behavioral Innovation			
Institutional Invention	+	±	±
Normative Invention	+	±	+
Operating Invention	+	+	±
Value Innovation			
Intellectual Invention	±	+	+
Organization Invention	±	±	+
Social Movement	±	+	±
Behavioral Ritualism			
Levelling of Aspirations	–	+	+
Institutional Moralist	–	+	–
Organization Automaton	–	–	+
Value Ritualism			
Demagogue	+	–	–
Normative Opportunist	+	–	+
Means Opportunist	+	+	–
Retreatism	–	–	–
Rebellion	+	+	–

+ = acceptance
– = rejection
± = rejection and substitution (active rejection)

Now we may consider examples of each of the fourteen types of deviant behavior set forth in Table 3. This is exactly the procedure followed by Merton in his original paper. Exemplification of concepts is designed to discover whether the analytical categories used for classifying the outcomes of behavior, in fact, are populated. If we can present reasonable examples of each proposed type, then the category becomes useful for analytical purposes in classifying social behavior. If the category is a vacuous one, then the attempt to exemplify it, by producing no results, leads to the rejection of the class without further test.

Behavioral Innovation

We examine behavioral innovation in a context of social change. Here we are concerned with innovating behavior as a form of invention. This is a context that Merton deliberately avoids, except obliquely in the last section of "Social Structure and Anomie." Its consideration, however, illuminates that general category of deviant behavior we call behavioral innovation.

The analysis of types of behavioral innovation is the problem of determining the functions of deviancies with respect to institutions. Our general conclusion is that behavioral innovations are constructive inventions in the institutional settings in which they occur.

Institutional Invention Institutional inventions take place when new standards of legitimacy come to be accepted, governing newly developed or formerly illegitimate behaviors. The historical point of invention of an institution occurs when the new norms achieve legitimacy and the behaviors conforming to them are practiced. Thus Table 3 indicates an active rejection of institutional norms *and* means in institutional invention. Not only are both rejected but men seek institutional substitutes.

The development of collective bargaining illustrates institutional invention. The relations in industry between management and men has been governed by the institution of collective bargaining in the United States for a period of less than half the history of the country. Indeed, collective bargaining as a dominant feature of the industrial milieu is a phenomenon of recent decades. The institutional norm of exclusive decision-making about the firm by management had to be modified to include joint decision-making, at least with respect to the destinies of employees, before collective bargaining could be established as an institution. Joint decision making as the institutional norm was preceded by experiments by workingmen to reach agreements on minimum working conditions, and then to seek employer acceptance of these unilaterally determined conditions. These attempts by workers extend back to the beginning of the 19th century in America and were characteristic of the earliest trade union behavior.[8] The evolution of collective bargaining also reveals that management, guided by the norm of unilateral managerial decision, tried such operating inventions (see below) as paternalism, company unionism, employee representation plans, and "consultative management" (now included in some applications of "group dynamics" to industry) in an effort to forestall the institution of collective bargaining.⁹

The acceptance by industrial managers of joint decision-making concerning employment was the normative foundation of collective bargaining. That this norm had to be forcibly imposed by a sympathetic Federal administration should not obscure the fact that bargaining between management and unions rests fundamentally on the social value that employees should have some voice, through union representatives, about their own employment destiny. It is not necessary here to catalog the institutional means invented so as to make operative the new norm. But it should be noted that the behaviors of management representatives, union officers, unionized employees, and the products of their bargaining interaction depart significantly from old behaviors and their legitimate outcomes.

Another example of institutional invention is the development of employer supported (or partially supported) health and welfare funds for employees. This innovation is of recent origin, almost exclusively a post-World War II phenomenon. The basic normative change in this case was the recognition that the employment contract established an explicit employer responsibility to support the welfare of his employees away from work as well as at work. Thus health and welfare benefits extend to illnesses, accidents, and other disabilities wholly unrelated to work; in some instances even family members are eligible for benefits.

A number of unanticipated consequences have resulted from the invention of this institution, associated with the behaviors appropriate to it (institutional means). The rapid growth of very large reserve funds, for example, opened important avenues for racketeering exploitation of unions, as the McClellan investigating committee of the Senate has so abundantly made clear. Another unanticipated development, consonant with the collective bargaining welfare institution, is the need for expert guidance in the investment of reserve funds. This investment function, a necessary means for consenting health and welfare funds, has "capitalized" labor unions, and has made such funds, which they control exclusively or jointly with management, an important source of investment capital in the whole economy.

These examples – there are of course many others – make it clear that institutions are invented when cultural goals are accepted but institutional norms and means are actively rejected.

Normative Invention In Table 3 it will be noted that this type of deviant adaptation is characterized by the fact that new norms are introduced into an old institutional setting without changes in the institutional means being actively sought. The new norms are typically the consequence of changed conditions under which the institution operates. Responses to the new conditions necessitate the replacement of old norms by new.¹⁰

An important illustration of normative invention is given in Bendix's excellent study of managerial ideology, specifically with reference to authority in the industrial setting.[11] In his analysis of American managerial ideology Bendix shows that new norms giving legitimacy to managerial authority have been the product of 20th century enterprise. His study traces out the history of conditions external to industry to which the new norms represent managerial responses. In general, he concludes that the old norm of "might makes right" has been replaced by the new norm that technical competence is necessary in managerial decisions, which justifies the authority of technically trained people to make industrial decisions. While this is an oversimplified summary of Bendix's main thesis regarding American managerial ideology, it illustrates normative invention in the industrial institution. This is not to claim that the change in norms represented in the shift in ideological justification of industrial authority has had no consequences for institutional behavior (means) in industry. Rather, and this is Bendix's central point of departure, the self-consciously changing element in the industrial institution was the norm governing authority of management over workers.

A more recent and still evolving normative invention is illustrated by hot-rodding. The prevalence of automobiles in the United States and the very limited functional uses to which teen-agers licensed to drive could put cars led to the development of "drag races," about which many youngsters became enthusiastic; but this development was viewed with alarm by many persons, who condemned drag racing as illegitimate behavior in operating cars. The initial response of civil authorities was to ban the activity, applying police sanctions against it. Sympathetic consideration by juvenile authorities led to the recognition of the play element in drag racing, and the consequent normative invention of a game to legitimize this dangerous pastime. Local communities set up drag strips and provided police or other supervision for approved drag races. Motor clubs of teen-agers rapidly developed as institutionally respectable organizations participating in the now legitimate sport. Within the institution governing the operation of motor vehicles, then, a normative invention occurred which gave to an already developed activity the moral sanction of legitimacy by surrounding it with an acceptable justification. More generally, it may be added, those programs dealing with juvenile delinquency that focus on "taming" the organizations and gangs of youth have as their objective a normative invention, one permitting incorporation of gang-centered behavior into some established institutional setting.

Operating Invention The most common form of behavioral innovation is the establishment of new activities which flow from the acceptance of institutional norms, an operating invention. We defined institutional means above, as "specific behaviors, prescribed or potential, that lie within the limits established by the institutional norms." Operating inventions are wholly concerned with innovating behaviors that represent the fulfillment of the potential behavior patterns possible within the limits established by the institutional norms.[12] Such operating inventions are almost daily occurrences in the institutionalized behavior of people. These operating inventions exhibit creativity in the routines of life.[13]

Fad and fashion are good examples of operating inventions. Folk fads and fashions in dress, language usage, and stylistic gestural behavior operate within normative prescriptions. Styles in clothing, for example, may approach, but do not exceed, the norm demanding minimum covering of "private parts." Complete nudism is reserved for such other institutional settings as the burlesque show, the artist's studio, the brothel, the marital bedroom, the nudist encampment. Each of these settings has its special norms legitimizing the undraped body.

Examples of operating invention abound. The special jargon of a group or occupation is a case in point. So are many technologies and craft secrets of working groups.[14] In social investigation the use of projective tests, the psychoanalytic interview, and some forms of content analysis of the subject's normal discourse, are operating inventions designed to explore the sub-conscious.

Sociologically, one of the most relevant features of the "Kinsey reports" is that in the privacy of their bed chambers conventional middle class Americans make operating inventions in the realm of sexual behavior. Of course, these may be discoveries only to those who make them, and simply replications from the standpoint of the institution in which they are made. This phenomenon has particular relevance to socialization, much of which occurs through the conscious transmittal to succeeding generations of the social practices of the present. But there is a realm of socialization in which the person privately experiments with behaviors (institutional means) which are not known to him as institutionally legitimate. Such operating inventions are "privatized" because the behaviors occur in areas of delicacy – here overt instruction is awkward or even embarrassing. While sexual behavior illustrates this situation in our society, it does not in Samoa, for example, where erotic performance is a matter of conscious instruction.[15]

In business a privatized realm is also marked by operating inventions. the tricks for making and closing retail sales. In this case, each salesman usually experiments with sales techniques or observes successful colleagues; a recent series of articles in an appliance sales trade journal describes some of these sales gimmicks in detail.[16] These articles stimulated two extreme types of responses in letters to the editor. There were those writers who considered the revelations immoral (that is, illegitimate in business dealings), but who were probably more nearly expressing their embarrassment that such matters of delicacy had escaped the realm of private operating invention. The second group of letters expressed enthusiasm for the revelations as useful and important for sales success.

Cohen, in taking issue with Merton's formulation of deviant behavior, points out that juvenile gang members often behave with wanton destruction and apparently pointless brutality.[17] Cohen suggests that this represents a repudiation of middle class norms, and in this fashion such behavior can be analytically oriented to the social system. Merton admits that his typology excludes this kind of deviant behavior.[18] I would contend that if we grant the existence of the institutional norms of a gang as including solidary relations and internal competition among members for status, then wanton destructiveness and brutality become explicable as operating inventions The whole gang follows this course in fulfilling the normative expectation that the activity of the group will be solidary. The apparent randomness of the acts themselves and their pointlessness from the standpoint of larger institutional norms or cultural goals may be explained as the consequence of the search by the individual for potential activities within the institutional norms of gangs the discovery of which is status-conferring for the inventor. Within these two normative prescriptions the wanton behavior of gang members become illustrations of behavioral innovation of the operating invention type.

Part of the adventure and mystery of growing up is a product of deviant behavior of this type. From the viewpoint of the actor, and not the social system, individually created operating inventions may be surrounded by a sense of uncertainty.[19] The private character of the behavior, which does not appear to accord with the publicly acknowledged institutional means (legitimate behaviors), may also produce a temporary guilt response in the actor. This guilt may be different in kind from that associated with illegitimate acts that clearly are proscribed by institutional norms. When an individual is experimenting with behaviors that potentially may fall within the prescribed normative limits, the occasion for guilt is his ignorance as to whether this in fact is so. Hence, the behavior is less likely to be suppressed as in the case of violations of normative proscriptions (when the norms are internalized), and is more likely to be carried on surreptitiously with attentive concern for evidence that others are doing the same thing and that the problematic behavior really falls within the prescribed normative limits. Thus, guilt engendered in operating invention is tentative and is not apt to result in suppression sublimation, or other permanent resolutions of conflicts between norms and proscribed conduct.

This analysis suggests the presence of areas of anxiety in social behavior that are a product of incomplete socialization. The person experiments with behaviors not clearly proscribed by institutional norms, but which he does not know to fall within the range of prescribed legitimate activity. Socialization becomes complete, and anxieties dissipate, when the actor learns that his operating invention, in fact, is a replication of delicate or "hidden" behaviors not readily transmitted through education or open instruction. The adventures of growing up, and of adult socialization, are heightened by private operating inventions and the anxiety they engender until the individual is finally "in the know" that his experiments are actually legitimate.[20]

Value Innovation

By value innovation we mean the self-conscious rejection of cultural goals and either institutional norms or institutional means and an active search for substitutes. Value innovation is relatively uncommon in all social systems. It is usually surrounded by open controversy between those espousing the new values and the vast majority wedded to the old. Indeed, value innovation constitutes the arena of social change in which the "big things" of a society are modified. The realm of value innovation is one in which new ideas, ideologies, and standards of right and wrong are introduced into the social system. We distinguish three types of value innovation as forms of deviant adaptation.

Intellectual Invention An intellectual invention results from the active rejection of a cultural goal and the search for a positive substitute. The history of ideas is replete with intellectual inventions.

Copernicus was responsible for shifting the orientation to the physical universe from an earth-centered to an earth-component viewpoint. Pasteur stirred the realms of biological science by changing the study of the etiology of disease to microscopic organisms. Einstein's concept of relativity made a great deal of difference in the goals towards which physical and chemical research were directed (providing, for example, a wholly new system of mechanics to replace the Newtonian mechanics, which in its day was also a major intellectual invention). Boole created a system of algebra which required almost a century to find application in the behavioral sciences as a precise logic and language for stating concepts and transformations of typology and classification. Freud made the analysis of the role of the sub-conscious in human behavior a central goal of scientific endeavor. Marx invented a dynamic model for analyzing social systems, some of the consequences of which are now the focal point of a world struggle. These are illustrations of widely known intellectual inventions of continuing influence.

There are two characteristic features of intellectual inventions: (1) the redefinition of cultural goals by the invention is limited to a given institution or complex of institutions; and (2) its originator considers his invention testable by the institutional norms and institutional means for which it has relevance.

Each institution or institutional complex of a social system has its own cultural goals. In the institution of science, for example, a modern goal is the accumulation of knowledge, including both the additions called new knowledge and the replications of old knowledge by the use of more refined technologies of investigation and knowing.[21] The cultural goal of "success" may be shared by several institutions in the same society. But the institutionally specific definition of success in science is quite different from that in the business institution. It follows that intellectual inventions, in changing the goals of behavior in a specific institution, may not necessarily conflict with the more general cultural goals of the whole society. Thus, the invention of the sub-conscious as a unit in the scientific model of the human personality had a profound and has a continuing influence. This intellectual invention declared a new objective for scientific investigation of personality; it set up a new goal for behavioral scientists — to build models incorporating the sub-conscious and to develop empirical methods for its study.

The second characteristic of an intellectual invention, it will be recalled, is that it is testable by the norms of the relevant institution according to the institution's legitimate means. (While the following examples are drawn from science, the point is applicable more broadly.) Thus, Einstein was constrained to assert that the tests of his general and special theories of relativity would depend on the canons of scientific investigation and the available empirical means. And Pasteur insisted on using the norms and means of scientific investigation, his original detractors concluding that his intellectual invention could be rejected out of hand without test according to the canons of science.

A major consequence of intellectual invention is that it usually gives rise to active, and sometimes bitter, controversy among the participants of the institution to which it applies. The history of all profound intellectual inventions shows that the initial opposition comes from within the institution to which they apply. There may be a subsequent popular castigation of the invention and its inventor.

Here we can not document intra-institutional conflict stimulated by intellectual invention; we nevertheless assert that this is demonstrably the case. But we can reach one important conclusion as to why controversy in an institution should center here. Intellectual inventions establish new goals for activity. They provide new rationalizations for institutionalized behavior. Part of the dynamic of a social system is that activity goals are more persistently adhered to than are the actual forms of behavior. This is another way of saying that ideology is more resistant to change than action. The intellectual inventor seeks to change the ideology of an institution and is therefore viewed by its participants as attacking the institution's most sacred feature. In general, behavioral innovation is more frequent than value innovation, and more frequently welcomed.

Organization Invention As a type of value innovation, an organization invention is characterized by the replacement of old cultural goals and institutional norms by new ones. The theoretical reason for the appearance of a new organizational form when cultural goals and institutional norms are simultaneously innovated is clear. An established institution and the organizations embodying it lose the coordinating influences of values when goals and norms are changed at the same time. Under these circumstances neither the aims of conduct nor the criteria for evaluating their legitimacy are stable; should the situation persist, chaotic behavior would result. We therefore conclude that when cultural goals and institutional norms change together a new organization is created.[22]

Organization invention may be illustrated in various realms. In the military services, for example, the Air Corps was originally developed as an auxiliary unit of ground forces providing a larger vista for observation of the enemy. During World War I plane-to-plane combat began to specialize the military function of aircraft. The development of heavier planes capable of carrying explosives to a target beyond the reach of conventional arms further specialized military aviation. It soon became apparent to some individuals, as the General Billy Mitchell controversy demonstrated, that the existing goals of military strategy, which made of aircraft ancillary rather than independent arms, were inadequate to guide the use of this weapon. Furthermore, the specific norms of aircraft operations, recruitment, and training of personnel no longer fitted the standard military mold. The strategic and tactical use of aircraft, together with their proper technological and doctrinal development, could no longer be satisfactorily achieved within the existing military organizations. The effective rejection of the cultural goals for military aviation as an extension of conventional ground arms and the organizational needs for distinctive technical usage and personnel development required the development of a new organizational form. These pressures ultimately led to the creation of an independent Air Force coordinate with the Army and Navy. The Air Force, then, can be viewed as the product of active rejection of military cultural goals and institutional norms, resulting in organization invention.

It should be noted, however, that the Air Force retained most of the means of the military institution. Thus conventional training with small arms and close order drill are a standard feature, although of no direct value in military operations. Similarly, the traditional military line authority structure was initially followed, although eventually it was modified in specific content to conform to the command functions required in Air Force operations.

Value innovation resulting in organization invention, as this example suggests, is a real category of deviant adaptation characterized by active rejection of existing cultural goals and institutional norms. Organization invention and normative invention (discussed above) are forms of deviant adaptation particularly significant for formal organizations. Organization invention leads to the development of new types of organizations. Normative inventions, on the other hand, lead to the legitimation of new functional specializations within existing organizations. This has the consequence of further elaborating organizational division of labor, evidenced, for example, by various technical specialties in business organizations – legitimized and firmly established through normative invention.

Social Movements As a form of group deviant behavior, social movements are characterized by an active search for new cultural goals and modification of existing institutional means. Social movements, however, remain attached to the existing social system through acceptance by their participants of institutional norms in the area of their interests – they are not wholly alienated from the society in which they appear.

Members of a social movement are singularly unconcerned with conversion of adversaries or the larger populace to their cause. Their strategy of action is to secure the extension of existing institutional norms to cover an excluded group, adherents of the movement. Indifference to conversion of those presently favored by the norms makes for high in-group solidarity among members by emphasizing their distinctive identity – women "righters" remain females; Negro "righters" do not give up their racial distinctiveness.

The social movement centering on women's rights had the objective of substantive equality for women and men[23] – clearly a rejection of existing cultural goals. But the action program in this case was focused on the alteration of institutional means. Thus in politics, the franchise was an actively sought goal, which assumed the legitimacy of the norms of the political institution, seeking only a change in institutional means to gain the vote for women. In the field of employment, programmatic goals concerned governmental protection of women from employer exploitation due to their unequal position in the society, thus leading to equality of treatment with men in terms of wages and working conditions for comparable jobs. Trivial illustrations of changes in institutional means sought by this movement include dress by active leaders simulating male attire and the disparagement of traditional male courtesies. In such manner the movement for women's rights actively rejected cultural goals and institutional means, while accepting institutional norms.

The Negro rights movement can be analyzed in similar terms. Here, the new cultural goal being sought is substantive equality with whites in the general treatment of Negroes. The programmatic features of the movement center on fair employment legislation and practice in industry, removal of restrictive covenants in housing, equal voting rights with whites, and equality of facilities in education. These are all attempts to change institutional means within established institutional norms so as to attain new cultural goals. Again, we see the analytically characteristic features of the deviant adaptation called a social movement.

Merton gives pre-eminence in his discussion of innovation to the negative aspects of the behavior of innovators from the standpoint of the social system. From this viewpoint innovating behavior may be dysfunctional for the stability of a social system.[24] In contrast, we have analyzed innovation as a feature of social change and thereby emphasize the lasting consequences of innovation. Individual and group innovators are concerned with changing existing social arrangements. We have delineated six categories of such innovating behavior, substantively different in kind, that have real counterparts in social life.

Behavioral Ritualism

Ritualism is distinguished from innovation by the fact that the person whose behavior or ideas are ritualized rejects facets of the social system without seeking substitutes, at the same time remaining "attached" to the system by over-conforming to other social and cultural elements.

In all six types of ritualism analyzed here, there is a large category of social behavior in which values are not directly linked to social behavior. In this connection, Durkheim's concept of anomie becomes useful. Normlessness has significance for social action when that action is not guided by values. This result may obtain if there is (1) a rejection of values, as in retreatism or (2) an over-conformity to values without reference to the behavioral consequences of such over-conformity. The problem of values as selectors of behavior is not simply the issue of whether any goals or norms are accepted by actors as guiding behavior. It is also necessary to examine situations of over-conformity to goals and norms which do not result in institutionally legitimate action. Both cases are forms of normlessness, or anomie.

Levelling of Aspirations Merton's analysis of ritualism elaborates this first type. He points out that rejection of cultural goals (for example. the success goal in American society) leads to a ritualism in which the person retreats into the institutional setting of primary significance to his own life interests and scales downward his aspirations concerning rewards available to him in that setting. Merton has clearly established the reality of this type of deviant adaptation and has provided numerous examples of it.[25]

Institutional Moralist This moralist centers his overconforming behavior on the norms of the institution in which he acts. This over-conformity is expressed in a persistent reiteration of these norms. Often the institutional moralist is found in an official position within an organization that gives legitimacy to his ritualistic "drumming" of the norms. Thus a clergyman, a business executive, a military commander, a labor union leader, or a government functionary may become an institutional moralist.

The hallmark of the institutional moralist is exhibited in the folk aphorism, "Do as I say, not as I do." The response may be, "Your actions speak so loud I can't hear what you're saying." These folk sayings capture both the subjective view that the institutional moralist takes of himself and a common reaction of those to whom his moralizing is addressed.

The institutional moralist plays the role of Jiminiy Cricket on the shoulders of an institution. His legitimate activities focus on the iteration of institutional norms, keeping them in the awareness of institutional participants. This may be highly functional for the institution as a whole, in spite of the fact that the institutional moralist himself displays a deviant adaptation. The labor leader who talks democracy but runs his union autocratically, the businessman who glorifies sales as the engine of the economy but uses illegitimate means to secure them, the government functionary who proclaims "hound-tooth cleanliness" while wearing a vicuna coat and treading on Persian rugs, reinforces the norms of his particular institutional setting even though he may concurrently, and incidentally, reject goals and means. Institutional norms are not always self-evident and may need such reaffirmation.[26]

The institutional moralist sees himself as acting to sustain norms, and in the process of over-conforming to them may adversely affect institutional functioning through rejection of goals and means. This may lead to stultification of the actions of others through failure to see the goal-relevance of their behavior, or simple fault-finding with the means they propose to use. But the institutional moralist does not use his moralizing stance as a cloak to subvert institutional goals and means. He is not an opportunist in disguise.

Organization Automaton This deviant is a person whose behaviors center on institutional means. This is the man in industry who does everything "by the book," the barracks room lawyer whose text is Army Regulations, the governmental bureaucrat for whom the beginning and end of all action are "the regulations," and the religious adherent for whom the ceremonies are the true content of piety. Merton, in pointing out that a deviant form of bureaucratic behavior transforms means into ends,[27] illustrates the type of deviant adaptation we call organization automaton.

If there is a category of deviant behavior that merits the term *anomic* in the literal sense that values do not guide behavior, it is to be found among organization automatons.[28] For both cultural goals and institutional norms are rejected in such deviant adaptation. Only the legitimacy of institutional means determine the range of behaviors displayed by the organization automaton.[29]

Before concluding that the organization automaton is wholly dysfunctional for any institutional setting in which he is found, one additional aspect of such behavioral ritualism must be considered. The very over-conformity to institutional means makes the automaton the "perfect'" organization man in Hughes' sense of the "thank God for" people.[30] Most of the routine business of organizations is carried out by people whose individual functional contribution is very small and whose work is most efficiently guided by rule and regulation. From the viewpoint of organization. the readiness with which rules and regulations may be changed is enhanced by the automatic legitimacy conferred on them in the eyes of the organization automaton. This deviant adaptation, when legitimized, permits marked and rapid behavioral shifts.[31] Thus over-conformity to institutional means by the organization automaton may be highly functional for organizations by reducing resistance to operational changes. In one sense the "best" soldier is an organization automaton and the "best" worker is his brother in civilian clothing: both are "thank God for" people.

Operating invention, as a form of behavioral innovation, may be distinguished from the type of behavioral ritualism represented by the organization automaton. In operating invention, the worker (or soldier or government functionary) seeks new and better institutional means for fulfilling his tasks. In contrast, the organization automaton accepts institutional means even though they may be changed by fiat, demanding only that they be labelled legitimate changes in the rules. This distinction is displayed in the goals of "group dynamics." The latter approach sees to make of every organizational participant an operating inventor so as to maximise his constructive contributions. That this is not always successful, and indeed may fail more often than not, is due to the fact that most participants lack the positive acceptance of cultural goals and institutional norms that characterize the operating inventor. More frequently, organizational members reject cultural goals and institutional means, major components in the orientation of organization automatons.[32]

Each type of behavioral ritualism has functional consequences for the organizations and institutions in which it operates.[33] Institutional *levelling of aspirations* makes the realities of the social system more congruent with the life chances of its members. The *institutional moralist* continually fortifies the institutional norms by his self-conscious iteration. The *organization automaton* is capable of ready modification of his behavior if these changes are given regulatory legitimacy. Behavioral ritualism in all three of its forms may, in fact, be highly functional for the social system. This general conclusion is consistent with Merton's treatment of institutional levelling of aspirations, the type of ritualism to which his discussion gives major attention.

We can better understand Parsons' analysis of Merton's typology of deviant behavior in the light of this discussion of behavioral ritualism.[34] Parsons contends that over-conformity is one central feature of deviant behavior, of which Merton's ritualism is a special case. Our depiction of three types of behavioral ritualism suggests that overconformity has two dimensions: (1) the ritualist is selective with respect to that facet of the social system to which he overconforms; and (2) over-conformity is visibly displayed in his words and action because ritualization makes it a self-conscious focus of attention.

Value Ritualism

The value ritualist centers the attention of his audiences on his espousal of values while he opportunistically rejects institutional norms or means or both. The value ritualist's appearance to others is that of a moralizer, when in fact his moralizing, *from his standpoint*, is a means of rejecting certain institutional expectations. The value ritualist can thus be contrasted with the institutional moralist because the latter sees himself, and is seen by others, as an active supporter of institutional norms.

We distinguish three types of value ritualism: the demagogue, the normative opportunist, and the means opportunist. Like our other typological distinctions, these three types of deviant adaptation are characterized by a logical combination of the actor's acceptances and rejections of facets of culture and institutions.

The Demagogue A demagogue takes advantage of strongly held beliefs in the society's cultural goals. He makes these goals the focus of attention irrespective of whether or not they conflict with norms in specific institutional settings. The demagogue claims absolute priority of cultural goals over institutional norms and means, resolving any conflicts in favor of the goals. Thus a demagogue's appeal is to the most general values of a society. "The ends justify the means" wholly applies to the demagogue.

The late Senator McCarthy, an outstanding example of the demagogue, wrapped himself in the flag and elevated "Americanism" to the pinnacle of all cultural goals. His actions, often appearing to be highly inconsistent, were altogether consistent with his laudation of "Americanism." McCarthy blatantly rejected institutional norms governing citizen-state relations, the constitutional rights of citizens, "due process," the right of legal representation, and the rules of evidence. It is noteworthy that criticisms of McCarthy designed to reveal his brand as not "true" Americanism were unsuccessful in modifying his influence. It was difficult, if not impossible, to demonstrate that his actions were in fact un-American because the tests proposed by his opponents referred to specific institutional norms. To urge that McCarthy violated constitutional rights in his investigations and allegations, for example, did not vitiate or contradict his claims of being the "true" American. McCarthy's influence was finally restrained when his conduct so flagrantly violated the institutional norms of the Senate that fellow Senators of both parties adopted increasingly restrictive sanctions (institutional means) against him within the Senate.

The case of McCarthy illustrates the central features of the demagogue as a value ritualist. In over-conforming to cultural goals, the demagogue rejects specific institutional norms and means, sometimes in several major institutions. However, for the demagogue, this is a simple rejection – his attack against institutions is unguided by conceptions of substitute norms or means. The demagogue's one consistency is the insistent demand that his espoused cultural goal or goals should override any institutional norms or means – a clear-cut case of over-conformity.

Moralizing by leaders of political, economic, military, and religious affairs reaches the extreme form of demagogic appeal when the moralizing centers wholly on cultural goals. The politician who "wraps himself in the flag" bases his appeal on the presumption that he will be voted into office because he symbolizes the "pure" advocacy of these goals. Indeed, there is a logic of demagogy which demands that the demagogue not attack specific institutional arrangements. For direct attack requires some positive program for their modification, ordinarily not within the purview of the demagogue.

Normative Opportunist This type temporarily rejects limiting institutional norms. He does so, however, under exigencies of an operating situation demanding action prevented by existing norms. After the crisis, the normative opportunist can readily become a conformist, his distinctive characteristic being the willingness, in certain situations, to reject limiting norms in order to act.

An example of the normative opportunist is the purchasing agent who operates in the "grey market" to secure needed supplies for his company. When supplies are short on the market, the purchasing agent is caught in the structural bind of having to secure materials for continuous production when they are not readily available through normal trade channels – he may then proceed to "make arrangements." This can be justified as satisfying the cultural goal of continuity of economic output, achieved through the institutional means of a market transaction, although at a price outside the legitimate norms for pricing materials. The purchase may be made at an exhorbitant price, or it may include side payments to unscrupulous suppliers in the form of bribes, or it may require "tie-in" purchases of unwanted materials.

Another normative opportunist is the man who accepts institutional means but who justifies them with norms from another institutional setting. For example, according to recent reports, some members of the Federal Communications Commission have addressed industrial conventions, accepting both governmental reimbursements and stipends from industry (for the same expenses plus an honorarium). The commissioners involved claimed that institutional arrangements for addresses to the "public" morally sanction such compensation, even if replicated. The allegations of conflict of interest made against these practices rest on the claim that while the cited norm may govern public speakers in general, they are in conflict with the institutional norm of a public regulative agency. As this case illustrates, perhaps, the normative opportunist may honestly fail to see a conflict of interests simply because his behavior (part of which fits the institutional means) is guided by norms from another institutional setting. In this instance, he does not actively seek to replace norms of a particular institution, but perceiving a limiting norm, makes a temporary choice from another institutional setting and claims its priority as a guide for conduct.

Means Opportunist This deviant encounters situations for which available institutional means demand actions he is unwilling or incapable of carrying out. When unwilling to follow prescribed methods, he will, for given situations, use illegitimate means, with the private reservation. "for this time only." Found more frequently is the man incapable of carrying out required actions, usually because of incompetence. He justifies inactivity or actions only vaguely related to his responsibilities on the ground that institutional norms and goals or both give him blanket protection against having to act out his responsibilities. Avoidance of responsibility usually takes place in specific situations, but if repeatedly successful, may become an habitual stance.

This form of deviant adaptation may be found in all institutional settings. A business executive may glorify the cultural goal of success and its institutional index of promotion and salary increase to the point where his rejection of institutional means may become flagrant. A college professor may be a means opportunist, wrapping himself in the norm of academic freedom to cover up intellectual mediocrity or (probably less frequently) to disguise radical leanings.[35] A church hierarchy may protect a functionary from a dissatisfied congregation on the ground that ordination grants legitimacy to carry on church office even though the manifest conduct of the functionary may no longer conform to his responsibilities. The profession of law or of medicine, or even of teaching, may be exceedingly reluctant to exercise internal discipline on members for professional failures except when their behavior openly violates legitimate institutional means or, in the more frequent case, when they have violated institutional norms outside the profession itself.[36]

Retreatism And Rebellion

We make no modification in Merton's two categories of retreatism and rebellion, as types of deviant adaptation. Merton's examples of retreatism include "the adaptive activities of psychotics, autists, pariahs, outcasts, vagrants, vagabonds, tramps, chronic drunkards, and drug addicts";[37] today's "beatnick" adaptation of San Francisco's pad denizens might be added. This listing is sufficient to establish the reality of this category of adaptive behavior, and it probably almost exhausts the possible forms that retreatism takes.

Rebellion is given cursory treatment by Merton. We will do no more. This summary treatment, however, does not imply that rebellion is unimportant in human affairs. Rebellion and revolution are linked with the most crucial types of social change, engendering both vast social dislocations in social process and, when successful, permanent modifications of social systems. But the common usage of "rebellion" to designate other forms of deviancy (for example, "the rebellion of modern youth," which in fact usually consists of operating inventions) should not be confused with the analytical use of this category as a distinctive type of deviant adaptation.

Theoretical Role Of Paradigm

A typology of deviant adaptations in social action specifies the *outcomes* of a theoretical model of deviant behavior. Thus Merton's typology and this extension of it indicate the forms that deviant behavior take. These typologies are only part-theories describing predictable states: they are *not* a theory of deviant behavior.

Both of us employ units in the construction of the typologies the definitions of which rest on common understandings among social scientists. Merton analyzes the person's actions with relation to cultural goals and institutionally prescribed means. I add *group* to the category of actors. The person and the group are conventionally defined units of the sociological frame of reference.

Merton *illustrates* cultural goals with the success motif in American life. That this is *the* goal of living Americans might be inferred from his discussion, although he rejects this monistic view.[38] Rebellion as a deviant adaptation clearly implies multiple cultural goals. I underscore this multiplicity in the three categories of value innovation which involve the substitution of new goals. Both of us avoid explicit definition of cultural goals.

Merton defines institutional means as legitimate behavior; I subdivide this category into institutional norms and means. *From the actor's viewpoint,* I also distinguish behavior from the values by which he makes preferential choices among alternatives. The addition of these analytical units provides the grounds for the extension of the typology of deviant adaptations beyond Merton's formulation.

Any whole or part-theory must specify its units, the *interaction* of which is exactly what the theoretical model undertakes to predict. Again, we both use units familiar to the sociological frame of reference.

But neither of us specifies *laws of interaction*. The lack of such specification precludes a closed theoretical model of deviant behavior. But our effort is to explore the range of outcomes of behavior called deviant, not to propound a theory of deviancy, that is, to establish the *boundary* within which a model of deviant behavior operates.

In order to establish the boundary between deviancy and conformity, we both use implicit laws of interaction among our units. Put otherwise, so as to relate the units, we must accept implicitly some connecting links among them. We use these interactional laws as "sensitizing" rather than explicit concepts because our focus is on outcomes of a theoretical model rather than its substantive content.

Merton, in fact, pitches his discussion at two levels. He presents a typology of deviant behavior using an implicit set of *social psychological* laws. He also considers a variety of instances in which structural imperatives are created the consequences of which are deviant behavior. The latter *sociological* analysis, although brilliantly set forth, remains wholly descriptive. When Merton combines the two levels of analysis, the lineage becomes a social psychological one. For the mechanisms by which persons or groups, subject to structural imperatives, *make decisions* in favor of deviant courses of conduct are social psychological. This is the only legitimate interpretation of the plusses and minuses in Merton's tables and my own.

The sociological level of Merton's analysis proceeds from the following sensitizing idea: "It is, indeed, my central hypothesis that aberrant behavior may be regarded sociologically as a symptom of dissociation between culturally prescribed aspirations and socially structured avenues for realizing these aspirations."[39] This depiction of the linkage between the person as one unit in the system of interaction and cultural goals and institutional means as the other units is hardly a law of interaction. Note that deviancy is defined as a "symptom:" and that the dynamic is "dissociation," a statement of outcome, not process. Using this formulation as the "law" of interaction among the units composing the system, it is impossible either to construct a closed theoretical system or to state any single proposition predicting a state of relationship between persons, cultural goals, and institutional means. Thus Merton's "central hypothesis" turns out to be "sensitizing" with respect to certain types of deviant behavior.

Both Merton and I employ two implicit laws of interaction: (1) A person (or group) either actively accepts, passively rejects, or actively rejects by seeking substitutes for the established features of his social system (defined as cultural goals, institutional norms. and means). As a limiting condition of this law, acceptance, rejection or active rejection are mutually exclusive states for the individual (group) in relation to any given facet of the established social system. (2) The action outcome for the person (group) is deviant behavior when rejection, active rejection, or both is displayed by the person towards at least one facet of the social system. As a limiting condition of the second law, types of deviant behavior can be defined by the logical and exhaustive combinations of acceptance, rejection, and active rejection displayed by a person (group) towards facets of the social system.

Stated in the form of these two laws, the consequences (not the content) of Merton's dissociation become clear, and are revealed as social psychological rather than sociological. For the individual's or group's *perception* determine acceptance, rejection, or active rejection of facets of social system. Merton avoids this issue by focussing on structural imperatives in the description of cases where cultural goals and institutional means somehow become (structurally) out of balance or dissociated.[40] While his examples are illuminating, he does not state any law or laws by which such structural strains in the social system are created. (Ogburn, for example, does this with his concept of cultural lag.[41]) So long as models of deviant behavior include the dynamic of the person or group accepting, rejecting or actively rejecting goals, norms, and means, they remain, perforce, social psychological models.[42]

We can now see the importance of Blumer's insistence that some concepts are *sensitizing* for the analyst.[43] Merton and I both use "sensitizing" social psychological laws to construct paradigms. We both also accept the sensitizing idea that something, "dissociation," happens in the social system so as to encourage particular perceptions by actors or to alter those formerly held. These sensitizing ideas have been used in constructing the typology presented in this paper – a typology of the outcomes of behavior called deviant.

This is *not* a theory of *how* deviant behavior occurs, nor why it occurs. It is simply a descriptive typology of the range of mutually exclusive types of non-conforming behavior.[44] In building any theoretical model, specification of outcomes of the model is an essential step. The order in which the elements of a theory is developed is irrelevant to the content of the theoretical model.

We conclude that Merton's typology can be extended, as shown, to catch up additional real categories of deviant behavior. Our extension of the typology, like the original, is grounded in implicit social psychological rather than sociological "laws of interaction." These typologies are part-theories. Theoretical models of deviant behavior which explain why and how such behavior occurs remain to be constructed. Perhaps these typologies, as component parts, will be useful in that effort.

Notes

Acknowledgement is made to the Graduate School, University of Oregon, for a grant in support of this and related papers on theory building, and for the able assistance of Samuel L. Johnson in preparing this paper. I am particularly indebted to Albert K. Cohen, whose extensive editorial comments resulted in important clarifications of initial obscurities. A companion paper, "Parsons' Actor: Continuities in Social Theory," to be published shortly, deals with a typology of units used in building a theory. The latter contrasts with the present paper, in which the concern is with a typology of outcomes of a theory.

1. Robert K. Merton, "Social Structure and Anomie." Here we use the version appearing as Chapter 4 in the revised edition of *Social Theory and Social Structure*, Glencoe, Ill.: Free Press, 1957. All references to this article and to its companion piece,

"Continuities in the Theory of Social Structure and Anomie," Chapter 5, are to page numbers in that volume.

2. This is clear in Merton's analysis of "sharp practices" in business, his comments on white collar crime, and his conclusion that outright criminal behavior is the substitution of illegitimate institutional means for legitimate ones in pursuing the cultural goal of success. See "Social Structure and Anomie," pp. 141–149.

3. In the following analysis we demonstrate that the combination of acceptance of cultural goals and simple rejection of institutional means (called "innovation" by Merton) is the general category of value ritualism. Analytically, we also show that innovation has a real set of counterparts in deviant behaviour, quite different from those proposed by Merton.

4. Talcott Parsons, "The Motivation of Economic Activities," *Canadian Journal of Economics and Political Science*, 6 (May, 1940), pp. 187–203.

5. "Social Structure and Anomie," p. 153. The same distinction is also noted in the introductory section of this essay, pp. 132–139.

6. See Ralph Turner, "Value Conflict in Social Disorganization," *Sociology and Social Research*, 38 (May, 1954), pp. 301–308, where the distinction between cultural goals and institutional norms is admirably set forth and made relevant to the analysis of deviant behavior.

7. There are 27 logically possible modes of adaptation, including conformity. Fourteen are contained in Table 3 as representing the modes of *active* deviant adaptation. All twelve of the remaining combinations of acceptances, rejections, and active rejections are viewed as possible subjective preconditions of action, which, if it eventuates, becomes one of the fourteen deviant adaptations presented in Table 3. For example: (+) (–) and (±) (+) (±) (–) may be states of anticipation of action, and when they eventuate in acts become (+) (±) (±), or institutional invention. Also: (–) (–) (±) and (–) (±) (–) and (±) (–) (–) may be subjective states of individuals in transit to retreatism; (–) (+) (±) and (–) (±) (+) are subjective pre-conditions to levelling of aspirations; while (±) (±) (–) and (±) (–) (±) and (–) (±) (±) are subjective preludes to rebellion. In the same way we conclude that (±) (+) (–) or (±) (–) (+) may be a subjective pre-condition to intellectual invention. Merton ("Social Structure and Anomie" p. 156) distinguishes *ressentiment* from rebellion and defines the former as a "sour grapes" posture amounting to simple rejection in the specific institutional setting – i.e., (±) (–) (–), one of the omitted categories listed above. He concludes that *ressentiment* may be the subjective prelude to rebellion. We would be inclined to argue, in the light of the above discussion, that *ressentiment* is more accurately described as the subjective prelude to retreatism.

8. See, e. g., John R. Commons, *et al., History of Labor in the United States*, New York: Macmillan, 1918–1935, 4 vols., especially volume 1.

9. See, e.g., Harry A. Millis and Royal E. Montgomery, *Organized Labor* New York: McGraw-Hill, 1945, Chapter 10.

10. Merton implies normative invention as a type but does not accord it the status of a deviant adaptation in his discussion of the social process linking anomie and deviant behavior. "Continuities" pp. 179–180. For example: "A mounting frequency of deviant but 'successful' behavior tends to lessen, and as an extreme potentiality, to eliminate the legitimacy of the institutional norms for others in the system." (p. 180) Incidentally, note that we have here the explicit distinction between behavior (institutional means) and institutional norms which constitutes the fundamental rationale of this revision of Merton's typology.

11. Reinhard Bendix, *Work and Authority in Industry*, New York, Wiley, 1956.

12. Merton recognizes operating invention, although obliquely, in his analysis of *role-set*. He points out that one of the mechanisms operating to resolve conflicting demands on a status occupant is the recognition and correction of these conflicts by the members of his role-set. Here the operating invention is produced by those who people a role-set rather than by the person beset by their conflicting demands. Robert K. Merton, "The Role-Set: Problems in Sociological Theory." *British Journal of Sociology*, 8 (June, 1957), pp. 106–121.

13. Celia Rosenthal in "Deviation and Social Change in the Jewish Community of a Small Polish Town," *American Sociological Review*, 15 (September, 1954), pp. 177–181, makes clear that the decline in Jewish orthodoxy was most evident in the abandonment of traditional dress and the use of arranged marriages. Both illustrate operating inventions which neither threaten the institutional norms nor the cultural goals of the Jewish community.

14. One of the important contributions of Peter Blau's study of bureaucracy is his attentive concern with operating inventions among bureaucrats. *Dynamics of Bureaucracy*, Chicago: University of Chicago Press, 1955, see especially pp. 24, 25, 169, 188, and 201.

15. See Margaret Mead, *Coming of Age in Somoa*, New York: Morrow, 1928.

16. As reported in *Consumer Reports*, 23 (October, 1958), pp. 546–547.

17. Albert K Cohen, *Delinquent Boys*, Glencoe, Ill.: Free Press. 1955, pp. 25–26, 30, 36, *et passim*.

18. "Continuities" pp. 178–179.

19. S. N. Eisenstadt, in *From Generation to Generation*, Glencoe, Ill.: Free Press, 196, pp. 292 ff., portrays the characteristic features of operating invention in his elaboration of Parsons' concept of "secondary institutionalization."

20. Cf. "Social Structure and Anomie," pp. 158–159, where Merton discusses the role of the family. He makes the general point that "children detect and incorporate cultural uniformities even when they remain implicit and have not been reduced to rules." (p. 158) For the actor, this is deviant behavior until he discovers its legitimacy.

21. Merton presents a penetrating analysis of innovation in "Priorities in Scientific Discovery: A Chapter in the Sociology of Science," *American Sociological Review*, 22 December, 1957), pp. 635–659, where he makes this among many other points. We can add the characteristic rarity and simplicity of intellectual inventions to his catalog of structural imperatives making for claims of "firstness" in scientific innovation. Many profound intellectual inventions have the face appearance of great simplicity and obviousness. This generates tension when the invention is first announced because its discoverer realizes that its very simplicity makes it readily available to colleagues and peers.

22. Merton discusses organization invention, but does not view it as a form of deviant behavior in "The Role-Set: Problems in Sociological Theory," *op. cit.* Here Merton points out that the mechanism of mutual social support among status occupants operates to create organizations specializing in their problems. These organizations are a structural response to the problems of coping with actual or potential demands on status occupants by those in their role-sets. The organizations develop normative systems (institutional norms) and cultural goals designed to anticipate and mitigate such conflicting demands.

23. See, e.g., Elizabeth Cady Stanton, *et al., The History of Woman Suffrage*, various places and publishers, 1889–1922, 6 vols.

24. Had Merton pursued such formulations as the following, he would have been constrained to search for types of innovation having positive functions "A certain degree of 'innovation,' for example, may result in the formation of new institutionalized patterns of behavior which are more adaptive than the old in making for realization of primary goals." "Continuities," p. 182.

25. See "Social Structure and Anomie," pp. 149-153. In "Continuities," pp. 183-187, Merton views levelling of aspirations as an alternate curb on deviant behavior, seemingly abandoning such levelling as a type of deviant adaptation. It seems more realistic to retain it as a mode of deviant adaptation in which broad cultural goals are renounced while still making possible rewards in a given institutional setting. This is the interpretation, essentially, made by Bernard Barber and Lyle S. Lobel in "'Fashion' in Women's Clothes and the American Social System," *Social Forces*, 31 (December, 1952), pp. 124-131, and also by L. A. Fallers in "A Note on the 'Trickle Effect'," *Public Opinion Quarterly* 18 (Fall, 1954), pp. 314-321. Levelling of aspirations is one of the central themes of Ely Chinoy's *Automobile Workers and the American Dream*, New York: Random House, 1955, where he points out that the retreat from the institution of production to that of consumption is one way of escaping the cultural imperative to get ahead at work.

26. Curiously, Merton uses moralizing tracts and self-help preachments to demonstrate cultural themes of American life without considering the social role of the moralizers. See "Social Structure and Anomie," pp. 136-139, and "Continuities," pp 166-170. I would interpret this same material as clearly portraying the institutional moralist in the persons of Andrew Carnegie, Rev. Conwell, Elbert Hubbard, Orison Marden, and others cited. Wyllie's excellent study, cited by Merton, is as much an analysis of institutional moralists as it is a history of cultural themes in American life.

27. *Social Theory and Social Structure, op. cit.*, Chapter 6.

28. Herbert H. Hyman's excellent secondary analysis of survey studies, "The Value Systems of Different Classes," in Reinhard Bendix and Seymour M. Lipset, editors, *Class, Status and Power*, Glencoe, Ill. Free Press, 1953, pp. 426-442, generally supports the interpretation that in the lower classes the deviant adaptation here called organization automaton is more likely to be found than levelling of aspirations. The reasoning is as follows. If we assume "upper class" responses to be conforming ones, then the problem is to determine what type of deviant adaptation is exhibited by "lower class" respondents where differences between the two classes are evidenced. The questions analyzed by Hyman deal with two institutional settings: education and work. We assume that past experience (for adults) and present or known-about experiences for youths are the basis for responses to questions about these institutions. The generally reported disinterest in advanced education and the non-financial incentives for work; (e.g. congenial atmosphere and intellectual challenge) represent an "organization automaton" response by "lower class" people. They have experienced the rules of participation in schools or occupation and therefore are realistically oriented to the rules as they know them rather than to institutional norms or cultural goals. In short, they are organization automatons. This conclusion is supported by Merton's contention that, Negro respondents "tend to be decidedly more pessimistic in appraising the opportunities where they themselves work" than their opportunities to get ahead in general ("Continuities," p. 173).

29. We can interpret Leo Srole's study, "Social Integration and Certain Corollaries: An Exploratory Study," *American Sociological Review*, 21 (December, 1956), pp. 709-716,

in this light. He reports the closest correlation between (his measure of) highest anomie and unfavorable attitudes towards minority groups. The first "anomie" question deals with an institutional norm, the remaining four with cultural goals: a high anomie score representing agreement with the statements all rejections of the goals and norm. In the minority attitude measure four of five of Srole's items deal with rules (e.g. legislation or folkways recognizable as rules), agreement with them representing a high negative attitude toward minority groups. The correlation between these two measures indicates that rejection of at least one institutional norm and four cultural goals is associated with acceptance of existing rules of behavior. This satisfies the condition defining the organization automaton, where the organization context is the neighborhood.

30. Everett C. Hughes, "Queries Concerning Industry and Society Growing Out of Study of Ethnic Relations in Industry," *American Sociological Review*, 14 (April, 1949), pp. 211–220.

31. Merton's citation of Liddell's experiments with goats ("Continuities," pp. 185–186) and Blau's treatment of overconforming behavior in bureaucracy (*op. cit.*, pp. 42, 17) are relevant instances of organization automatons. Blau depicts over-conformity to rules as a result of lack of security in important social relations within the organization; this is a psychological, not a sociological explanation. See in this connection the final section of the present paper

32. Cf. Robert Dubin, "Industrial Workers' Worlds: A Study of the 'Central Life Interests' of Industrial Workers," *Social Problems*, 3 (January, 1956), pp. 131–142.

33. Merton's recognition of the functional consequences of deviation is illustrated by such statements as the following: ". . . not all such deviation from the dominant norms of the group is necessarily dysfunctional to the basic values and adaptation of the group" ("Continuities," p. 182) We examine specific types of deviation that may be highly functional for the group.

34. See, e.g., Talcott Parsons, *The Social System*, Glencoe, Ill.: Free Press, 1951, pp 249–267

35. This point is made beautifully by Stringfellow Barr in his satire, *Purely Academic*, New York: Simon and Schuster, 1958; while the problem of the radical is set forth in Mary McCarthy's novel *Groves of Academe*, New York: Harcourt, Brace, 1952.

36. A standard basis for disbarment or revocation of medical or teaching license is the commission of a felony. Recommendations for disbarment are likely to be most frequent (aside from an act of felony) in cases of conversion of client's funds while loss of teaching license is least likely to be protested by teachers' associations in instances of immoral behavior with students.

37. "Social Structure and Anomie " p. 153.

38. Merton makes clear his own pluralistic position. "Continuities" p. 181.

39. "Social Structure and Anomie" p. 134 See also "Continuities" p. 162.

40. Merton modifies his original position in "Continuities," pp. 165–166, where he acknowledges that the subjective and the social structural aspects of the problem of deviant behavior can be separately analyzed. He does not satisfactorily show how these two levels of analysis can be brought together. Nor does this analysis, since my concern, like Merton's, is the delineation of types of deviant adaptations of persons and groups grounded in social psychological law.

41. W. F. Ogburn, *Social Change*, New York: Viking, 1922.

42. In "Social Structure and Anomie," Merton repeatedly casts his discussion in social psychological terms: "The victims of this contradiction between the cultural emphasis

on pecuniary ambition and the social bars to full opportunity are not always aware of the structural sources of their thwarted aspirations." (p 11) "Since the adaptation [ritualism] is in effect an internal decision...." (p. 150) "It is, in short, a mode of adaptation of individually seeking a *private* escape...." (p. 151) "The severe training leads many to carry a heavy burden of anxiety. The socialization patterns of the lower middle class thus promote the very character structure most predisposed toward ritualism...." (p. 151) And in summarizing retreatism: "... their adaptations were largely private and isolated rather than unified under the aegis of a new cultural code." (p 155)

43. Herbert Blumer, "What is Wrong With Social Theory"? American *Sociological Review*, 19 (February, 1954), pp. 8–10.

44. Merton makes this point in "Continuities": "Merely to identify some types of deviation is itself a difficult problem of sociological theory which is being progressively clarified." (pp. 181–182) Again: "As the *typology* of responses to anomie is intended to make clear, there are distinct kinds of behavior which, in contrast to their manifest appearance of conformity to institutionalized expectations can be shown upon further sociological analysis to represent departures from these expectations." (p. 182)

53

The Curious Importance of Small Groups in American Sociology

Allan Silver

The small group occupies a distinctive position in American sociology, past and present. To show this requires sustained comparisons with other Western nations, but an essay of this scope can offer only indicative illustrations. The story involves a conjuncture of two strands in the Anglo-American heritage – one religious, the other secular – which came together with far more force in America than in Britain. First, the core religious culture in America during its formative period was uniquely dominated by congregational doctrines and forms of church government. The congregational churches have long not been majoritarian, but their cultural and doctrinal influence continues, usually as unspoken cultural and intellectual assumptions. Second, the secular Anglo-American idea of "social control" has been biased in favor of face-to-face relations rather than control by institutional authority, religious or secular. The confluence of these two currents in America, as nowhere else, endowed the small group with a sociological significance in America that elsewhere it has largely lacked. I discuss, first, the impact of congregational forms of religion and, second, of the secular notion of social control.

It is widely said that the meliorist tendencies of American sociology were much influenced by reformist Protestant impulses, one evidence of this being the number of early American sociologists who began as clergymen or were the sons of clergy. This is true, but insufficient. Religion has constituted a "deep structure" influencing the assumptions of secular sociologists, even as they sought to offer a scientific account of the moral order (see Vidich and Lyman 1985). In the American case the most influential religious "deep structure" – for the culture and for sociological thought – has been congregational doctrine and church government. In congregational doctrine, there is something sacred and irreducibly ultimate about the moral texture of face-to-face relationships organized as local congregations. In religious language – for example, that of the Constitution of the Congregational Churches of the United States

---

Source: H. J. Gans, (ed.), *Sociology in America*, (Newbury Park: Sage, 1990).

of 1871 – the idea sounds like this: "The right of government resides in local churches, or congregations of believers, who are responsible directly to the Lord Jesus Christ, the One Head of the church universal and of all particular churches" (Walker 1960, p. 573). On this view, the church is composed of compacts made among freely choosing persons; there is no valid distinction between the personal and the institutional aspects of religious life. Thomas Hooker's *A Survey of the Somme of Church Discipline*, published in 1648, makes the point concisely:

> Amongst such who ... have power each over other, *there must of necessity be an engagement*, each of the other by their free consent, before [in] any rule of God they have any right or power, or can exercise either, each toward the other. (Quoted in Morgan 1966, p. 26; emphasis in the original)

This perspective is not limited to rejecting the radical distinction in Catholicism and other hierarchical churches between office and person, priesthood and laity, *ecclesia* and the world. For hierarchical churches, marriage is in essence a sacrament – an expression of the church's action on the world. The congregational perspective considers personal emotions key to marriage (Morgan 1966, pp. 29–64; Schücking 1970). Personal affinities between spouses, accidental to the sacramental conception, are essential to the congregational view of marriage as a voluntary relationship. Husband and wife are doctrinally commanded to love each other (Leites 1982), but doctrine also provides a legitimate role for elective affinities in drawing them together and contributing toward marriage as a sacred arrangement.

In congregational relationships, face-to-face relationships are simultaneously ideological and personal: They are constituted both by the voluntary consent of particular persons to enter into relationships – marriage, congregation, local polity – and by the idea of communion in Christ. Despite vicissitudes in congregational theology, and the emergence in America of other religious traditions on a very large scale, this "deep structure" defining the linkages among person, community, and larger society has persisted as a model in American society and social theory. In the language of a churchly commentator:

> True *koinonia* [communion] occurs when the local church has the same authority as the communion as a whole [so that] the two, in deep mutual respect, maintain continual dialogue with one another ... [L]ocal churches do not create the communion any more than the communion creates the local churches. ... Christ gives the Church power, feeding strength to the local church through the whole company of churches and to the whole company through the local church ... [T]he whole is not itself except as it is made up of free and autonomous parts with direct access to Christ, but the parts are not themselves except as they

belong to the whole which is also informed by Christ. (Walker 1960, p. ix; see also Atkins and Fagley 1942, pp. 340392)

Projected as secular social thought: Small groups of interacting persons are both constituted by the larger society and, in turn, constitute it. It follows that the small group, like the congregation, is essential to understanding society as a whole.

This is not true of French sociology – neither of the passionately secular Durkheim nor of the foremost sociologist of French Catholicism, Gabriel Le Bras. Durkheim's account of the normative order accords causal priority not to the interacting small group but to impersonal dynamics constituting the secular moral order and to the administrative governance of the lay state. Le Bras's sociology of Catholicism drew a clear distinction between social interaction and the formal aspects of the church. A short passage gives the flavor of his approach.

> The parish is something other than living men . . . [and] individual souls. . . . A church is not a parish, a people is not a parish. But if the church is bound [*est affecté*] to a people, a parish exists. The parochial bond is . . . the essence of the parish. . . . This bond is constituted by all the judicial obligations, spiritual or temporal, of the parishioner toward his church. (Le Bras 1955, p. 107; my translation)

Obviously, Le Bras's sociology is cast in theological terms: The parish, the smallest unit of the church, is understood not as the product of its human interactions, nor solely as an aspect of the church, but as a distinct phenomenon constituted by the relationship of individuals to the parish, not to each other. In contrast, the American Catholic sociologist Joseph H. Fichter's analysis of the parish (Fichter 1964) treats it precisely as constituted by what Le Bras called "living men . . . [and] individual souls" – as the sum of social interactions with its bounds.

What I have called the characteristically American, or "congregational," sociology of face-to-face relationships provides simultaneously for individualism and community. The view that America in particular normatively provides for individualism but not community derives from incomplete historical and theological assumptions. Joining in the constitution of congregations by personal interaction is not religiously valid unless based on individual choice. In the congregational perspective, community is constituted by individualism; the congregation is created by the consent of individuals not merely to join it but to create it continuously by their continuous consent.

In the Old World, community was sustained by hierarchical churches, intricate systems of patronage and clientage, the powers of landlords and princes, and the imperatives of collective life in town and country. In the European setting, neither freewill theologies nor notions of political agency and consent were understood to create the structures of sacred and secular community;

rather, they signified participation in structures constituted by "tradition." With the important exception of merchant cities and artisinal and merchant guilds, these did not require the consent of participants for continued existence. Churches based on hierarchy and sacrament understood themselves as constituted by divine decree and apostolic succession; and the necessitous imperatives of community among aristocrats, artisans and peasants, rather than personal volition, accounted for communal ethos and practices.

Translating this into sociological terms means that a purely Lockean view of America as a liberal and capitalist society par excellence overlooks its indigenous theory and practice of community, one that has had a strong and continuing impact on American sociology. This theory of community, unlike that of the Old World, is based on interaction at the face-to-face level of an essentially voluntaristic character. To be sure, the coexistence of community and individualism in the congregational model does not imply romantic or "antisocial" forms of individualism, but an individualism consistent with – indeed, constituting – consensual values. It is precisely this idea that informs the idea of the primary group, the face-to-face community and socialization as they appear, variously elaborated, in the foundational work of Charles Horton Cooley, E. A. Ross, George Herbert Mead, Mary Parker Follett, and later in that of Robert Park and W. I. Thomas. For all these seminal figures, part and whole simultaneously constitute each other, as in congregational theology, endowing the small, face-to-face group with a strategic significance it lacks in the European tradition. No major tradition in European social thought and theory, whether inspired by the class-oriented left, market-oriented liberalism, or the organicist right, has accorded so causally decisive a role to small groups in understanding the larger society and the total polity.

The self-understanding of the American polity has also been shaped by these conceptions. Writing in 1915, Herbert Croly – an influential publicist for Progressive liberalism – drew on the work of "recent social psychologists [who] give a concrete account of the way social minds are formed, and consequently . . . bring the idea of social minds into relation with the fundamental idea of society as a process." Croly's writing illustrates how the congregationalist view of social structure sustains a sort of political pluralism distinctive to America and also evokes the emphasis on the germinal role of small-scaled groups characteristic of American reform movements:

> A society is not made up primarily of individuals . . . [but] of an innumerable number of smaller societies . . . [each of which] . . . constitutes a society, whose reality is determined by [its] . . . purposes. Every church, every club, every political and military association, every labor union, every family, even every temporary social gathering, constitutes a society of a kind. . . . They acquire joint responsibilities and seek the realization of common purposes . . . [out of which] a social ideal gradually emerges. (Croly 1915, p. 197)

Congregationalists have long claimed that their theology and church government are seminal not only for religious but for political democracy (Heermance 1906). American social psychologists made an analogous claim, proposing that proper socialization in interpersonal relations of small scale is key to the development of democratic citizens; the idea is pervasive in Cooley, implicit in Mead, and reaches its fullest development in John Dewey. But while Croly drew such political consequences in Wilsonian America, contemporary British social psychologists like Wilfred Trotter and William MacDougall advanced theories of instinct, including that of the "herd," unconcerned with the small group and its distinctive attributes, and at odds with the texture of democracy (Soffer 1978, pp. 217–51).

Obviously, to take the small group as central for understanding society diminishes the interpretive force both of class and tradition. Less obviously, it also diminishes the dominance of market individualism. The congregational concept of social structure involves a form of individualism-in-solidarity that does not uncritically celebrate the utilitarian or self-regarding individualism of classical market theory. Illustratively, consider a passage of Cooley's:

> It is . . . not my aim to depreciate the self-assertive passions. I believe they are fierce, inextinguishable, indispensable. Competition and the survival of the fittest are as righteous as kindness and cooperation, and not necessarily opposed to them . . . [because] the normal self is moulded in primary groups to be a social self whose ambitions are formed by the common thought of the group. (Cooley [1909] 1962, pp. 35–36)

To take as a model of "community" an image based on tradition and imperative necessity – as in peasant villages, manors, merchant guilds, clientalism, endemic war – rules out an appreciation of American models of community and, in particular, of the central role played in them by voluntaristic small groups.

I have already turned to the second, and secular, aspect of the story – the idea of "social control" and its sociological flowering in America. Especially in discussions and polemics in and after the 1960s, "social control" has been taken to refer to authoritative control from above, as by state bureaucracies. The assumption is that "control" is necessarily exercised by powerful authorities – emphasizing the noun, *control*. However, the original emphasis of "social control" lay rather in its adjective, *social*. It reflected the celebration by nineteenth-century liberal thought of moral self-regulation rather than governance from above, despotic or traditional. I know no earlier appearance of the phrase than in John Stuart Mill's *On Liberty* ([1859] 1956, p. 8), which applauds the possibility of normative regulation emerging from within civil society through mutual influence among citizens, replacing the historic governance of clergy, landlords, guild masters, and princes.

The classical idea of social control arose in Britain but came to flourish in America as the prevalence of both social and religious hierarchy, and classical market theory in Britain accorded it less intellectual space. It has few and weak counterparts in continental Europe, where principalities and absolutist monarchies were succeeded by strong administrative states. Two assumptions are key to the social control perspective. The first is that social relationships generated by price systems are insufficient in both fact and value as an account of social structure and the moral order. The second is that small-scale, face-to-face groups are of crucial interpretive importance in any account of modern societies (Janowitz 1975). These ideas – key to the formative American sociology of Cooley, Mead, Ross, Baldwin, and John Dewey – are rooted in the moral social psychology of the earliest secular social psychology to emerge in the setting of a thoroughly commercial society, that of the eighteenth-century Scottish Enlightenment, of which Adam Smith and Hume are the preeminent figures (see Bryson 1945).

The Scots and Americans both sought an empirical basis for the moral order, for the genesis of a restraining but not oppressive morality, in an arena that, until the emergence of market and liberal society, had been merely residual or interstitial: face-to-face, informal, small-scaled relationships. Families, churches, schools, and formal associations are understood essentially as "sites" of personal relations; the socializing and moralizing effect of institutions are understood to derive not from their formal properties and claims but from the personal relationships found within them.

The anti-institutional idea that the moral order is constituted essentially by the effects of personal relations emerges clearly in changing conceptions of the family. That the family is the "basic unit" of the moral order has become a platitude. But what this idea sought to overcome when it was new were two historically dominant notions of the family: first, that the father's domination of the family expresses the principle of social and political hierarchy, and, second, that the family was a solidary unit in alliance or conflict with others in a pervasively contestatory world, in which family resources were indispensable to collective defense and advancement (see Alberti [1935] 1969, and Giesey 1977, for illustrations, respectively, from the Italian Renaissance and eighteenth-century France). In their place was put the idea of the family as a small group constituted by interaction. For example, here is Adam Ferguson, the eighteenth-century Scottish moralist and social theorist, showing how family loyalty – which in the Scottish Highlands contributed to the pervasive antagonisms of clan society – could provide the basis of a universal and pacific moral order:

> The fortunes of men are sometimes involved in those of their kindred. Although we distinguish therefore the specific principle of consanguinity from indiscriminate [general] affection and good will to mankind, yet it appears, that nature in planting the instinctive affections which united the members of a family together, and which may extend to a numerous kindred, has in this manner sown the seeds of a boundless society. Or seeming only to connect individuals of a narrow circle

together, has formed a chain, whose links being continued in every direction, extend far beyond where personal acquaintance or choice would reach. (Ferguson, 1792, Vol. 2, p. 364)

Cooley undertakes a similar project in ascribing "primary ideals" to a reformed America: "Americans may surely claim that there was never before a great nation in which the people felt so much like a family, had so kindly and cheerful a sense of a common life" (Cooley [1909]1962, p. 196). John Dewey's language in his early textbook in psychology, published in 1889, is directly descended from Ferguson's:

> Sympathy is the sole means by which persons come within the range of our life. It is thus an extremely universal feeling. . . . It may be limited at first to those of our own family, our own rank in society, our own neighborhood, but this is because of a defective sympathy . . . [for] as our nature widens and becomes developed there must be a corresponding increase of sympathy. . . . Such a sympathy can, of course, recognize no distinction of social rank, wealth, or learning, or anything that tends to cut off one person from another. (Dewey, [1889] 1927, p. 332)

On this view, the morality of the small group, socialized in persons and extended over the polity, is key to democracy. The localism of the American polity, never the threat or obstacle to nationhood that it was in Europe, encouraged this outlook. Indeed, in the American case, the decline of localism has often meant the decline of a vigorous concept of nationhood; as illustrated by John Dewey's pessimistic meditation on these themes in *The Public and Its Problems*, published in 1926, this concern – today the province of conservatives – characterized American liberalism as well.

The morality of small groups is often contrasted with that of market society, but both are expressions of liberal society. The social control perspective assigns central importance to small-scale interactions in a manner paralleling the postulate of classical market theory that a multitude of small exchanges in the market results in a general order. In both cases, the unmediated governance of institutions such as religions and states is irrelevant, inefficient, or harmful. The moral order is constantly being re-created, on this view, by an indefinitely large number of encounters between people who meet in an arena defined not by institutions but by their own sentiments and interactions. Thus the web of social interaction, of which small groups are pulsing nodes, resembles the classical notion of the market: It is not regulated but re-creates itself; its indefinitely many transactions occur between people who are formally and juridically equal, all of whom may therefore "influence" each other.

Indeed, the democratization of "influence" is a central feature of the sociology of the small group and, in general, of a social world constituted by interaction. In principle, all may influence everyone else; the sources and distribution of influence are understood as the results of interaction and taken as phenomena for social science to explain. It had not always been thus. In the English language, influence was reserved for patrons and power brokers and, like its origins in astrology, was intrinsically vertical, describing the power of the mighty to exercise "influence" over others. Thus, until the electoral reforms of the 1880s, an English landlord might exercise what the political language of the time called "legitimate influence" over his enfranchised tenants (Davis 1972; Hanham 1978). In that setting, "influence" is not constituted by interaction but by status – the privileges associated with the ownership of landed property, and the obligations of tenants toward a landlord who, for example, does not always seek the highest possible rent. From the moment that the social world was conceived in terms of interaction, or mutual influence, best observed in the small group and small-scaled interaction, a profound transformation in a democratic direction is effected. It becomes possible to imagine society *as if* it were continuously created by an uncountable number of small-scaled interactions among persons of equal jural status; one task of empirical sociology becomes to investigate the varieties of interpersonal influences and their sources within such a world – according to some contemporary "microsociologists," its distinctive task.

These ideas are current in modern sociology. In *Union Democracy*, Lipset, Trow, and Coleman (1956) interpret their data to mean that optimal forms of personal groups among printers are vital to a democratic labor union. The spontaneous relations of neighbors and friends, according to Litwak (1985), may be integrated with the provision of public services in ways that enhance both efficiency and community. Fischer (1977, 1982) holds that the pattern of face-to-face relations in American cities largely contributes to urban community. These, and many other instances, manifest the continuity of the "congregational" model.

I have yet to address the familiar notion that the texture of face-to-face life in America is distinctively characterized not by latent "congregationalism" but a pervasive market orientation. Here is a recent statement of this idea:

> Social life is mutual negotiation and society, social order, relies on this mutual negotiation between individuals; this represents both creed and particular reality in American society. In no other society is this creed and the corresponding reality as prominent as the United States. (Münch 1986, p. 43)

Münch argues that, both in reality and in theory, "exchange and competition are thus in the United States the basic forms of interaction not only in economic life but in social life as a whole" (Münch 1986, p. 44) and traces their impact on the American preference for accounts of interaction in terms of exchange relations.

However, attributing exchange and competition solely or largely to market relations is ahistorical. European notions of instrumental exchange in personal interaction were deeply formed by practices and institutions that preceded the modern market – for example, deference, clientilism, honor – and are, therefore, embedded in nonmarket practices, though, of course, no less driven by instrumental imperatives. Many of La Rochefoucauld's *Maximes*, first published in 1665, seek to unmask such behavior as love and faithfulness in such terms; two examples of many:

> What men have called friendship is only a partnership, only a reciprocal managing of interests, and an exchange of services; it is after all only a transaction [*commerce*] in which self-love always seeks to gain something.

> The loyalty that most men show is only a device of self-love to gain trust; it is a means of surpassing others and to make us agents in the most important affairs. (La Rochefoucauld [1665,1678]1964, nos. 83, 247; my translation)

The *Maximes* are sometimes cited by exchange theorists as striking anticipations of scientific hypotheses (for example, Blau 1964) but without considering the historical setting to which they refer. Consider only a passage from Norbert Elias's analysis of the court of Versailles:

> The whole bustle of activity had a certain resemblance to a stock exchange. In it, too, a society actually present formed changing assessments of value. But at a stock exchange what is at stake is the value of commercial houses in the opinion of investors; at court it was the value of the people present in each others' opinion. And while at the former even the slightest fluctuation can be expressed in figures, in the latter a person's value was expressed primarily in the nuances of social intercourse. (Elias 1983, p. 91)

At Versailles, the competition for advantage and power was not only expressed but conducted through the dynamics of interaction rather than markets based on price systems; but it was hardly the less instrumental in its time and place. Capitalism, markets, or a "Lockean" America are not necessary for highly developed exchange or instrumental orientations in interpersonal relations, although, to be sure, the instrumentalism of premarket societies is profoundly different in cultural meaning from that prevailing in modern market society. If Old World notions of status, dignity, honor, loyalty, and "tradition" sometimes appear incompatible with instrumentality and exchange, it is because they have, with modernization, "floated free" from their historical settings and also, in retrospect, have become vulnerable to ahistorical or sentimental interpretations. Every culture has its own way, in life and theory, to express and understand instrumentality; of these, the rational concept of interest intrinsic to market society (Hirschman 1977) is but one.

The continuing distinctiveness of the sociology of small groups and personal interaction in American does not lie only in its alleged propensity to project market relations onto personal ones – as in the American taste, which Münch well documents, for exchange theories. Rather, it lies in a vision of personal interaction that separates the utility of persons for each other from their worth as individuals engaged in the continuous creation with others of a multitude of small moral worlds. This vision endows small moral worlds with an ultimate significance in creating, sustaining, and improving the nation. In the statist regimes of continental Europe, the possibilities for moral reform flowed from the idea that the state represents a higher form of social organization – an idea held alike by reactionary nationalists like Treitschke, reformist liberals like Jules Ferry, and socialists like Jean Jaurès. All in varying ways were statists because they understood a properly constituted state to be the key source of reform and improvement, an idea shared, among other European sociologists, by Durkheim.

The American way was different. The Progressive reformers to whom the formative sociologists, among many others, supplied congenial ideas, largely understood the reformist and moral possibilities of the state to reflect the noblest values of relationships of small scale, because these were distinctively the basic source of social values. What made the state a worthy and effective agent of reform was its capacity to absorb and reflect, as it were, moral aspirations stemming from the social relations of small scale in which they are created at their source and, therefore, in their purest form.

To be sure, the small group perspective is not the only way in which sociology in America has addressed the significance of face-to-face relationships for the moral order; three others, of varying age and provenance, can be distinguished. The Parsonian "theory of action" sought to develop the counterpart of a Durkheimian sociology of social control, taking as its object the American polity conceived of as a "society," as Durkheim conceived of Republican France. Here, the "congregationalist" aspect of small groups is not essential; "action theory" does not denote a process of mutual moral control among persons creating and sharing a moral history, as does the small group perspective, but among anonymous and interchangeable citizens, reflecting the move from a nation of communities to a national polity – a comparatively recent event in the United States. Analogously, in what I will call, in an undiscriminating phrase, the "California school" – symbolic interaction, conversation analysis, ethnomethodology – the creation and sharing of a moral history with others is not a core problematic; this is, rather, symbolic and cognitive processes shaping behavior in interaction. Issues of social control centering on problematics of the moral order are replaced by those of mutual adjustment in symbolic and cognitive dynamics. Network analysis continues the impulse to construct the larger society out of small-scale interactions but does so in terms of structures generated by interactions, not in substantive, much less in moral, terms. The "subtext" underlying these perspectives is the irreducibility and ultimate significance of individual experience, whether in its subjective, interactional, or structural aspects:

> Everyone's life, experientially, is a sequence of microsituations, and the sum of individual experience in the world would constitute all the possible sociological data. . . . *Sociological concepts can be made fully empirical only by grounding them in a sample of the typical micro-events that make them up.* (Collins 1981, pp. 987–88; emphasis in original)

In all these literatures, an American strain continues in varying, even incompatible ways, to emphasize the fundamental character of the small. In each case, the claim is made that central features of total societies are best or uniquely understood by investigating properties of small-scale interaction between persons, albeit that those properties are differently conceived. The study of small-scaled interaction, now "micro-sociology," in relation to the larger society, now "macro-sociology," has clearly entered a new phase, as the "linkage" between the two has become a defined problematic – it being assumed that such a "linkage" is a central problematic for sociology (Alexander, Giesen, Münch, and Smelser 1987; Knorr-Cetina and Cicourel 1981).

The "congregational" sociology of small groups assumes that their members come to know and to deal with each other over time, forming groups with moral histories, which, cumulatively, are crucial for the moral order. Approaches appearing after Parsonian "action theory" do not take as central the problematic of moral order, and all are indifferent to a categorical distinction between strangers and those whose knowledge of each other informs their interactions. The Parsonian concern with an impersonal morality, microsociology's with interactional nuance, network theory's with the logic of structure – all, in varying ways, reflect massive changes in American society and culture intervening in the near century since the discipline shook free of religion and philosophy. The "congregational" tradition, deeply grounded in American culture as well as sociology, persists. In these respects, as in so many others, America both is and is not what it was a century ago, when sociology was born in the new world.

References

Alberti, Leon Battista. [1435]. *I Libri della Famiglia.* Translated by Renée Watkins (1969) as *The Family in Renaissance Florence.* Columbia: University of South Carolina Press.

Alexander, Jeffrey C., Bernhard Giesen, Richard Münch, and Neil Smelser, eds. 1987. *The Micro-Macro Link.* Berkeley: University of California Press.

Atkins, Gaius Glenn and Frederick L. Fagley. 1942. *History of American Congregationalism.* Boston: Pilgrim.

Blau, Peter. 1964. *Exchange and Power in Social Life.* New York: John Wiley.
Bryson, Gladys. 1945. *Man and Society: The Scottish Inquiry of the Eighteenth Century.* Princeton, NJ: Princeton University Press.
Collins, Randall. 1981. "On the Microfoundations of Macrosociology." *American Journal of Sociology* 86: 984–1015.
Cooley, Charles Horton. [1909]1962. *Social Organization.* New York: Schocken.
Croly, Herbert. 1915. *Progressive Democracy.* New York: Macmillan.
Davis, Richard W. 1972. *Political Change and Continuity 1760–1885.* Hamdon, CT: Archon.
Dewey, John. [1889]1926. *The Public and Its Problems.* New York: Holt.
Dewey, John. 1927. *Psychology.* New York: Harper.
Elias, Norbert. 1983. *The Court Society.* New York: Blackwell.
Ferguson, Adam. 1792. *Principles of Moral and Political Science.* 2 vols. Edinburgh: Creech.
Fichter, Joseph H. 1964. *Parochial School: A Sociological Study.* New York: Anchor.
Fischer, Claude. 1977. *Networks and Places: Social Relations in Urban Settings.* New York: Free Press.
Fischer, Claude. 1982. *To Dwell Among Friends: Personal Relations in Town and City.* Berkeley: University of California Press.
Giesey, Ralph E. 1977. "Rules of Inheritance and Strategies of Mobility in Prerevolutionary France." *American Historical Review* 82: 271–89.
Hanham, H. J. 1978. *Elections and Party Management: Politics in the Time of Disraeli and Gladstone.* Sussex, United Kingdom: Harvester.
Heermmance, Edgar. 1906. *Democracy in the Church.* Boston: Pilgrim.
Hirschman, Albert O. 1977. *The Passions and the Interests.* Princeton, NJ: Princeton University Press.
Janowitz, Morris. 1975. "Sociological Theory and Social Control." *American Journal of Sociology* 81: 82–108.
Knorr-Cetina, Karen and Aaron Cicourel, eds. 1981. *Advances in Sociological Theory and Methodology: Toward an Integration of Micro- and Macro-Sociology.* Boston: Routledge & Kegan Paul.
Le Bras, Gabriel. 1955. *Etudes de sociologie Religieuse.* Tome Premier. Paris: Presses Universitaires de France.
La Rochefoucauld. [1665, 1678] 1964. "Maximes". In *Oeuvres Complètes.* Paris: Éditions Gallimard.
Leites, Edmund. 1982. "The Duty to Desire: Love, Friendship and Sexuality in Some Puritan Theories of Marriage." *Journal of Social History* 15: 381–408.
Litwak, Eugene. 1985. *Helping the Elderly: The Complementary Role of Informal Networks and Formal Systems.* New York: Guilford.
Mill, John Stuart. [1859] 1956. *On Liberty.* Indianapolis: Bobbs-Merrill.
Morgan, Edmund S. 1966. *The Puritan Family: Religion and Domestic Relations in Seventeenth Century New England.* New York: Harper.
Münch, Richard. 1986. "The American Creed in Sociological Theory." *Sociological Theory* 4: 44–60.
Schücking, Levin. 1970. *The Puritan Family.* New York: Schocken.
Soffer, Reba N. 1978. *Ethics and Society in England: The Revolution in the Social Sciences 1870–1914.* Berkeley: University of California Press.
Vidich, Arthur J. and Stanford Lyman. 1985. *American Sociology: Worldly Rejections of Religion and Their Directions.* New Haven, CT: Yale University Press.
Walker, Williston. 1960. *The Creeds and Platforms of Congregationalism.* Boston: Pilgrim.

54

The Authoritarian Personality

T. W. Adorno, Else Frankel-Brunswik, Daniel J. Levinson and R. Nevitt Sanford

Introduction

A. The Problem

The research to be reported in this volume was guided by the following major hypothesis: that the political, economic, and social convictions of an individual often form a broad and coherent pattern, as if bound together by a "mentality" or "spirit," and that this pattern is an expression of deep-lying trends in his personality.

The major concern was with the *potentially fascistic* individual, one whose structure is such as to render him particularly susceptible to antidemocratic propaganda. We say "potential" because we have not studied individuals who were avowedly fascistic or who belonged to known fascist organizations. At the time when most of our data were collected fascism had just been defeated in war and, hence, we could not expect to find subjects who would openly identify themselves with it; yet there was no difficulty in finding subjects whose outlook was such as to indicate that they would readily accept fascism if it should become a strong or respectable social movement.

In concentrating upon the potential fascist we do not wish to imply that other patterns of personality and ideology might not profitably be studied in the same way. It is our opinion, however, that no politico-social trend imposes a graver threat to our traditional values and institutions than does fascism, and that knowledge of the personality forces that favor its acceptance may ultimately prove useful in combating it. A question may be raised as to why, if we wish to explore new resources for combating fascism, we do not give as much attention to the "potential antifascist." The answer is that we do study trends that stand in opposition to fascism, but we do not conceive that they constitute any single pattern. It is one of the major findings of the present study that individuals who show extreme susceptibility to fascist propaganda have a

---

Source: T. W. Adorno, Else Frankel-Brunswik, Daniel J. Levinson and R. Nevitt Sanford, *The Authoritarian Personality*, (New York: Harper & Row, 1950).

great deal in common. (They exhibit numerous characteristics that go together to form a "syndrome" although typical variations within this major pattern can be distinguished.) Individuals who are extreme in the opposite direction are much more diverse. The task of diagnosing potential fascism and studying its determinants required techniques especially designed for these purposes; it could not be asked of them that they serve as well for various other patterns. Nevertheless, it was possible to distinguish several types of personality structure that seemed particularly resistant to antidemocratic ideas, and these are given due attention in later chapters.

If a potentially fascistic individual exists, what, precisely, is he like? What goes to make up antidemocratic thought? What are the organizing forces within the person? If such a person exists, how commonly does he exist in our society? And if such a person exists, what have been the determinants and what the course of his development?

These are questions upon which the present research was designed to throw some light. Though the notion that the potentially antidemocratic individual is a totality may be accepted as a plausible hypothesis, some analysis is called for at the start. In most approaches to the problem of political types two essential conceptions may be distinguished: the conception of ideology and the conception of underlying needs in the person. Though the two may be thought of as forming an organized whole within the individual, they may nonetheless be studied separately. The same ideological trends may in different individuals have different sources, and the same personal needs may express themselves in different ideological trends.

The term ideology is used in this book, in the way that is common in current literature, to stand for an organization of opinions, attitudes, and values – a way of thinking about man and society. We may speak of an individual's total ideology or of his ideology with respect to different areas of social life: politics, economics, religion, minority groups, and so forth. Ideologies have an existence independent of any single individual; and those which exist at a particular time are results both of historical processes and of contemporary social events. These ideologies have for different individuals, different degrees of appeal, a matter that depends upon the individual's needs and the degree to which these needs are being satisfied or frustrated.

There are, to be sure, individuals who take unto themselves ideas from more than one existing ideological system and weave them into patterns that are more or less uniquely their own. It can be assumed, however, that when the opinions, attitudes, and values of numerous individuals are examined, common patterns will be discovered. These patterns may not in all cases correspond to the familiar, current ideologies, but they will fulfill the definition of ideology given above and in each case be found to have a function within the over-all adjustment of the individual.

The present inquiry into the nature of the potentially fascistic individual began with anti-Semitism in the focus of attention. The authors, in common with most social scientists, hold the view that anti-Semitism is based more largely upon factors in the subject and in his total situation than upon actual characteristics of Jews, and that one place to look for determinants of anti-Semitic opinions and attitudes is within the persons who express them. Since this emphasis on personality required a focusing of attention on psychology rather than on sociology or history – though in the last analysis the three can be separated only artificially – there could be no attempt to account for the existence of anti-Semitic ideas in our society. The question was, rather, why is it that certain individuals accept these ideas while others do not? And since from the start the research was guided by the hypotheses stated above, it was supposed (1) that anti-Semitism probably is not a specific or isolated phenomenon but a part of a broader ideological framework, and (2) that an individual's susceptibility to this ideology depends primarily upon his psychological needs.

The insights and hypotheses concerning the antidemocratic individual, which are present in our general cultural climate, must be supported by a great deal of painstaking observation, and in many instances by quantification, before they can be regarded as conclusive. How can one say with assurance that the numerous opinions, attitudes, and values expressed by an individual actually constitute a consistent pattern or organized totality? The most intensive investigation of that individual would seem to be necessary. How can one say that opinions, attitudes, and values found in groups of people go together to form patterns, some of which are more common than others? There is no adequate way to proceed other than by actually measuring, in populations, a wide variety of thought contents and determining by means of standard statistical methods which ones go together.

To many social psychologists the scientific study of ideology, as it has been defined, seems a hopeless task. To measure with suitable accuracy a single, specific, isolated attitude is a long and arduous proceeding for both subject and experimenter. (It is frequently argued that unless the attitude is specific and isolated, it cannot properly be measured at all.) How then can we hope to survey within a reasonable period of time the numerous attitudes and ideas that go to make up an ideology? Obviously, some kind of selection is necessary. The investigator must limit himself to what is most significant, and judgments of significance can only be made on the basis of theory.

The theories that have guided the present research will be presented in suitable contexts later. Though theoretical considerations had a role at every stage of the work, a beginning had to be made with the objective study of the most observable and relatively specific opinions, attitudes, and values.

Opinions, attitudes, and values, as we conceive of them, are expressed more or less openly in words. Psychologically they are "on the surface." It must be recognized, however, that when it comes to such affect-laden questions as those concerning minority groups and current political issues, the degree of openness with which a person speaks will depend upon the situation in which he finds himself. There may be a discrepancy between what he says on a particular occasion and what he "really thinks." Let us say that what he really thinks he can express in confidential discussion with his intimates. This much, which is still relatively superficial psychologically, may still be observed directly by the psychologist if he uses appropriate techniques – and this we have attempted to do.

It is to be recognized, however, that the individual may have "secret" thoughts which he will under no circumstances reveal to anyone else if he can help it; he may have thoughts which he cannot admit to himself, and he may have thoughts which he does not express because they are so vague and ill-formed that he cannot put them into words. To gain access to these deeper trends is particularly important, for precisely here may lie the individual's potential for democratic or antidemocratic thought and action in crucial situations.

What people say and, to a lesser degree, what they really think depends very largely upon the climate of opinion in which they are living; but when that climate changes, some individuals adapt themselves much more quickly than others. If there should be a marked increase in antidemocratic propaganda, we should expect some people to accept and repeat it at once, others when it seemed that "everybody believed it," and still others not at all. In other words, individuals differ in their *susceptibility* to antidemocratic propaganda, in their readiness to exhibit antidemocratic tendencies. It seems necessary to study ideology at this "readiness level" in order to gauge the potential for fascism in this country. Observers have noted that the amount of outspoken anti-Semitism in pre-Hitler Germany was less than that in this country at the present time; one might hope that the potentiality is less in this country, but this can be known only through intensive investigation, through the detailed survey of what is on the surface and the thorough probing of what lies beneath it.

A question may be raised as to what is the degree of relationship between ideology and action. If an individual is making antidemocratic propaganda or engaging in overt attacks upon minority group members, it is usually assumed that his opinions, attitudes, and values are congruent with his action; but comfort is sometimes found in the thought that though another individual expresses antidemocratic ideas verbally, he does not, and perhaps will not, put them into overt action. Here, once again, there is a question of potentialities. Overt action, like open verbal expression, depends very largely upon the situation of the moment – something that is best described in socio-economic and political terms – but individuals differ very widely with respect to their readiness to be provoked into action. The study of this potential is a part of the study of the individual's over-all ideology; to know what kinds and what intensities of belief, attitude, and value are likely to lead to action, and to know what forces within the individual serve as inhibitions upon action are matters of the greatest practical importance.

There seems little reason to doubt that ideology-in-readiness (ideological receptivity) and ideology-in-words and in action are essentially the same stuff.

The description of an individual's total ideology must portray not only the organization on each level but organization among levels. What the individual consistently says in public, what he says when he feels safe from criticism, what he thinks but will not say at all, what he thinks but will not admit to himself, what he is disposed to think or to do when various kinds of appeal are made to him – all these phenomena may be conceived of as constituting a single structure. The structure may not be integrated, it may contain contradictions as well as consistencies, but it is *organized* in the sense that the constituent parts are related in psychologically meaningful ways.

In order to understand such a structure, a theory of the total personality is necessary. According to the theory that has guided the present research, personality is a more or less enduring organization of forces within the individual. These persisting forces of personality help to determine response in various situations, and it is thus largely to them that consistency of behavior – whether verbal or physical – is attributable. But behavior, however consistent, is not the same thing as personality; personality lies *behind* behavior and *within* the individual. The forces of personality are not responses but *readiness for response*, whether or not a readiness will issue in overt expression depends not only upon the situation of the moment but upon what other readinesses stand in opposition to it. Personality forces which are inhibited are on a deeper level than those which immediately and consistently express themselves in overt behavior.

What are the forces of personality and what are the processes by which they are organized? For theory as to the structure of personality we have leaned most heavily upon Freud, while for a more or less systematic formulation of the more directly observable and measurable aspects of personality we have been guided primarily by academic psychology. The forces of personality are primarily *needs* (drives, wishes, emotional impulses) which vary from one individual to another in their quality, their intensity, their mode of gratification, and the objects of their attachment, and which interact with other needs in harmonious or conflicting patterns. There are primitive emotional needs, there are needs to avoid punishment and to keep the good will of the social group, there are needs to maintain harmony and integration within the self.

Since it will be granted that opinions, attitudes, and values depend upon human needs, and since personality is essentially an organization of needs, then personality may be regarded as a *determinant* of ideological preferences. Personality is not, however, to be hypostatized as an ultimate determinant. Far from being something which is given in the beginning, which remains fixed and acts upon the surrounding world, personality evolves under the impact of the social environment and can never be isolated from the social totality within which it occurs. According to the present theory, the effects of environmental forces in moulding the personality are, in general, the more profound the earlier in the life history of the individual they are brought to bear. The major influences upon personality development arise in the course of child training as carried forward in a setting of family life. What happens here is profoundly influenced by economic and social factors. It is not only that each family in trying to rear its children proceeds according to the ways of the social, ethnic, and religious groups in which it has membership, but crude economic factors affect directly the parents' behavior toward the child. This means that broad changes in social conditions and institutions will have a direct bearing upon the kinds of personalities that develop within a society.

The present research seeks to discover correlations between ideology and sociological factors operating in the individual's past – whether or not they continue to operate in his present. In attempting to explain these correlations the relationships between personality and ideology are brought into the picture, the general approach being to consider personality as an agency through which sociological influences upon ideology are mediated. If the role of personality can be made clear, it should be possible better to understand which sociological factors are the most crucial ones and in what ways they achieve their effects.

Although personality is a product of the social environment of the past, it is not, once it has developed, a mere object of the contemporary environment. What has developed is a *structure* within the individual, something which is capable of self-initiated action upon the social environment and of selection with respect to varied impinging stimuli, something which though always modifiable is frequently very resistant to fundamental change. This conception is necessary to explain consistency of behavior in widely varying situations, to explain the persistence of ideological trends in the face of contradicting facts and radically altered social conditions, to explain why people in the same sociological situation have different or even conflicting views on social issues, and why it is that people whose behavior has been changed through psychological manipulation lapse into their old ways as soon as the agencies of manipulation are removed.

The conception of personality structure is the best safeguard against the inclination to attribute persistent trends in the individual to something "innate" or "basic" or "racial" within him. The Nazi allegation that natural, biological traits decide the total being of a person would not have been such a successful political device had it not been possible to point to numerous instances of relative fixity in human behavior and to challenge those who thought to explain them on any basis other than a biological one. Without the conception of personality structure, writers whose approach rests upon the assumption of infinite human flexibility and responsiveness to the social situation of the moment have not helped matters by referring persistent trends which they could not approve to "confusion" or "psychosis" or evil under one name or another. There is, of course, some basis for describing as "pathological" patterns of behavior which do not conform with the most common, and seemingly most lawful, responses to momentary stimuli. But this is to use the term pathological in the very narrow sense of deviation from the average found in a particular context and, what is worse, to suggest that everything in the personality structure is to be put under this heading. Actually, personality embraces variables which exist widely in the population and have lawful relations one to another. Personality patterns that have been dismissed as "pathological" because they were not in keeping with the most common manifest trends or the most dominant ideals within a society, have on closer investigation turned out to be but exaggerations of what was almost universal below the surface in that society. What is "pathological" today may with changing social conditions become the dominant trend of tomorrow.

It seems clear then that an adequate approach to the problems before us must take into account both fixity and flexibility; it must regard the two not as mutually exclusive categories but as the extremes of a single continuum along which human characteristics may be placed, and it must provide a basis for understanding the conditions which favor the one extreme or the other. Personality is a concept to account for relative permanence. But it may be emphasized again that personality is mainly a potential; it is a readiness for behavior rather than behavior itself; although it consists in dispositions to behave in certain ways, the behavior that actually occurs will always depend upon the objective situation. Where the concern is with antidemocratic trends, a delineation of the conditions for individual expression requires an understanding of the total organization of society.

It has been stated that the personality structure may be such as to render the individual susceptible to antidemocratic propaganda. It may now be asked what are the conditions under which such propaganda would increase in pitch and volume and come to dominate in press and radio to the exclusion of contrary ideological stimuli, so that what is now potential would become actively manifest. The answer must be sought not in any single personality nor in personality factors found in the mass of people, but in processes at work in society itself. It seems well understood today that whether or not antidemocratic propaganda is to become a dominant force in this country depends primarily upon the situation of the most powerful economic interests, upon whether they, by conscious design or not, make use of this device for maintaining their dominant status. This is a matter about which the great majority of people would have little to say.

The present research, limited as it is to the hitherto largely neglected psychological aspects of fascism, does not concern itself with the production of propaganda. It focuses attention, rather, upon the consumer, the individual for whom the propaganda is designed. In so doing it attempts to take into account not only the psychological structure of the individual but the total objective situation in which he lives. It makes the assumption that people in general tend to accept political and social programs which they believe will serve their economic interests. What these interests are depends in each case upon the individual's position in society as defined in economic and sociological terms. An important part of the present research, therefore, was the attempt to discover what patterns of socioeconomic factors are associated with receptivity, and with resistance, to antidemocratic propaganda.

At the same time, however, it was considered that economic motives in the individual may not have the dominant and crucial role that is often ascribed to them. If economic self-interest were the only determinant of opinion, we should expect people of the same socioeconomic status to have very similar opinions, and we should expect opinion to vary in a meaningful way from one socioeconomic grouping to another. Research has not given very sound support for these expectations. There is only the most general similarity of opinion among people of the same socioeconomic status, and the exceptions are glaring; while variations from one socioeconomic group to another are rarely simple or clear-cut. To explain why it is that people of the same socioeconomic status so frequently have different ideologies, while people of a different status often have very similar ideologies, we must take account of other than purely economic needs.

More than this, it is becoming increasingly plain that people very frequently do not behave in such a way as to further their material interests, even when it is clear to them what these interests are. The resistance of white-collar workers to organization is not due to a belief that the union will not help them economically; the tendency of the small businessman to side with big business in most economic and political matters cannot be due entirely to a belief that this is the way to guarantee his economic independence. In instances such as these the individual seems not only not to consider his material interests, but even to go against them. It is as if he were thinking in terms of a larger group identification, as if his point of view were determined more by his need to support this group and to suppress opposite ones than by rational consideration of his own interests. Indeed, it is with a sense of relief today that one is assured that a group conflict is merely a clash of economic interests – that each side is merely out to "do" the other – and not a struggle in which deep-lying emotional drives have been let loose. When it comes to the ways in which people appraise the social world, irrational trends stand out glaringly. One may conceive of a professional man who opposes the immigration of Jewish refugees on the ground that this will increase the competition with which he has to deal and so decrease his income. However undemocratic this may be, it is at least rational in a limited sense. But for this man to go on, as do most people who oppose Jews on occupational grounds, and accept a wide variety of opinions, many of which are contradictory, about Jews in general, and to attribute various ills of the world to them, is plainly illogical. And it is just as illogical to praise all Jews in accordance with a "good" stereotype of them. Hostility against groups that is based upon real frustration, brought about by members of that group, undoubtedly exists, but such frustrating experiences can hardly account for the fact that prejudice is apt to be generalized. Evidence from the present study confirms what has often been indicated: that a man who is hostile toward one minority group is very likely to be hostile against a wide variety of others. There is no conceivable rational basis for such generalization; and, what is more striking, prejudice against, or totally uncritical acceptance of, a particular group often exists in the absence of any experience with members of that group. The objective situation of the individual seems an unlikely source of such irrationality; rather we should seek where psychology has already found the sources of dreams, fantasies, and misinterpretations of the world – that is, in the deep-lying needs of the personality.

Another aspect of the individual's situation which we should expect to affect his ideological receptivity is his membership in social groups – occupational, fraternal, religious, and the like. For historical and sociological reasons, such groups favor and promulgate, whether officially or unofficially, different patterns of ideas. There is reason to believe that individuals, out of their needs to conform and to belong and to believe and through such devices as imitation and conditioning, often take over more or less ready-made the opinions, attitudes, and values that are characteristic of the groups in which they have membership. To the extent that the ideas which prevail in such a group are implicitly or explicitly antidemocratic, the individual group member might be expected to be receptive to propaganda having the same general direction. Accordingly, the present research investigates a variety of group memberships with a view to what general trends of thought – and how much variability – might be found in each.

It is recognized, however, that a correlation between group membership and ideology may be due to different kinds of determination in different individuals. In some cases it might be that the individual merely repeats opinions which are taken for granted in his social milieu and which he has no reason to question; in other cases it might be that the individual has chosen to join a particular group because it stood for ideals with which he was already in sympathy. In modern society, despite enormous communality in basic culture, it is rare for a person to be subjected to only one pattern of ideas, after he is old enough for ideas to mean something to him. Some selection is usually made, according, it may be supposed, to the needs of his personality. Even when individuals are exposed during their formative years almost exclusively to a single, closely knit pattern of political, economic, social, and religious ideas, it is found that some conform while others rebel, and it seems proper to inquire whether personality factors do not make the difference. The soundest approach, it would seem, is to consider that in the determination of ideology, as in the determination of any behavior, there is a situational factor and a personality factor, and that a careful weighing of the role of each will yield the most accurate prediction.

Situational factors, chiefly economic condition and social group memberships, have been studied intensively in recent researches on opinion and attitude, while the more inward, more individualistic factors have not received the attention they deserve. Beyond this, there is still another reason why the present study places particular emphasis upon the personality. Fascism, in order to be successful as a political movement, must have a mass basis. It must secure not only the frightened submission but the active cooperation of the great majority of the people. Since by its very nature it favors the few at the expense of the many, it cannot possibly demonstrate that it will so improve the situation of most people that their real interests will be served. It must therefore make its major appeal, not to rational self-interest, but to emotional needs – often to the most primitive and irrational wishes and fears. If it be argued that fascist propaganda fools people into believing that their lot will be improved, then the question arises: Why are they so easily fooled? Because, it may be supposed, of their personality structure; because of long-established patterns of hopes and aspirations, fears and anxieties that dispose them to certain beliefs and make them resistant to others. The task of fascist propaganda, in other words, is rendered easier to the degree that antidemocratic potentials already exist in the great mass of people. It may be granted that in Germany economic conflicts and dislocations within the society were such that for this reason alone the triumph of fascism was sooner or later inevitable; but the Nazi leaders did not act as if they believed this to be so; instead they acted as if it were necessary at every moment to take into account the psychology of the people – to activate every ounce of their antidemocratic potential, to compromise with them, to stamp out the slightest spark of rebellion. It seems apparent that any attempt to appraise the chances of a fascist triumph in America must reckon with the potential existing in the character of the people. Here lies not only the susceptibility to antidemocratic propaganda but the most dependable sources of resistance to it.

The present writers believe that it is up to the people to decide whether or not this country goes fascist. It is assumed that knowledge of the nature and extent of antidemocratic potentials will indicate programs for democratic action. These programs should not be limited to devices for manipulating people in such a way that they will behave more democratically, but they should be devoted to increasing the kind of self-awareness and self-determination that makes any kind of manipulation impossible. There is one explanation for the existence of an individual's ideology that has not so far been considered: that it is the view of the world which a reasonable man, with some understanding of the role of such determinants as those discussed above, and with complete access to the necessary facts, will organize for himself. This conception, though it has been left to the last, is of crucial importance for a sound approach to ideology. Without it we should have to share the destructive view, which has gained some acceptance in the modern world, that since all ideologies, all philosophies, derive from nonrational sources there is no basis for saying that one has more merit than another.

But the rational system of an objective and thoughtful man is not a thing apart from personality. Such a system is still motivated. What is distinguishing in its sources is mainly the *kind of personality organization* from which it springs. It might be said that a mature personality (if we may for the moment use this term without defining it) will come closer to achieving a rational system of thought than will an immature one; but a personality is no less dynamic and no less organized for being mature, and the task of describing the structure of this personality is not different in kind from the task of describing any other personality. According to theory, the personality variables which have most to do with determining the objectivity and rationality of an ideology are those which belong to the ego, that part of the personality which appreciates reality, integrates the other parts, and operates with the most conscious awareness.

It is the ego that becomes aware of and takes responsibility for nonrational forces operating within the personality. This is the basis for our belief that the object of knowing what are the psychological determinants of ideology is that men can become more reasonable. It is not supposed, of course, that this will eliminate differences of opinion. The world is sufficiently complex and difficult to know, men have enough real interests that are in conflict with the real interests of other men, there are enough ego accepted differences in personality to insure that arguments about politics, economics, and religion will never grow dull. Knowledge of the psychological determinants of ideology cannot tell us what is the *truest* ideology; it can only remove some of the barriers in the way of its pursuit.

B. Methodology

1. General Characteristics of the Method

To attack the problems conceptualized above required methods for describing and measuring ideological trends and methods for exposing personality, the contemporary situation, and the social background. A particular methodological challenge was imposed by the conception of *levels* in the person; this made it necessary to devise techniques for surveying opinions, attitudes, and values that were on the surface, for revealing ideological trends that were more or less inhibited and reached the surface only in indirect manifestations, and for bringing to light personality forces that lay in the subject's unconscious. And since the major concern was with *patterns* of dynamically related factors – something that requires study of the total individual – it seemed that the proper approach was through intensive clinical studies. The significance and practical importance of such studies could not be gauged, however, until there was knowledge of how far it was possible to generalize from them. Thus it was necessary to perform group studies as well as individual studies, and to find ways and means for integrating the two.

Individuals were studied by means of interviews and special clinical techniques for revealing underlying wishes, fears, and defenses; groups were studied by means of questionnaires. It was not expected that the clinical studies would be as complete or profound as some which have already been performed, primarily by psychoanalysts, nor that the questionnaires would be more accurate than any now employed by social psychologists. It was hoped, however – indeed it was necessary to our purpose – that the clinical material could be conceptualized in such a way as to permit its being quantified and carried over into group studies, and that the questionnaires could be brought to bear upon areas of response ordinarily left to clinical study. The attempt was made, in other words, to bring methods of traditional social psychology into the service of theories and concepts from the newer dynamic theory of personality and in so doing to make "depth psychological" phenomena more amenable to mass-statistical treatment, and to make quantitative surveys of attitudes and opinions more meaningful psychologically.

In the attempt to integrate clinical and group studies, the two were carried on in close conjunction. When the individual was in the focus of attention, the aim was to describe in detail his pattern of opinions, attitudes, and values and to understand the dynamic factors underlying it, and on this basis to design significant questions for use with groups of subjects. When the group was in the focus of attention, the aim was to discover what opinions, attitudes, and values commonly go together and what patterns of factors in the life histories and in the contemporary situations of the subjects were commonly associated with each ideological constellation; this afforded a basis on which to select individuals for more intensive study: commanding first attention were those who exemplified the common patterns and in whom it could be supposed that the correlated factors were dynamically related.

In order to study potentially antidemocratic individuals it was necessary first to identify them. Hence a start was made by constructing a questionnaire and having it filled out anonymously by a large group of people. This questionnaire contained, in addition to numerous questions of fact about the subject's past and present life, a variety of antidemocratic statements with which the subjects were invited to agree or disagree. A number of individuals who showed the greatest amount of agreement with these statements – and, by way of contrast, some who showed the most disagreement or, in some instances, were most neutral – were then studied by means of interviews and other clinical techniques. On the basis of these individual studies the questionnaire was revised, and the whole procedure repeated.

The interview was used in part as a check upon the *validity* of the questionnaire, that is to say, it provided a basis for judging whether people who obtained the highest antidemocratic scores on the questionnaire were usually those who, in a confidential relationship with another person, expressed antidemocratic sentiments with the most intensity. What was more important, however, the clinical studies gave access to the deeper personality factors behind antidemocratic ideology and suggested the means for their investigation on a mass scale. With increasing knowledge of the underlying trends of which prejudice was an expression, there was increasing familiarity with various other signs or manifestations by which these trends could be recognized. The task then was to translate these manifestations into questionnaire items for use in the next group study. Progress lay in finding more and more reliable indications of the central personality forces and in showing with increasing clarity the relations of these forces to antidemocratic ideological expression.

Prejudice in the Interview Material

A. Introduction

Our study grew out of specific investigations into anti-Semitism. As our work advanced, however, the emphasis gradually shifted. We came to regard it as our main task not to analyze anti-Semitism or any other antiminority prejudice as a sociopsychological phenomenon *per se*, but rather to examine the relation of antiminority prejudice to broader ideological and characterological patterns. Thus anti-Semitism gradually all but disappeared as a topic of our questionnaire and in our interview schedule it was only one among many topics which had to be covered.

Another investigation, carried through parallel to our research and partly by the same staff members of the Institute of Social Research, i.e., the study on anti-Semitism within labor (57b), concentrated on the question of anti-Semitism, but at the same time was concerned with sociopsychological issues akin to those presented in the present volume. While the bulk of the material to be discussed in this chapter is taken from the section on prejudice of the Berkeley interviews, an attempt was made to utilize, at least in a supplementary form, some of the ideas of the Labor Study as hypotheses for further investigation. This was done as a part of the work carried out in Los Angeles. In collaboration with J. F. Brown and F. Pollock we drew up an additional section of the interview schedule devoted to specific questions about Jews. These questions were derived for the most part from the material gathered through the "screened interviews" of the Labor Study. The aim of this new section of the interview schedule was to see if it was possible to establish certain differential patterns within the general structure of prejudice.

The list of questions follows. Not all of these questions were put to every subject, nor was the exact wording of the questions always the same, but most of the ground marked off by the questions was covered in each case.

List of Questions Pertaining to Jews

Do you think there is a Jewish problem? If yes, in what sense?
Do you care about it?
Have you had any experience with Jews? What kind?
Do you remember names of persons involved and other specifi data?
If not, on what is your opinion based?
Did you have any contrary experiences (or hear about such experiences) with Jewish individuals?

If you had – would it change your opinion? If not, why not?
Can you tell a Jew from other people? How?
What do you know about the Jewish religion?
Are there Christians that are as bad as Jews?
Is their percentage as high or higher than the percentage of bad Jews?
How do Jews behave at work? What about the alleged Jewish industriousness?
Is it true that the Jews have an undue influence in movies, radio, literature, and universities?
If yes – what is particularly bad about it? What should be done about it?
Is it true that the Jews have an undue influence in business, politics, labor, etc.?
If yes – what kind of an influence? Should something be done to curb it?
What did the Nazis do to the German Jews? What do you think about it? Is there such a problem here? What would you do to solve it?
What do you blame them most for? Are they: aggressive, bad-mannered; controlling the banks; black marketeers; cheating; Christ killers; clannish; Communists; corrupting; dirty; draft dodgers; exploiters; hiding their identity; too intellectual; Internationalists; overcrowding many jobs; lazy; controlling movies; money-minded; noisy; overassimilative; overbearing; oversexed; looking for privileges; quarrelsome; running the country; too smart; spoiling nice neighborhoods; owning too many stores; undisciplined; unethical against Gentiles; upstarts; shunning hard manual labor; forming a world conspiracy?
Do you favor social discrimination or special legislation?
Shall a Jew be treated as an individual or as a member of a group?
How do your suggestions go along with constitutional rights?
Do you object to personal contacts with individual Jews?
Do you consider Jews more as a nuisance or more as a menace?
Could you imagine yourself marrying a Jew?
Do you like to discuss the Jewish issue?
What would you do if you were a Jew?
Can a Jew ever become a real American?

The additional interview material taught us more about prevailing overt patterns of anti-Semitism than about its inner dynamics. It is probably fair to say that the detailed questions proved most helpful in understanding the phenomena of psychological *conflict* in prejudice – the problems characterized in Chapter V as "pseudo-democratism." Another significant observation has to do with the reactions of our interviewees to the list of "bad Jewish traits" presented to them. Most answers to this list read "all-inclusive," that is to say, very little differentiation takes place. The prejudiced subjects tend to subscribe to any reproach against the Jews, provided they do not have to produce these objections themselves but rather find them pre-established, as if they were commonly accepted. This observation could be interpreted in different ways. Either it may be indicative of the "inner consistency" of anti-Semitic ideology, or it may testify to the mental rigidity of our high scorers, and this apart from the fact that the method of multiple choice may itself make for automatic reactions. Although our questionnaire studies gave evidence of marked consistency within anti-Semitic ideology, it would hardly be enough to account for the all-inclusiveness of the present responses. It seems that one must think in terms of automatization, though it is impossible to say conclusively whether this is due to the "high" mentality or to the shortcomings of our procedure. In all probability, the presentation of extreme anti-Semitic statements as if they were no longer disreputable but rather something which can be sensibly discussed, works as a kind of antidote for the superego and may stimulate imitation even in cases where the individual's "own" reactions would be less violent. This consideration may throw some light upon the phenomenon of the whole German people tolerating the most extreme anti-Semitic measures, although it is highly to be doubted that the individuals themselves were more anti-Semitic than our high-scoring subjects. A pragmatic inference to be drawn from this hypothesis would be that, in so far as possible, pseudorational discussions of anti-Semitism should be avoided. One might refute factual anti-Semitic statements or explain the dynamics responsible for anti-Semitism, but he should not enter the sphere of the "Jewish problem." As things stand now, the acknowledgment of a "Jewish problem," after the European genocide, suggests, however subtly, that there might have been some justification for what the Nazis did.

The whole material on ideology has been taken from 63 Los Angeles interviews in addition to the pertinent sections of those gathered in Berkeley.

It should be stressed that once again the *subjective* aspect is in the foreground. The selection of our sample excluded an investigation into the role played by the "object" – that is to say, the Jews – in the formation of prejudice. We do not deny that the object plays a role, but we devote our attention to the forms of reaction directed towards the Jew, not to the basis of these reactions within the "object." This is due to a hypothesis with which we started and which has been given strong support in Chapter III, namely, that anti-Semitic prejudice has little to do with the qualities of those against whom it is directed. Our interest is centered in the high-scoring subjects.

In organizing the present chapter, we start with the general assumption that the – largely unconscious – hostility resulting from frustration and repression and socially diverted from its true object, *needs* a substitute object through which it may obtain a realistic aspect and thus dodge, as it were, more radical manifestations of a blocking of the subject's relationship to reality, e.g., psychosis. This "object" of unconscious destructiveness, far from being a superficial "scapegoat," must have certain characteristics in order to fulfill its role. It must be tangible enough; and yet not *too* tangible, lest it be exploded by its own realism. It must have a sufficient historical backing and appear as an indisputable element of tradition. It must be defined in rigid and well-known stereotypes. Finally, the object must possess features, or at least be capable of being perceived and interpreted in terms of features, which harmonize with the destructive tendencies of the prejudiced subject. Some of these features, such as "clannishness" aid rationalization; others, such as the expression of weakness or masochism, provide psychologically adequate stimuli for destructiveness. There can be hardly any doubt that all these requirements are fulfilled by the phenomenon of the Jew. This is not to say that Jews *must* draw hatred upon themselves, or that there is an absolute historical necessity which makes them, rather than others, the ideal target of social aggressiveness. Suffice it to say that they *can* perform this function in the psychological households of many people. The problem of the "uniqueness" of the Jewish phenomenon and hence of anti-Semitism could be approached only by recourse to a theory which is beyond the scope of this study. Such a theory would neither enumerate a diversity of "factors" nor single out a specific one as "the" cause but rather develop a unified framework within which all the "elements" are linked together consistently. This would amount to nothing less than a theory of modern society as a whole.

We shall first give some evidence of the "functional" character of anti-Semitism, that is to say, its relative independence of the object. Then we shall point out the problem of *cui bono*: anti-Semitism as a device for effortless "orientation" in a cold, alienated, and largely ununderstandable world. As a parallel to our analysis of political and economic ideologies, it will be shown that this "orientation" is achieved by stereotypy. The gap between this stereotypy on the one hand and real experience and the still-accepted standards of democracy on the other, leads to a *conflict* situation, something which is clearly set forth in a number of our interviews. We then take up what appears to be the resolution of this conflict: the underlying anti-Semitism of our cultural climate, keyed to the prejudiced person's own unconscious or preconscious wishes, proves in the more extreme cases to be stronger than either conscience or official democratic values. This leads up to the evidence of the destructive character of anti-Semitic reactions. As remnants of the conflict, there remain traces of sympathy for, or rather "appreciation" of, certain Jewish traits which, however, when viewed more closely, also show negative implications.

Some more specific observations about the structure of anti-Jewish prejudice will be added. Their focal point is the differentiation of anti-Semitism according to the subject's own social identifications. This survey of anti-Semitic features and dynamics will then be supplemented by a few remarks on the attitudes of low-scoring subjects. Finally, we shall offer some evidence of the broader social significance of anti-Semitism: its intrinsic denial of the principles of American democracy.

B. The "Functional" Character of Anti-Semitism

The psychological dynamisms that "call for" the anti-Semitic outlet – most essentially, we believe, the ambivalence of authoritarian and rebellious trends – have been analyzed in detail in other sections of this book. Here we limit ourselves to some extreme but concrete evidence of the fact that anti-Semitism is not so much dependent upon the nature of the object as upon the subject's own psychological wants and needs.

There are a number of cases in which the "functional" character of prejudice is obvious. Here we find subjects who are prejudiced *per se*, but with whom it is relatively accidental against what group their prejudice is directed. We content ourselves with two examples. *5051* is a generally high-scoring man, one of a few Boy Scout leaders. He has strong, though unconscious, fascist leanings. Although anti-Semitic, he tries to mitigate his bias by certain semirational qualifications. Here, the following statement occurs:

> "Sometimes we hear that the average Jew is smarter in business than the average white man. I do not believe this. I would hate to believe it. What the Jews should learn is to educate their bad individuals to be more cooperative and agreeable. Actually there is more underhandedness amongst Armenians than there is amongst Jews, but the Armenians aren't nearly as conspicuous and noisy. Mind you, I have known some Jews whom I consider my equal in every way and I like very much."

This is somewhat reminiscent of Poe's famous story about the double murder in the Rue Morgue where the savage cries of an orangutan are mistaken by bystanders as words of all kinds of different foreign languages, to wit, languages particularly strange to each of the listeners who happen to be foreigners themselves. The primary hostile reaction is directed against foreigners *per se*, who are perceived as "uncanny." This infantile fear of the strange is only subsequently "filled up" with the imagery of a specific group, stereotyped and handy for this purpose. The Jews are favorite stand-ins for the child's "bad man." The transference of unconscious fear to the particular object, however, the latter being of a secondary nature only, always maintains an aspect of accidentalness. Thus, as soon as other factors interfere, the aggression may be deflected, at least in part, from the Jews and to another group, preferably one of still greater social distance. Pseudodemocratic ideology and the professed desire to promote militantly what he conceives to be American ideals are marked in our Boy Scout leader, *5051*, and he considers himself not conservative but "predominantly liberal"; hence he tempers his anti-Semitism and anti-Negroism by referring to a third group. He summons the Armenians in order to prove that he is not "prejudiced," but at the same time his formulation is such that the usual anti-Semitic stereotypes can easily be maintained. Even his exoneration of the Jews with regard to their supposed "smartness" is actually a device for the glorification of the ingroup: he hates to think that "we are less smart than they." While anti-Semitism is functional with regard to the object choice on a more superficial level, its deeper determinants still seem to be much more rigid.

An extreme case of what might be called "mobile" prejudice is *M1225a*, of the Maritime School group. Though his questionnaire scores are only medium, the interview shows strong traces of a "manipulative" anti-Semite. The beginning of the minorities section of his interview is as follows:

> (What do you think of the race-minority problem?) "I definitely think there is a problem. I'd probably be prejudiced there. Like the Negro situation. They could act more human. . . . It would be less of a problem."

His aggression is absorbed by the Negroes, in the "idiosyncratic" manner that can otherwise be observed among extreme anti-Semites, all of whose aggression appears to be directed against Jews.

> "I wouldn't sail on a ship if I had to sail with a Negro. To me, they have an offensive smell. Course, the Chinese say we smell like sheep."

It may be mentioned that a subject of the Labor Study, a Negro woman, complained about the smell of the Jews. The present subject concentrates on the Negroes, exonerating the Jews, though in an equivocal way:

> (What about the Jewish problem?) "I don't believe there is much of a problem there. They're too smart to have a problem. Well, they are good business men. (Too much influence?) I believe they have a lot of influence. (In what areas?) Well, motion picture industry. (Do they abuse it?) Well, the thing you hear an awful lot about is help the Jews, help the Jews. But you never hear anything about helping other races or nationalities. (Do they abuse their influence in the movies?) If they do, they do it in such a way that it is not offensive."

Here again, anti-Semitic stereotypy is maintained descriptively whereas the shift of actual hatred to the Negroes – which cannot be accounted for by the course of the interview – affects the superimposed value judgments. The twist with regard to the term "problem" should be noted. By denying the existence of a "Jewish problem," he consciously takes sides with the unbiased. By interpreting the word, however, as meaning "having difficulties," and emphasizing that the Jews are "too smart to *have* a problem," he expresses unwittingly his own rejection. In accordance with his "smartness" theory, his pro-Jewish statements have a rationalistic ring clearly indicative of the subject's ambivalence: all race hatred is "envy" but he leaves little doubt that in his mind there is some reason for this envy, e.g., his acceptance of the myth that the Jews controlled German industry.

This interview points to a way in which our picture of ethnocentrism may be differentiated. Although the correlation between anti-Semitism and anti-Negroism is undoubtedly high, a fact which stands out in our interviews as well as in our questionnaire studies (cf. Chapter IV), this is not to say that prejudice is a single compact mass. Readiness to accept statements hostile to minority groups may well be conceived as a more or less unitary trait, but when, in the interview situation, subjects are allowed to express themselves spontaneously it is not uncommon for one minority more than the others to appear, for the moment at least, as an object of special hatred. This phenomenon may be elucidated by reference to persecution mania which, as has been pointed out frequently, has many structural features in common with anti-Semitism. While the paranoid is beset by an over-all hatred, he nevertheless tends to "pick" his enemy, to molest certain individuals who draw his attention upon themselves: he falls, as it were, negatively in love. Something similar may hold good for the potentially fascist character. As soon as he has achieved a specific and concrete countercathexis, which is indispensable to his fabrication of a social pseudoreality, he may "canalize" his otherwise free-floating aggressiveness and then leave alone other potential objects of persecution. Naturally, these processes come to the fore in the dialectics of the interview rather than in the scales, which hardly allow the subject freely to "express" himself.

It may be added that subjects in our sample find numerous other substitutes for the Jew, such as the Mexicans and the Greeks. The latter, like the Armenians, are liberally endowed with traits otherwise associated with the imagery of the Jew.

One more aspect of the "functional" character of anti-Semitism should be mentioned. We encountered quite frequently members of other minority groups, with strong "conformist" tendencies, who were outspokenly anti-Semitic. Hardly any traces of solidarity among the different outgroups could be found. The pattern is rather one of "shifting the onus," of defamation of other groups in order to put one's own social status in a better light. An example is *5023*, a "psychoneurotic with anxiety state," Mexican by birth:

> Being an American of Mexican ancestry, he identifies with the white race and feels "we are superior people." He particularly dislikes the Negroes and completely dislikes Jews. He feels that they are all alike and wants as little as possible to do with them. Full of contradiction as this subject is, it is not surprising to find that he would marry a Jewess if he really loved her. On the other hand he would control both Negroes and Jews and "keep them in their place."

5068 is regarded by the interviewer as representing a "pattern probably quite frequent in second-generation Americans who describe themselves as Italian-Americans." His prejudice is of the politico-fascist brand, distinctly colored by paranoid fantasies:

He is of pure Italian extraction and naturalized here at the time of the first World War. He is very proud of this extraction and for a long time in the early days of Mussolini was active in Italian-American organizations. He still feels that the war against Italy was very unfortunate. Concerning the other minorities he is quite prejudiced. The Mexicans he feels are enough like the Italians so that if they were educated enough it would be all right. At the present time, however, he feels that they need much education. He believes that the California Japanese were more than correctly handled and that those about whom there is no question should be gradually allowed back. He described the Negro situation as a tough one. He believes there should be definite laws particularly with regard to racial intermarriage and that the color line should also be drawn "regarding where people can live." "Despite what they say, the Southern Negroes are really the happiest ones." "The trouble with Jews is that they are all Communists and for this reason dangerous." His own relations with them have only been fair. In his business relations he says they are "chiselers" and "stick together." Concerning a solution to this problem, he says, "The Jews should actually educate their own. The way the Jews stick together shows that they actually have more prejudice against the Gentiles than the Gentiles have against them." He illustrates this with a long story which I was not able to get in detail about some acquaintance of his who married into a Jewish family and was not allowed to eat off the same dishes with them.

We may mention, furthermore, *5052*, an anti-Semitic man of Spanish Negro descent, with strong homosexual tendencies. He is a nightclub entertainer, and the interviewer summarizes his impression in the statement that this man wants to say, "I am not a Negro, I am an entertainer." Here the element of social identification in an outcast is clearly responsible for his prejudice.

Finally, reference should be made to a curiosity, the interview of a Turk, otherwise not evaluated because of his somewhat subnormal intelligence. He indulged in violent anti-Semitic diatribes until it came out near the end of the interview that he was Jewish himself. The whole complex of anti-Semitism among minority groups, and among Jews themselves, offers serious problems and deserves a study of its own. Even the casual observations provided by our sample suffice to corroborate the suspicion that those who suffer from social pressure may frequently tend to transfer this pressure onto others rather than to join hands with their fellow victims.

C. *The Imaginary Foe*

Our examples of the "functional" character of anti-Semitism, and of the relative ease by which prejudice can be switched from one object to another, point in one direction: the hypothesis that prejudice, according to its intrinsic content, is but superficially, if at all, related to the specific nature of its object. We shall now give more direct support for this hypothesis, the relation of which to clinical categories such as stereotypy, incapacity to have "experience," projectivity, and power fantasies is not far to seek. This support is supplied by statements which are either plainly self-contradictory or incompatible with facts and of a manifestly imaginary character. Since the usual "self-contradictions" of the anti-Semite can, however, frequently be explained on the basis that they involve different layers of reality and different psychological urges which are still reconcilable in the over-all "*Weltanschauung*" of the anti-Semite, we concern ourselves here mainly with evidence of imaginary constructs. The fantasies with which we shall deal are so well known from everyday life that their significance for the structure of anti-Semitism can be taken for granted. They are merely highlighted by our research. One might say that these fantasies occur whenever stereotypes "run wild," that is to say, make themselves completely independent from interaction with reality. When these "emancipated" stereotypes are forcibly brought back into relation with reality, blatant distortions appear. The content of the examples of stereotyped fantasy which we collected has to do predominantly with ideas of excessive power attributed to the chosen foe. The disproportion between the relative social weakness of the object and its supposed sinister omnipotence is by itself evidence that the projective mechanism is at work.

We shall first give some examples of omnipotence fantasies projected upon a whole outgroup abstractly, as it were, and then show how the application of such ideas to factual experience comes close to paranoid delusion.

5054, a middle-aged woman with fairly high scores on all the scales, who is greatly concerned with herself and characterized by a "domineering" manner, claims that she has always tried "to see the other side" and even to "fight prejudice on every side." She derives her feelings of tolerance from the contrast with her husband whom she characterized as extremely anti-Jewish (he hates all Jews and makes no exceptions) whereas she is willing to make exceptions. Her actual attitude is described as follows:

> She would not subscribe to a "racist theory," but does not think that the Jews will change much, but rather that they will tend to become "more aggressive." She also believes that "they will eventually run the country, whether we like it or not."

The usual stereotype of undue Jewish influence in politics and economy is inflated to the assertion of threatening over-all domination. It is easy to guess that the countermeasures which such subjects have in mind are no less totalitarian than their persecution ideas, even if they do not dare to say so in so many words.

Similar is case *5061a*, chosen as a mixed case (she is high-middle on E, but low on F and PEC), but actually, as proved by the interview, markedly ethnocentric. In her statement, the vividness of the fantasies about the almighty Jew seems to be equalled by the intensity of her vindictiveness.

> "My relations with the Jews have been anything but pleasant." When asked to be more specific it was impossible for her to name individual incidents. She described them, however, as "pushing everybody about, aggressive, clannish, money-minded.... The Jews are practically taking over the country. They are getting into everything. It is not that they are smarter, but they work so hard to get control. They are all alike." When asked if she did not feel that there were variations in the Jewish temperament as in any other, she said, "No, I don't think so. I think there is something that makes them all stick together and try to hold on to everything. I have Jewish friends and I have tried not to treat them antagonistically, but sooner or later they have also turned out to be aggressive and obnoxious.... I think the percentage of very bad Jews is very much greater than the percentage of bad Gentiles.... My husband feels exactly the same way on this whole problem. As a matter of fact, I don't go as far as he does. He didn't like many things about Hitler but he did feel that Hitler did a good job on the Jews. He feels that we will come in this country to a place where we have to do something about it."

Sometimes the projective aspect of the fantasies of Jewish domination comes into the open. Those whose half-conscious wishes culminate in the idea of the abolition of democracy and the rule of the strong, call those antidemocratic whose only hope lies in the maintenance of democratic rights. *5018* is a 32-year-old ex-marine gunnery sergeant who scores high on all the scales. He is suspected by the interviewer of being "somewhat paranoid." He knows "one cannot consider Jews a race, but they are all alike. They have too much power but I guess it's really our fault." This is followed up by the statement:

> He would handle the Jews by outlawing them from business domination. He thinks that all others who feel the same could get into business and compete with them and perhaps overcome them, but adds, "it would be better to ship them to Palestine and let them gyp one another. I have had some experiences with them and a few were good soldiers but not very many." The respondent went on to imply that lax democratic methods cannot solve the problem because "they won't cooperate in a democracy."

The implicitly antidemocratic feelings of this subject are evidenced by his speaking derogatorily about lax democratic methods: his blaming the Jews for lack of democratic cooperation is manifestly a rationalization.

One more aspect of unrealistic imagery of the Jew should at least be mentioned. It is the contention that the Jews "are everywhere." Omnipresence sometimes displaces omnipotence, perhaps because no actual "Jewish rule" can be pretended to exist, so that the image-ridden subject has to seek a different outlet for his power fantasy in ideas of dangerous, mysterious ubiquity. This is fused with another psychological element. To the highly prejudiced subject the idea of the total right of the ingroup, and of its tolerating nothing which does not strictly "belong," is all-pervasive. This is projected upon the Jews. Whereas the high scorer apparently cannot stand any "intruder" – ultimately nothing that is not strictly like himself – he sees this totality of presence in those whom he hates and whom he feels justified in exterminating because one otherwise "could not get rid of them." The following example shows the idea of Jewish omnipresence applied to personal experience, thus revealing its proximity to delusion.

6070, a 40-year-old woman, is high-middle on the E scale and particularly vehement about the Jews:

> "I don't like Jews. The Jew is always crying. They are taking our country over from us. They are aggressive. They suffer from every lust. Last summer I met the famous musician X, and before I really knew him he wanted me to sign an affidavit to help bring his family into this country. Finally I had to flatly refuse and told him I want no more Jews here. Roosevelt started bringing the Jews into the government, and that is the chief cause of our difficulties today. The Jews arranged it so they were discriminated for in the draft. I favor a legislative discrimination against the Jews along American, not Hitler lines. Everybody knows that the Jews are back of the Communists. This X person almost drove me nuts. I had made the mistake of inviting him to be my guest at my beach club. He arrived with ten other Jews who were uninvited. They always cause trouble. If one gets in a place, he brings two more and those two bring two more."

This quotation is remarkable for more reasons than that it exemplifies the "Jews are everywhere" complex. It is the expression of Jewish *weakness* – that they are "always crying" – which is perverted into ubiquity. The refugee, forced to leave his country, appears as he who *wants* to intrude and to expand over the whole earth, and it is hardly too far-fetched to assume that this imagery is at least partly derived from the fact of persecution itself. Moreover, the quotation gives evidence of a certain ambivalence of the extreme anti-Semite which points in the direction of "negatively falling in love." This woman had *invited* the celebrity to her club, doubtless attracted by his fame, but used the contact, once it had been established, merely in order to personalize her aggressiveness.

Another example of the merging of semipsychotic idiosyncrasies and wild anti-Jewish imagery is the 26-year-old woman, *5004*. She scores high on the F scale and high-middle on E and PEC. Asked about Jewish religion, she produces an answer which partakes of the age-old image of "uncannyness." "I know very little, but I would be afraid to go into a synagogue." This has to be evaluated in relation to her statement about Nazi atrocities:

"I am not particularly sorry because of what the Germans did to the Jews. I feel Jews would do the same type of thing to me."

The persecution fantasy of what the Jews *might* do to her, is used, in authentic paranoid style, as a justification of the genocide committed by the Nazis.

Our last two examples refer to the distortions that occur when experience is viewed through the lens of congealed stereotypy. *M732c* of the Veterans Group, who scores generally high on the scales, shows this pattern of distorted experience with regard to both Negroes and Jews. As to the former:

"You never see a Negro driving (an ordinary car of which subject mentions a number of examples) but only a Cadillac or a Packard.... They always dress gaudy. They have that tendency to show off.... Since the Negro has that feeling that he isn't up to par, he's always trying to show off.... Even though he can't afford it, he will buy an expensive car just to make a show...." Subject mentions that the brightest girl in a class at subject's school happens to be a Negro and he explains her outstandingness in the class in terms of Negro overcompensation for what he seems to be implying is her inherent inferiority.

The assertion about the Negro's Cadillac speaks for itself. As to the story about the student, it indicates in personalized terms the aspect of inescapability inherent in hostile stereotypy. To the prejudiced, the Negro is "dull"; if he meets, however, one of outstanding achievement, it is supposed to be mere over-compensation, the exception that proves the rule. No matter what the Negro is or does, he is condemned.

As to the "Jewish problem":

"As far as being good and shrewd businessmen, that's about all I have to say about *them*. They're *white* people, that's one thing.... Of course, they have the Jewish instinct, whatever that is.... I've heard they have a business nose.... I imagine the Jewish people are more *obsequious*... For example, *somehow* a Jewish barber will entice you to come to *his* chair." Subject elaborates here a definite fantasy of some mysterious influence by Jews.... "They're mighty shrewd businessmen, and you don't have much chance" (competing with Jews).

The story about the barber seems to be a retrogression towards early infantile magical patterns of thinking.

F359, a 48-year-old accountant in a government department, is, according to the interviewer, a cultured and educated woman. This, however, does not keep her from paranoid story-telling as soon as the critical area of race relations, which serves as a kind of free-for-all, is entered. (She is in the high quartile on E, though low on both F and PEC.) Her distortions refer both to Negroes and to Jews:

> Subject considers this a very serious problem and she thinks that it is going to get worse. The Negroes are going to get worse. She experienced a riot in Washington; there was shooting; street-car windows were broken, and when a white would get into the Negro section of the car, the shooting would start. The white man would have to lie on the floor. She did not dare to go out at night. One day the Negroes were having a procession and some of them started pushing her off the sidewalk. When she asked them not to push, they looked so insolent that she thought they would start a riot, and her companion said, "Let's get out of here or we will start a riot." A friend of hers told her that she had asked her maid to work on a Thursday but the maid had refused because she said it was "push and shove" day – the day they shoved the whites off the sidewalk. Another friend of hers in Los Angeles told her not to let her maid use her vacuum cleaner because they tamper with it in such a way as to cause it to tear your rugs. One day she caught the maid using a file on her vacuum cleaner and asked her what she was doing. The maid replied, "Oh, I'm just trying to fix this thing." They just want to get revenge on whites. One cannot give them equal rights yet, they are not ready for it; we will have to educate them first. Subject would not want to sit next to a Negro in a theatre or restaurant. She cited the case of a drugstore man who addressed a Negro janitor, a cleaner, as "Mr." You just can't do that to them or they will say, "Ah'm as good as white folks." (Outcome?) "I think there will be trouble." She expects riots and bloodshed.
>
> (Jews?) "Well, they are to blame too, I think. They just cannot do business straight, they have to be underhanded – truth has no meaning for them in business." (What has been your personal experience?) She cited the case of a friend who is interested in photography and bought some second-hand cameras from pawn shops. One day when he was in one, a woman came in with a set of false teeth. She was told that they were not worth anything (there was some gold in them). Finally, the Jew gave her a few dollars for them. As soon as she had gone out, he turned to the man and said, "She didn't know it, but see that platinum under here? " In other words the teeth were worth many times what he gave for them. Subject's friend did not get gypped because he knew them and called their bluff.

It is often advocated as the best means of improving intercultural relations that as many personal contacts as possible be established between the different groups. While the value of such contacts in some cases of anti-Semitism is to be acknowledged, the material presented in this section argues for certain qualifications, at least in the case of the more extreme patterns of prejudice. There is no simple gap between experience and stereotypy. Stereotypy is a device for looking at things comfortably; since, however, it feeds on deep-lying unconscious sources, the distortions which occur are not to be corrected merely by taking a *real* look. Rather, experience itself is predetermined by stereotypy. The persons whose interviews on minority issues have just been discussed share one decisive trait. Even if brought together with minority group members as different from the stereotype as possible, they will perceive them through the glasses of stereotypy, and will hold against them whatever they are and do. Since this tendency is by no means confined to people who are actually "cranky" (rather, the whole complex of the Jew is a kind of recognized red-light district of legitimatized psychotic distortions), this inaccessibility to experience may not be limited to people of the kind discussed here, but may well operate in much milder cases. This should be taken into account by any well-planned policy of defense. Optimism with regard to the hygienic effects of personal contacts should be discarded. One cannot "correct" stereotyping by experience; he has to reconstitute the capacity for *having* experiences in order to prevent the growth of ideas which are malignant in the most literal clinical sense.

55

Some Types of Character and Society

David Riesman

> ... nor can the learned reader be ignorant, that in human nature, though here collected under one general name, is such prodigious variety, that a cook will sooner have gone through all the several species of animal and vegetable food in the world, than an author will be able to exhaust so extensive a subject.
>
> Fielding, *Tom Jones*

> I speak of the American in the singular, as if there were not millions of them, north and south, east and west, of both sexes, of all ages, and of various races, professions, and religions. Of course the one American I speak of is mythical; but to speak in parables is inevitable in such a subject, and it is perhaps as well to do so frankly.
>
> Santayana, *Character and Opinion in the United States*

This is an article about social character and about the differences in social character between men of different regions, eras, and groups. It considers the ways in which different social character types, once they are formed at the knee of society, are then deployed in the work, play, politics, and child-rearing activities of society. More particularly, it is about the way in which one kind of social character, which dominated America in the nineteenth century, is gradually being replaced by a social character of quite a different sort. Why this happened; how it happened; and what are its consequences in some major areas of life.

Just what do we mean when we speak of "social character"? We do not speak of "personality," which in current social psychology is used to denote the total self, with its inherited temperaments and talents, its biological as well as psychological components, its evanescent as well as more or less permanent attributes. Nor even do we speak of "character" as such, which, in one of its contemporary uses, refers to only a part of personality – that part which is formed not by heredity but by experience (not that it is any simple matter to

---

Source: David Riesman, *The Lonely Crowd*, (New Haven: Yale University Press, 1961).

draw a line between the two): Character, in this sense, is the more or less permanent socially and historically conditioned organization of an individual's drives and satisfactions – the kind of "set" with which he approaches the world and people.

"Social character" is that part of "character" which is shared among significant social groups and which, as most contemporary social scientists define it, is the product of the experience of these groups. The notion of social character permits us to speak, as I do throughout, of the character of classes, groups, regions, and nations.

I do not plan to delay over the many ambiguities of the concept of social character – whether it may properly be ascribed to experience rather than to heredity; whether there is any empirical proof that it really exists; whether it deserves to be regarded here as more important than the elements of character and personality that bind all people everywhere in the world together, or those other elements of character and personality that separate each individual from every other, even the closest. The assumption that a social character exists has always been a more or less invisible premise of ordinary parlance and is becoming today a more or less visible premise of the social sciences. It will consequently be familiar under one name or another to any of my readers who are acquainted with the writings of Erich Fromm, Abram Kardiner, Ruth Benedict, Margaret Mead, Geoffrey Gorer, Karen Horney and many others who have written about social character in general, or the social character of different people and different times

Most of these writers assume – as I do – that the years of childhood are of great importance in molding character. Most of them agree – as I do – that these early years cannot be seen in isolation from the structure of society, which affects the parents who raise the children, as well as the children directly. My collaborators and I base ourselves on this broad platform of agreement, and do not plan to discuss in what way these writers differ from each other and we from them.

I. Character and Society

What is the relation between social character and society? How is it that every society seems to get, more or less, the social character it "needs"? Erik H. Erikson writes in a study of the social character of the Yurok Indians, that ". . . systems of child training . . . represent unconscious attempts at creating out of human raw material that configuration of attitudes which is (or once was) the optimum under the tribe's particular natural conditions and economic–historic necessities."[1]

From "economic–historic necessities" to "systems of child training" is a long jump. Much of the work of students of social character has been devoted to closing the gap and showing how the satisfaction of the largest "needs" of society is prepared, in some half-mysterious way, by its most intimate practices.

Erich Fromm succinctly suggests the line along which this connection between society and character training may be sought: "In order that any society may function well, its members must acquire the kind of character which makes them *want* to act in the way they *have* to act as members of the society or of a special class within it. They have to *desire* what objectively is *necessary* for them to do. *Outer force* is replaced by *inner compulsion*, and by the particular kind of human energy which is channeled into character traits."[2]

Thus, the link between character and society – certainly not the only one, but one of the most significant, and the one I choose to emphasize in this discussion – is to be found in the way in which society ensures some degree of conformity from the individuals who make it up. In each society, such a mode of ensuring conformity is built into the child, and then either encouraged or frustrated in later adult experience. (No society, it would appear, is quite prescient enough to ensure that the mode of conformity it has inculcated will satisfy those subject to it in every stage of life.) I shall use the term "mode of conformity" interchangeably with the term "social character" – though certainly conformity is not all of social character: "mode of creativity" is as much a part of it. However, while societies and individuals may live well enough – if rather boringly – without creativity, it is not likely that they can live without some mode of conformity – even be it one of rebellion.

My concern in this book is with two revolutions and their relation to the "mode of conformity" or "social character" of Western man since the Middle Ages. The first of these revolutions has in the last four hundred years cut us off pretty decisively from the family- and clan-oriented traditional ways of life in which mankind has existed throughout most of history; this revolution includes the Renaissance, the Reformation, the Counter-Reformation, the Industrial Revolution, and the political revolutions of the seventeenth, eighteenth, and nineteenth centuries. This revolution is, of course, still in process, but in the most advanced countries of the world, and particularly in America, it is giving way to another sort of revolution – a whole range of social developments associated with a shift from an age of production to an age of consumption.

The first revolution we understand moderately well; it is, under various labels, in our texts and our terminology. The second revolution, which is just beginning, has interested many contemporary observers, including social scientists, philosophers, and journalists. Both description and evaluation are still highly controversial; indeed, many are still preoccupied with the first set of revolutions and have not invented the categories for discussing the second set. I try to sharpen the contrast between, on the one hand, conditions and character in those social strata that are today most seriously affected by the second revolution, and, on the other hand, conditions and character in analogous strata during the earlier revolution; in this perspective, what is briefly said about the traditional and feudal societies which were overturned by the first revolution is in the nature of backdrop for these later shifts.

One of the categories I make use of is taken from demography, the science that deals with birth rates and death rates, with the absolute and relative numbers of people in a society, and their distribution by age, sex, and other variables, for I tentatively seek to link certain social and characterological developments, as cause and effect, with certain population shifts in Western society since the Middle Ages.

It seems reasonably well established, despite the absence of reliable figures for earlier centuries, that during this period the curve of population growth in the Western countries has shown an S-shape of a particular type (as other countries are drawn more closely into the net of Western civilization, their populations also show a tendency to develop along the lines of this S-shaped curve). The bottom horizontal line of the S represents a situation where the total population does not increase or does so very slowly, for the number of births equals roughly the number of deaths, and both are very high. In societies of this type, a high proportion of the population is young, life expectancy is low, and the turnover of generations is extremely rapid. Such societies are said to be in the phase of "high growth potential"; for should something happen to decrease the very high death rate (greater production of food, new sanitary measures, new knowledge of the causes of disease, and so on), a "population explosion" would result, and the population would increase very rapidly. This in effect is what happened in the West, starting with the seventeenth century. This spurt in population was most marked in Europe, and the countries settled by Europeans, in the nineteenth century. It is represented by the vertical bar of the S. Demographers call this the stage of "transitional growth," because the birth rate soon begins to follow the death rate in its decline. The rate of growth then slows down, and demographers begin to detect in the growing proportion of middle-aged and aged in the population the signs of a third stage, "incipient population decline." Societies in this stage are represented by the top horizontal bar of the S, again indicating, as in the first stage, that total population growth is small – but this time because births and deaths are low.

The S-curve is not a theory of population growth so much as an empirical description of what has happened in the West and in those parts of the world influenced by the West. After the S runs its course, what then? The developments of recent years in the United States and other Western countries do not seem to be susceptible to so simple and elegant a summing up. "Incipient population decline" has not become "population decline" itself, and the birth rate has shown an uncertain tendency to rise again, which most demographers think is temporary.[3]

It would be very surprising if variations in the basic conditions of reproduction, livelihood, and chances for survival, that is, in the supply of and demand for human beings, with all these imply for change in the spacing of people, the size of markets, the role of children, the society's feeling of vitality or senescence, and many other intangibles, failed to influence character.

My thesis is, in fact, that each of these three different phases on the population curve appears to be occupied by a society that enforces conformity and molds social character in a definably different way.

The society of high growth potential develops in its typical members a social character whose conformity is insured by their tendency to follow tradition: these I shall term *tradition-directed* people and the society in which they live *a society dependent on tradition-direction.*

The society of transitional population growth develops in its typical members a social character whose conformity is insured by their tendency to acquire early in life an internalized set of goals. These I shall term *inner-directed* people and the society in which they live *a society dependent on inner-direction.*

Finally, the society of incipient population decline develops in its typical members a social character whose conformity is insured by their tendency to be sensitized to the expectations and preferences of others. These I shall term *other-directed* people and the society in which they live one *dependent on other-direction.*

Let me point out, however, before embarking on a description of these three "ideal types" of character and society, that I am not concerned here with making the detailed analysis that would be necessary before one could prove that a link exists between population phase and character type. Rather, the theory of the curve of population provides me with a kind of shorthand for referring to the myriad institutional elements that are also – though usually more heatedly – symbolized by such words as "industrialism," "folk society," "monopoly capitalism," "urbanization," "rationalization," and so on. Hence when I speak here of transitional growth or incipient decline of population in conjunction with shifts in character and conformity, these phrases should not be taken as magical and comprehensive explanations.

My reference is as much to the complex of technological and institutional factors related – as cause or effect – to the development of population as to the demographic facts themselves. It would be almost as satisfactory, for my purposes, to divide societies according to the stage of economic development they have reached. Thus, Colin Clark's distinction between the "primary," "secondary," and "tertiary" spheres of the economy (the first refers to agriculture, hunting and fishing, and mining; the second to manufacturing; the third to trade, communications, and services) corresponds very closely to the division of societies on the basis of demographic characteristics. In those societies which are in the phase of "high growth potential," the "primary" sphere is dominant (for example, India); in those that are in the phase of "transitional" growth, the "secondary" sphere is dominant (for example, Russia); in those that are in the phase of "incipient decline," the "tertiary" sphere is dominant (for example, the United States). And of course, no nation is all of a piece, either in its population characteristics or its economy – different groups and different regions reflect different stages of development, and social character reflects these differences.

High Growth Potential: Tradition-Directed Types

The phase of high growth potential characterizes more than half the world's population: India, Egypt, and China (which have already grown immensely in recent generations), most preliterate peoples in Central Africa, parts of Central and South America, in fact most areas of the world relatively untouched by industrialization. Here death rates are so high that if birth rates were not also high the populations would die out.

Regions where the population is in this stage may be either sparsely populated, as are the areas occupied by many primitive tribes and parts of Central and South America; or they may be densely populated, as are India, China, and Egypt. In either case, the society achieves a Malthusian bargain with the limited food supply by killing off, in one way or another, some of the potential surplus of births over deaths – the enormous trap which, in Malthus' view, nature sets for man and which can be peaceably escaped only by prudent cultivation of the soil and prudent uncultivation of the species through the delay of marriage. Without the prevention of childbirth by means of postponement of marriage or other contraceptive measures, the population must be limited by taking the life of living beings. And so societies have "invented" cannibalism, induced abortion, organized wars, made human sacrifice, and practiced infanticide (especially female) as means of avoiding periodic famine and epidemics.

Though this settling of accounts with the contradictory impulses of hunger and sex is accompanied often enough by upheaval and distress, these societies in the stage of high growth potential tend to be stable at least in the sense that their social practices, including the "crimes" that keep population down, are institutionalized and patterned. Generation after generation, people are born, are weeded out, and die to make room for others. The net rate of natural increase fluctuates within a broad range, though without showing any long-range tendency, as is true also of societies in the stage of incipient decline. But unlike the latter, the average life expectancy in the former is characteristically low: the population is heavily weighted on the side of the young, and generation replaces generation far more rapidly and less "efficiently" than in the societies of incipient population decline.

In viewing such a society we inevitably associate the relative stability of the man–land ratio, whether high or low, with the tenacity of custom and social structure. However, we must not equate stability of social structure over historical time with psychic stability in the life span of an individual: the latter may subjectively experience much violence and disorganization. In the last analysis, however, he learns to deal with life by adaptation, not by innovation. With certain exceptions conformity is largely given in the "self-evident" social situation. Of course nothing in human life is ever really self-evident; where it so appears it is because perceptions have been narrowed by cultural conditioning. As the precarious relation to the food supply is built into the going culture, it helps create a pattern of conventional conformity which is reflected in many, if not in all, societies in the stage of high growth potential. This is what I call tradition-direction.

A definition of tradition-direction. Since the type of social order we have been discussing is relatively unchanging, the conformity of the individual tends to reflect his membership in a particular age-grade, clan, or caste; he learns to understand and appreciate patterns which have endured for centuries, and are modified but slightly as the generations succeed each other. The important relationships of life may be controlled by careful and rigid etiquette, learned by the young during the years of intensive socialization that end with initiation into full adult membership. Moreover, the culture, in addition to its economic tasks, or as part of them, provides ritual, routine, and religion to occupy and to orient everyone. Little energy is directed toward finding new solutions of the age-old problems, let us say, of agricultural technique or medicine, the problems to which people are acculturated.

It is not to be thought, however, that in these societies, where the activity of the individual member is determined by characterologically grounded obedience to traditions, the individual may not be highly prized and, in many instances, encouraged to develop his capabilities, his initiative, and even, within very narrow time limits, his aspirations. Indeed, the individual in some primitive societies is far more appreciated and respected than in some sectors of modern society. For the individual in a society dependent on tradition-direction has a well-defined functional relationship to other members of the group. If he is not killed off, he "belongs" – he is not "surplus," as the modern unemployed are surplus, nor is he expendable as the unskilled are expendable in modern society. But by very virtue of his "belonging," life goals that are *his* in terms of conscious choice appear to shape his destiny only to a very limited extent, just as only to a limited extent is there any concept of progress for the group.

In societies in which tradition-direction is the dominant mode of insuring conformity, relative stability is preserved in part by the infrequent but highly important process of fitting into institutionalized roles such deviants as there are. In such societies a person who might have become at a later historical stage an innovator or rebel, whose belonging, as such, is marginal and problematic, is drawn instead into roles like those of the shaman or sorcerer. That is, he is drawn into roles that make a socially acceptable contribution, while at the same time they provide the Individual with a more or less approved niche. The medieval monastic orders may have served in a similar way to absorb many characterological "mutations."

In some of these societies certain individuals are encouraged toward a degree of individuality from childhood, especially if they belong to families of high status. But, since the range of choice, even for high-status people, is minimal, the apparent social need for an individuated type of character is also minimal. It is probably accurate to say that character structure in these societies is very largely "adjusted," in the sense that for most people it appears to be in tune with social institutions. Even the few misfits "fit" to a degree; and only very rarely is one driven out of his social world.

This does not mean, of course, that the people are happy; the society to whose traditions they are adjusted may be a miserable one, ridden with anxiety, sadism, and disease. The point is rather that change, while never completely absent in human affairs, is slowed down as the movement of molecules is slowed down at low temperature; and the social character comes as close as it ever does to looking like the matrix of the social forms themselves.

In western history the Middle Ages can be considered a period in which the majority were tradition-directed. But the term tradition-directed refers to a common element, not only among the people of precapitalist Europe but also among such enormously different types of people as Hindus and Hopi Indians Zulus and Chinese, North African Arabs and Balinese. There is comfort in relying on the many writers who have found a similar unity amid diversity, a unity they express in such terms as "folk society" (as against "civilization"), "status society" (as against "contract society"), "*Gemeinschaft*" (as against "*Gesellschaft*"), and so on. Different as the societies envisaged by these terms are, the folk, status, and *Gemeinschaft* societies resemble each other in their relative slowness of change, their dependence on family and kin organization, and – in comparison with later epochs – their tight web of values. And, as is now well recognized by students, the high birth rate of these societies in the stage of high growth potential is not merely the result of a lack of contraceptive knowledge or techniques. A whole way of life – an outlook on chance, on children, on the place of women, on sexuality, on the very meaning of existence – is the basis of distinction between the societies in which human fertility is allowed to take its course and toll and those which prefer to pay other kinds of toll to cut down on fertility by calculation, and, conceivably, as Freud and other observers have suggested, by a decline in sexual energy itself.

Transitional Growth: Inner-Directed Types

Except for the West, we know very little about the cumulation of small changes that can eventuate in a breakup of the tradition directed type of society, leading it to realize its potential for high population growth. As for the West, however, much has been learned about the slow decay of feudalism and the subsequent rise of a type of society in which inner-direction is the dominant mode of insuring conformity.

Critical historians, pushing the Renaissance ever back into the Middle Ages, seem sometimes to deny that any decisive change occurred at all. On the whole, however, it seems that the greatest social and characterological shift of recent centuries did indeed come when men were driven out of the primary ties that bound them to the western medieval version of tradition-directed society. All later shifts, including the shift from inner-direction to other-direction, seem unimportant by comparison, although of course this latter shift is still under way and we cannot tell what it will look like when – if ever – it is complete.

A change in the relatively stable ratio of births to deaths, which characterizes the period of high growth potential, is both the cause and consequence of other profound social changes. In most of the cases known to us a decline takes place in mortality prior to a decline in fertility; hence there is some period in which the population expands rapidly. The drop in death rate occurs as the result of many interacting factors, among them sanitation, improved communications (which permit government to operate over a wider area and also permit easier transport of food to areas of shortage from areas of surplus), the decline, forced or otherwise, of infanticide, cannibalism, and other inbred kinds of violence. Because of improved methods of agriculture the land is able to support more people, and these in turn produce still more people.

Notestein's phrase, "transitional growth," is a mild way of putting it. The "transition" is likely to be violent, disrupting the stabilized paths of existence in societies in which tradition-direction has been the principal mode of insuring conformity. The imbalance of births and deaths puts pressure on the society's customary ways. A new slate of character structures is called for or finds its opportunity in coping with the rapid changes – and the need for still more changes – in the social organization.

A definition of inner-direction. In western history the society that emerged with the Renaissance and Reformation and that is only now vanishing serves to illustrate the type of society in which inner-direction is the principal mode of securing conformity. Such a society is characterized by increased personal mobility, by a rapid accumulation of capital (teamed with devastating technological shifts), and by an almost constant *expansion*: intensive expansion in the production of goods and people, and extensive expansion in exploration, colonization, and imperialism. The greater choices this society gives – and the greater initiatives it demands in order to cope with its novel problems – are handled by character types who can manage to live socially without strict and self-evident tradition-direction. These are the inner-directed types.

The concept of inner-direction is intended to cover a very wide range of types. Thus, while it is essential for the study of certain problems to differentiate between Protestant and Catholic countries and their character types, between the effects of the Reformation and the effects of the Renaissance, between the puritan ethic of the European north and west and the somewhat more hedonistic ethic of the European east and south, while all these are valid and, for certain purposes, important distinctions, the concentration of this study on the development of modes of conformity permits their neglect. It allows the grouping together of these otherwise distinct developments because they have one thing in common: *the source of direction for the individual is "inner" in the sense that it is implanted early in life by the elders and directed toward generalized but nonetheless inescapably destined goals.*

We can see what this means when we realize that, in societies in which tradition-direction is the dominant mode of insuring conformity, attention is focused on securing strict conformity in generally observable words and actions, that is to say, behavior. While behavior is minutely prescribed, individuality of character need not be highly developed to meet prescriptions that are objectified in ritual and etiquette – though to be sure, a social character *capable* of such behavioral attention and obedience is requisite. By contrast, societies in which inner-direction becomes important, though they also are concerned with behavioral conformity, cannot he satisfied with behavioral conformity alone. Too many novel situations are presented, situations which a code cannot encompass in advance. Consequently the problem of personal choice, solved in the earlier period of high growth potential by channeling choice through rigid social organization, in the period of transitional growth is solved by channeling choice through a rigid though highly individualized character.

This rigidity is a complex matter. While any society dependent on inner-direction scenes to present people with a wide choice of aims – such as money, possessions, power, knowledge, fame, goodness – these aims are ideologically interrelated, and the selection made by any one individual remains relatively unalterable throughout his life. Moreover, the means to those ends, though not fitted into as tight a frame of social reference as in the society dependent on tradition-direction, are nevertheless limited by the new voluntary associations – for instance, the Quakers, the Masons, the Mechanics' Associations – to which people tie themselves. Indeed, the term "tradition-direction" could be misleading if the reader were to conclude that the force of tradition has no weight for the inner-directed character. On the contrary, he is very considerably bound by traditions: they limit his ends and inhibit his choice of means. The point is rather that a splintering of tradition takes place, connected in part with the increasing division of labor and stratification of society. Even if the individual's choice of tradition is largely determined for him by his family, as it is in most cases, he cannot help becoming aware of the existence of competing traditions – hence of tradition as such. As a result he possesses a somewhat greater degree of flexibility in adapting himself to ever changing requirements and in return requires more from his environment.

As the control of the primary group is loosened – the group that both socializes the young and controls the adult in the earlier era – a new psychological mechanism appropriate to the more open society is "invented": it is what I like to describe as a psychological gyroscope.[4] This instrument, once it is set by the parents and other authorities, keeps the inner-directed person, as we shall see, "on course" even when tradition, as responded to by his character, no longer dictates his moves. The inner-directed person becomes capable of maintaining a delicate balance between the demands upon him of his life goal and the buffetings of his external environment.

This metaphor of the gyroscope, like any other, must not be taken literally. It would be a mistake to see the inner-directed man as incapable of learning from experience or as insensitive to public opinion in matters of external conformity. He can receive and utilize certain signals from outside, provided that they can be reconciled with the limited maneuverability that his gyroscope permits him. His pilot is not quite automatic.

Huizinga's *The Waning of the Middle Ages* gives a picture of the anguish and turmoil, the conflict of values, out of which the new forms slowly emerged. Already by the late Middle Ages people were forced to live under new conditions of awareness. As their self-consciousness and their individuality developed, they had to make themselves at home in the world in novel ways. They still have to.

Incipient Decline of Population: Other-Directed Types

The problem facing the societies in the stage of transitional growth is that of reaching a point at which resources become plentiful enough or are utilized effectively enough to permit a rapid accumulation of capital. This rapid accumulation has to be achieved even while the social product is being drawn on at an accelerated rate to maintain the rising population and satisfy the consumer demands that go with the way of life that has already been adopted. For most countries, unless capital and techniques can be imported from other countries in still later phases of the population curve, every effort to increase national resources at a rapid rate must actually be at the expense of current standards of living. We have seen this occur in the U.S.S.R., now in the stage of transitional growth. For western Europe this transition was long-drawn-out and painful. For America, Canada, and Australia – at once beneficiaries of European techniques and native resources – the transition was rapid and relatively easy.

The tradition-directed person, as has been said, hardly thinks of himself as an individual. Still less does it occur to him that he might shape his own destiny in terms of personal, lifelong goals or that the destiny of his children might be separate from that of the family group. He is not sufficiently separated psychologically from himself (or, therefore, sufficiently close to himself), his family, or group to think in these terms. In the phase of transitional growth, however, people of inner-directed character do gain a feeling of control over their own lives and see their children also as individuals with careers to make. At the same time, with the shift out of agriculture and, later, with the end of child labor, children no longer become an unequivocal economic asset. And with the growth of habits of scientific thought, religious and magical views of human fertility – views that in an earlier phase of the population curve made sense for the culture if it was to reproduce itself – give way to "rational." individualistic attitudes. Indeed, just as the rapid accumulation of productive capital requires that people be imbued with the "Protestant ethic" (as Max Weber characterized one manifestation of what is here termed inner-direction), so also the decreased number of progeny requires a profound change in values – a change so deep that, in all probability, it has to be rooted in character structure.

As the birth rate begins to follow the death rate downward, societies move toward the epoch of incipient decline of population. Fewer and fewer people work on the land or in the extractive industries or even in manufacturing. Hours are short. People may have material abundance and leisure besides. They pay for these changes however – here, as always, the solution of old problems gives rise to new ones – by finding themselves in a centralized and bureaucratized society and a world shrunken and agitated by the contact – accelerated by industrialization – of races, nations, and cultures.

The hard enduringness and enterprise of the inner-directed types are somewhat less necessary under these new conditions. Increasingly, *other people* are the problem, not the material environment. And as people mix more widely and become more sensitive to each other, the surviving traditions from the stage of high growth potential – much disrupted, in any case, during the violent spurt of industrialization – become still further attenuated. Gyroscopic control is no longer sufficiently flexible, and a new psychological mechanism is called for.

Furthermore, the "scarcity psychology" of many inner-directed people, which was socially adaptive during the period of heavy capital accumulation that accompanied transitional growth of population, needs to give way to an "abundance psychology" capable of "wasteful" luxury consumption of leisure and of the surplus product. Unless people want to destroy the surplus product in war, which still does require heavy capital equipment, they must learn to enjoy and engage in those services that are expensive in terms of man power but not of capital – poetry and philosophy, for instance.[5] Indeed, in the period of incipient decline, nonproductive consumers, both the increasing number of old people and the diminishing number of as yet untrained young, form a high proportion of the population, and these need both the economic opportunity to be prodigal and the character structure that allows it.

Has this need for still another slate of character types actually been acknowledged to any degree? My observations lead me to believe that in America it has.

A definition of other-direction. The type of character I shall describe as other-directed seems to be emerging in very recent years in the upper middle class of our larger cities: more prominently in New York than in Boston, in Los Angeles than in Spokane, in Cincinnati than in Chillicothe. Yet in some respects this type is strikingly similar to the American, whom Tocqueville and other curious and astonished visitors from Europe, even before the Revolution, thought to be a new kind of man. Indeed, travelers' reports on America impress us with their unanimity. The American is said to be shallower, freer with his money, friendlier, more uncertain of himself and his values, more demanding of approval than the European. It all adds up to a pattern which, without stretching matters too far, resembles the kind of character that a number of social scientists have seen as developing in contemporary, highly industrialized, and bureaucratic America: Fromm's "marketer," Mills's "fixer," Arnold Green's "middle class male child."[6]

It is my impression that the middle-class American of today is decisively different from those Americans of Tocqueville's writings who nevertheless strike us as so contemporary. It is also my impression that the conditions I believe to be responsible for other-direction are affecting increasing numbers of people in the metropolitan centers of the advanced industrial countries. My analysis of the other-directed character is thus at once an analysis of the American and of contemporary man. Much of the time I find it hard or impossible to say where one ends and the other begins. Tentatively, I am inclined to think that the other-directed type does find itself most at home in America, due to certain unique elements in American society, such as its recruitment from Europe and its lack of any feudal past. As against this, I am also inclined to put more weight on capitalism, industrialism, and urbanization – these being international tendencies – than on any character-forming peculiarities of the American scene.

Bearing these qualifications in mind, it seems appropriate to treat contemporary metropolitan America as our illustration of a society – so far, perhaps, the only illustration – in which other-direction is the dominant mode of insuring conformity. It would be premature, however, to say that it is already the dominant mode in America as a whole. But since the other-directed types are to be found among the young, in the larger cities, and among the upper income groups, we may assume that, unless present trends are reversed, the hegemony of other-direction lies not far off.

If we wanted to cast our social character types into social class molds, we could say that inner-direction is the typical character of the "old" middle class – the banker, the tradesman, the small entrepreneur, the technically oriented engineer, etc. – while other-direction is becoming the typical character of the "new" middle class – the bureaucrat, the salaried employee in business, etc. Many of the economic factors associated with the recent growth of the "new" middle class are well known. They have been discussed by James Burnham, Colin Clark, Peter Drucker, and others. There is a decline in the numbers and in the proportion of the working population engaged in production and extraction – agriculture, heavy industry, heavy transport – and an increase in the numbers and the proportion engaged in white-collar work and the service trades. People who are literate, educated, and provided with the necessities of life by an ever more efficient machine industry and agriculture, turn increasingly to the "tertiary" economic realm. The service industries prosper among the people as a whole and no longer only in court circles.

Education, leisure, services, these go together with an increased consumption of words and images from the new mass media of communications.

While societies in the phase of transitional growth step up the process of distributing words from urban centers, the flow becomes a torrent in the societies of incipient population decline. This process, while modulated by profound national and class differences, connected with differences in literacy and loquacity, takes place everywhere in the industrialized lands. Increasingly, relations with the outer world and with oneself are mediated by the flow of mass communication. For the other-directed types political events are likewise experienced through a screen of words by which the events are habitually atomized and personalized – or pseudo-personalized. For the inner-directed person who remains still extant in this period the tendency is rather to systematize and moralize this flow of words.

These developments lead, for large numbers of people, to changes in paths to success and to the requirement of more "socialized" behavior both for success and for marital and personal adaptation. Connected with such changes are changes in the family and in child-rearing practices. In the smaller families of urban life, and with the spread of "permissive" child care to ever wider strata of the population, there is a relaxation of older patterns of discipline. Under these newer patterns the peer-group (the group of one's associates of the same age and class) becomes much more important to the child, while the parents make him feel guilty not so much about violation of inner standards as about failure to be popular or otherwise to manage his relations with these other children. Moreover, the pressures of the school and the peer-group are reinforced and continued – in a manner whose inner paradoxes I shall discuss later – by the mass media: movies, radio, comics, and popular culture media generally. Under these conditions types of character emerge that we shall here term other-directed. *What is common to all the other-directed people is that their contemporaries are the source of direction for the individual either those known to him or those with whom he is indirectly acquainted, through friends and through the mass media. This source is of course "internalized" in the sense that dependence on it for guidance in life is implanted early. The goals toward which the other-directed person strives shift with that guidance: it is only the process of striving itself and the process of paying close attention to the signals from others that remain unaltered throughout life.* This mode of keeping in touch with others permits a close behavioral conformity, not through drill in behavior itself, as in the tradition-directed character, but rather through an exceptional sensitivity to the actions and wishes of others.

Of course, it matters very much who these "others" are: whether they are the individual's immediate circle or a "higher" circle or the anonymous voices of the mass media; whether the individual fears the hostility of chance acquaintances or only of those who "count." But his need for approval and direction from others – and contemporary others rather than ancestors – goes beyond the reasons that lead most people in any era to care very much what others think of them. While all people want and need to be liked by some of the people some of the time, it is only the modern other-directed types who make this their chief source of direction and chief area of sensitivity.[7]

It is perhaps the insatiable force of this psychological need for approval that differentiates people of the metropolitan, American upper middle class, whom we regard as other-directed, from very similar types that have appeared in capital cities and among other classes in previous historical periods, whether in Imperial Canton, in eighteenth- and nineteenth-century Europe, or in ancient Athens, Alexandria, or Rome. In all these groups fashion not only ruled as a substitute for morals and customs, but it was a rapidly changing fashion that held sway. It could do so because, although the mass media were in their infancy, the group corresponding to the American upper middle class was comparably small and the elite structure was extremely reverberant. It can be argued, for example, that a copy of *The Spectator* covered its potential readership more thoroughly in the late eighteenth century than *The New Yorker* covers its readership today. In eighteenth- and nineteenth-century English, French, and Russian novels, we find portraits of the sort of people who operated in the upper reaches of bureaucracy and had to be prepared for rapid changes of signals. Stepan Arkadyevitch Oblonsky in *Anna Karenina* is one of the more likable and less opportunistic examples, especially striking because of the way Tolstoy contrasts him with Levin, a moralizing, inner-directed person. At any dinner party Stepan manifests exceptional social skills; his political skills as described in the following quotation are also highly social:

> Stepan Arkadyevitch took in and read a liberal newspaper, not an extreme one, but one advocating the views held by the majority. And in spite of the fact that science, art, and politics had no special interest for him, he firmly held those views on all subjects which were held by the majority and by his paper, and he only changed them when the majority changed them – or, more strictly speaking, he did not change them, but they imperceptively changed of themselves within him.
>
> Stepan Arkadyevitch had not chosen his political opinions or his views; these political opinions and views had come to him of themselves, just as he did not choose the shapes of his hats or coats, but simply took those that were being worn. And for him, living in a certain society – owing to the need, ordinarily developed at years of discretion, for some degree of mental activity – to have views was just as indispensable as to have a hat. If there was a reason for his preferring liberal to conservative views, which were held also by many of his circle, it arose not from his considering liberalism more rational, but from its being in closer accord with his manner of life ... And so liberalism had become a habit of Stepan Arkadyevitch's, and he liked his newspaper, as he did his cigar after dinner, for the slight fog it diffused in his brain.

Stepan, while his good-natured gregariousness makes him seem like a modern middle-class American, is not fully other-directed. This gregariousness alone, without a certain sensitivity to others as individuals and as a source of direction, is not the identifying trait. Just so, we must differentiate the nineteenth-century American – gregarious and subservient to public opinion though he was found to be by Tocqueville, Bryce, and others – from the other-directed American as he emerges today, an American who in his character is more capable of and more interested in maintaining responsive contact with others both at work and at play. This point needs to be emphasized, since the distinction is easily misunderstood. The inner-directed person, though he often sought and sometimes achieved a relative independence of public opinion and of what the neighbors thought of him, was in most cases very much concerned with his good repute and, at least in America, with "keeping up with the Joneses." These conformities, however, were primarily external, typified in such details as clothes, curtains, and bank credit. For, indeed, the conformities were to a standard, evidence of which was provided by the "best people" in one's milieu. In contrast with this pattern, the other-directed person, though he has his eye very much on the Joneses, aims to keep up with them not so much in external details as in the quality of his inner experience. That is, his great sensitivity keeps him in touch with others on many more levels than the externals of appearance and propriety. Nor does any ideal of independence or of reliance on God alone modify his desire to look to the others – and the "good guys" as well as the best people – for guidance in what experiences to seek and in how to interpret them.

The three types compared. One way to see the structural differences that mark the three types is to see the differences in the emotional sanction or control in each type.

The tradition-directed person feels the impact of his culture as a unit, but it is nevertheless mediated through the specific, small number of individuals with whom he is in daily contact. These expect of him not so much that he be a certain type of person but that he behave in the approved way. Consequently the sanction for behavior tends to be the fear of being *shamed*.

The inner-directed person has early incorporated a psychic gyroscope which is set going by his parents and can receive signals later on from other authorities who resemble his parents. He goes through life less independent than he seems, obeying this internal piloting. Getting off course, whether in response to inner impulses or to the fluctuating voices of contemporaries, may lead to the feeling of *guilt*.

Since the direction to be taken in life has been learned in the privacy of the home from a small number of guides and since principles, rather than details of behavior, are internalized, the inner-directed person is capable of great stability. Especially so when it turns out that his fellows have gyroscopes too, spinning at the same speed and set in the same direction. But many inner-directed individuals can remain stable even when the reinforcement of social approval is not available – as in the upright life of the stock Englishman isolated in the tropics.

Contrasted with such a type as this, the other-directed person learns to respond to signals from a far wider circle than is constituted by his parents. The family is no longer a closely knit unit to which he belongs but merely part of a wider social environment to which he early becomes attentive. In these respects the other-directed person resembles the tradition-directed person: both live in a group milieu and lack the inner-directed person's capacity to go it alone. The nature of this group milieu, however, differs radically in the two cases. The other-directed person is cosmopolitan. For him the border between the familiar and the strange – a border clearly marked in the societies depending on tradition-direction – has broken down. As the family continuously absorbs the strange and reshapes itself, so the strange becomes familiar. While the inner-directed person could be "at home abroad" by virtue of his relative insensitivity to others, the other-directed person is, in a sense, at home everywhere and nowhere, capable of a rapid if sometimes superficial intimacy with and response to everyone. The tradition-directed person takes his signals from others, but they come in a cultural monotone; he needs no complex receiving equipment to pick them up. The other-directed person must be able to receive signals from far and near; the sources are many, the changes rapid. What can be internalized, then, is not a code of behavior but the elaborate equipment needed to attend to such messages and occasionally to participate in their circulation. As against guilt-and-shame controls, though of course these survive, one prime psychological lever of the other-directed person is a diffuse *anxiety*. This control equipment, instead of being like a gyroscope, is like a radar.[8]

The Case of Athens. Could other civilizations, such as the ancient Hebrew, Greek, and Roman, also be characterized at successive stages in their population-subsistence development as tradition-directed, inner-directed, and other-directed? In all likelihood the tremendous growth of world population since about 1650 – and consequently the S-curve of population growth – is unique in the history of mankind and the consequence of an altogether new (industrialized) type of technological, economic, and social organization. Nonetheless, the fact that every society has some form of organization and some "technology," be it the most unscientific ritual, constitutes proof of an effort, more or less successful, to bring down the death rate and improve the standard of living over that of mere animal existence. And an exploratory study of the Athenian empire suggests that there, too, a correlation between population growth and social character of the type we have described for the recent West may be discerned.[9]

What scant evidence we have of the long-term trend of population growth in the empire must be derived from the patient studies of present-day demographers and from the remarks of ancient Greek authors. The Homeric epics depict a volatile society in which the institution of private property had already disrupted the tradition-directed communal organization of tribe, phratry, and clan. Revolutionary improvements in cultivation of the soil, made possible by continued settlement in one place, increased the standard of living and, as a corollary, initiated a phase of population growth that was to continue for several centuries. Private ownership, the development of an exchange economy, and the patrilineal inheritance of property encouraged the concentration of wealth and produced economic and social inequality. A new, three-fold social stratification interpenetrated the traditional organization and not only loosened the hold of the clan upon its members but also encouraged the coalescence of individuals with like economic status from different tribes and phratries. The reform measures taken by Solon and others in succeeding generations also clearly imply that some individuals and families were far more successful than others in achieving the new economic goals of leisure and material wealth.

During the five hundred years after the founding of the Athenian state there seems to have existed an expanding "frontier" economy, based in part upon the exploitation of internal resources, made possible by technological improvement and the institution of slavery, and in greater part upon the conquest of other peoples and the incorporation of their wealth into the domestic economy. One might well adduce as indications of inner-direction during this period the changing attitudes toward the family and the upbringing of children; the laws which enhanced the freedom of the individual, for example, the significant reforms which permitted the free alienation of property and the initiation of a criminal prosecution by a "third party"; the multiplication of opportunities for profitable employment in commerce, agriculture, and industry; the drift from country to city; the enthusiasm for exploration and conquest; and the increasing interest in philosophic speculation and science.

By the turn of the fifth century the Athenian empire had reached the zenith of its power; and the Greeks of this period were familiar with the idea of an expanding population. Both Plato and Aristotle advocated a stationary population. Two centuries later we find that the problem has radically shifted and the fear of overpopulation has been replaced by the fear of depopulation. Polybius, writing in the second century, declared that the population of Greece was dying out because of the practice of infanticide. This is undoubtedly an overstatement; infanticide was confined, as contraception tends to be today, largely to the upper and upper middle classes. Nevertheless, it indicates the trend toward artificial limitation of the size of the family and suggests that the population had reached the period not only of incipient but of actual decline. It is as an expanding population begins to reach its peak that we see the rise of social forms that seem to indicate the presence of the other-directed mode of conformity.

For example, the institution of ostracism, introduced as a means of preventing tyranny, became in the fifth century a formidable weapon of public opinion, wielded capriciously as a means of insuring conformity of taste and "cutting down to size" those statesmen, playwrights, and orators of markedly superior ability. In addition, the common people produced a numerous brood of informers "who were constantly accusing the better and most influential men in the State, with a view to subjecting them to the envy of the multitude."

In *The Jealousy of the Gods and Criminal Law in Athens* Svend Ranulf has meticulously traced the incidence and development of the "disinterested tendency to inflict punishment" which, based upon a diffuse characterological anxiety, could perhaps be described as the ascendancy of an omnipotent "peer-group."

All this was accompanied by a decline in inner-directed dutifulness toward the political sphere. In spite of the deference shown by many authors to Athenian "democracy" of the fifth century, one is struck by the apathy of the voting population. What had earlier been a hard-won privilege of the lower classes – attendance at the ecclesia or popular assembly – became during the rule of the demos an obligation. Various punitive measures were introduced to insure a quorum; and when these failed, the "right to vote" became a paid service to the state.

Here in the history of the Athenian empire we have an area in which more detailed research and analysis might very profitably be undertaken; obviously, no more has been done in these remarks than to suggest certain problems that would be relevant for such research. Similarly, the problems of Rome during the reign of Augustus suggest the emergence and ascendancy of the other-directed character type as the population reached the phase of incipient decline. The importation of a new poetic language legitimating the importance of subtle states of personal feeling, in the Alexandrian-influenced work of such poets as Catullus, and probably Gallus, may evidence shifts toward other-direction in the dominant classes.

Some necessary qualifications. The limitations of language lead me to speak as if I saw societies as always managing to produce the social organization and character types they need in order to survive. Such an assumption, raising the image of a separate body "society," making certain demands on people and testing out various processes, would introduce an unwarranted teleology into social change. What seems to happen is that by sheer "accident" any of a number of ways of insuring characterological conformity may exist in a given society. Those which have been successful in preserving a coherent society are transmitted as unconsciously as they arose; but, since by their historical success they present themselves for study and investigation, it appears as if some teleological force, serving the interest of society, has introduced the successful – or fairly successful – mode of insuring conformity. Yet we must recognize that societies do disintegrate and die out despite what may appear to be successful methods of insuring the perpetuation of the social character. Correspondingly, it would seem that societies can continue to endure enormous strains and fissures, and grave incompatibilities between the social character and the societal requirements, without succumbing to total ruin and disorganization.

Nor must we overestimate the role of character in the social process. It is not a sufficient explanation, for instance, to say, as some students have said, that the German army held together because "the Germans" had an authoritarian character, since armies of very diverse character type do in fact hold together under given conditions of battle and supply. Nor will it do to assume, as American aptitude-testers sometimes do, that certain jobs can be successfully handled only by a narrowly limited range of character types: that we need "extrovert" or "oral" salesmen and administrators, and "introvert" or "anal" chemists and accountants. Actually, people of radically different types can adapt themselves to perform, adequately enough, a wide variety of complex tasks. Or, to put the same thing in another way, social institutions can harness a gamut of different motivations, springing from different character types, to perform very much the same kinds of socially demanded jobs. And yet, of course, this is not to say that character is merely a shadowy factor in history, like some Hegelian spirit. Character will affect the style and psychic costs of job performances that, in economic or political analysis, look almost identical.

Thus we are forced to take account of the possibility that people may be compelled to behave in one way although their character structure presses them to behave in the opposite way. Society may change more rapidly than character, or vice versa. Indeed, this disparity between socially required behavior and characterologically compatible behavior is one of the great levers of change. Fortunately we know of no society like the one glumly envisaged by Aldous Huxley in *Brave New World*, where the social character types have been completely content in their social roles and where consequently, barring accident, no social change exists.

Finally, it is necessary to point out that social character types are abstractions. To be sure, they refer back to the living, concrete human being, but in order to arrive at them, as we saw at the beginning of this chapter, it is necessary first to abstract from the real individual his "personality," then to abstract from that his "character," finally to abstract from that the common element that forms "social character."

In fact, the discerning reader may already have realized that in the nature of the case there can be no such thing as a society or a person wholly dependent on tradition-direction, inner-direction, or other-direction: each of these modes of conformity is universal, and the question is always one of the degree to which an individual or a social group places reliance on one or another of the three available mechanisms. Thus, all human beings are inner-directed in the sense that, brought up as they are by people older than themselves, they have acquired and internalized some permanent orientations from them. And, conversely, all human beings are other-directed in the sense that they are oriented to the expectations of their peers and to the "field situation" (Kurt Lewin) or "definition of the situation" (W. I. Thomas) that these peers at any moment help to create.[10]

Since, furthermore, each of us possesses the capacity for each of the three modes of conformity, it is possible that an individual may change, in the course of his life, from greater dependence on one combination of modes to greater dependence on another (though radical shifts of this kind, even when circumstances encourage them, are unlikely). For, unless individuals are completely crazy – and, indeed, they are never *completely* crazy – they both organize the cues in their social environment and attend to those cues. Thus, if a predominantly other-directed individual were placed in an environment without peers, he might fall back on other patterns of direction. Similarly, it is clear that no individual, and assuredly no society, ever exists without a heavy reliance on tradition, much as this may appear to be overlaid by swings of fashion.

It is important to emphasize these overlappings of the several types in part because of the value judgments that readers are likely to attach to each type in isolation. Since most of us value independence we are likely to prefer the inner-directed type and overlook two things. First, the gyroscopic mechanism allows the inner-directed person to appear far more independent than he really is: he is no less a conformist to others than the other-directed person, but the voices to which he listens are more distant, of an older generation, their cues internalized in his childhood. Second, as just indicated, this type of conformity is only one, though the predominant, mechanism of the inner-directed type: the latter is not characteristically insensitive to what his peers think of him, and may even be opportunistic in the highest degree. Thus, he need not always react to other people as if they were merely stand-ins for his parents. Rather, the point is that he is somewhat less concerned than the other-directed person with continuously obtaining from contemporaries (or their stand-ins: the mass media) a flow of guidance, expectation, and approbation.

Let me repeat: the types of character and society dealt with here are *types*: they do not exist in reality, but are a construction, based on a selection of certain historical problems for investigation. By employing more types, or subtypes, one could take account of more facts (or mayhap, the same facts with less violence!), but my collaborators and I have preferred to work with a minimum of scaffolding; throughout, in seeking to describe by one interrelated set of characteristics both a society and its typical individuals, we have looked for features that connect the two and ignored those aspects of behavior – often striking – which did not seem relevant to our task.

II. The Characterological Struggle

We can picture the last few hundred years of western history in terms of a gradual succession to dominance of each of the later two types. The tradition-directed type gives way to the inner-directed, and the inner-directed gives way to the other-directed. Shifts in type of society and type of character do not, of course, occur all at once. Just as within a given culture one may find groups representing all phases of the population curve, so, too, we may find a variety of characterological adaptations to each particular phase. This mixture is made even more various by the migration of peoples, by imperialism, and by other historical developments that constantly throw together people of different character structures, people who "date," metaphorically, from different points on the population curve.

These character types, like geological or archaeological strata, pile one on top of the other, with outcroppings of submerged types here and there. A cross section of society at any given time reveals the earlier as well as the later character types, the earlier changed through the pressure of being submerged by the later. Tradition-direction seems to be dominant in Latin America, agricultural southern Europe, in Asia and Africa. Inner-directed types seem to be dominant in rural and small-town United States and Canada, in north-western Europe, and to a degree in Central Europe. One notices an energetic campaign to introduce the inner-directed pattern in eastern Europe, in Turkey, and in parts of Asia. And one notices the beginnings of dominance by other-directed types in the metropolitan centers of the United States and, more doubtfully, their emergence in the big cities of north-western Europe. This last and newest type is spreading outward into areas where inner-direction still prevails, just as the latter is spreading into unconquered areas where tradition-directed types still hang on.

Such a view may help us to understand American character structures. In America it is still possible to find southern rural groups, Negro and poor white, in the phase of high growth potential – and it is here that we look for the remnants of tradition-directed types. Similarly, immigrants to America who came from rural and small-town areas in Europe carried their fertility rates and character patterns with them to our major cities as well as to the countryside. In some cases these people were and are forced to make, in one lifetime, the jump from a society in which tradition-direction was the dominant mode of insuring conformity to one in which other-direction is the dominant mode. More frequently the jump is made in two generations: the peasant is converted to inner-directed ways; his children then make the jump to other-direction.

The mixing of people of different character types, as of different races and religions, as a result of industrialization and colonization, is to be found everywhere in the world. Character types that would have been well adapted to their situation find themselves under pressure from newer, better-adapted types. They may resign themselves to a subordinate position. Or they may be tempted by the new goals which enter their view and may even seek these goals without reference to the culturally prescribed means of attaining them.

Inner-directed types, for instance, in the urban American environment may be forced into resentment or rebellion. They may be unable to adapt because they lack the proper receiving equipment for the radar signals that increasingly direct attitude and behavior in the phase of incipient population decline. They may refuse to adapt because of moral disapproval of what the signals convey. Or they may be discouraged by the fact that the signals, though inviting enough, do not seem meant for them. This is true, for instance, of minority groups whose facial type or coloring is not approved of for managerial or professional positions, or in the hierarchy of values portrayed in the mass media of communication. The same thing holds for those whose ancestry is adequate but whose personality in subtle ways lacks the pliability and sensitivity to others that is required.

Studies of American Indians provide analogies for some of the things that may happen when an older character type is under pressure from a newer one. Among Sioux reservation children, as described by Erik H. Erikson, there seem to be two reactions to white culture: one is resentful resistance, the other is what might be termed compliant resistance. The behavior of the former seems, to the white educator, incorrigible; of the latter, almost too ingratiating, too angelic. In both cases, because he has at least the tacit approval of his parents and other Sioux adults, the child preserves something of the Sioux character and tradition whether or not he yields overtly to the whites. The conflict, however, drains the child of emotional energy; often he appears to be lazy. Both the resistant and the seemingly compliant are apathetic toward the white culture and white politics.

I think that there are millions of inner-directed Americans who reject in similar fashion the values that emanate from the growing dominance of other-directed types. Their resentment may be conscious and vocal. As with the Sioux, this resentment is culturally supported both by the old-timers and by the long memory of the past which is present to all in rural and small-town areas. This past is carried in the tales of the old men and the editorials of the rural press, not yet blotted out by urban sights and sounds. Hence, the resentment can express itself and win local victories over the representatives of other-directed types. Nevertheless, the "moralizers," as we will later term them, do not feel secure – the weight of the urban world outside is against them – and their resentment hardens until these residual inner-directed persons are scarcely more than caricatures of their characterological ancestors in the days of their dominance.

A second locus of resistance and resentment is to be found among the vanishing tradition-directed migrants to America – migrants both from America's colonies: Puerto Rico, the deep South, and previously the Philippines, and from Mexico, Italy, and the Orient. Here it is more difficult to find cultural support for one's resistance to the enforced change of signals called "Americanization." The southern poor white or the poor Negro who moves North does not have to learn a new language, but he is usually about as deracinated as are the migrants from abroad. The costume and manners of the zoot-suiter were a pathetic example of the effort to combine smooth urban ways with a resentful refusal to be completely overwhelmed by the inner-directed norms that are still the official culture of the city public schools.

A similar style of resentment is to be found among miners, lumberjacks, ranch hands, and some urban factory workers. As in many other societies, the active dislike of these workers for the dominant culture is coupled with a feeling of manly contempt for smooth or soft city ways. These men have their own cocky legends as the Sioux have stories of the cowboy as well as of their own belligerent past. We must ask to what extent all these groups may be dying out, like their Sioux counterparts, as other-direction spreads down the class ladder and beyond the metropolitan areas. In the absence of a home base, a reservation, these people have their choice, if indeed there be a choice, between homelessness and rapid acculturation to other-directed values.

The "characterological struggle" does not go on only within a single country and among the groups within that country who stand at different points on the curve of character and population. Whole countries in the phase of incipient decline also feel threatened by the pressure of population and expansion from other countries that are in the phase of transitional growth, and even more by the huge oriental countries still in the phase of high growth potential. These international tensions, acting in a vicious circle, help to preserve, in countries of incipient decline, the inner-directed character types and their scarcity psychology, appropriate in the earlier era of transitional growth. Thus the slate of character types befitting a society of abundance – a society of which men have dreamed for centuries – is held in historical abeyance, and the gap between character structure and the potentialities of the economic structure remains.

It is possible to take various attitudes toward this gap. One would be that, because another world war – this time between the two highly polarized world powers – is possible or even probable, it makes little sense to talk about the age of abundance, its character types, and its anticipated problems. Or, the same conclusion might be reached by a different route, arguing that in effect it is immoral, if not politically impractical, to discuss abundance *in America* when famine and misery remain the lot of most of the world's agriculturists and many of its city dwellers. These are real issues. But I would like to point out as to the first – the imminence and immanence of war – that to a slight degree nations, like neurotics, bring on themselves the dangers by which they are obsessed, the dangers that, in place of true vitality and growth, help structure their lives; though obviously the decision, war or not, does not rest with the United States alone. As to the second issue, it seems to me that to use world misery as an argument against speculation about possible abundance is actually to help prolong the very scarcity psychology that, originating in misery, perpetuates it. Pushed to its absurd extreme, the argument would prevent leadership in human affairs except by those who are worst off. On the other hand, those who are best off may fail as models not only out of surfeit but out of despair. Contrary to the situation prevailing in the nineteenth century, pessimism has become an opiate, and the small chance that the dangers so obviously menacing the world can be avoided is rendered even smaller by our use of these menaces in order to rationalize our resignation and asceticism.

Fundamentally, I think the "unrealistic" Godwin was correct who, in contrast to his great opponent Malthus, thought that we would someday be able to grow food for the world in a flower pot. Technologically, we virtually have the flowerpots.

Notes

1. "Observations on the Yurok: Childhood and World Image," *University of California Publications in American Archaeology and Ethnology*, XXXV (1943), iv.

2. "Individual and Social Origins of Neurosis," *American Sociological Review*, IX (1944), 380; reprinted in *Personality in Nature, Society and Culture*, edited by Clyde Kluckhohn and Henry Murray (New York, Alfred A. Knopf, 1948).

3. The terminology used here is that of Frank W. Notestein. See his "Population – The Long View," in *Food for the World*, edited by Theodore W. Schultz (University of Chicago Press, 1945).

4. Since writing the above I have discovered Gardner Murphy's use of the same metaphor in his volume *Personality* (New York, Harper, 1947).

5. These examples are given by Allan G. B. Fisher, *The Clash of Progress and Security* (London, Macmillan, 1935).

6. See Erich Fromm, *Man for Himself*; C. Wright Mills, "The Competitive Personality," *Partisan Review*, XIII (1946), 433; Arnold Green, "The Middle Class Male Child and Neurosis," *American Sociological Review*, XI (1946), 31. See also the work of Jurgen Ruesch, Martin B. Loeb, and co-workers on the "infantile personality."

7. This picture of the other-directed person has been stimulated by, and developed from, Erich Fromm's discussion of the "marketing orientation" in *Man for Himself*, pp. 67–82. I have also drawn on my portrait of "The Cash Customer," *Common Sense*, XI (1942), 183.

8. The "radar" metaphor was suggested by Karl Wittfogel.

9. The following discussion draws on an unpublished monograph by Sheila Spaulding, "Prolegomena to the Study of Athenian Democracy" (Yale Law School Library, 1949).

10. In this connection, it is revealing to compare the conceptions of the socialization process held by Freud and Harry Stack Sullivan. Freud saw the superego as the internalized source of moral life-directions, built in the image of the awesome parents, and transferred thereafter to parent-surrogates such as God, the Leader, Fate. Sullivan does nor deny this happens but puts more emphasis on the role of the peer-group – the chum and group of chums who take such a decisive hand in the socialization of the American child. Sullivan's very insistence on the importance of interpersonal relations – which led him to believe, much more than Freud, in the adaptability of men and the possibilities of social peace and harmony – may itself be viewed as a symptom of the shift toward other-direction.

56

Contributions to the Theory of Reference Group Behavior

Robert K. Merton and Alice S. Kitt

This paper proceeds on the assumption that there is two-way traffic between social theory and empirical research. Systematic empirical materials help advance social theory by imposing the task and by affording the opportunity for interpretation along lines often unpremeditated, and social theory, in turn, defines the scope and enlarges the predictive value of empirical findings by indicating the conditions under which they hold. The systematic data of *The American Soldier*, in all their numerous variety, provide a useful occasion for examining the interplay of social theory and applied social research.

More particularly, we attempt to identify and to order the fairly numerous researches in *The American Soldier* which, by implication or by explicit statement, bear upon the theory of *reference group behavior*. (The empirical realities which this term denotes will presently be considered in some detail. It should be said here, however, that although the *term* "reference group" is not employed in these volumes, any more than it has yet found full acceptance in the vocabulary of sociology as distinct from social psychology, reference group *concepts* play an important part in the interpretative apparatus utilized by the Research Branch.)

At two points, we deal briefly with related subjects which are not, however, part and parcel of reference group theory. We review the statistical indices of group attributes and social structure as variously adopted in these researches, and attempt to indicate, though very briefly and programmatically, the specific value of *systematically* incorporating such indices in further research. And, in equally brief fashion, we point out how data analyzed by the Research Branch from a psychological standpoint can be supplemented and usefully re-worked from the standpoint of functional sociology.

A common procedure for extracting and attempting to develop the theoretical implications of *The American Soldier* is adopted throughout the paper.

Source: Robert K. Merton and Paul F. Lazarsfeld, (eds.), *Continuities in Social Research*, (Glencoe, Ill.: The Free Press, 1950).

This entails the intensive re-examination of *cases* of research reported in these volumes, with an eye to subsuming the findings under higher-level abstractions or generalizations. In the volumes themselves, the authors austerely (and, in our judgment, wisely) limit their analysis to the interpretation of the behavior of soldiers and to the organizational contexts in which that behavior occurred. But manifestly, the analytical concepts hold not merely for the behavior of soldiers. By provisionally generalizing these concepts, we may be in a position to explore the wider implications of the materials for social theory.

Our discussion thus grows out of an internal analysis of every research study in these volumes in which some reference group concept was used by the authors as an interpretative variable. The object of collating these cases is to determine the points at which they invite extensions of the theory of reference group behavior which can be followed up through further strategically focused research. Occasionally, the effort is made to suggest how these theoretical extensions might be incorporated into designs for empirical research which will thus build upon the findings of the Research Branch. In this way, there may be provision for continuity in the interplay between cumulative theory and new research.

The inductive re-examination of cases admits also the linking of these reference group conceptions with other conceptions prevalent in social psychology and sociology which have not ordinarily been connected with the theory of reference group behavior. In the degree that such connections are established, *The American Soldier* will have served a further function of empirical research: the provisional consolidation of presently scattered fragments of theory.[1]

Along these lines, an effort will be made to indicate the coherence between reference group theory and conceptions of functional sociology. It appears that these deal with different facets of the same subject: the one centers on the processes through which men relate themselves to groups and refer their behavior to the values of these groups; the other centers on the consequences of the processes primarily for social structures, but also for the individuals and groups involved in these structures. It will be found that reference group theory and functional sociology address different questions to the same phenomena but that these questions have reciprocal relevance.

Throughout, then, this essay aims to learn from *The American Soldier* what it has to yield for the current state of reference group theory and related theoretical problems. Committed as we are to the notion that the development of social theory requires a large measure of continuity, rather than a collection of self-contained and allegedly definitive results, this means that the present reworking of some of the materials in *The American Soldier* is itself a highly provisional phase in an ongoing development rather than a stable stopping point. Nor is it assumed, of course, that each and all of the extensions of reference group theory here proposed will in fact turn out to be sound; for like any other form of human activity, theorizing has its quota of risk. Indeed, it is when every hypothesis provisionally advanced at a given stage in the development of a discipline turns out to be apparently confirmed that the theorist has cause for alarm, since a record of unvarying success may indicate a defective and overly-compliant apparatus for confirmation rather than an unexceptionably sound theory.

The Concept Of Relative Deprivation

Of the various concepts employed by the authors of *The American Soldier* to interpret their multiform materials, there is one which takes a major place. This is the concept of relative deprivation. Its central significance is in some measure evidenced by its being one of the two concepts expressly called to the attention of the reader in the chapter introducing the two volumes. As the authors themselves put it, after a brief allusion to the conception of varying profiles, "Other conceptual tools, notably a theory of *relative deprivation*, also are introduced to help in more generally ordering otherwise disparate empirical findings." (I, 52)

Although the concept of relative deprivation is periodically utilized for the interpretation of variations in attitudes among different categories of men, varying, for example, with respect to age, education and marital status, it nowhere finds formal definition in the pages of these volumes. Nevertheless, as we shall presently discover, the outlines of this conception gradually emerge from the various instances in which it is put to use. It is in the very first instance of such use, for example, that the authors refer to the nature of the theoretical utility of the conception and to its possible kinship to other, established concepts of sociological theory:

> "The idea [of relative deprivation] is simple, almost obvious, but its utility comes in reconciling data, especially in later chapters, where its applicability is not at first too apparent. The idea would seem to have a kinship to and, in part, include such well-known sociological concepts as 'social frame of reference,' 'patterns of expectation,' or 'definitions of the situation.'" (I, 125)

This absence of a formal definition of relative deprivation is no great handicap. In any case, the authors escape the well-established tradition of works in sociological theory to be replete with numerous definitions which remain unemployed. In place of an explicit definition of the concept we can assemble an array of all those occasions, scattered through the volumes and dealing with seemingly unrelated types of situations, in which the concept has been put to use by the authors, and in this way we can learn something of the actual operational character of the concept.

The following list represents, albeit in much abbreviated form, every research in which some version of the concept of relative deprivation (or a kindred concept, such as relative status) is explicitly drawn upon in *The American Soldier*.

1. *With reference to the drafted married man:* "Comparing himself with his unmarried associates in the Army, he could feel that induction demanded greater sacrifice from him than from them; and *comparing himself with his married civilian friends*, he could feel that he had been called on for sacrifices which they were escaping altogether." (I, 125)
2. "The average high school graduate or college man was a clear-cut candidate for induction; marginal cases on occupational grounds probably occurred much more often in groups with less educational attainment. On the average, the non high school man who was inducted *could point to more acquaintances* conceivably no more entitled to deferment than himself, who nonetheless had been deferred on occupational grounds . . . when they *compared themselves with their civilian friends* they may have been more likely to feel that they were required to make sacrifices which *others like them* were excused from making." (I, 127)
3. "The concept of *relative deprivation* is particularly helpful in evaluating the role of education in satisfaction with status or job, as well as in some aspects of approval or criticism of the Army. . . . With higher levels of aspiration than the less educated, *the better educated man had more to lose in his own eyes and in the eyes of his friends* by failure to achieve some sort of status in the Army. Hence, frustration was greater for him than for others if a goal he sought was not attained. . . ." (I, 153)
4. ". . . the concept of differential deprivation and reward . . . may help us understand some of the psychological processes relevant to this problem. In general, it is of course true that the overseas soldier, *relative to soldiers still at home*, suffered a greater break with home ties and with many of the amenities of life in the United States to which he was accustomed. But it was also true that, *relative to the combat soldier*, the overseas soldier [in rear areas of an active theater] not in combat and not likely to get into combat suffered far less deprivation than the actual fighting man." (I, 172)
5. "The concept of differential deprivation would lead us to look further for a reason why the actually more deprived group of soldiers seemed little more critical than the less deprived group . . . the less *the differential between officers and men* in the enjoyment of scarce privileges – the extreme case being that of actual combat – the less likely was the enlisted man to be critical of the officers and the easier it was for him to accept the inevitability of deprivation."
6. ". . . as would be expected . . . those soldiers who had advanced slowly *relative to other soldiers of equal longevity* in the Army were the most critical of the Army's promotion opportunities. *But relative rate of advancement can be based on different standards by different classes of the Army population.* For example, a grade school man who became a corporal after a year of service would have had a more rapid rate of promotion *compared with most of his friends at the same educational level* than would a college man

who rose to the same grade in a year. Hence we would expect, at a given rank and a given longevity, that the better educated would be more likely than others to complain of the slowness of promotion.... A similar phenomenon appeared to operate between different branches of the service." (I, 250)

7. "From the studies of enlisted men reported previously in this chapter, it would be expected that attitudes of officers about promotion, like those of enlisted men, would reflect some relationship with level of expectation and with level of achievement *relative to that of one's acquaintances.* Thus we would expect a captain who had been in grade a long time *compared with other captains* to be less happy about the promotion situation than a lieutenant in grade a relatively short time." (I, 279)

8. "... it seems likely that both Northern and Southern Negroes may have been considerably influenced in their overall adjustment by other psychological compensations in being stationed in the South, which can be understood if we look at their situation as one of *relative status.*

"Relative to most Negro civilians whom he saw in Southern towns, the Negro soldier had a position of comparative wealth and dignity." (I, 563)

9 "Putting it simply, the psychological values of Army life to the Negro soldier in the South *relative to the Southern Negro civilian* greatly exceeded the psychological values of Army life to the Negro soldier in the North *relative to the Northern Negro civilian."* (I, 564)

These nine excerpts touch upon the core interpretative statements in which the notion of relative deprivation or affiliated concepts were expressly utilized to interpret otherwise anomalous or inconsistent findings.[2] To these explicit uses of the concept we shall later add several research cases not subjected by the authors to interpretation in terms of reference group concepts which nevertheless seem explicated by such concepts.

In all these cases, it should be noted, the concept of relative deprivation serves the same theoretical purpose: it is used as an interpretative intervening variable. The researches were designed to study the sentiments and attitudes of American soldiers – their attitudes toward induction, for example, or their appraisals of chances for promotion. These attitudes are typically taken as the *dependent variables.* The analysis of data finds that these attitudes differ among soldiers of varying status – for example, older or married men exhibited more resentment toward induction than younger or unmarried men; those enjoying the status of high school and college graduates were less likely to be optimistic about their prospects for promotion in the Army. These status attributes are in general taken provisionally as the *independent variables.* Once these relationships between independent and dependent variables are established, the problem is one of accounting for them: of inferring how it comes to be that the better educated are typically less optimistic about their chances for promotion or how it comes to be that the married man exhibits greater resentment over his induction into military service. At this point of interpretation, the concept of relative deprivation is introduced, so that the pattern of analysis becomes somewhat as follows: the married man (independent variable) more often questions the legitimacy of his induction (dependent variable), because he appraises the situation within the frame of reference (interpretative variable) yielded by comparing himself with other married men still in civilian life, who escaped the draft entirely, or with unmarried men in the Army, whose induction did not call for comparable sacrifice. We may thus tag the major function of the concept of relative deprivation as that of a provisional after-the-fact interpretative concept which is intended to help explain the variation in attitudes expressed by soldiers of differing social status. And since after-the-fact interpretations have a distinctive place in the ongoing development of theory, we shall later want to consider this characteristic of the concept of relative deprivation at some length.[3]

The collation of these key excerpts serves as something more than a thin summary of the original materials. Since the studies employing the concept of relative deprivation deal with diverse subject matters, they are scattered through the pages of *The American Soldier* and thus are not likely to be examined in terms of their mutual theoretical linkages. The juxtaposition of excerpts admits of a virtually *simultaneous inspection* of the several interpretations and, in turn, permits us to detect the central categories which were evidently taken by the Research Branch as the *bases of comparison* presumably implicit in the observed attitudes and evaluations of soldiers. And once the categories of analysis employed by the Research Branch are detected, their logical connections can be worked out, thus leading to formulations which seem to have significance for the further development of reference group theory.

If we proceed inductively, we find that the frames of reference for the soldiers under observation by the Research Branch were provisionally assumed to be of three kinds. First of all are those cases in which the attitudes or judgments of the men were held to be influenced by comparison with the situation of others with whom they were in *actual association*, in sustained social relations, such as the "married civilian friends" of the soldier in excerpt 1, or the "acquaintances" of the non-high-school man in excerpt 2.

A second implied basis of comparison is with those men who are in some pertinent respect *of the same status* or in the *same social category*, as in the case of the captain who compares his lot "with other captains" in excerpt 7 without any implication that they are necessarily in direct social interaction.

And third, comparison is assumed with those who are in some pertinent respect of *different status* or in a *different social category*, as in the case of the non-combat soldier compared with combat men in excerpt 4, or the enlisted men compared with officers in excerpt 5 (again without social interaction between them being necessarily implied).

For the most part, as we learn from this inspection of cases, the groups or individuals presumably taken as bases for comparison by soldiers do not fall simply into one *or* another of these three types, but involve various combinations of them. Most commonly, presumed comparison is with *associates* of the same status, as the gradeschool man compared with friends of the same educational level in excerpt 6, or with various unassociated "others" who are of a *status similar in some salient respect and dissimilar in other respects*, such as the Negro soldier who compares himself with the Negro civilian in excerpts 8 and 9.

If these attributes of the individuals or groups serving as presumed frames of reference are arranged in a matrix, then the conceptual structure of the notion of relative deprivation (and affiliated concepts) becomes more readily visible. The schematic arrangement enables us to locate, not only the frames of comparative reference most often utilized in the interpretation of data by the Research Branch, but additional possible frames of reference which found little place in their interpretation. It thus affords an occasion for systematically exploring the theoretical nature of relative deprivation as an interpretative tool and for indicating the points at which it possibly deepens and broadens the apposite theory of reference group behavior.

In substance, the groups or individuals taken as points of reference in the nine excerpts are explicitly characterized by these few attributes. The presence of sustained social relations between the individual and those taken as a basis for comparison indicates that they are to this degree, in a common *membership group* or *in-group*, and their absence, that they are in a *non-membership* or *out-group*. When it comes to comparative status, the implied classification is slightly more complex: the individuals comprising the base of comparison may be of the same status as the subject or different, and if different, the status may be higher, lower, or unranked. The array of reference points implied in the interpretations of the Research Branch thus appears as in Table 1.

Examination of this matrix of variables implied by the notion of relative deprivation at once directs attention to several empirical and theoretical problems. These problems, as will presently become evident, not only bear specifically upon the concept of relative deprivation but more generally upon a theory of reference group behavior.

It will be noted from the preliminary survey of cases contained in the matrix that, at times, the authors of *The American Soldier* assume that individuals take as a base for self-reference the situation of people with whom they are in direct social interaction: primarily, the in-group of friends and associates. At others, the assumed frame of reference is yielded by social categories of people – combat soldiers, other captains, etc. – with whom the individual is not in sustained social relations. In order to highlight the connection of the concept of relative deprivation with reference group theory, these "others" with whom the individual does not interact are here designated as non-membership groups or out-groups.[4] Since both membership groups and non-membership groups, in-groups and out-groups, have in fact been taken as assumed social frames of reference in these interpretations, this at once leads to a general question of central importance to a developing theory of reference group behavior:

under which conditions are associates within one's own groups taken as a frame of reference for self-evaluation and attitude-formation, and under which conditions do out-groups or non-membership groups provide the significant frame of reference?

Table 1
Attributes of Individuals, Social Categories and Groups Taken as a Frame of Comparative Reference by Individuals

In Sustained Social Relations with Individual	Same Status	Different Social Status		
		Higher	Lower	Unranked
Yes (membership- or in-group)	# 1 married friends # 2 non high school acquaintances # 6 friends at same educational level	# 5 officers	# 8, 9 Negro civilians in South	# 3 friends # 7 acquaintances
	ORIENTATION OF INDIVIDUAL TO			
No (non-membership or out-group)	# 4 soldiers in U.S. or in active combat # 6 soldiers of equal longevity # 7 other captains	# 5 officers	# 8, 9 Negro civilians in South	

The numbers refer to the appropriate excerpts which are here being provisionally classified.

Reference groups are, in principle, almost innumerable: any of the groups of which one is a member, and these are comparatively few, as well as groups of which one is not a member, and these are, of course, legion, can become points of reference for shaping one's attitudes, evaluations and behavior. And this gives rise to another set of problems requiring theoretical formulation and further empirical inquiry. For, as the matrix arrangement of cases drawn from *The American Soldier* plainly suggests, the individual may be oriented toward any one *or more* of the various kinds of groups and statuses – membership groups and non-membership groups, statuses like his own or if different, either higher, lower, or not socially ranked with respect to his own. This, then, locates a further problem: if *multiple* groups or statuses, with their possibly divergent or even contradictory norms and standards, are taken as a frame of reference by the individual, how are these discrepancies resolved?[5]

These initial questions may help establish the range of our inquiry. That men act in a social frame of reference yielded by the groups of which they are a part is a notion undoubtedly ancient and probably sound. Were this alone the concern of reference group theory, it would merely be a new term for an old focus in sociology, which has always been centered on the group determination of behavior. There is, however, the further fact that men frequently orient themselves to groups *other than their own* in shaping their behavior and evaluations, and it is the problems centered about this fact of orientation to non-membership groups that constitute the distinctive concern of reference group theory. Ultimately, of course, the theory must be generalized to the point where it can account for *both* membership- and non-membership-group orientations, but immediately its major task is to search out the processes through which individuals relate themselves to groups to which they do *not* belong.

In general, then, reference group theory aims to systematize the determinants and consequences of those processes of evaluation and self-appraisal in which the individual takes the values or standards of other individuals and groups as a comparative frame of reference.[6]

From our brief preliminary examination, it appears that the researches in *The American Soldier* utilizing the concept of relative deprivation can act as a catalyst quickening theoretical clarification and the formulation of problems for further empirical study. But the precise nature of these formulations can be better seen through a detailed examination of several of these cases after we have more definitely connected the concept of relative deprivation with the theory of reference group behavior.

Relative *Deprivation* or *Relative* Deprivation

In developing their concept of relative deprivation, the authors of *The American Soldier* have, on the whole, centered their attention on the deprivation component rather than the relative component of the concept. They have, so to say, focused on relative *deprivation* rather than on *relative* deprivation. The reason for this seems both apparent and understandable, in view of the conspicuously deprivational character of the Army situations with which they dealt. By and large, American men viewed service in the armed forces as at best a grim and reluctantly accepted necessity:

> "The vast majority of men did not come into the Army voluntarily . . . the acceptance of the soldier role probably tended to be passive in character, at least with respect to initial attitudes . . . the passive attitude

toward military service implied a relative absence of identification with broad social goals which would serve to deflect attention away from the day-to-day frustrations in the new environment. Recruits were therefore likely to be sharply aware of the deprivational features of Army life." (I, 208–9)

It was, then, the patterns of response to a basically deprivational situation which most often called for study and it was primarily in the service of interpreting these patterns of response that the concept of relative deprivation was developed. As the term, relative deprivation, itself suggests, the concept was primarily utilized to help account for feelings of dissatisfaction, particularly in cases where the objective situation would at first glance not seem likely to provoke such feelings. This is not to say that the concept was wholly confined to interpreting the feelings of dissatisfaction, deprivation, or injustice among soldiers, since the presumed practice of comparing one's own situation with that of others often resulted in a state of relative satisfaction. In the main, however, satisfactions stemming from such comparison with others are seen in the role of offsetting excessive dissatisfaction in cases of multiple comparison: for example, the dissatisfaction of the noncombat man overseas, presumably reinforced by comparison with those serving in the United States, is tempered by satisfaction with his status as compared with the combat man. (I, 173)

As the authors themselves evidently recognize, "deprivation" is the incidental and particularized component of the concept of relative deprivation, whereas the more significant nucleus of the concept is its stress upon social and psychological experience as "relative." This may be seen from the text at the point where the authors introduce the notion of relative deprivation and suggest its kinship to such other sociological concepts as "social frame of reference, patterns of expectation, or definitions of the situation." (I, 125) It is the *relative* component, the standards of comparison in self-evaluation, that these concepts have in common.

By freeing the concept of relative deprivation from confinement to the particular data which it was initially designed to interpret, it may become generalized and related to a larger body of theory. Relative deprivation can provisionally be regarded as a special concept in reference group theory. And since *The American Soldier* provides systematic empirical data and not merely discursive views on the concept of relative deprivation, the way is possibly opened for progressively clarifying crucial variables so that further cumulative research bearing on the theory can be mapped out.

All this, however, is still programmatic. Whether *The American Soldier* does indeed have these functions for reference group theory can only be determined through inspection, at closer range than we have yet attempted, of the researches in these volumes bearing upon the theory.

The analysis of these several cases is intended to document and to elaborate the emergence of those problems of reference group theory briefly foreshadowed in the foregoing pages and to indicate further related problems which have not yet received notice. Toward this end, the essential facts and basic interpretation as these are set out by the Research Branch will be summarized for each case, and followed by a statement of its apparent implications for the advancement of reference group theory.

By way of preview, it may be said that these cases generate the formulation of a wide range of specific problems which will be taken up in detail and which are here roughly indicated by the following list of headings:

Membership-groups operating as reference groups;
Conflicting reference groups and mutually sustaining reference groups;
Uniformities of behavior derived from reference group theory;
Statistical indices of social structure;
Reference group theory and social mobility;
Functions of positive orientations to non-membership groups;
Social processes sustaining or curbing these orientations;
Psychological and social functions of institutions regulating passage from one membership-group to another; and
A review of concepts kindred to reference group theory.

Membership-Group as Reference Group

Case #1. This research deals with soldiers' evaluations of promotion opportunities as these were elicited by the question, "Do you think a soldier with ability has a good chance for promotion?" A generalized finding, necessarily and too much abbreviated in this summary, holds that for each level of longevity, rank and education, "the *less* the promotion opportunity afforded by a branch or combination of branches, the *more favorable* the opinion tends to be toward promotion opportunity." (I, 250) Within the limits of the data in hand,[7] this paradoxical response of greater satisfaction with opportunities for mobility in the very branches characterized by less mobility finds clear demonstration. Thus, although the Air Corps had a conspicuously high rate of promotion, Air Corps men were definitely far more critical of chances for promotion than, say, men in the Military Police, where the objective chances for promotion "were about the worst in any branch of the Army." So, too, at any given rank and longevity, the better educated soldiers, despite their notably higher rates of promotion in general, were the more critical of opportunities for promotion.

This paradox is provisionally explained by the Research Branch as a result of evaluations occurring within the frame of reference provided by group rates of promotion. A generally high rate of mobility induces excessive hopes and expectations among members of the group so that each is more likely to experience a sense of frustration in his present position and disaffection with the chances for promotion. As it is put by the authors, "Without reference to the theory that such opinions represent a relationship between their expectations and their achievements *relative to others in the same boat with them*, such a finding would be paradoxical indeed." (I, 251, italics supplied)

Theoretical implications. First of all, it should be noted that it was an anomalous finding which apparently elicited the hypothesis that evaluations of promotion chances are a function of expectations and achievements "relative to others in the same boat with them." And, in turn, the raw uninterpreted finding appears anomalous only because it is inconsistent with the commonsense assumption that, in general, evaluations will correspond to the objective facts of the case. According to common sense, marked differences in objective rates of promotion would presumably be reflected in corresponding differences in assessments of chances for promotion. Had such correspondences been empirically found, there would seemingly have been little occasion for advancing this hypothesis of a group frame of reference. As it turns out, the data suggest that men define the situation differently. But it is not enough to mention these "definitions of the situation"; it is necessary to *account for* them. And the function of the concept of relative deprivation (as with other concepts of reference groups) is precisely that of helping to account for observed definitions of a situation.

In this case, it required *systematic* empirical data, such as those assembled in *The American Soldier*, to *detect* the anomalous pattern, not detectable through impressionistic observation. And this illustrates a basic role of systematic empirical research in reaching unanticipated, anomalous and strategic findings that exert pressure for initiating or extending theory.[8] The data and the hypothesis advanced to account for them open up further theoretical and research problems, which can here receive bare mention rather than the full exposition they deserve.

The hypothesis makes certain important assumptions about *the* group taken as a point of reference by the soldiers and thus affecting their level of satisfaction with promotion opportunities. This assumption is stated, as we have seen, in the form that evaluations are "relative to others in the same boat." And the data are consistent with the view that four groups or social categories have presumably been taken as a context or frame of reference: men with similar longevity, similar educational status, similar rank, and in the same branch of the Service.

Now, this hypothesis, suitably generalized, raises all manner of further questions germane to reference group theory and requiring renewed inquiry and analysis. Which conditions predispose toward this pattern of selecting people of the same status or group as significant points of reference? The idiomatic phrase, "in the same boat," raises the same sociological problems as the idiomatic phrase, "keeping up with the Joneses." Who are the specific Joneses, in various social structures, with whom people try to keep up? their close associates? people in immediately higher social or income strata with whom they have contact? When are the Joneses people whom one never meets, but whom one hears about (through public media of communication, for example)? How does it happen that some select the Joneses to keep up with, others the Cabots, or the Cassidys, and finally that some don't try to keep up at all?

In other words, the hypothesis advanced in *The American Soldier* regarding individuals of similar status being taken as frames of reference for self-evaluations at once opens up an interrelated array of problems, amenable to research and constituting important further links in the development of reference group theory. When are one's membership-groups *not* taken as reference groups in arriving at evaluations? After all, many men were apparently aware of the differences between the table of organization of the Air Corps and their own branch. When would these mobility rates among men *not* in the same boat affect their own level of satisfaction? And these sociological problems, though they might have originated elsewhere, were in fact generated by the anomalous empirical findings developed and provisionally interpreted in this study.

That new systematic experience, such as that represented by the data and hypothesis of *The American Soldier*, does indeed generate the formulation of further theoretical questions is suggested by glancing briefly at the somewhat contrasting work of a notable theorist in social psychology, George H. Mead, who did not steep himself in *systematic* empirical materials. Mead was, of course, a forerunner and an important forerunner in the history of reference group theory, particularly with respect to his central conception, variously expressed in his basic writings, but adequately enough captured in the statement that "The individual experiences himself as such, not directly, but only indirectly, from the particular standpoints of other individual members *of the same group*, or from the generalized standpoint of the social group as a whole *to which he belongs*."[9]

In this formulation and in numerous others like it,[10] Mead in effect advances the hypothesis that it is the groups of which the individual *is a member* that yield the significant frame of reference for self-evaluations. And this he *illustrates* abundantly with anecdotal instances drawn from his varied personal experience and insightful reflection. But, possibly because he was not exposed to *systematic* empirical evidence, which might prove seemingly inconsistent with this formulation *at specific points*, he was not driven to ask whether, indeed, the group taken as a point of reference by the individual is invariably the group of which he is a member. The terms "another," "the other" and "others" turn up on literally hundreds of occasions in Mead's exposition of the thesis that the development of the social self entails response to the attitudes of "another" or of "others." But the varying status of "these others" presumably taken as frames of self-reference is glossed over, except for the repeated statement that they are members of "the" group. Thus, Mead, and those of his followers who also eschew empirical research, had little occasion to move ahead to the question of conditions under which non-membership-groups may also constitute a significant frame of reference.

Not only does the research from *The American Soldier* point directly to that question, but it leads further to the problems raised by the facts of *multiple* group affiliations and *multiple* reference groups. It reminds us that theory and research must move on to consider the *dynamics of selection* of reference groups among the individual's several membership groups: when do individuals orient themselves to others in their occupational group, in their congeniality groups, or in their religious group? How can we characterize the *structure of the social situation* which leads to one rather than another of these several group affiliations being taken as the significant context?

Following out the hypothesis advanced in the text, we note as well the problem raised by the simultaneous operation of multiple reference groups. Further steps call for study of the *dynamic processes* involved in the theoretically supposed counter-tendencies induced by multiple reference groups. For example, what are the dynamics of evaluation, and not merely the final evaluation, of the mobility system among college graduates relatively new to the Military Police: on the hypothesis advanced in *The American Soldier*, they would be moved, through reference to the status of other college graduates, toward dissatisfaction, but as comparatively new replacements and as M.P.'s they would be moved toward relative satisfaction. How are these counter-tendencies ultimately resolved in the evaluation which comes to the notice of the observer?

Turning finally to the dependent variable in this study, we note that it consists in soldiers' evaluations of the *institutional system* of promotion in the Army, and not to *self-evaluations* of personal achievement within that system.[11] The men were in effect asked to appraise the system of promotion in terms of its effectiveness and legitimacy, as can be seen from the carefully worded question which elicited their judgments: "Do you think a soldier with ability has a good chance for promotion?"

This introduces a problem, deserving attention which it has not yet received: do the two types of evaluations, self-appraisals and appraisals of institutional arrangements, involve similar mechanisms of reference group behavior? At this point, it is clear that research is needed to discover the structure of those social situations which typically elicit self-evaluations or internalized judgments – for example, where comparison with the achievements of specified others leads to invidious self-depreciation, to a sense of personal inadequacy – and the structure of those situations which typically lead to evaluations of institutions or externalized judgments – for example, where comparison with others leads to a sense of institutional inadequacies, to the judgment that the social system militates against any close correspondence between individual merit and social reward.

Here, as with many of *The American Soldier* researches, the implications of procedure, analysis, and interpretation are of course not confined to further studies of behavior of soldiers. They bear upon some of the more strategic areas of study in the larger social system. For example, the sociological factors which lead men to consider their own, relatively low, social position as legitimate, as well as those which lead them to construe their position as a result of defective and possibly unjustified social arrangements clearly comprise a problem area of paramount theoretical and political importance. When are relatively slim life-chances taken by men as a normal and expectable state of affairs which they attribute to their own personal inadequacies and when are they regarded as the results of an arbitrary social system of mobility, in which rewards are not proportioned to ability?[12] The concepts of relative deprivation and of relative reward help transfer these much-discussed but little-analyzed patterns of behavior from the realm of impressionistic speculation to that of systematic research.

Multiple Reference Groups

Several researches in *The American Soldier* afford occasion for looking into theoretical problems arising from the conception that multiple reference groups provide contexts for evaluations by individuals. Two of these cases have been selected for attention here because they apparently exhibit different patterns of multiple comparison: in the first of these, multiple reference groups provide contexts which operate at cross-purposes; in the second, they provide contexts which are mutually sustaining.

Conflicting reference groups. Case #2. During the latter part of 1943 and the early part of 1944, the Research Branch conducted a series of surveys from which they developed a picture of differences in attitudes (reflecting personal adjustment) of noncombat men overseas and of men stationed in the United States. Though consistent, the differences in attitudes were not large. Among noncoms still in the United States, for example, 41 per cent reported themselves as "usually in good spirits" in comparison with 32 per cent of those overseas; 76 per cent of the one held that the "Army is run pretty well or very well" compared with 63 per cent of the other. (I, 167, Chart IV) But since other surveys found that the major concern of the men overseas was to get back home (I, 187), the authors observe that considerably greater differences in attitudes expressing personal adjustment might well have been expected.

Three factors are tentatively adduced to account for the absence of greater differences, factors operating to curb the expectable[13] degree of dissatisfaction expressed by the noncombat soldier overseas. Of these, we attend only to the interpretative concept of "differential deprivation and reward"[14] which, it will be remembered from an earlier excerpt,

> "may help us understand some of the psychological processes relevant to this problem. In general, it is of course true that the overseas soldier, *relative to soldiers still at home*, suffered a greater break with home ties and with many of the amenities of life in the United States to which he was accustomed. But it was also true that, *relative to the combat soldier*, the overseas soldier not in combat and not likely to enter into combat suffered far less deprivation than the actual fighting man." (I, 172)

Theoretical implications. In effect, the authors suggest that two contexts of comparison, operating at cross-purposes, affected the evaluations of overseas noncombat troops. What, then, can be learned from this case about the grounds on which certain contexts rather than others become pertinent for such evaluations?

It should be noted at the outset that the status of those constituting the contexts of evaluation is, in some significant respect, *similar* to the status of the men making the evaluation. Thus, the soldiers still at home are similar in that they too are not in combat, and the combat soldiers are similar in that they too are overseas. Beyond this, other similarities and dissimilarities, pertinent to the situation, affect the resulting evaluations in contrasting ways. Thus, the overseas noncombat soldier is, by the standards of Army life, worse off than the soldier at home in that he is comparatively deprived of amenities and cut off from social ties, and better off than the combat soldier in that he is not exposed to the same measure of deprivation and risk. It is as though he had said, "Bad off as we are, the others are worse off," a comparison not seldom adopted by those who would accommodate themselves to their position. His definition of his situation is then presumably the resultant of these counteracting patterns of comparison.

This suggests the general hypothesis that some similarity in status attributes between the individual and the reference group must be perceived or imagined, in order for the comparison to occur at all. Once this minimal similarity obtains,[15] other similarities and differences pertinent to the situation, will provide the context for shaping evaluations. Consequently, this focuses the attention of the theorist immediately upon the factors which produce a sense of pertinent similarity between statuses, since these will help determine which groups are called into play as comparative contexts. The underlying similarities of status among members of in-groups, singled out by Mead as *the* social context, thus appear as only one special, though obviously important, basis for the selection of reference groups. Out-groups may also involve *some* similarity of status.

By implication, the hypothesis of the Research Branch at this point provides a clue to the factors affecting the selection of reference groups. The hypothesis does not hold that the two categories of men – the combat men overseas and the noncombat men at home – constituted the *only* ones with which *any particular individual* among the overseas combat men compared himself. He may indeed have compared his lot with that of numerous and diverse others – a civilian friend in a cushy job back home, a cousin enjoying life as a war correspondent, an undrafted movie star whom he had read about in a magazine. But such comparisons by an individual, precisely because they involve personal frames of reference, might well be idiosyncratic. They would not provide contexts *common* to (many or most of) the individuals in the status of overseas non-combat men. To the degree that they are idiosyncratic, they would vary at random among the various categories of soldiers.

Consequently, they would not aggregate into statistically significant differences of attitudes between *groups* or *social categories* of soldiers.

In other words, the statistics of *The American Soldier* on differential definitions of their situation among combat men,[16] overseas noncombat men and men still in the United States are taken to manifest the impact of *socially structured* reference groups more or less common to men in each category. It is not mere indolence or lack of insight which keeps the sociologist from seeking to track down all the comparative contexts which hold for any given individual; it is, rather, that many of these contexts are idiosyncratic, not shared by a large fraction of other individuals within the same group or social category. The comparative statistics in *The American Soldier* are plainly not intended to manifest and cannot manifest those numerous private contexts peculiar to individuals and hence varying at random to the social category. One does not look to these sociological data for idiosyncratic contexts of appraisal.

The reference groups here hypothesized, then, are not mere artifacts of the authors' arbitrary scheme of classification. Instead, they appear to be frames of reference held in common by a proportion of individuals within a social category sufficiently large to give rise to definitions of the situation characteristic of that category. And these frames of reference are common because they are patterned by the social structure. In the present case, for example, the degree of closeness to combat provides a socially organized and socially emphasized basis of comparison among the three categories of soldiers – overseas combat, overseas noncombat, and troops back home. It is, accordingly, categories such as these which provide the *common* comparative contexts for definition of the situation among these men. This is not to deny that other contexts may be of great consequence to particular individuals within each of these social categories. But these become relevant for the sociologist only if they are shared sufficiently to lead to group differences in evaluations.

In these pages, *The American Soldier* affords a clue, and possibly an important clue, for solving the sociological problem of finding the common residual which constitutes the reference groups distinctive for those in social status category.

There is another problem implicit here about which little can be learned from this case: what are the patterns of response among members of a group or status category when they are subject to multiple reference groups operating at cross-purposes? In the present case, the net evaluation of their lot among overseas noncombat men apparently represented a compromise, intermediate between the evaluations of noncombat men at home and of men in actual combat. But it is not implied by the authors of *The American Soldier* that this is the only pattern of response under such circumstances. It is possible, for example, that when several membership groups exert diverse and conflicting pressures for self-appraisal, the individual tends to adopt other, non-membership groups as a frame of reference. In any event, there arises the large and imperfectly defined problem, previously alluded to, of searching out the processes of coming to terms with such conflicting pressures.[17] That the social scientists of the Research Branch were cognizant of this line of inquiry, emerging from their wartime studies, is suggested by the fact that the director, Stouffer, is now developing researches on the varying patterns of response to the simultaneous but conflicting demands of primary groups and of formal organizational authorities.[18]

Mutually sustaining reference groups. Case #3. In its bare outlines, this study (I, 122–130) is concerned with the feelings of legitimacy ascribed by men to their induction into service. Patterns of response to the question, "At the time you came into the Army,[19] did you think you should have been deferred?" showed that married men, over 20 years of age, who had not been graduated from high school were most likely to maintain that they should have been deferred. In this status category, 41 per cent, as compared, for example, with only 10 per cent of unmarried high school graduates under 20 years of age, claimed that they should not have been inducted at all. More generally, it is found that the statuses of age, marital condition and educational level are consistently related with willingness for military service.

Since the hypotheses advanced to account for these findings are essentially of the same type for each of the three status categories, we need concern ourselves here with only one of these for illustrative purposes. As we have seen in an excerpt from this case, the authors provisionally explain the greater reluctance for service of married men in terms of the standards of comparison yielded by reference to two other status categories. The key interpretative passage bears repetition at this point:

> "*Comparing himself with his unmarried associates* in the Army, he could feel that induction demanded greater sacrifice from him than from them; and *comparing himself with his married civilian friends* he could feel that he had been called on for sacrifices which they were escaping altogether. Hence the married man, on the average, was more likely than others to come into the Army with reluctance and, possibly, a sense of injustice." (I, 125, italics supplied)

Theoretical implications. However brief and tentative the interpretation, it helps us to locate and to formulate several further problems involved in developing a theory of reference group behavior.

First of all, it reinforces the supposition, hinted in the preceding case, that it is the institutional definitions of the social structure which may focus the attention of members of a group or occupants of a social status upon certain *common* reference groups. Nor does this refer only to the fact that soldiers will take the official institutional norms (the rules governing induction and exemption) as a *direct* basis for judging the legitimacy of their own induction into the service. These same rules, since they are defined in terms of such statuses as marital condition and age, also focus attention on certain groups or statuses with which individuals subject to service will compare themselves. This is, in effect, implied by the authors who, referring to the greater sacrifices entailed by induction of the married man, go on to say: "This was officially recognized by draft boards.... The very fact that draft boards were more liberal with married than with single men provided numerous examples to the drafted married man of *others in his shoes* who got relatively better breaks than he did." (I, 125, italics supplied) The institutional norms evoke comparisons with others similar in *particular* aspects of status – "others in his shoes" – thus encouraging *common* reference groups for these married soldiers. In addition to these common reference groups, as previously stated, there may well have been all manner of idiosyncratic reference groups, which, since they vary at random, would not have resulted in the statistically discernible reluctance for service which was comparatively marked among married men.

A second problem is highlighted by the hypothesis which uniformly assumes that the married soldier compares himself with like statused individuals with whom he is or has been in *actual social relations: associates* in the Army or civilian *friends*. This, then, raises a question concerning reference group behavior when the frame of comparative reference is provided by *impersonal status categories* in general (other married men, noncoms, *etc.*) and by those representatives of these status categories with whom he is in *sustained social relations*. Which, for example, most affects the evaluations of the individual when these operate at cross-purposes (a problem clearly visible in the matrix of variables set out earlier in this paper)?

This question leads at once to the comparative significance of general status categories and intimate subgroups of which one is a member. Suppose, for example, that all or almost all of a married soldier's married associates have also been drafted, even though, *in general*, this status category has a smaller proportion of inductions than the category of the unmarried male. Which basis of comparison will, on the average, prove more effective? Will he compare himself with the other drafted benedicts in his clique or subgroup and consequently be the more ready to accept induction for himself, or will he compare himself with the larger status category of married men, who are in general more often deferred, and consequently feel aggrieved over his own induction? The question has, of course, more general bearing. For example, are workers' expectations regarding their personal prospects of future employment shaped more by the present employment of themselves and their associates on the job or by high rates of unemployment prevailing in the occupation at large?

This case from *The American Soldier* thus points to the need for cumulative research on *the relative effectiveness of frames of reference yielded by associates and by more general status categories*. It suggests the salient items of observation which must be incorporated in such projected studies, so that this problem, at least in its major outlines, can lend itself to research, here and now, not in some remote future. Such projected studies could readily include items of data on the norms or situation of close associates as well as data on knowledge about the norms or situation prevailing in the given status at large. Subsequent analysis would then be in terms of systematic comparison of individuals in the *same status* but with immediate *associates* who have distinctly opposed norms or who are in contrasting situations. Replicated studies including such materials would substantially advance our present understanding of the workings of reference group behavior.[20]

Third, the theory assumes that individuals comparing their own lot with that of others have some *knowledge* of the situation in which these others find themselves. More concretely, it assumes that the individual knows about the comparative rates of induction among married and single men, or the degree of unemployment in their occupation at large.[21] Or, if the individual is taken to be positively oriented toward the norms of a non-membership group, the theory of course assumes that he has some knowledge of these norms. Thus, the theory of reference group behavior must include in its fuller psychological elaboration some treatment of the dynamics of perception (of individuals, groups and norms) and in its sociological elaboration, some treatment of channels of communication through which this knowledge is gained. Which processes make for accurate or distorted images of the situation of other individuals and groups (taken as a frame of reference)? Which forms of social organization maximize the probabilities of correct perception of other individuals and groups, and which make for distorted perception? Since *some* perceptual and cognitive elements are definitely *implied* even in a description of reference group behavior, it will be necessary for these elements to be explicitly incorporated into the theory.

A fourth problem emerging from this case concerns the empirical status of reference group concepts. In this study, as well as in others we consider here, the interpretative concept of relative deprivation was introduced *after* the field research was completed.[22] This being the case, there was no provision for the collection of *independent systematic*[23] *evidence* on the operation of such social frameworks of individual judgments. That a significant proportion of married soldiers did indeed compare their lot with that of married civilian friends and unmarried associates in the Army in arriving at their judgment remains, so far as the data in hand go, an assumption. These comparisons are inferred, rather than factually demonstrated, intervening variables. But they need not remain assumptions. They not only happen to square with the facts in hand, but are of a kind which can be directly tested in future inquiries employing the concept of reference group.[24] These studies can be designed to incorporate systematic data on the groups which individuals actually do take as frames of reference for their behavior and can thus determine whether variations in attitude and behavior correspond to variations in reference group contexts.

This possibility of converting the intervening variable of reference groups from assumption into fact brings us to a fifth problem. Before plunging into research on the conditions under which individuals compare themselves with *specified* other individuals or groups, it is necessary to consider the psychological status of these comparisons. For when individuals *explicitly* and consciously adopt such frames of reference, sociological researches involving interviews with large numbers of people face no great procedural difficulties. Appropriate questions can elicit the needed information on the groups, status categories or individuals which are taken as a frame of reference. But there is, of course, no reason to assume that comparisons of self with others are uniformly conscious. Numerous experimental studies in social psychology have shown that individuals *unwittingly* respond to different frames of reference introduced by the experimenter. To the extent that unwitting reference groups are involved in the ordinary routines of daily life, research techniques must be extended to detect their operation.

Appropriate research procedures must also be designed to discover which reference groups are spontaneously and explicitly brought into play, as distinguished from the study of responses to reference group contexts provided by the experimenter or suggested by the interviewer. Both interview and experimental studies have heretofore been largely centered on responses to reference group contexts supplied for the subjects. These studies can be further advanced by providing ordered arrays of comparative contexts, somewhat as follows:

> "Compared with others on your work-team [or other membership group], do you feel you are getting a fair income for what you do?"
> "Compared with the men in the front office, do you . . . etc . . .?"
> "Compared with the president of the firm, do you . . . etc . . .?"

Or similarly, information about the salaries of various individuals and groups could be given an experimental group and withheld from a matched group of workers to determine whether the subsequent self-appraisals and satisfactions of the experimental group are modified by possible reference groups supplied by the investigator.

But such tentative types of inquiry, in which the particular reference groups are provided, do not, of course, enter into the uncharted region of the *spontaneous selection of reference groups* in varying situations. Why will A, in one situation, compare himself with B, and in another, with C? Or, more concretely and illustratively: when do workers compare their lot with that of fellow workers in close association, and when with others of markedly different status? which aspects of the social structure and which psychological processes limit the range of individuals and groups regarded as pertinent frames of reference? It is this type of problem – the processes shaping the selection of reference groups – that stands in most conspicuous need of research.[25]

Notes

1. On this function, see Robert K. Merton, *Social Theory and Social Structure*, (Glencoe, Illinois, The Free Press, 1949) Chapter III, "The Bearing of Empirical Research on Sociological Theory."

2. It thus appears, as we shall have occasion to note in some detail, that the concept of relative deprivation grows out of what has been called "the serendipity pattern" of the impact of empirical research upon theory, namely, "the fairly common experience of observing an *unanticipated, anomalous and strategic datum* which becomes the occasion for developing a new theory or for extending an existing theory." See Merton, *op. cit.*, 98.

3. At this point it need be noted only in passing that it is premature to assume that *ex post facto* interpretations are *in principle* not susceptible to empirical nullification. To argue this, as Nathan Glazer does in his overly-quick rejection of the concept of relative deprivation, is to be opaque to the interplay between theory and research in the *historical development* of a discipline. As we shall see, there is no foundation for saying, as Glazer does, that the notion of relative deprivation cannot conceivably be nullified: "Thus, [with the concept of relative deprivation] a little imagination will permit us to cover any conceivable outcome . . ." And later, he claims, that the conception "cannot be refuted by facts, and it will be found to hold true whatever the outcome of a given set of data." It will presently become clear that propositions incorporating the concept of relative deprivation are readily subject to empirical nullification, if they are in fact untrue. To appreciate one reason for our stress on empirically-oriented sociological theory as an ongoing *development*, see the consequences of neglecting this fact as exhibited in Nathan Glazer, " 'The American Soldier' as Science," *Commentary*, 1949, 8, 487–96.

4. We recognize that this sentence is replete with implicit problems which it would be premature to consider at this point. It involves, for example, the problem of criteria of "membership" in a group. Insofar as frequency of social interaction is one such criterion, we must recognize that the boundaries between groups are anything but sharply drawn. Rather, "members" of given groups are variously connected with other groups of which they are not *conventionally* regarded as members, though the sociologist might have ample basis for including them in these latter groups, by virtue of their frequent social interaction with its conventional membership. So, too, we are here momentarily by-passing the question of distinctions between social *groups* and social *categories*, the latter referring to established statuses between the occupants of which there may be little or no interaction. It will also be noticed by some that the formulation contained in *The American Soldier* extends the formulations by such theorists of social psychology as George H. Mead who confined himself to *membership groups* as significant frames of reference in his concept of the "generalized other" and in his account of the formation of self-attitudes. All this bears only passing mention at this point since it will be considered at a more appropriate place.

5. Though this problem is reminiscent of the traditional but only slightly clarified problem of conflict between multiple group *affiliations* or multiple *roles*, it is by no means identical with it. For, as we have seen, frames of reference are yielded not only by one's own membership groups or one's own statuses, but by non-membership groups and other statuses, as well.

6. This summary and elliptical statement will be amplified in later sections of the paper.

7. It is important that we introduce this caveat, for it is scarcely probable that this relationship between actual mobility rates and individual satisfaction with mobility chances holds throughout the entire range of variation. If promotion rates were reduced to practically zero in some of these groups, would one then find an even more "favorable opinion" of promotion chances? Presumably, the relationship is curvilinear, and this requires the sociologist to work out toward the conditions under which the observed linear relation fails to obtain.

8. This "creative function" of empirical research for theory warrants greater attention than is accorded it in Merton, *op. cit.*, 98–102, 374–5.

9. George H. Mead, *Mind, Self and Society* (The University of Chicago Press, 1934), 138 (italics supplied).

10. For example, see *ibid.*, 151–156, 193–194.

11. True, as the text implies, the institutional evaluations probably reflect soldiers' assessments of their own position as compared with their legitimate expectations, but this is not at issue here. The reference group hypothesis attempts to account for variations in the nature of these expectations in terms of the social contexts provided by the distribution of statuses in significant in-groups.

12. Such questions have of course been raised on numerous previous occasions. But they have ordinarily been regarded as distinct and self-contained problems of interest in their own right and not as special problems subsumable under a theory of reference group behavior. For example, it has been suggested that conspicuously "successful" individuals who have risen rapidly in a social hierarchy and who are much in the public eye, function as models or reference figures testifying to a mobility-system in which, apparently, careers are still open to talents. For some, these success-models are living testimony to the legitimacy of the institutional system and in this comparative context, the individual deflects criticism of the system onto himself. See R. K. Merton, M. Fiske and A. Curtis, *Mass Persuasion* (New York: Harper, 1946), 152ff.; Merton, *op. cit.*, 137 ff. But these observations remain impressionistic and anecdotal, since they do not provide *systematic* designs for inquiry into this behavior along the lines suggested by the researches of *The American Soldier*.

13. Here we see again that the concept of relative deprivation (just as the notion of "definition of the situation" generally) is introduced to account for an apparently anomalous finding. In this case, the finding seemingly deviates, not from common sense expectation merely, but from other facts uncovered in the course of research. It would thus seem to illustrate the type of serendipity pattern in research in which "the observation is anomalous, surprising, either because it seems inconsistent with prevailing theory or with other established facts. In either case, the seeming inconsistency provokes curiosity; it stimulates the investigator to 'make sense of the datum.'" Merton, *Social Theory and Social Structure*, 98–99.

14. The other two are, first, physical selection since men overseas had to meet more rigorous standards and second, "a sense of the significance of one's army job." In this latter connection, the authors remark: "While the difference between theaters . . . cannot prove or disprove hypotheses, the fact that, on the average, United States-overseas differences on attitudes toward Army jobs were negligible or reversed – as compared with United States-overseas differences in personal esprit or attitudes toward the Army – is a fact not to be overlooked." (I, 173)

15. This minimum of status similarity apparently presupposed by reference group behavior clearly requires systematic study. *Some* similarity in status can of course always

be found, depending only on the breadth of the status category. One can compare oneself with others, if only in the most general social capacity of "human being." And more germane to the case in question, the overseas combat man could (and did) compare himself with the noncombat man back home by virtue of their similar status as soldiers, and with civilians by virtue of their similar status as young adult American males. The theoretical and research problem at this point is to determine how the structure of the social situation encourages certain status-similarities to become the basis for such comparisons, and leads other status-similarities to be ignored as "irrelevant."

16. *The American Soldier* does not supply data on the attitudes of combat men at this point in the text, although apposite data are found at other places in the volumes. (*e.g.*, I, 111)

17. Thus, a study of political behavior found that individuals, under cross pressure, were more likely to delay their final vote decision. And as the senior author goes on to say: "But such delay is not the only possible reaction. Other alternatives range all the way from individual neurotic reactions, such as an inability to make any decision at all, to intellectual solutions which might lead to new social movements. Many of the baffling questions about the relationship between individual attitudes and social environment may be answered when these problems of cross-pressures and reactions to them are thoroughly and properly studied." P. F. Lazarsfeld, Bernard Berelson, and Hazel Gaudet, *The People's Choice* (New York: Columbia University Press, 1948, second edition), xxii.

18. Samuel Stouffer, "An analysis of conflicting social norms," *American Sociological Review*, 1949, 14, 707–717.

19. Since it is not germane to our chief purpose, we have made no effort throughout this paper to report the numerous technical steps taken by the Research Branch to determine the adequacy of their data. But readers of *The American Soldier* will be well aware of the diverse and often imaginative procedures adopted to cross-check each set of data. In the present case, for example, it is shown that the responses to this question were not merely a reflection of the soldiers' sentiments *subsequent* to induction. For "when asked of new recruits, whose report on their feelings about induction could not be colored by months or years of subsequent Army experience, the [same kind of] question discriminated significantly between recruits who *later* became psychoneurotics and other men." (I, 123n) This note is intended to emphasize, once and for all, that our summary of a research case does not at all reproduce those subtle and cumulative details which often lend weight to the data in hand. For these details, rather than the more general questions to which they give rise, a first-hand study of *The American Soldier* is necessary.

20. Thus, a current unpublished research in the sociology and social psychology of housing by R. K. Merton, P. J. S. West, and M. Jahoda includes a study of the comparative effectiveness of "primary environment of opinion" (constituted by the opinions of one's close associates) and of "secondary environment of opinion" (constituted by the opinions of those with whom one is not in close association). When these operate at cross-purposes, it appears that the primary environment does take some measure of precedence.

21. It may of course turn out that, under certain conditions, individuals extrapolate their knowledge of the situation of associates in a given social category to that social category at large. Or, it may develop that the situation of one's associates is accorded greater weight by the individual than the contrasting situation which he knows to obtain

in the social category at large. These are questions amenable to empirical research and salient for reference group theory.

22. Although the concept is after-the-fact of *data collection*, it was introduced early enough in the *analysis* to permit its use in suggesting types of tabulations which would otherwise not have been undertaken. From the interpretative standpoint, therefore, relative deprivation was not confined to use as an *ex post facto* conception.

23. The emphasis on *systematic* data is essential, for *The American Soldier* has abundant indications that *in many cases* assumed reference groups were indeed taken as a context of comparison. For example, their text includes remarks by overseas soldiers which clearly indicate that the soldiers back home are sometimes taken as a point of reference in assessing their own situation: "I think I've had my share being overseas over two years. That's plenty for any man . . . Let them USO boys get some of this chow once in a while, then they will know what it is to sleep in the mud with mosquitoes buzzing around them like a P-88." "We should have a chance to breathe a little fresh air for a while. But I guess you better keep them USO boys back there or there won't be any USO." "It is hard as hell to be here and read in every paper that comes from home where Pvt. Joe Dokes is home again on furlough after tough duty as a guard in Radio City." "We receive letters from soldiers who have not yet left the States and who are on their second furlough." (I, 188) These remarks also contain passing allusions to the source of information regarding the situation of the men back home: "read in every paper," "we receive letters," *etc.* But such telling anecdotal materials are properly enough not regarded as a basis for *systematic* analysis by the authors of *The American Soldier*.

24. A recent example of the possibility of now anticipating the need for data on reference group behavior is provided by the 1948 voting study in Elmira. Under a grant from the Rockefeller Foundation for the study of panel techniques in social research, a conference at Swarthmore on reference group concepts was arranged, with an eye to having materials bearings on these concepts introduced into the Elmira voting study. *The American Soldier* provides numerous further conceptions which can be similarly incorporated in further research. It is this process of an ongoing interplay between theory and empirical research which is overlooked by verdicts such as Glazer's that the concept of relative deprivation "cannot be refuted by facts." (See note 3 of this paper.) A theoretical concept emerging or developed in the course of one inquiry, if it has any empirical relevance at all, can then be utilized (and if defective, modified or nullified) in subsequent researches. If it is to be creative at all, research cannot be *confined* to the testing of predetermined hypotheses. New concepts and hypotheses emerge in the process of inquiry, and these become the basis for further inquiry. This, we take it, is precisely how continuity in science occurs. For a general statement of this view, see Merton, *Social Theory and Social Structure*, 3–16, 97–111.

25. A notable beginning is found in the pioneering study by Herbert H. Hyman, *The Psychology of Status*, Archives of Psychology, No. 269, 1942. Hyman sought to have his subjects report the groups or individuals which they had taken for comparison with their own status. This kind of direct questioning can of course elicit only the conscious and remembered frames of comparison. But the advancement of reference group theory has suffered by the general failure to follow up Hyman's suggestive lead on spontaneously emerging frames of group reference.

57

TVA and the Grassroots

Philip Selznick

Introduction: TVA and Democratic Planning

In this country we are very vain of our political institutions, which are singular in this, that they sprung, within the memory of living men, from the character and condition of the people, which they still express with sufficient fidelity. . . .

Emerson

Whatever the ultimate outcome, it is evident that modern society has already moved rather far into the age of control. It is an age marked by widening efforts to master a refractory industrial system. That a technique for control will emerge, that there is and will be planning, is hardly in question. What is more doubtful is the character and direction of the new instruments of intervention and constraint. For these have been born of social crisis, set out piecemeal as circumstances have demanded; they have not come to us as part of a broad and conscious vision. As a consequence, the foundations of a clear-cut choice between totalitarian and democratic planning have not been adequately laid; nor has the distinction been altogether clear between planning directed toward some acceptable version of the common good and planning for the effective maintenance of existing and emerging centers of privilege and power.

Democracy has to do with means, with instruments, with tools which define the relation between authority and the individual. In our time, new and inescapable tasks demand a choice among available means within the framework of increased governmental control. It is therefore especially important to examine those organizations which are proposed as contributions to the technique of democratic planning. An example of such a proposed contribution is the Tennessee Valley Authority.

On June 25, 1942, *The Times* (London) published a brief review of TVA under the heading "The Technique of Democratic Planning." *The Times*

Source: Philip Selznick, *TVA and the Grassroots*, (New York: Harper & Row, 1966 [Los Angeles: University of California Press, 1949]).

correspondent reported that he was impressed by the physical accomplishments of dam and power plant construction, but what interested him most was "the technique which the TVA had adopted with the deliberate aim of reconciling over-all planning with the values of democracy." Here *The Times* reflected what many feel to be the enduring significance of this much discussed government agency. The theme of democracy in government administration was also prominent in a widely distributed book, *TVA: Democracy on the March*, written by David E. Lilienthal, and in numerous speeches and pamphlets emanating from the Authority. In addition, much of the comment friendly to the agency has stressed its contribution to a new synthesis, one which would unite positive government – the welfare or service state – with a rigorous adherence to the principles of democracy.

What is this organization which is thought to embody an ideal so eagerly sought? What is the nature of this democratic technique? What are its implications and consequences? What will a close and critical study of the organization in action tell us about these problems? These questions have yet to be satisfactorily answered. To seek a partial answer, a study was undertaken, during 1942–1943, with attention focused primarily upon the Authority's "democratic" or "grass roots" method. This inquiry was based upon the assumption that no prior personal commitment to the TVA as a political symbol ought to interfere with a realistic examination. It was an inquiry which did not hesitate to seek out informal and unofficial sources of information. And it began with certain ideas about the nature of the administrative process which seem helpful in uncovering the underlying forces shaping leadership and policy.

The Tennessee Valley Authority was created by Congress in May, 1933, as a response to a long period of pressure for the disposition of government-owned properties at Muscle Shoals, Alabama. During the First World War, two nitrate plants and what was later known as Wilson Dam were constructed, at a cost of over $100,000,000. For the next fifteen years, final decision as to the future of these installations hung fire. The focal points of contention related to the production and distribution of fertilizer and electric power, and to the principle of government versus private ownership. Two presidential commissions and protracted congressional inquiries recorded the long debate. At last, with the advent of the Roosevelt administration in 1933, the government assumed responsibility for a general resolution of the major issues.

The TVA Act as finally approved was a major victory for those who favored the principle of government operation. The Muscle Shoals investment was to remain in public ownership, and this initial project was to be provided with new goals and to be vastly extended. A great public power project was envisioned, mobilizing the "by-product" of dams built for the purpose of flood control and navigation improvement on the Tennessee River and its tributaries. Control and operation of the nitrate properties, to be used for fertilizer production, was also authorized, although this aspect was subordinated in importance to electricity. These major powers – authority to construct dams, deepen the river channel produce and distribute electricity and fertilizer – were delegated by Congress to a corporation administered by a three-man board of directors.

If this had been all, the project would still have represented an important extension of government activity and responsibility. But what began as, and what was generally understood to be, primarily the solution of a problem of fertilizer and power emerged as an institution of far broader meaning. A new regional concept – the river basin as an integral unit – was given effect, so that a government agency was created which had a special responsibility neither national nor state-wide in scope. This offered a new dimension for the consideration of the role of government in the evolving federal system. At the same time, the very form of the agency established under the Act was a new departure. There was created a relatively autonomous public corporation free in important aspects from the normal financial and administrative controls exercised over federal organs. Further, and in one sense most important, a broad vision of regional resource development – in a word, planning – informed the conception, if not the actual powers, of the new organization.

The Message of the President requesting the TVA legislation did much to outline that perception: "It is clear," wrote Mr. Roosevelt, "that the Muscle Shoals development is but a small part of the potential public usefulness of the entire Tennessee River. Such use, if envisioned in its entirety, transcends mere power development: it enters the wide fields of flood control, soil erosion, afforestation, elimination from agricultural use of marginal lands, and distribution and diversification of industry. In short, this power development of war days leads logically to national planning for a complete river watershed involving many States and the future lives and welfare of millions. It touches and gives life to all forms of human concerns." To carry out this conception, the President recommended "legislation to create a Tennessee Valley Authority – a corporation clothed with the power of government but possessed of the flexibility and initiative of private enterprise. It should be charged with the broadest duty of planning for the proper use, conservation, and development of the natural resources of the Tennessee River drainage basin and its adjoining territory for the general social and economic welfare of the Nation."

This special regional focus and broad scope of the project have given it a character which rejects one of the major motifs of our time: the need for some sort of integral planning, especially in key problem areas. It is that character which has been caught up as a model for similar projects in other areas. For the uniqueness of TVA is not that it is a government-owned power business or conservation agency, but that it was given some responsibility for the unified development of the resources of a region.

Yet it must be said that although the agency and its program have symbolized concentrated effort and planning, in fact the TVA has had little direct authority to engage in large-scale regional planning. The powers delegated to it were for the most part specific in nature, related to the primary problems of good control, navigation, fertilizer, and power. In addition, authority to conduct studies and demonstrations of a limited nature, but directed toward general welfare objectives, was delegated to the President and by him to the Authority. This became the basis for some general surveys and demonstration work in forestry, local industrial development, community planning, and for work with cooperatives.

More important, however, is that the Act permitted such discretion in the execution of the primary purposes as would invite those in charge to recognize the social consequences of specific activities – such as the effect upon farm populations and urban communities of the creation of large reservoirs – and to assume responsibility for them. This assumption of responsibility invests the administration with an important planning function, though it is indirect and remains modifiable as circumstances may demand. In addition, there remained administrative freedom to devise methods of dealing with local people and institutions which would reflect the democratic process at work. Perhaps of equal importance is that the idea of planning associated with TVA accords this agency a central status in the consideration of the problems and the future of the Tennessee Valley region.

In the light of this weak delegation of broad planning powers, and the tendency of Congress to restrict developmental functions, it is probable that the significance of TVA in relation to democratic planning comes primarily from the infusion of specific tasks with a sense of social responsibility. In the purchase of lands, in the distribution of fertilizer and power, in personnel policy – in those functions which are a necessary part of the execution of its major and clearly delegated responsibilities – the TVA has normally taken account of the people of the area, with a view to adjusting immediate urgencies to long-term social policy. This, of course, is not the same as devising and executing a frontal plan for the reconstruction of the economy or institutions of an area. And yet, whichever view is emphasized – whether one conceives of TVA's limited regional planning as a portent of fuller ventures along that line, or whether one thinks of planning as simply an adjunct of specific responsibilities – we have something to learn from a study of the organization itself and of the methods developed in the execution of its tasks.

"Organization" and "method" are key words. Wherever we turn in considering the implications of a program for democracy these terms are inevitably involved. No democratic program can be unconcerned about the objectives of a course of action, especially as they affect popular welfare. But the crucial question for democracy is not what to strive for, but by what means to strive. And the question of means is one of what to do now and what to do next – and these are basic questions in politics.

If the problem of means is vital, it is also the most readily forgotten. "Results," "achievement," and "success" are heady words. They induce submission and consent, thus summoning rewards for diligence and labor – and they also enfeeble the intellect. For the results which most readily capture the imagination are external, colorful, concrete. They are the stated goals of action. Their achievement lends reality, wholesomeness, and stature to the enterprise as a whole.

But methods are more elusive. They have a corollary and incidental status. A viable enterprise is sustained in the public eye by its goals, not its methods. Means are variable and expedient. Their history is forgotten or excused. Here again the concrete and colourful win easiest attention. Where incorrect methods leave a visible residue – a rubbled city or wasted countryside, – then methods may gain notice. But those means which have long-run implications for cultural values, such as democracy, are readily and extensively ignored.

When we speak of methods, we speak in the same breath of instruments. Policies, decisions as to "how to proceed," require execution. Execution in turn implies a technology. We are familiar with the kind of technology which includes machines and tools of all sorts, handled and manipulated in more or less obvious ways. We are even reasonably familiar with the technology of economic and military organization, geared to the achievement of technical objectives, qualified and informed by the criteria of efficiency. But when we move into that area of technology which is related to the creation, defense, or reintegration of values, such as democracy, we find ourselves less assured. Yet the significance of this noneconomic technology, under the conditions of mass society and cultural disintegration, is of primary importance for whatever we may wish to do about that vague but demanding reality which we call our "way of life." Propaganda agencies, mass parties, unions, educational systems, churches, and governmental structures have a common aspect in that, more or less directly, they work upon and seriously affect the evolving values, the spirit, of contemporary society. Furthermore, there is a growing tendency for this effect to be conscious, to become an ordered technology available to those who have a stake in changing sentiment or social policy.

One of the pervasive obstacles to the understanding and even the inspection of this technology is ideology or official doctrine. By the very nature of their function, all those forces which are concerned about the evolution of value-impregnated methods, or public opinion itself, have a formal program, a set of ideas for public consumption. These ideas provide a view of the stated goals of the various organizations – political or industrial democracy, or decentralization, or the like – as well as of the methods which are deemed crucial for the achievement of these goals. It is naturally considered desirable for the attention of observers to be directed toward these avowed ideas, so that they may receive a view of the enterprise consistent with the conception of its leadership. All this in the often sincere conviction that precisely this view is in accord with the realities of the situation and best conveys the meaning and significance of the project under inspection.

However much we may be impressed by what a group says about its methods or its work, there is adequate justification for uneasiness and doubt. This doubt has its source in our general understanding of the persistent tendency for words to outrun deeds, for official statement and doctrine to raise a halo over the events and activities themselves. That this is a natural disposition among responsible men is well understood, and a gap of some sort between the idea and the act is normally expected. But what is less well understood, or at least less generally applied to objects of public esteem, is the tendency for ideas to reflect something more than enthusiasm or more or less pardonable pride. The functions of a doctrine may be more subtle and more significant, related to the urgent needs of leadership and to the security of the organization itself. Such functions, when relevant, cast a deeper shadow and indicate the need for more searching questions. In Part I of this study, we have critically analyzed TVA's official doctrine in relation to democratic planning – the policy of grass-roots administration as a contribution to democracy. The analysis points to underlying issues and problems not directly evident when we speak of the normal and anticipated gap between avowed statement and actual practice.

Though official statements and theories are important, an undue concentration upon what men say diverts attention from what they do. This is especially true with respect to the methods utilized in the execution of a program, for these are particularly difficult to view realistically. It is often sufficiently troublesome to attain a clear picture of the formal, stated methods in use, without pressing inquiry as to the less obvious but vital informal behavior of key participants. Yet it is precisely into the realm of actual behavior and its significance for evolving structures and values that we must move if this kind of inquiry is to realize its possibilities.

The instruments of planning are vitally relevant to the nature of the democratic process. The TVA is many things, but most significant for our purposes is its status as a social instrument. It is this role as instrument with which this study is directly concerned. Or, to emphasize another word, it is TVA as an organization to which our attention is directed. Thus it is not dams or reservoirs or power houses or fertilizer as such, but the nature of the Authority as an ordered group of working individuals, as a living institution, which is under scrutiny.

In searching out organizational behavior and problems as keys to understanding the implications of TVA for democratic planning, we are entering a field of inquiry which probes at the heart of the democratic dilemma. If democracy as a method of social action has any single problem, it is that of enforcing the responsibility of leadership or bureaucracy. A faith in majorities does not eliminate the necessity for governance by individuals and small groups. Wherever there is organization, whether formally democratic or not, there is a split between the leader and the led, between the agent and the initiator. The phenomenon of abdication to bureaucratic directorates in corporations, in trade unions, in parties, and in cooperatives is so widespread that it indicates a fundamental weakness of democracy. For this trend has the consequence of thrusting issues theoretically decided by a polity into the field of bureaucratic decision.

The term "bureaucracy" has an invidious connotation, signifying arbitrary power, impersonality, red tape. But if we recognize that all administrative officials are bureaucrats, the bishop no less than the tax collector, then we may be able to understand the general nature of the problem, separating it from the personal qualities or motives of the individuals involved. Officials, like other individuals, must take heed of the conditions of their existence. Those conditions are, for officials, organizational: in attempting to exercise some control over their own work and future they are offered the opportunity of manipulating personnel, funds, and symbols. Among the many varied consequences of this manipulation, the phenomena of inefficiency and arbitrariness are ultimately among the least significant. The difference between officials and ordinary members of an organized group is that the former have a special access to and power over the machinery of the organization; while those outside the bureaucratic ranks lack that access and power.

If we are to comprehend these bureaucratic machines, which must play an indispensable role in any planning venture, it is essential to think of an organization as a dynamic conditioning field which effectively shapes the behavior of those who are attempting to remain at the helm. We can best understand the behavior of officials when we are able to trace that behavior to the needs and structure of the organization as a living social institution.

The important point about organizations is that, though they are tools, each nevertheless has a life of its own. Though formally subordinated to some outside authority, they universally resist complete control. The use of organizational instrumentalities is always to some degree precarious, for it is virtually impossible to enforce automatic response to the desires or commands of those who must employ them. This general recalcitrance is recognized by all who participate in the organizational process. It is this recalcitrance, with its corollary instability, which is in large measure responsible for the enormous amount of continuous attention which organizational machinery requires. There are good reasons, readily grasped, for this phenomenon.

The internal life of any organization tends to become, but never achieves, a closed system. There are certain needs generated by organization itself which command the attention and energies of leading participants. The moment an organization is begun, problems arise from the need for some continuity of policy and leadership, for a homogeneous outlook, for the achievement of continuous consent and participation on the part of the ranks. These and other needs create an intricate system of relationships and activities, formal and informal, which have primarily an internal relevance. Thus leadership is necessarily turned in upon itself. But at the same time, no organization subsists in a vacuum. Large or small, it must pay some heed to the consequences of its own activities (and even existence) for other groups and forces in the community. These forces will insist upon an accounting, and may in self-defense demand a share in the determination of policy. Because of this outside pressure, from many varied sources, the attention of any bureaucracy must be turned outward, in defending the organization against possible encroachment or attack.

These general considerations, which have been stated here in a summary way, should lead to a more discerning study of any administrative agency. They direct us (1) to seek the underlying implications of the official doctrine of the agency, if it has one; (2) to avoid restriction to the formal structure of the organization, as that may be outlined in statutes, administrative directives, and organization charts; and (3) to observe the interaction of the agency with other institutions in its area of operation. Throughout, a search for the internally relevant in organizational behavior, especially that which is related to self-defensive needs, is a primary tool of such analysis.[1]

It will probably bear emphasis that the significance of TVA for democratic planning lies not so much in its program, or in its accomplishments, as in its methods and in its nature as an organization. Even though its planning powers are limited, the TVA does represent an experiment, an adventure in executing broad social responsibilities for the development of a unified area. Furthermore, its type of organization is proffered as a model for governmental planning in other areas. This point has been clearly recognized within TVA itself:

> Few of the activities of TVA are unique as public responsibilities. The Government of the United States has been constructing waterways and building works for flood control for more than a century. State and Federal agencies have engaged in technical research, and surveys of mineral and forestry resources have been carried on with public funds for many years. The TVA is not the first instance in which the Federal Government has sold electric power. Aid to and stimulation of business opportunities in industrial development, employment, farming, and other fields has become a familiar role of Government, State and National.
>
> It is in the integration and the correlation on a regional basis of these various activities under a single, unified management that the Tennessee Valley Authority represents a pioneer undertaking of government. For the first time a President and Congress created an agency which was directed to view the problems of a region as a whole.[2]

If the power granted to the Authority was not sufficient fully to execute that broad responsibility, still the vision has remained. It is the conception of an administrative instrument created to fulfill necessary planning functions within the framework of democratic values.

If TVA as instrument is the focus of attention, and if we are prepared to think of the Authority as a living social organization, we may expect that in one way or another the Authority will have been caught up in and shaped by its institutional environment. This expectation becomes especially relevant as we note (1) the TVA's official avowal of a special democratic relation to certain local institutions "close to the people," a doctrine which will be discussed in detail below; and (2) that TVA did not arise out of the expressed desires of the local area, and consequently was faced with a special problem of adjustment. Each of these points lends weight to the anticipation that in the Authority's relation to its own grass roots we may find significant material of general interest to those who wish to learn the lessons of the TVA experience.

Given such an anticipation, the problem for this inquiry became one of finding a significant vantage point from which to examine this grassroots relationship. The question thus posed required some sort of theory, a set of ideas which could point a way to the most vital aspects of the situation. The theory which seemed to make sense in the light of a general understanding of the materials was so formulated as to bring together in a single over-all analysis (1) the avowed contribution of TVA to democratic planning, through a grass-roots method of executing its responsibilities; (2) the self-defensive behavior of the organization as it faced the need to adjust itself to the institutions of its area of operation; (3) the consequences for policy and action which must follow upon any attempt to adjust an organization to local centers of interest and power. Put in a few words, this involved the hypothesis that the Authority's grass-roots policy as doctrine and as action must be understood as related to the need of the organization to come to terms with certain local and national interests; and that in actual practice this procedure resulted in commitments which had restrictive consequences for the policy and behavior of the Authority itself.

In order to handle this problem most effectively, it has been found necessary to introduce a concept which, while not new, is somewhat unfamiliar. This is the idea of *cooptation*[3] – often the realistic core of avowedly democratic procedures. To risk a definition: *cooptation is the process of absorbing new elements into the leadership or policy determining structure of an organization as a means of averting threats to its stability or existence.* With the help of this concept, we are enabled more closely and more rigorously to specify the relation between TVA and some important local institutions and thus uncover an important aspect of the real meaning and significance of the Authority's grass-roots policy. At the same time, it is clear that the idea of cooptation plunges us into the field of bureaucratic behavior as that is related to such democratic ideals as "local participation."

Cooptation tells us something about the process by which an institutional environment impinges itself upon an organization and effects changes in its leadership, structure, or policy. Cooptation may be formal or informal, depending upon the specific problem to be solved.

Formal cooptation. – When there is a need for the organization to publicly absorb new elements, we shall speak of formal cooptation. This involves the establishment of openly avowed and formally ordered relationships. Appointments to official posts are made, contracts are signed, new organizations are established – all signifying participation in the process of decision and administration. There are two general conditions which lead an organization to resort to formal cooptation, though they are closely related:

1. When the legitimacy of the authority of a governing group or agency is called into question. Every group or organization which attempts to exercise control must also attempt to win the consent of the governed. Coercion may be utilized at strategic points, but it is not effective as an enduring instrument. One means of winning consent is to coopt into the leadership or organization elements which in some way reflect the sentiment or possess the confidence of the relevant public or mass and which will lend respectability or legitimacy to the organs of control and thus reestablish the stability of formal authority. This device is widely used, and in many different contexts. It is met in colonial countries, where the organs of alien control reaffirm their legitimacy by coopting native leaders into the colonial administration. We find it in the phenomenon of "crisis-patriotism" wherein normally disfranchised groups are temporarily given representation in the councils of government in order to win their solidarity in a time of national stress. Cooptation has been considered by the United States Army in its study of proposals to give enlisted personnel representation in the courts-martial machinery – a clearly adaptive response to stresses made explicit during World War II. The "unity" parties of totalitarian states are another form of cooptation; company unions or some employee representation plans in industry are still another. In each of these examples, the response of formal authority (private or public, in a large organization or a small one) is an attempt to correct a state of imbalance by formal measures. It will be noted, moreover, that what is shared is the responsibility for power rather than power itself.

2. When the need to invite participation is essentially administrative, that is, when the requirements of ordering the activities of a large organization or state make it advisable to establish the forms of self-government. The problem here is not one of decentralizing decision but rather of establishing orderly and reliable mechanisms for reaching a client public or citizenry. This is the "constructive" function of trade unions in great industries where the unions become effective instruments for the elimination of absenteeism or the attainment of other efficiency objectives. This is the function of self-government committees in housing projects or concentration camps, as they become reliable channels for the transmission of managerial directives. Usually, such devices also function to share responsibility and thus to bolster the legitimacy of established authority. Thus any given act of formal cooptation will tend to fulfill both the political function of defending legitimacy and the administrative function of establishing reliable channels for communication and direction.

In general, the use of formal cooptation by a leadership does not envision the transfer of actual power. The forms of participation are emphasized but action is channeled so as to fulfill the administrative functions while preserving the locus of significant decision in the hands of the initiating group. The concept of formal cooptation will be utilized primarily in the analysis of TVA's relation to the voluntary associations established to gain local participation in the administration of the Authority's programs.

Informal cooptation. – Cooptation may be, however, a response to the pressure of specific centers of power within the community. This is not primarily a matter of the sense of legitimacy or of a general and diffuse lack of confidence. Legitimacy and confidence may be well established with relation to the general public, yet organized forces which are able to threaten the formal authority may effectively shape its structure and policy. The organization faced with its institutional environment, or the leadership faced with its ranks, must take into account these outside elements. They may be brought into the leadership or policy-determining structure, may be given a place as a recognition of and concession to the resources they can independently command. The representation of interests through administrative constituencies is a typical example of this process. Or, within an organization, individuals upon whom the group is dependent for funds or other resources may insist upon and receive a share in the determination of policy. This type of cooptation is typically expressed in informal terms, for the problem is not one of responding to a state of imbalance with respect to the "people as a whole" but rather one of meeting the pressure of specific individuals or interest groups which are in a position to enforce demands. The latter are interested in the substance of power and not necessarily in its forms. Moreover, an open acknowledgment of capitulation to specific interests may itself undermine the sense of legitimacy of the formal authority within the community. Consequently, there is a positive pressure to refrain from explicit recognition of the relationship established. This concept will be utilized in analyzing the underlying meaning of certain formal methods of cooperation initiated in line with the TVA's grass-roots policy.

Cooptation reflects a state of tension between formal authority and social power. This authority is always embodied in a particular structure and leadership, but social power itself has to do with subjective and objective factors which control the loyalties and potential manipulability of the community. Where the formal authority or leadership reflects real social power, its stability is assured. On the other hand, when it becomes divorced from the sources of social power its continued existence is threatened. This threat may arise from the sheer alienation of sentiment or because other leaderships control the sources of social power. Where a leadership has been accustomed to the assumption that its constituents respond to it as individuals, there may be a rude awakening when organization of those constituents creates nucleuses of strength which are able to effectively demand a sharing of power.

The significance of cooptation for organizational analysis is not simply that there is a change in or a broadening of leadership, and that this is an adaptive response, but also *that this change is consequential for the character and role of the organization or governing body.* Cooptation results in some constriction of the field of choice available to the organization or leadership in question. The character of the coopted elements will necessarily shape the modes of action available to the group which has won adaptation at the price of commitment to outside elements. In other words, if it is true that the TVA has, whether as a defensive or as an idealistic measure, absorbed local elements into its policy determining structure, we should expect to find that this process has had an effect upon the evolving character of the Authority itself. From the viewpoint of the initiators of the project, and of its public supporters, the force and direction of this effect may be completely unanticipated.

The important consideration is that the TVA's choice of methods could not be expected to be free of the normal dilemmas of action. If the sentiment of the people (or its organized expression) is conservative, democratic forms may require a blunting of social purpose. A perception of the details of this tendency is all important for the attempt to bind together planning and democracy. Planning is always positive – for the fulfillment of some program, – but democracy may negate its execution. This dilemma requires an understanding of the possible unanticipated consequences which may ensue when positive social policy is coupled with a commitment to democratic procedure. The description and analysis which follows, in tracing the consequences of TVA's grass-roots policy for the role and character of the organization, may cast some light upon that problem.[4]

Conclusion: Guiding Principles and Interpretation – A Summary

The entire science considered as a body of formulae having coherent relations to one another is just a system of possible predicates – that is, of possible standpoints or methods to be employed in qualifying some particular experience whose nature or meaning is unclear to us.[5]

John Dewey

It is believed that the interpretation set forth in the preceding chapters provides a substantially correct picture of a significant aspect of the TVA's grass-roots policy at work. Far from remote, or divorced from what is considered pertinent by informed participants, the analysis reflects what is obvious to those who "know the score" in TVA.[6] Of course, this exposition is more explicit and systematic, and the relevant implications are more fully drawn out, but in main outline it can come as no surprise to leading officials of the Authority. This is not to suggest that there are are no errors of detail, perhaps even of important detail. The nature of this kind of research precludes any full assurance on that. While much of the material is derived from documentary (though largely unpublished) sources, much is also based upon interviews with members of the organization and with those nonmembers who were in a position to be informed. Care was taken to rely upon only those who had an intimate, as opposed to hearsay, acquaintance with the events and personalities involved. Those who are familiar with the shadowland of maneuver in large organizations will appreciate the difficulties, and the extent to which ultimate reliability depends upon the ability of the investigator to make the necessary discriminations. They will also recognize the need for insight and imagination if the significance of behavior, as it responds to structural constraints, is to be grasped. All this involves considerable risk.

If the use of personal interviews, gossip channels, working papers,[7] and participation[8] opens the way for error, it remains, however, the only way in which this type of sociological research can be carried on. A careful investigator can minimize error by such means as checking verbal statements against the documentary records appraising the consistency of information supplied to him, and avoiding reliance on any single source. On the other hand, he will not restrict his data to that which is publicly acknowledged.

The possibilities of factual error, however great, are probably less important as hazard than the theoretical orientation of the study. To be sure, an empirical analysis of a particular organization, of its doctrine, of a phase of policy in action, of its interaction with other structures, was our objective. But in order to trace the dynamics of these events, it has been necessary to attempt a reconstruction, which is to say, a theory, of the conditions and forces which appear to have shaped the behavior of key participants.

Theoretical inquiry, when it is centered upon a particular historical structure or event, is always hazardous. This is due to the continuous tension between concern for a full grasp and interpretation of the materials under investigation as history, and special concern for the induction of abstract and general relations. Abstractions deal harshly with "the facts," choosing such emphases and highlighting such characteristics as may seem factitious, or at least distorted, to those who have a stake in an historically well-rounded apprehension of the events themselves. This is especially true in the analysis of individual personalities or social institutions, for these demand to be treated as wholes, with reference to their own central motives and purposes, rather than as occasions for the development of theoretical systems. This general, and perhaps inescapable, source of misunderstanding being admitted, let us review the concepts which have been used to order the materials of our inquiry.

Sociological Directives

This volume has been subtitled "A Study in the Sociology of Formal Organization." This means that the inquiry which it reports was shaped by sociological directives, more especially by a frame of reference for the theory of organization.[9] These directives are operationally relevant without, however, functioning as surrogates for inductive theory itself. That is, while they provide criteria of significance, they do not tell us what is significant; while they provide tools for discrimination, they do not demand any special conclusions about the materials under investigation.[10] The fundamental elements of this frame of reference are these:

1. All formal organizations are molded by forces tangential to their rationally ordered structures and stated goals. Every formal organization – trade union, political party, army, corporation, etc. – attempts to mobilize human and technical resources as means for the achievement of its ends. However, the individuals within the system tend to resist being treated as means. They interact as wholes, bringing to bear their own special problems and purposes; moreover, the organization is imbedded in an institutional matrix and is therefore subject to pressures upon it from its environment, to which some general adjustment must be made. As a result, the organization may be significantly viewed as an adaptive social structure, facing problems which arise simply because it exists as an organization in an institutional environment, independently of the special (economic, military, political) goals which called it into being.

2. It follows that there will develop an informal structure within the organization which will reflect the spontaneous efforts of individuals and subgroups to control the conditions of their existence. There will also develop informal lines of communication and control to and from other organizations within the environment. It is to these informal relations and structures that the attention of the sociologist will be primarily directed. He will look upon the formal structure, e.g., the official chain of command, as the special environment within and in relation to which the informal structure is built. He will search out the evolution of formal relations out of the informal ones.[11]

3. The informal structure will be at once indispensable to and consequential for the formal system of delegation and control itself. Wherever command over the responses of individuals is desired, some approach in terms of the spontaneous organization of loyalty and interest will be necessary. In practice this means that the informal structure will be useful to the leadership and effective as a means of communication and persuasion. At the same time, it can be anticipated that some price will be paid in the shape of a distribution of power or adjustment of policy.

4. Adaptive social structures are to be analyzed in structural functional terms.[12] This means that contemporary and variable behavior is related to a presumptively stable system of needs[13] and mechanisms. Every such structure has a set of basic needs and develops systematic means of self-defense. Observable organizational behavior is deemed explained within this frame of reference when it may be interpreted (and the interpretation confirmed) as a response to specified needs. Where significant, the adaptation is dynamic in the sense that the utilization of self-defensive mechanisms results in structural transformations of the organization itself. The needs in question are organizational, not individual, and include: the security of the organization as a whole in relation to social forces in its environment; the stability of the lines of authority and communication; the stability of informal relations within the organization; the continuity of policy and of the sources of its determination; a homogeneity of outlook with respect to the meaning and role of the organization.

5. Analysis is directed to the internal relevance of organizational behavior. The execution of policy is viewed in terms of its effect upon the organization itself and its relations with others. This will tend to make the analysis inadequate as a report of program achievement, since that will be deemphasized in the interests of the purely organizational consequences of choice among alternatives in discretionary action.

6. Attention being focused on the structural conditions which influence behavior, we are directed to emphasize constraints, the limitation of alternatives imposed by the system upon its participants. This will tend to give pessimistic overtones to the analysis, since such factors as good will and intelligence will be deemphasized.

7. As a consequence of the central status of constraint, tensions and dilemmas will be highlighted. Perhaps the most general source of tension and paradox in this context may be expressed as the recalcitrance of the tools of action. Social action is always mediated by human structures, which generate new centers of need and power and interpose themselves between the actor and his goal. Commitments to others are indispensable in action: at the same time, the process of commitment results in tensions which have always to be overcome.

These principles define a frame of reference, a set of guiding ideas which at once justify and explain the kind of selection which the sociologist will make in approaching organizational data. As we review some of the key concepts utilized in this study, the operational relevance of this frame of reference will be apparent.

Unanticipated Consequences in Organized Action

The foregoing review of leading ideas directs our attention to the meaning of events. This leads us away from the problem of origins.[14] For the meaning of an act may be spelled out in its consequences, and these are not the same as the factors which called it into being. The meaning of any given administrative policy will thus require an excursion into the realm of its effects. These effects ramify widely, and those we select for study may not always seem relevant to the formal goals in terms of which the policy was established. Hence the search for meanings may seem to go rather far afield, from the viewpoint of those concerned only with the formal program. Any given event, such as the establishment of a large army cantonment, may have a multitude of effects in different directions: upon the economy of the area, upon the morals of its inhabitants, upon the pace of life, and so on. The free-lance theorist may seek out the significance of the event in almost any set of consequences. But in accordance with the principle stated above, we may distinguish the random search for meanings which can be, at one extreme, an aesthetic interest – from the inquiry of the organizational analyst. The latter likewise selects consequences, but his frame of reference constrains his view: it is his task to trace such consequences as redound upon the organization in question; that is, such effects as have an internal relevance. Thus, only those consequences of the establishment of the army cantonment in a given area which result in adjustments of policy or structure in the administration of the cantonment will be relevant.

There is an obvious and familiar sense in which consequences are related to action: the articulation of means and ends demands that we weigh the consequences of alternative courses of action. Here consequences are anticipated. But it is a primary function of sociological inquiry to uncover systematically the sources of unanticipated consequence in purposive action.[15] This follows from the initial proposition in our frame of reference: "All formal organizations are molded by forces tangential to their rationally ordered structures and stated goals" (p. 251, above). Hence the notion of unanticipated consequence is a key analytical tool: where unintended effects occur, there is a presumption, though no assurance,[16] that sociologically identifiable forces are at work.

There are two logically fundamental sources of unanticipated consequence in social action, that is, two conditions which define the inherent predisposition for unanticipated consequences to occur:

1. *The limiting function of the end-in-view.* – A logically important but sociologically insignificant source of unanticipated consequence exists because the aim of action limits the perception of its ramified consequences.[17] This is legitimate and necessary, for not all consequences are relevant to the aim. But here there arises a persistent dilemma. This very necessity to "keep your eye on the ball" – which demands the construction of a rational system explicitly relating means and ends – will restrain the actor from taking account of those consequences which indirectly shape the means and ends of policy. Because of the necessarily abstract and selective character of the formal criteria of judgment, there will always be a minimum residue of unanticipated consequence.[18]

2. *Commitment as a basic mechanism in the generation of unanticipated consequences.* – The sociologically significant source of unanticipated consequences inherent in the organizational process may be summed up in the concept of "commitment." This term has been used throughout this study to focus attention upon the structural conditions which shape organizational behavior. This is in line with the sociological directive, stated above, that constraints imposed by the system will be emphasized. A commitment in social action is an enforced line of action; it refers to decision dictated by the force of circumstance with the result that the free or scientific adjustment of means and ends is effectively limited. The commitment may be to goals, as where the existence of an organization in relation to a client public depends on the fulfillment of certain objectives;[19] or, less obviously, to means, derived from the recalcitrant nature of the tools at hand. The commitments generated by the use of self-activating and recalcitrant tools are expressed in the proliferation of unintended consequences.[20]

The types of commitment in organizational behavior identify the conditions under which a high frequency of unanticipated consequences may be expected to occur:

i) *Commitments enforced by uniquely organizational imperatives.* – An organizational system, whatever the need or intent which called it into being, generates imperatives derived from the need to maintain the system. We can say that once having taken the organizational road we are committed to action which will fulfill the requirements of order, discipline, unity, defense, and consent. These imperatives may demand measures of adaptation unforeseen by the initiators of the action, and may, indeed, result in a deflection of their original goals. Thus the tendency to work toward organizational unity will commit the organization as a whole to a policy originally relevant to only a part of the program. This becomes especially true where a unifying doctrine is given definite content by one subgroup: in order to preserve its special interpretation the subgroup presses for the extension of that interpretation to the entire organization so that the special content may be institutionalized.[21]

ii) *Commitments enforced by the social character of the personnel.* – The human tools of action come to an organization shaped in special but systematic ways. Levels of aspiration and training, social ideals, class interest – these and similar factors will have molded the character of the personnel. This will make staff members resistant to demands which are inconsistent with their accustomed views and habits; the freedom of choice of the employer will be restricted, and he will find it necessary in some measure to conform to the received views and habits of the personnel. Thus, in recruiting, failure to take into account initial commitments induced by special social origins will create a situation favorable to the generation of unanticipated consequences. The TVA's agricultural leadership brought with it ideological and organizational commitments which influenced over-all policy. This was a basically uncontrolled element in the organization. It is noteworthy that where the character of any organization is self-consciously controlled, recruitment is rigidly qualified by the criterion of social (class, familial, racial) origin.

iii) *Commitments enforced by institutionalization.* – Because organizations are social systems, goals or procedures tend to achieve an established value-impregnated status. We say that they become institutionalized. Commitment to established patterns is generated, thus again restricting choice and enforcing special lines of conduct. The attempt to commit an organization to some course of action utilizes this principle when it emphasizes the creation of an established policy, or other forms of precedent. Further, the tendency of established relations and procedures to persist and extend themselves, will create the unintended consequence of committing the organization to greater involvement than provided for in the initial decision to act.[22] Where policy becomes institutionalized as doctrine, unanalyzed elements will persist, and effective behavior will be framed in terms of immediate necessities. An official doctrine whose terms are not operationally relevant will be given content in action, but this content will be informed by the special interests and problems of those to whom delegation is made. Hence doctrinal formulations will tend to reinforce the inherent hazard of delegation.[23]

A variation of this situation occurs when the role of participants comes to overshadow in importance the achievement of formal goals. Action then becomes irresponsible, with respect to the formal goals, as in the "fanatical" behavior of the TVA agriculturists.[24]

iv) *Commitments enforced by the social and cultural environment.* – Any attempt to intervene in history will, if it is to do more than comment upon events, find it necessary to conform to some general restraints imposed from without. The organizers of this attempt are committed to using forms of intervention consistent with the going social structure and cultural patterns. Those who ascend to power must face a host of received problems; shifts in public opinion will demand the reformulation of doctrine; the rise of competing organizations will have to be faced; and so on. The institutional context of organizational decision, when not taken into account, will result in unanticipated consequences. Thus intervention in a situation charged with conflict will mean that contending forces will weigh the consequences of that intervention for their own battle lines. The intervening organization must therefore qualify decision in terms of an outside controversy into which it is drawn despite itself. More obviously, the existence of centers of power and interest in the social environment will set up resistances to, or accept and shape to some degree, the program of the organization.

v) *Commitments enforced by the centers of interest generated in the course of action.* – The organizational process continuously generates subordinate and allied groupings whose leaderships come to have a stake in the organizational status quo. This generation of centers of interest is inherent in the act of delegation. The latter derives its precarious quality from the necessity to permit discretion in the execution of function or command. But in the exercise of discretion there is a tendency for decisions to be qualified by the special goals and problems of those to whom delegation is made. Moreover, in the discretionary behavior of a section of the apparatus, action is taken in the name of the organization as a whole; the latter may then be committed to a policy or course of action which was not anticipated by its formal program. In other words, the lack of executive control over the tangential informal goals of individuals and subgroups within an organization tends to divert it from its initial path. This holds true whether delegation is to members and parts of a single organization, or to other organizations, as in the TVA's relation to the land-grant colleges.

These types of commitment create persistent tensions or dilemmas.[25] In a sense, they set the problems of decision and control, for we have identified here the key points at which organizational control breaks down. Operationally, a breakdown of control is evidenced in the generation of observable unanticipated consequences. This is the same as to say that significant possibilities inherent in the situation have not been taken into account. The extension of control, with concomitant minimization of unintended consequence, is achieved as and if the frame of reference for theory and action points the way to the significant forces at work.

The problems indicated here are perennial because they reflect the interplay of more or less irreconcilable commitments: to the goals and needs of the organization and at the same time to the special demands of the tools or means at hand. Commitment to the tools of action is indispensable; it is of the nature of these tools to be dynamic and self activating; yet the pursuit of the goals which initiated action demands continuous effort to control the instruments it has generated. This is a general source of tension in all action mediated by human, and especially organizational, tools.

The systematized commitments of an organization define its character. Day-to-day decision, relevant to the actual problems met in the translation of policy into action, create precedents, alliances, effective symbols, and personal loyalties which transform the organization from a profane, manipulable instrument into something having a sacred status and thus resistant to treatment simply as a means to some external goal. That is why organizations are often cast aside when new goals are sought.

The analysis of commitment is thus an effective tool for making explicit the structural factors relevant to decision in organized action. Attention is directed to the concrete process of choice, selecting those factors in the environment of decision which limit alternatives and enforce uniformities of behavior. When we ask, "To what are we committed?" we are speaking of the logic of action, not of contractual obligations freely assumed. So long as goals are given, and the impulse to act persists, there will be a series of enforced lines of action demanded by the nature of the tools at hand. These commitments may lead to unanticipated consequences resulting in a deflection of original goals.[26]

Notes

1. It appears that this institutional approach (not, of course, original with the author) to the study of administrative organization may be the avenue to an enlargement of the horizon of inquiry in this field. In a sense, this approach and this study are a response to such criticism as that voiced by Donald Morrison in his review of the series, *Case Reports in Public Administration*: "To put the matter succinctly, the subject-matter of public administration has been defined so as to leave a no-man's land of significant problems, flanked on one side by the students of administration and on the other by political theorists. The problems thus isolated have their origin in the fact that in its fundamental aspect administration is governance. . . . One such problem, perhaps the most urgent, is to develop and strengthen ways of insuring that government by the bureaucracy does not destroy the democratic pattern of our society. Unless it is assumed that such insurance lies in the perfection of organizational structure and techniques of fiscal and personnel management, the present series of case studies does not deal with

this matter. Many persons believe that the TVA experiment is suggestive of ways of democratizing bureaucratic government. Ten TVA studies are published in *Case Reports*, but none deals with the integration of the TVA program into the social and economic life of the area" (*Public Administration Review*, V, 1 [Winter, 1945], 85).

2. "The Widening of Economic Opportunity through TVA," pamphlet adapted from an address by David E. Lilienthal, Director, TVA, at Columbia University, New York, N. Y., January, 1940 (Washington: Government Printing Office, 1940), p. 15.

3. With some modifications, the following statement of the concept of cooptation is a repetition of that presented in the author's "Foundations of the Theory of Organization," *American Sociological Review*, XIII, 1 (February, 1948), pp. 33-35. For a further discussion of cooptation see, Philip Selznick, *TVA and the Grassroots*, (New York: Harper & Row, 1966), pp. 259–261.

4. The notion of "unanticipated consequence" referred to in this section is central to this study. See above, pp. 143–147, for a theoretical statement of the problem.

5. John Dewey, *Problems of Men* (New York: Philosophical Library, 1946), p. 221.

6. Although responsibility for the analysis rests solely with the author, it should be emphasized that this study was made possible by the willingness of TVA to make its records and personnel available. This is a happy precedent which we may hope will be followed by other organizations, public and private.

7. Some of the materials quoted in the study are unofficial in the sense that they would be vigorously edited before receiving even the public status of a memorandum sent to another department within TVA. This would be so with comparable documents in any large organization, public or private.

8. The author spent most of his year's stay at TVA in daily contact with personnel of the agency. A number of weeks was spent in intensive contact with extension service personnel in the field.

9. For a fuller statement than the summary which follows see Philip Selznick, "Foundations of the Theory of Organization," *American Sociological Review*, XIII (February, 1948).

10. Thus, while approaching his materials within a guiding frame of reference, the author was not committed by this framework to any special hypothesis about the actual events. Indeed, he began his work with the hypothesis that informally the grass roots policy would mean domination by TVA because of its resources, energy, and program. After the first two months in the field, however, this hypothesis was abandoned as a major illuminating notion.

11. For discussion of informal organization, see F. J. Roethlisberger and W. J. Dickson, *Management and the Worker* (Cambridge: Harvard University Press, 1941), pp. 524 ff; also Chester I. Barnard, *The Functions of the Executive* (Cambridge: Harvard University Press, 1938), chap. ix; Wilbert E. Moore, *Industrial Relations and the Social Order* (New York: The Macmillan Co., 1946), chap. xv.

12. See Talcott Parsons, "The Present Position and Prospects of Systematic Theory in Sociology," in George Gurvitch and Wilbert E. Moore (eds.), *Twentieth Century Sociology* (New York: Philosophical Library, 1945).

13. As Robert K. Merton has pointed out to the author, the concept of "basic needs" in organizational analysis may be open to objections similar to those against the concept of instinct. To be sure, the needs require independent demonstration; they should be theoretically grounded independently of imputations from observed responses. However, we may use the notion of "organizational need" if we understand that it refers

to stable systems of variables which, with respect to many changes in organizational structure and behavior, are independent.

14. In terms of origins, the TVA's policy – though not the grass-roots doctrine *qua* doctrine – of channeling its agricultural program through the land-grant colleges of the Valley states may be adequately referred to such factors as the nature of the formal agricultural program, the resources available for its implementation, and the administrative rationale which seemed conclusive to leading participants. Moreover, these factors may sustain the continued existence of the policy, and it may therefore seem superfluous when extraneous factors are brought in and somewhat tangential explanations are offered. But when we direct our attention to the meaning of the policy in terms of certain indirect but internally relevant consequences – as for the role of TVA in the agricultural controversy, – we have begun to recast our observation of the policy (taken as a set of events) itself. We are then concerned not with the question, "how did the grass-roots policy come into being?" but with the question, "what are the implications of the grass-roots policy for the organizational position and character of TVA?"

15. Consequences emancipated from the viewpoint of the formal structure are not necessarily undesired. On the contrary, the result may be a satisfactory adjustment to internal and external circumstances, upon which the leadership may find it convenient to declare that the resulting were actually intended, though close analysis might show that this is actually a rationalization. In this type of unintended consequence, some need is fulfilled. The same unintended consequence may fulfill a need for a part of the organization and at the same time cause difficulties for the whole, and conversely. Many unintended consequences are, of course, sociologically irrelevant. For an early statement of this general problem, see Robert K. Merton, "The Unanticipated Consequences of Purposive Social Action," *American Sociological Review*, Vol. I (December, 1936).

16. Where unintended consequences occur due to error, or to individual idiosyncrasy, they are sociologically irrelevant. However, there is often, though not always, a systematically non-rational factor at work whose presence is manifested by mistakes and personality problems.

17. This follows, of course, from the hypothetical, and therefore discriminating and ordering, status of the end-in-view. See John Dewey, *Logic: The Theory of Inquiry* (New York: Henry Holt, 1938), pp. 496–497.

18. The use of the terms "end-in-view" and "anticipated" may easily lead to the fallacy of formulating this problem as one of the subjective awareness of the participants. This is a serious error. What is really involved is that which is anticipated or unanticipated by the system of discrimination and judgment which is applied to the means at hand. This may, and very often does, involve subjective anticipation or its want, but need not do so. Moreover, the system may be adjusted so as to be able to take account of factors previously unpredicted and uncontrolled. This addition of systematically formulated criteria of relevance occurs continuously, as in the recognition of morale factors in industry. In the situation detailed above, the high self-consciousness of the American Farm Bureau Federation apparently led it to anticipate the possible rivalry from a new organization set up under the Agricultural Adjustment Administration, since it took steps to ward off this threat. See above, p. 161. This is no accidental perspicacity but a result of the systematic consideration of just such possible consequences from the implementation of new legislation. However, the tendency to ignore factors not considered by the formal system – not so much subjectively as in regard to the competence of the

system to control them – is inherent in the necessities of action and can never be eliminated.

19. As in the TVA's commitment to become a successful electric power business; this type of commitment was much milder in the distribution of fertilizer, permitting adaptation in this field which would contribute to the fulfillment of the prior commitment to electricity.

20. Our use of the notion of unanticipated consequence assumes that the functional significance of such consequences is traceable within a specific field of influence and interaction. Thus price decisions made by a small enterprise affect the market (cumulatively with others), with ultimate unanticipated and uncontrolled consequence for future pricing decision. This is not an organizational process. When, however, the retailer builds up good will or makes decisions which will enforce his dependence upon some manufacturer, these are organizational acts within a theoretically controllable field, and are analyzable within the frame of reference set forth above.

21. In the TVA, the agriculturists made vigorous efforts to extend their interpretation of the grass-roots policy to the Authority as a whole; in respect to the federal government, the TVA attempts to have its special interpretation of administrative decentralization become general public policy.

22. See *TVA and the Grassroots*, p. 70 f.

23. We have reviewed above, *TVA and the Grassroots*, pp. 59-64, the unanalyzed abstractions in TVA's grassroots doctrine, which are given content and meaning by the pressure of urgent organizational imperatives.

24. See *TVA and the Grassroots*, pp. 205 ff.

25. In effect, we have related here some of the basic points made in the discussion above of the inherent dilemmas of the TVA doctrine. see *TVA and the Grassroots*, pp. 69-74.

26. The British Labor Party, when it assumed power in 1945, had to accept a large number of commitments which followed simply from the effort to govern in those circumstances, independently of its special program. "Meeting a crisis," in a women's club as well as in a cabinet, is a precondition for the institution of special measures. To assume leadership is to accept these conditions.

58

Democracy and Oligarchy in Trade Unions

Seymour Martin Lipset, Martin A. Trow and James S. Coleman

In recent years political democracy has proved so vulnerable to changes in social structure that the better understanding of these processes has become one of the major tasks of social science. Few still believe (as the American negotiators in Paris in 1919 seemed to believe) that formal guarantees and written constitutions can insure democracy. The most carefully worded guarantees have been swept aside, and the most intelligent of constitutions ignored, until now men seem liable to the opposite error of considering guarantees and constitutions worthless.

In few areas of political life is the discrepancy between the formal juridical guarantees of democratic procedure and the actual practice of oligarchic rule so marked as in private or voluntary organizations such as trade unions, professional and business associations, veterans' groups, and cooperatives. In fact, as many observers have noted, almost all such organizations are characterized internally by the rule of a one-party oligarchy. That is, one group, which controls the administration, usually retains power indefinitely, rarely faces organized opposition, and when faced with such opposition often resorts to undemocratic procedures to eliminate it. This is especially true for national organizations.

There is, however, one trade union – the International Typographical Union (ITU), the organization of the shops of North America – which does not fit this pattern. It is the only American trade union in which organized parties regularly oppose each other for election to the chief union posts, and in which a two-party system has been institutionalized. Since the beginning of this century, the officers of the international union and of most of the larger locals have been chosen in biennial elections, in which two or more political parties have offered a complete slate of candidates for all offices. The two major parties of the union operate much as do the Democratic and Republican Parties in American politics, though they have no connection with any group or party

---

Source: Seymour Martin Lipset, Martin A. Trow and James S. Coleman, *Union Democracy: The Internal Politics of the International Typographical Union*, (New York: Free Press: 1959).

outside the union. The parties have been of roughly equal strength in the international since 1920, so that turnover in office occurs at least as frequently as in national politics. In the thirty-five years since 1920, five incumbent presidents of the international have been defeated for re-election. In the New York local of the union, the largest local of the ITU, containing 10% of the membership, seven out of the last fourteen elections have resulted in defeat for the incumbent president. Probably nothing like this has happened in any other trade union or other of the private governments (as we may call voluntary organizations) anywhere in the world.

The Theory of Oligarchy

The pattern which characterizes almost all voluntary organizations was generalized over forty years ago by the German sociologist, Robert Michels, when he laid down his famous "iron law of oligarchy" in the following terms: "It is organization which gives birth to the dominion of the elected over the electors, of the mandataries over the mandators, of the delegates over the delegators. Who says organization says oligarchy."[1]

The experience of most people as well as the studies of social scientists concerned with the problem of organization would tend to confirm Michels' generalization. In their trade unions, professional societies, business associations, and cooperatives – in the myriad nominally democratic voluntary organizations – men have learned an learn again every day, that the clauses in the constitutions which set forth the machinery for translating membership interests and sentiments into organizational purpose and action bear little relationship to the actual political processes which determine what their organizations do. At the head of most private organizations stands a small group of men most of whom have held high office in the organization's government for a long time., and whose tenure and control is rarely threatened by a serious organized internal opposition. In such organizations, regardless of whether the membership has a nominal right to control through regular elections or conventions, the real and often permanent power rests with the men who hold the highest positions.

Since Michels first wrote, many books and articles have been written about oligarchy in voluntary organizations, but almost invariably they have documented the operation of his iron law in another set of circumstances. They have shown how control of the organizational machinery, combined with membership passivity, operates to perpetuate oligarchic control. From these studies it is clear that unions and other voluntary organizations more closely resemble one-party states in their internal organization than they do democratic societies with organized legitimate opposition and turnover in office. Indeed, the pattern of one-party oligarchy is so common in the labor movement that one defender of the Soviet Union has pointed to it as a justification of the one-party regime in that country:

> What is totalitarianism? A country that has a totalitarian government operates like our union operates. There are no political parties. People are elected to govern the country based upon their records. . . . That is totalitarianism. If we started to divide up and run a Republican set of officers, a Democratic set, a Communist set and something else we would have one hell of a time.[2]

Oligarchy becomes a problem only in organizations which assume as part of their public value system the absence of oligarchy, that is, democracy. In societies or organizations in which the self-perpetuation of the governing elite is the norm few people will raise questions regarding the determinants or consequences of oligarchy. In such organizations oligarchy is a thing given, not a phenomenon to be explained. However, when one finds an organization ostensibly devoted to the extension of democracy which is nevertheless itself undemocratically governed, some explanation seems demanded. Thus in his *Political Parties* Michels, himself a socialist at the time he was writing, raised the question of why the German Social-Democratic Party and the German labor movement, though ideologically committed to a completely democratic society and actively engaged in fighting for democratic rights within Germany, were themselves oligarchic in their internal structures. To Michels, oligarchy within the democratic socialist movement was significant because it was an "unintended consequence" of organization. For him, the fact that the conservative German political parties or other organizations were also oligarchic was not a problem, since they did not believe in democracy to the same degree as the socialists, and in fact often upheld the principle of oligarchy for the larger society. In the same way and at about the same time the oligarchic structure of American political parties attracted the interest of some observers such as Moise Ostrogorski, who were struck by the apparent contradiction between American democratic ideals and the reality of the boss and the machine.[3]

The problem had been recognized earlier, of course, but until Michels, European socialists took a generally optimistic view of the problem of machine domination of workers' organizations. Marx and Engels themselves viewed oligarchy as part of the early stage of the political emergence of the working class. They believed that the workers could come to control their institutions as soon as large numbers of them acquired class consciousness and political sophistication. Clique domination of socialist groups could not survive when workers really understood the facts of political life.[4]

American political scientists, with their generally liberal and optimistic outlook, took a similar point of view. They saw the boss and the machine as social problems which would gradually be solved as democracy advanced, the immigrant was assimilated, and education was extended. They viewed the American political party as progressively moving out of close control of a small group of leaders, first to the caucus, then to open conventions, and finally to the ultimate stage of the preferential primary. During the first period of this century, this point of view found expression in a movement to extend formal popular control through the direct primary, initiative, referendum, and recall.

In Europe where the idea of a popular democracy did not actually come to fulfillment in terms of universal adult or male suffrage without class restrictions until after World War I, few efforts were made to formally democratize the structure of political parties. But the left and labor groups, which were concerned with achieving a more complete democracy, invariably set up formal blueprints which provided for a high degree of popular control over the selection of leaders and formation of policy by way of regular conventions, discussion periods, and elections.

Despite the optimistic hopes of early socialist bodies and the institution of formal democratic control, the problem remained. As the trade-union and the socialist movement grew in size and power, members who came to disagree with the policies of incumbent leaders found, with rare exceptions, that it was impossible to dislodge those leaders from office. They discovered that offices whose authority originally and formally derived from the consent of the members gave officials power over the members. In most cases, however, the opponents of an existing oligarchy did not generalize from their own experience, nor did they raise the question, is there something in the nature of large-scale organizations which engenders oligarchic control?[5] Rather, like Karl Marx they tended to view the problem in terms of evil or weak men who were corrupted by power, and to place the democratic solution in a change of personnel.

By itself the existence of oligarchy in voluntary organizations rarely leads to great concern even in democratic societies and organizations. In most cases where men have forcefully and articulately opposed oligarchy, their concern has usually arisen from disagreement with the policies of a specific oligarchy. Thus the critics of the American party machine were not basically incensed by boss control *per se*, but rather by the fact that the machine was linked to corruption and inefficient government or refused to support the various social and economic reforms favored by the critics. In the pre-World War I socialist movement Lenin, for example, attacked the leadership of the German Social Democratic Party, not primarily for being oligarchic, but for having betrayed "Marxism." The CIO critics of AFL leadership in the mid-1930's in the United States were obviously not concerned with the lack of democracy within the AFL, but with the fact that the AFL was not organizing the mass production industries. Two American books which first brought Michels' analysis to the attention of the American labor movement were written by supporters of left-wing labor groups, and they objected more to the fact that many union leaders were restraining the post-World War I strike wave than to the fact that they were dictatorial.[6]

Occasionally the criticism of oligarchic control within the labor movement led to successful attempts to further democratize the constitutional structure of unions so as to reduce the power of the officials. A favored remedy introduced in some unions before World War I was to replace convention election of officers by a direct vote of the membership and to require referenda for constitutional changes, as well as to make it possible for members to directly initiate referenda. The Industrial Workers of the World (IWW) tried to insure turnover in office by limiting the number of years that a man might hold office and requiring that he return to the shop after his term as an official.

With very few significant exceptions all the efforts to reduce oligarchic control by formal mechanisms have failed. In those cases where an entrenched oligarchy was finally dislodged, the new leaders soon reverted to the same tactics as they had denounced in the old in order to guarantee their own permanent tenure in office and reduce or eliminate opposition. Even anarchist political and labor groups, whom we might expect to be highly sensitive to the dangers of oligarchy on the basis of their ideology, have succumbed to the blight. In pre-Franco Spain and in other countries where the anarchists had large organizations, a small semipermanent group of leaders maintained itself in power and selected its own replacements through a process of cooptation (selection by the leaders themselves). There is no more persuasive illustration of the unanticipated consequences of men's purposeful social actions than the recurrent transformations of nominally democratic private organizations into oligarchies more concerned with preserving and enhancing their own power and status than in satisfying the demands and interests of the members.[7]

What are the factors that account for the lack of democracy in labor unions? Why do opposition groups find it so difficult to survive? Michels and others who have dealt with the problem have summed it up in broad generalizations: The nature of large-scale organizations is such as to give the incumbent officials overwhelming power as compared with that of the opposition; the situation of the leaders of most unions is such that they wish to stay in office and will adopt dictatorial tactics to do so; and the relationship of the members to their union results in a low level of participation by the members. These factors have been discussed in considerable detail in another publication by the senior author.[8] Some of these generalizations are deserving of treatment here.

Large-Scale Organizations Give Union Officials a Near Monopoly of Power

(a) Unions, like all other large-scale organizations, tend to develop a bureaucratic structure, that is, a system of rational (predictable) organization which is hierarchically organized. Bureaucracy is inherent in the sheer problem of administration, in the requirement that unions be "responsible" in their dealings with management (and responsible for their subordinate units),[9] in the need to parallel the structures of business and government, in the desire of workers to eliminate management arbitrariness and caprice, and in the desire of the leaders of unions to reduce the hazards to their permanent tenure of office.

The price of increased union bureaucracy is increased power at the top, decreased power among the ordinary members. With the increase in the power of the top officials over local units and members, the sources of organized opposition are controlled or reduced. Most unions have given their executive boards the right to suspend local officials for violating policies of the central bodies. Whether they follow a conciliatory tone (as when they call for intra-union discipline and responsibility) or a militant one (as when they call for union solidarity in a dispute with management, union leaders strengthen their own hands and justify their monopolization of internal power in the course of articulating organizational needs and purposes.

(b) Control over the formal means of communication within the organization is almost exclusively in the hands of the officials. The individual member's right of free speech is not an effective check on administrative power if the union leaders control all public statements made by members of the administrative or field staff and the union newspaper. Since the only viewpoints about union matters that are widely available to the members are those of the administration, even widespread discontent which might result in organized opposition cannot be effectively expressed.[10]

(c) In most unions, one of the chief factors perpetuating the power of the incumbents is the administration's almost complete monopoly of political skills and the absence of those skills among the rank and file.[11] Within a trade union the principal source of leadership training is the union administrative and political structure itself. The union official, to maintain his position, must become adept in political skills. The average worker, on the other hand, has little opportunity or need to acquire them. Rarely if ever is he called upon to make a speech before a large group, put his thoughts down in writing, or organize a group's activities.[12] To the extent that union officers possess a monopoly of political skills, they inhibit the rise of an effective opposition.

The Leaders Want to Stay in Office

There is a basic strain between the values inherent in society's stratification system and the democratic values of the trade-union movement. With few significant exceptions, every trade-union official has moved up in the status hierarchy by becoming an official. The leader of a large local or national union has the income and prestige of a member of the upper-middle class,[13] and often wields more power than the average upper-middle class person. Most high-status positions carry with them some security of tenure. Democracy, on the other hand, implies permanent insecurity for those in governing positions: the more truly democratic the governing system, the greater the insecurity. Thus every incumbent of a high-status position of power within a democratic system must of necessity anticipate a loss of position.

It is hard for the persons in such positions to accept this insecurity with equanimity. Once high status is secured, there is usually a pressing need to at least retain and protect it.[14] This is particularly true if the discrepancy between the status and the position to which one must return on losing the status is very great. In other words, if the social distance between the trade-union leader's position as an official and his position as a regular worker is great, his need to retain the former will be correlatively great.[15]

The strenuous efforts on the part of many trade-union leaders to eliminate democracy (the possibility of their defeat) from their unions are, for them, necessary adaptive mechanisms. The insecurity of leadership status endemic in democracy, the pressures on leaders to retain their achieved high status, and the fact that by their control over the organizational structure and the use of their special skills they can often maintain their office, all help in the creation of dictatorial oligarchies.

The Members Do Not Participate in Union Politics

Although high participation is not necessarily a sign of democracy (dictatorships also find participation useful), the maintenance of effective opposition to incumbent leaders requires membership participation and interest. Ordinarily, however, few members show much interest in the day-to-day political process within the union; apathy of the members is the normal state of affairs. There are good reasons for this. Most union members, like other people, must spend most of their time at work or with their families. Their remaining free time is generally taken up by their friends, commercial entertainment, and other personally rewarding recreational activities.[16]

Most trade unions in addition are concerned with technical administrative matters, which cannot be of deep interest to the average member. The typical union appears to its members as an administrative agency doing a specific technical job for them. Union leaders will often attempt to sustain this image to prevent "interference" with their conduct of their job. Consequently only a small minority finds the rewards for participation in union affairs great enough to sustain a high level of interest and activity.

The leaders of the trade unions and other formally democratic organizations must in some way explain and justify the suppression, and to do so they make two points: that trade unions are organized for political or industrial conflicts; and that their membership is more homogeneous in background and interests than the citizens of a nation or some other civic political unit. Officials of trade unions have argued that since the group is engaged in perpetual conflict with management, internal opponents only serve the objective interests of the external enemy. They argue further that there is no basis for factionalism in their organization (other than the illegitimate selfish desire for office of ambitious individuals, or the outside interference of Communists) since all the members are workers and have common interests and objectives. According to this thesis, organized political conflict should take place only among classes, not within them. These same two arguments are, of course, used by the Communists to justify the contradiction between the one-party state and democratic values in the Soviet Union. They explain that since the Soviet Union is surrounded by the capitalist enemy, any domestic opposition is in effect treason; and that in any case in a one-class workers' state there is no legitimate basis for disagreement.

Strengthening the force of these arguments is the fact that the political decisions of trade unions and of other groups which are totally or in part political pressure groups, such as the American Legion or the American Medical Association, often fall into the realm of "foreign policy": that is, they involve the tactics and relations that these groups should adopt towards outside groups or the state. And just as in national politics there are many pressures toward a unified bipartisan foreign policy, so in trade unions and other voluntary groups we find similar pressures. Potential oppositionists are consequently faced with the likelihood that if they exercise their constitutional democratic rights, they will be denounced for harming the organization and helping the enemy.

The fact remains, however, that the democratic political system of the International Typographical Union does exist. It is obviously no temporary exception, for the party system of the union has lasted for half a century, and regular political conflict in North American printing unions can be dated back to 1815. As we shall note in later sections of this book, there are also a few other unions which deviate from the iron law of oligarchy. Up to now almost all analysts of the political systems of private governments have devoted their energies to documenting further examples of oligarchy. Rather than do this we have undertaken an analysis of the major deviant cases. From the point of view of the further development of social research in the area of organizational structure, and indeed, the general expansion of our understanding of society, these deviant cases – cases which operate in ways not anticipated by theory – supply the most fruitful subjects for study. Kendall and Wolf have noted that the analysis of deviant cases

> can by refining the theoretical structure of empirical studies, increase the predictive value of their findings. In other words, deviant case analysis can and should play a *positive* role in empirical research, rather than being merely the "tidying up" process through which exceptions to the empirical rule are given some plausibility and thus disposed of.[17]

In the course of our analysis of the ITU we have systematically looked for the various *oligarchic mechanisms* – the elements and processes which Michels and others found operative in the organizations which they studied. Many of these mechanisms – for example, the monopolies of power, status, funds, and communications channels which the officials of most unions ordinarily possess – are not found in the ITU, or if present their effects are greatly mitigated by other elements in the system. A large part of our analysis is directed at specifying those elements in the structure of the ITU and the printing industry which work against oligarchic mechanisms, and at spelling out the processes by which they contribute to the maintenance of the union democracy. And as we look for those attributes and patterns in the ITU which work to nullify the oligarchic tendencies present in large organizations, we are implicitly or explicitly setting forth the conditions necessary for the maintenance of democratic politics within private organizations. In this our purpose is not, of course, to "refute" Michels or other previous workers in this area, but rather to refine and build on their insights and findings, paying them the respect of using them more often than we quote them.

A Theory of Democracy

The problem of democratic or oligarchic political institutions may be approached from two vantage points. We may ask, as we have asked in the previous section, what are the conditions which are responsible for the development and institutionalization of oligarchy, or alternatively we may ask under what conditions democracy arises and becomes institutionalized All the literature that deals with political institutions in private governments deals with the determinants of oligarchy. We have found only one article that raises the question of under what conditions democracy, the institutionalization of opposition, can exist in voluntary organizations.[18] There is of course a voluminous literature discussing democracy as a system of civil government, but we must ask ourselves whether a variable which seems related to the existence of democracy in states is relevant to the existence of democracy in organizations.

Aristotle, for example, suggested that democracy can exist only in a society which is predominantly middle class.[19] In essence he and later theorists argued that only in a wealthy society with a roughly equal distribution of income could one get a situation in which the mass of the population would intelligently participate in politics and develop the self-restraint necessary to avoid succumbing to the appeals of irresponsible demagogues. A society divided between a large impoverished mass and a small favored elite would result either in a dictatorship of the elite or a dictatorship of demagogues who would appeal to the masses against the elite. This proposition still appears to be valid. Political democracy has had a stable existence only in the wealthier countries, which have large middle classes and comparatively well-paid and well-educated working classes. Applying this proposition to trade-union government, we would expect to find democracy in organizations whose members have a relatively high income and more than average security, and in which the gap between the organizational elite and the membership is not great.

A second proposition which has been advanced about democracy is that it works best in relatively small units, in which a large proportion of the citizenry can directly observe the operation of their governments:[20] for example, the small Greek city-states, the New England town meetings, and the Swiss cantons. While historical research has indicated that much of the popular mythology about the democratic character of these societies is untrue, it is probably true that the smaller a political unit, the greater the possibility of democratic control. Increased size necessarily involves the delegation of political power to professional rulers and the growth of bureaucratic institutions. The translation of this proposition of the level of private government is clear: The smaller the association or unit, the greater membership control. There can be little doubt that this is true in the trade-union movement.[21]

Both of these approaches to democracy, that in terms of internal stratification, and that in terms of size, however, are somewhat unsatisfactory as solutions to the problem of democracy in complex societies or large private organizations. Clearly democratic political institutions do exist in large, complex, and bureaucratically run societies and in societies which have wide variations in the distribution of income, status, and power. There is a third proposition about the conditions that favor democracy that seems to be of greater value for our understanding of democracy in large private organizations. We know it under two names, the theory of political pluralism, and the theory of the mass society. Writers in English-speaking countries, trying to explain why democracy exists in these countries, have developed the theory of political pluralism. European writers, trying to explain why democracy seems so weak in Germany and other countries, have developed the theory of the mass society. Both theories say in essence the same thing. They argue that in a large complex society the body of the citizenry is unable to affect the policies of the state. If citizens do not belong to politically relevant *groups*, if they are "atomized," the controllers of the central power apparatus will completely dominate the society. Translated to the realm of the internal politics of private organizations, this theory suggests that democracy is most likely to become institutionalized in organizations whose members form organized or structured subgroups which while maintaining a basic loyalty to the larger organization constitute relatively independent and autonomous centers of power within the organization. Or to put it in another way, democracy is strengthened when members are not only related to the larger organization but are also affiliated with or loyal to subgroups within the organization.[22] Since it is this approach which we have found most useful in understanding the internal political system of the ITU, we will briefly characterize it here.

Democratic rights have developed in societies largely through the struggles of various groups – class, religious, sectional, economic, professional, and so on – against one another and against the group which controls the state. Each interest group may desire to carry out its own will, but if no one group is strong enough to gain complete power, the result is the development of tolerance. In large measure the development of the concept of tolerance, of recognition of the rights of groups with whom one disagrees to compete for adherents or power, arose out of conflicts among strong and indestructible groups in different societies. There were a number of processes through which tolerance became legitimate. In some situations groups such as the Catholic and the Protestant churches attempted to destroy the opposing faction, but finally recognized that the complete victory of one group was impossible or could occur only at the risk of destroying the very fabric of society. In these conflicts minority or opposition groups developed a democratic ideology, an insistence on specific minority rights, as a means of legitimating their own right to exist. These groups might then force the dominant power group to grant these rights in order to prevent a revolutionary upsurge or achieve power themselves. For them to reject their own program may then mean a considerable loss of support from adherents who have come to hold the democratic values.

Once democracy is established in a society, private organizations continue to play a positive role. These organizations serve as channels of communication among different groups in the population, crystallizing and organizing conflicting interests and opinions. Their existence makes more difficult the triumph of such movements as Communism and Fascism, for a variety of groups lay claim to the allegiance of the population, reinforcing diversity of belief and helping mobilize such diversity in the political arena.[23] This brief discussion of theories of political pluralism and of mass society does not pretend to be an adequate summary. A fuller discussion of these concepts as applied to voluntary organizations will be found in Chapter 4 and other parts of this book (*Union Democracy*). We have discussed them here to sensitize the reader to the type of factors which we were looking for in our analysis of the political system of the ITU.

Notes

1. Robert Michels: *Political Parties*, Glencoe, Ill., Free Press, 1949, p. 401. This book was first published in Germany in 1911.

2. Harry Bridges, in *Proceedings of the Seventh Biennial Convention I.L.W.U.*, April 7–11, 1947 (San Francisco, 1947) p. 178.

3. Moise Ostrogorski: *Democracy and the Organization of Political Parties*, New York, The Macmillan Company, 1902. Bryce, examining the oligarchy endemic to political organizations, considers boss control normal. Cf. James Bryce: *Modern Democracies*, New York, The Macmillan Company, 1921, Vol. 2, Chap. 75.

4. "The fact that here too [in the British Independent Labour Party] people like Keir Hardy, Shaw Maxwell, and others are pursuing all sorts of secondary aims of personal ambition is, of course, obvious. But the danger arising from this becomes less as the Party itself becomes stronger and gets more of a mass character." – Engels to Sorge, in Karl Marx and Frederick Engels: *Selected Correspondence*, New York, International Publishers Co., Inc., 1942, p. 507. Cf. also Nicolai Bukharin: *Historical Materialism*, New York, International Publishers Co., Inc., 1925, Chap. 8.

5. Bukharin, op. cit., pp. 306–7, explicitly notes this fact that critics of oligarchy are concerned only with policy, not with oligarchy.

6. Sylvia Kopald: *Rebellion in Labor Unions*, New York, Boni & Liveright, 1924; William Z. Foster: *Misleaders of Labor*, Chicago, Trade Union Educational League, 1927.

7. It is, of course, true that the leaders' objectives of personal power and permanent tenure need not conflict with the needs of the members. Most voluntary organizations do in fact represent their members' interests in conflicts with other groups But there may arise a situation in which the needs and goals of the leaders or simply their desire for peace and quiet as they remain in office lead them to oppose or not fight for membership objectives. In an organization in which the members cannot vote on alternative procedures or courses of action, it is impossible to know whether a leadership decision is in fact something that the members desire.

8. "The Political Process in Trade Unions: A Theoretical Statement," in Monroe Berger et al., *Freedom and Social Control in Modern Society*, New York, D. Van Nostrand Company. Inc., 1954, pp. 82–124; cf. also Philip Selznick: "An Approach to the Theory of Bureaucracy," *American Sociological Review*, 8:47–54 (1943).

9. Cf. Joseph Shister: "The Laws of Union Control in Collective Bargaining," *Quarterly Journal of Economics*, 60:513–545 (August 1946).

10. Cf. in this connection P. F. Lazarsfeld and R. K. Merton, "Mass Communication, Popular Taste and Organized Social Action," in Lyman Bryson (ed.), *The Communication of Ideas*, New York, Harper & Brothers, 1948, pp. 95–118.

11. Cf. Max Weber: "Politics as a Vocation," in H. Gerth and C. W. Mills (eds.), *From Max Weber: Essays in Sociology*, New York, Oxford University Press, 1946, pp. 77–128.

12. The history of the British labor movements testifies to the value of such training. Many of its early leaders were men who first served as officers or Sunday-school teachers in the Methodist or other nonconformist churches. Cf. A. P. Belden: *George Whitefield the Awakener*, London, S. Low, Marston & Co., Ltd., , pp. 247 ff.

13. Cf. Cecil C. North and Paul K. Hatt: "Jobs and Occupations: A Popular Evaluation," in Logan Wilson and William A. Kolb (eds.), *Sociological Analysis*, New York, Harcourt, Brace and Company, Inc., 1949, pp. 464–73.

14. Furthermore, as Shepard points out, "The demands on leadership are heavy and their positions precarious. . . . To survive, leaders must be extraordinarily able, and able leaders are capable of consolidating their positions." Cf. Herbert A. Shepard: "Democratic Control in a Labor Union," *American Journal of Sociology*, 54: 311–316 (1949).

15. Public officials in a democratic society are also faced with this problem. Most of them, however, come from occupational positions or social strata which permit them to return to private life without a sharp decline in income.

16. Cf. Bernard Barber "Participation and Mass Apathy in Associations," in A. W. Gouldner, *Studies in Leadership*, New York, Harper & Brothers, 1950, pp. 477–504.

17. Patricia Kendall and Katherine Wolf: "The Analysis of Deviant Cases in Communications Research 1948–1949," in Paul F. Lazarsfeld and Frank Stanton (eds.), *Communications Research, 1948–1949*, New York, Harper & Brothers 1949, p. 153.

18. Philip Selznick, "The Iron Law of Bureaucracy," *Modern Review*, January, 1950 pp. 157–165.

19. Aristotle: *Politics*, IV, 11.

20. Thomas Jefferson advocated "general political organization on the basis of small units, small enough so that all members could have direct communication with one another and take care of all community affairs." – John Dewey: *Freedom and Culture*, New York, G. P. Putnam's Sons, 1939, p. 159. Cf. also Gunnar Myrdal: *An American Dilemma*, New York, Harper & Brothers, 1944, pp. 716–19; John Dewey: *The Public and Its Problems*, New York, Henry Holt and Company, Inc., 1927, Chap. 5; "The Federalist, No. 10," in *The Federalist*, New York, Modern Library, Inc., 1937.

21. It has been pointed out as well that in small homogeneous societies a political democracy often succumbs to the danger of extreme democracy: intolerance of the minority by the majority. The authors of the *Federalist Papers* were well aware of this and pointed out the dangers of a small "pure" democracy. See *The Federalist*, pp. 57–59.

22. "The stability of any democracy depends not on imposing a single unitary loyalty and viewpoint but on maintaining conflicting loyalties and viewpoints in a state of tension." – R. H. S. Crossman: "On Political Neuroses," *Encounter*, 2:66 (May 1954).

23. Calhoun thought these factors so important he wanted to institutionalize faction by means of the concept *concurrent majority*. Cf. John C. Calhoun: *A Disquisition on Government*, New York, Political Science Classics, 1947.

The Dynamics of Bureaucracy

Peter Blau

The Empirical Study of Bureaucratic Structure and Function

The fully developed bureaucratic mechanism compares with other organizations exactly as does the machine with the non-mechanical modes of production. Precision, speed, unambiguity, knowledge of the files, continuity, discretion, unity, strict subordination, reduction of friction and of material and personal costs – these are raised to the optimum point in the strictly bureaucratic administration.

Its specific nature . . . develops the more perfectly the more the bureaucracy is "dehumanized," the more completely it succeeds in eliminating from official business, love, hatred, and all purely personal, irrational, and emotional elements which escape calculation.

In these words Max Weber characterized the bureaucratic form of organization.[1] It is designed to induce an impersonal and rational orientation toward tasks which is conducive to efficient administration. Weber specified the following requirements that an organization must meet to be considered a bureaucracy:

1. "The regular activities required for the purposes of the bureaucratically governed structure are distributed in a fixed way as official duties."[2]

2. "A specified sphere of competence . . . has been marked off as part of a systematic division of labor. . . ."

3. The official "is subject to strict and systematic discipline and control in the conduct of his office."

4. All operations are governed by "a consistent system of abstract rules . . . [and] consist in the application of these rules to particular cases."

5. "The organization of offices follows the principle of hierarchy; that is, each lower office is under the control and supervision of a higher one."

6. Officials are "subject to authority only with respect to their impersonal official obligations."

Source: Peter Blau, *The Dynamics of Bureaucracy*, (Chcago: University of Chicago Press, 1963).

7. "Candidates [for bureaucratic positions] are selected on the basis of technical qualifications. In the most rational case, this is tested by examinations, or guaranteed by diplomas certifying technical training, or both. They are *appointed*, not elected."

8. Being a bureaucratic official "constitutes a career. There is a system of 'promotions' according to seniority or to achievement, or both."[3]

In his analysis of bureaucratic structure, Weber focused on official regulations and requirements and their significance for administrative efficiency. Of course, he knew that the behavior of the members of an organization does not precisely correspond to its blueprint. But he was not concerned with this problem and did not investigate systematically the way in which operations actually are carried out. Consequently, his analysis ignored the fact that, in the course of operations, new elements arise in the structure that influence subsequent operations. Recent students of organization have emphasized the importance of these emergent factors, such as informal relations or unofficial norms. Chester I. Barnard, for instance, showed that "personal contacts and interactions" always develop within formal organizations and called them "informal organizations." He concluded that "informal organizations are necessary to the operations of formal organizations as a means of communication, of cohesion, and of protecting the integrity of the individual."[4]

This concept has greatly influenced recent research in factories[5] and other organizations, but its crucial insight has hardly been exploited. Most discussions on the subject contrast informal relations and practices with the formal blueprint of the organization. This emphasizes the least interesting aspect of the concept of "informal organization," namely, that behavior and relationships often fail to conform exactly to formal prescriptions, which is certainly not a novel discovery. Much more significant is the insight that such activities and interactions are not simply idiosyncratic deviations but form consistent patterns that are new elements of the organization. In other words, Barnard's concept calls attention to the fact that organizations do not statically remain as they had been conceived but always develop into new forms of organization.

The objective of this study is to analyze these processes of organizational development on the basis of an examination of the daily operations and the interpersonal relations of government officials. Two segmental structures are analyzed in detail: a departmental group of two dozen individuals in a state employment agency and a slightly smaller department in a federal agency of law enforcement. It will be essential to note which practices correspond to official procedure and which do not and to determine how formally institutionalized patterns differ from others. But, whether recurrent activities and interactions exactly follow official rules or directly violate them, they are part of the bureaucratic organization. It is hoped that this book will contribute to an understanding of the dynamic character of this type of organization.

The Case-Study Method

This is an empirical study based on the direct observation of the behavior of officials in two government agencies. The field work was conducted in the second half of 1948 in the federal agency and in the first half of 1949 in the state agency. At first, in each case, administrative officials explained the organization and its procedures to the observer, and he familiarized himself with official regulations and other written documents pertaining to operations. After this period of orientation, a department was selected for intensive study.

In both agencies the observer was introduced to the staff as a sociologist by a senior official at a departmental meeting, and he was given an opportunity briefly to explain that he was interested in studying the interpersonal relations of civil servants. However, the fact that top administrators permitted the presence of the observer – a prerequisite for doing this study – made officials suspicious. Many believed that he was a member of a government commission (in the federal agency, it was the "Hoover Commission") and not a social scientist, as he claimed. But after some time his role as a researcher was accepted as genuine by most officials, if not all. This shift in role perception originated primarily in the course of informal social intercourse, in which the observer could not help revealing his ignorance of civil service and government agencies and some knowledge of academic and scientific matters.

The activities in each departmental office were observed daily for over three months. The observer also accompanied officials on their field visits to clients and participated in their informal get-togethers, notably at lunch. Small "side-studies" of related departments were subsequently made. The examination of operational records provided additional data. Throughout, the observer attempted to collect systematic information. For example, to determine the pattern of interaction in the department, all social contacts of its members were tallied during one week; to compare the productivity of officials, a quantitative index was derived from performance records.

All members of these two departments were interviewed in their homes immediately after the observation period in each case. Interviews were not designed to obtain attitude frequencies but to clarify the social relations and operating practices in the two departments. Most questions elicited the respondent's opinions and feelings about his work, his career, and his clients. A few direct questions concerning attitudes to colleagues provided the basis for sociometric indices. For comparative purposes, a similar interview was administered to three other groups, clerks in the federal agency and members of two other departments in the state agency. Not counting brief interviews at the office, sixty-nine operating and sixteen supervisory officials were interviewed.

For the most part, then, this is a case study of two bureaucratic departments. The limitations of this approach must be recognized at the outset. Of course, the findings of such a study are not representative. How typical the processes investigated are of American bureaucracies cannot be ascertained by this method. Moreover, the focus on a small segment within each bureaucratic structure makes it impossible to determine *systematically* the functional significance of all observed practices *for the larger organization.* To minimize this limitation, the implications of the processes examined for the agency as a whole are explored whenever possible.

On the other hand, case studies of small groups have the major advantage of lending themselves to interlocking various research procedures. Direct observation, documents, and interviews can be used to obtain a variety of systematic empirical data on any particular problem. An impressionistic study of bureaucracy may show that informal relations between officials influence their work, but it cannot determine the exact network of informal relations in a group or the extent to which the competence of an official affects his informal relations or the processes through which his position in the group influences his performance. This requires precise information about very different phenomena, available only if several systematic research techniques can be used. In this respect, the case study is also superior to the interview survey, which is confined to those data that can be obtained from responses to questions.

Social processes can be examined directly in a case study, and explanatory hypotheses can be tested immediately. For example, the observer's impression that competitive practices in the state agency interfered with productivity was confirmed through the analysis of records. The more competitive a group was, the lower was its productivity. A plausible explanation of this relationship is that competition reduced social cohesion, the condition most conducive to elective performance. Observation and interviews provided data to test these inferences. An index of social cohesion that was independent of competitive practices could be obtained, which showed that the less competitive group actually was more cohesive. Moreover, the processes responsible for this relationship could be determined, that is, how competitive tendencies created tensions and conflicts and how the resulting strained relations interfered with efficient performance.

Access to different research techniques improves the accuracy of the data collected as well as their range. The most pertinent technique to ascertain a given fact can be used. If the concern is with the extent of contact between officials at work, it is not necessary to rely on procedure manuals stating how many contacts officials *should* have or on their own statements of how many contacts they *remember*, but the frequency and duration of interactions can be determined by direct observation. This is especially important when a bias distorts the information obtainable with a particular research tool. Thus the concealment of illegitimate competitive practices made it impossible to determine the extent of competition either by direct observation or from interview responses. Analysis of the case files, however, yielded an unbiased index of competitive practices.

The case-study method also provides an opportunity for comparing the reliability of different research techniques. For example, the extent of association between officials during their free time at noon was determined by asking in the interview which colleagues an official had never joined for lunch, by observing which ones went to lunch together, and from a record of his luncheon partners each member of the department kept for two weeks. Interview responses proved to be unreliable indices of social interaction in this and in similar comparisons. This does not mean, of course, that people's actions always provide more accurate data than their statements do. Systematic questioning rather than making inferences from overt behavior reveals most clearly certain types of information, such as the relative esteem each individual enjoys among the other members of the group. However, the recurrent interactions that constitute the most direct expression of social relationships are not fully within the awareness of participants and thus cannot be reported accurately by them. Most officials in these groups did not know whether they talked more often to the colleague who sat on their left or to their neighbor on the right, or whether they or he usually started their conversations. They even forgot that they had occasionally spent a lunch period with a particular colleague. These patterns must, therefore, be determined largely by observation. The examination of interpersonal relations in this study will be based on observational indices of interaction and on indices of mutual attitudes derived from interview responses.

The Functional Approach

Data do not speak for themselves but only answer questions the investigator puts to them. Conceptions of functional analysis are used to organize the data of this study, taking as a starting point the conceptual scheme developed by Robert K. Merton.[6] The basic tenet of this theoretical framework is that the social consequences of phenomena, not merely their origins, must be taken into account in sociological inquiry. Specifically, their contribution to and interference with adjustment or functioning in the social structure must be examined. This approach helps clarify the relationships between seemingly disparate observations and the processes of structural change.

The first concept, that of function, directs the researcher to ascertain the consequences of a given phenomenon and to evaluate their significance for the structure. For example, statistical records provided superior officials with accurate information about the operations of their subordinates in both agencies studied. They supplied a rational basis for supervision, which was intended to improve operations. Did they actually fulfil this function?

It is possible to answer questions like this one empirically because the main organizational objectives in these agencies were clearly defined. This is a peculiar advantage of the analysis of bureaucratic structures, not shared by investigations of institutions that have not been deliberately established, where it is often impossible to find unequivocal standards for deciding whether a given consequence enhances structural adjustment. But in the employment agency an exact criterion for determining the function of statistical records existed, since its major objective was officially specified as locating jobs for clients. The finding that the introduction of statistical records increased the proportion of clients placed in jobs therefore indicates that these records served the function of improving operations.

The second functional consideration is: What are the mechanisms or processes through which a contribution is effected? Originally, it may have seemed that statistical records promoted efficiency because the better-informed superior can correct deficiencies more easily by giving the appropriate directives to his subordinates. Actually, however, more complex processes were involved. It suffices to state here that the official's knowledge that statistical records provided his superior with accurate information on his operations induced him to improve his performance *without* direct intervention of the superior.

Third, latent functions are the unanticipated consequences of social behavior that contribute to structural adjustment. The discussion of mechanisms assumes new significance for the analyst sensitized by this concept. The existence of statistical records, since it constrained officials to improve their performance on their own initiative, enabled supervisors to criticize subordinates less often than their responsibility for operations would otherwise require. One of them put it aptly by saying, "I let the figures speak for themselves." With fewer criticisms, more cordial relations between supervisor and subordinates could develop, a latent function of performance records.

The tracing of unanticipated consequences is especially important for the understanding of unofficial practices that appear, at first, irrational and irrelevant to operations. Why did officials, though rushed for time, voluntarily perform tasks for which they were not responsible? Why did some white officials, no less prejudiced than others, treat Negro clients more impartially? Why did many officials ridicule clients when among themselves? Why did the very officials least familiar with regulations most strongly object to their being replaced by new regulations? The examination of latent functions provides answers to such questions.

The distinction between manifest and latent function raises the problem of the significance of awareness. What difference does it make whether a contribution is effected by deliberate effort or unintentionally? At several points in this study two different practices will be examined that had virtually the same function, but in one case participants were aware of this consequence of their behavior, and in the other they were not. These comparisons will indicate how recognition influences the way in which, and the extent to which, a given function is served.

Fourth, since behavior patterns have not only beneficial results, attention must also be paid to "*dysfunctions*, those observed consequences which lessen the adaptation or adjustment of the system."[7] The introduction of statistical records in the employment agency, for instance, generated competition among officials and made them reluctant to part with the job openings needed for serving clients. A group of specialists had no job openings of their own but were expected to serve their clients by obtaining openings from their colleagues. Competitive officials, however, tended to refuse such cooperation. This made it most difficult for the specialists to discharge their duties. Record-keeping was dysfunctional for the adjustment among officials and for providing employment service to the clients of the specialists.

The study of dysfunctions is of particular interest because they frequently are indicators of potential modifications of the structure. The distribution of specialized tasks in bureaucratic organizations makes each official responsible for the accomplishment of explicitly specified objectives.[8] In this context, a dysfunction that interferes with operations is experienced as a disturbance by certain members of the organization. The specialists, in the illustration cited, had to cope with the problem posed by the lack of co-operation of their colleagues in order to fulfil their responsibilities. A practice developed that seemed to be unrelated to this difficulty. Specialists voluntarily accepted the cases of the most unpopular clients of other officials. This put these officials under obligation to the specialists, constraining them, despite their competitive tendencies, to co-operate with specialists who looked for job openings. As a result, specialists were able to discharge their duty of providing employment service to their clients.

Dysfunctions often give rise to structural change. The disruption of operations consequent to the use of statistical records evoked new practices and interpersonal relations, in effect, a modification of the departmental structure. Similarly, performance records had been originally instituted in this department in response to practices that interfered with employment service. The very innovation introduced to cope with one disturbance may in due course have consequences that create new problems and lead to new adjustments.

The central thesis of this study is that bureaucratic structures continually create conditions that modify these structures. In the study of larger social systems, it is now generally acknowledged that processes of social development must be taken into account, but bureaucracy is still too often regarded as a rigid equilibrium exempt from these processes. It, as well as other social structures, however, contains the seeds, not necessarily of its own destruction, but of its own transformation. The analysis of bureaucracies as organizations in flux is facilitated by the conceptions of functionalism.

Functional Analysis of Processes of Social Change

Functionalism was conceived by anthropologists as an alternative to the evolutionary approach. It was intended to substitute explanations of cultural phenomena on the basis of empirical evidence for interpretations in terms of speculations about historical origins and evolutionary progress.[9] This was an advance in scientific method. However, the limitations of the specific research situation – namely, that historical developments cannot be empirically traced in illiterate societies – were elevated into a scientific principle: past conditions are irrelevant for investigations of social systems. This ahistorical orientation and the parallel assumption of social equilibrium, which prevented systematic treatment of historical trends and social change, were serious deficiencies of functionalism.

Merton's paradigm constitutes a fundamental departure, which directs functional thinking toward problems of disequilibrium and social change. Empirical research benefits from these conceptions and simultaneously provides a testing ground for them. The concrete problems that arose in the analysis of the data of this study indicated some limitations of Merton's theoretical framework. There are insights that he does not make explicit and issues that he fails to consider, and these offer a challenge to extend his conceptual scheme.

By defining "function" as a type of *consequence* of a social pattern, Merton implicitly calls attention to the fact that social phenomena must be examined in the time sequence in which they occur. This requires the transformation of functional analysis from a synchronic into a diachronic approach, which is primarily concerned with the effects of patterns of social behavior on subsequent patterns. When specialists did favors for other interviewers, for example, this influenced the subsequent interaction between these two groups; the others became more co-operative. Of course, the expectation of the recurrence of favors was a main determinant of this co-operative behavior, but the doing of favors had preceded the emergence of these expectations as well as the co-operative practices. The recurrence of socially standardized acts obscures the time differential between antecedent and consequence, but it becomes apparent and can be empirically tested when the development of new patterns is examined.

Merton proposes to distinguish between functions and dysfunctions on the basis of whether consequences enhance or lessen "the adaptation or adjustment of the system."[10] This definition does not furnish precise criteria for making the distinction in empirical investigations. Whether a certain condition constitutes adjustment or maladjustment is by no means self-evident. The absence, or reduction, of social conflict is not a sufficient criterion of adjustment, as is apparent in cultures in which some types of competitive conflict are defined as socially desirable. It would be absurd to consider monopolistic practices as functional for a free-enterprise system, although they eliminate competitive conflicts. Indeed, the same social condition may be experienced as adjustment or as maladjustment, depending on the value-orientation of participants. Ultimately, therefore, the distinction between functions and dysfunctions rests on value judgments.

Of course, scientists should not introject their own values into scientific analysis. Quite the contrary, they must guard against the intrusion of their personal prejudices by recognizing that functional analysis involves value judgments and specifying the value criteria employed. Arbitrary standards are preferable to none, but they are not satisfactory. Consequences of social patterns are experienced by people in terms of their value orientations, and not neutrally. Functional analysis takes this crucial aspect of social life into account by determining not merely the objective consequences of patterns but also their evaluative significance for participants. This necessitates that the values that prevail in the social system under consideration be ascertained and that they be used as criteria for defining function and dysfunction. The greater the precision with which value standards specify objectives, the greater their utility for scientific research. The explicit objectives of bureaucratic organizations, therefore, facilitate functional analysis.

Functions, then, can be defined as observed consequences of social patterns that change existing conditions in the direction of socially valued objectives or, more briefly, as consequences that contribute to the attainment of valued objectives. Dysfunctions, conversely, are those observed consequences of social patterns that change existing conditions in the direction opposite to socially valued objectives or consequences that interfere with the attainment of valued objectives.

Both functions and dysfunctions modify social conditions, but in opposite ways. The conditions *produced* by a dysfunctional pattern are identical, in one important respect, with those *relieved* by a functional pattern; both are experienced, in terms of prevailing values, as necessitating some improvement. Such conditions can be defined as social needs. Functions meet existing needs, whereas dysfunctions generate new needs.[11]

What happens if new social needs arise? There are three possibilities. First, the need may persist without being met. Many problems in bureaucratic organizations as well as in societies continue to require solutions for long periods of time. To be sure, if social needs were defined as prerequisites for survival, as they often are, it would be impossible to speak of needs that have not been met in an enduring social system. The advantage of the more limited concept adopted here is that it permits the empirical testing of functional hypotheses even when no information about extinct social systems is available.

To test the hypothesis that a pattern of behavior has a given function, it must be demonstrated that a condition necessitating improvement persists in structures in which this pattern does not occur, but does not exist in those in which it prevails. An alternative method is to show that the emergence of the pattern in a social structure eliminates this condition. Correspondingly, the test of a dysfunction of a social pattern requires evidence that a condition in need of improvement develops only in the presence of this pattern and not in its absence. In the study of prerequisites for survival, such comparisons have to be made between extinct social structures and enduring ones. Since this is rarely possible in the social sciences, functional imputations have often remained unproved assumptions. In the study of needs for the achievement of valued objectives, on the other hand, the comparison required is one between different surviving social structures which have attained a specific objective with varying degrees of success. Reliable data of this nature are much more readily accessible, which greatly increases the chances of being able to test functional hypotheses systematically.

A second possibility is that social needs disappear as a result of changes in value orientations. This involves more than becoming resigned to living under troublesome conditions, which indicates merely an adaptation to persisting needs. It means that situations that were once experienced as objectionable are now felt to be satisfactory because a new orientation has emerged. Learning is one of the processes through which such changes are brought about. As officials in the federal agency, for instance, learned to cope with the difficult problems of their work, their attitudes toward these problems changed, transforming them from disruptive threats into stimulating challenges.[12]

Finally, social needs may give rise to new social patterns that serve to meet them. Since this is only one of three alternatives, the existence of a need for improvement is not a sufficient condition for the development of such improvements. To explain their emergence, the conditions in social structures under which the need persisted and those under which it was met in a certain way must be contrasted. This analysis of structural constraints entails the comparison of historical developments in different structures, since past social experiences do, of course, influence present behavior.

A further specification of social needs and functions is important for this purpose, namely, an indication of the substructures particularly affected.[13] Which groups in a differentiated structure suffer from the existence of a given need, and which ones are relatively immune to it? Which groups benefit from the specific way a need is met, and which ones are not advantaged or are even disadvantaged? It is not possible to account for the persistence of needs, for practices that have serious dysfunctions, or for the fact that one pattern rather than another serves a given function, without inquiring into their differential effect on groups variously located in the power structure.

When a social pattern has a series of consequences, its dysfunctions may be looked upon as the social cost of its contributions. Presumably, once the cost outweighs the functions, the pattern will be abandoned. Often, however, social action is more constructive and less patient. People attack troublesome conditions, even if they cannot, or will not, eliminate the factors that produced them, and without waiting for a negative net balance of their consequences. We try to reduce highway accidents by means other than junking all cars and before their toll becomes so great that it would be preferable to give up motor transportation. Many emergent needs, in the two agencies studied, gave rise to social innovations that met the need without disturbing the pattern that had created it or the positive contributions of this pattern. The new practices, in turn, sometimes had dysfunctions as well as functions. Since the same social pattern that meets some needs frequently also generates others and since problems often lead to new solutions rather than to the elimination of their source, social structures continuously develop into different social structures.

The Dynamics of Bureaucratic Structure

"One cannot step twice into the same river," said Heraclitus, twenty-five centuries ago, and if one returns to the same riverbed, it also has imperceptibly changed. The only permanence in bureaucratic structure is the occurrence of change in predictable patterns, and even these are not unalterably fixed.

The two government agencies studied had been established by law to achieve designated purposes. One was responsible for providing employment service, the other for enforcing legal standards of employment. The external situations in which different segments of each organization found themselves differed, and these situations continually changed. Finding jobs for accountants and finding work for day laborers called for different procedures, and practices that sufficed for enforcing the law during a war might not do so in a period of recession. In order to discharge prescribed responsibilities under varying conditions, adjustments of the bureaucratic organization were necessary.

Changes in the external situation were not the only reason for making modifications in the structure. Most procedures, even if instituted for a specific purpose, had several unintended consequences. Statistical records of performance, for example, not only furnished a means for evaluating operations but also had a variety of other effects. Some of these – latent functions of record-keeping – furthered the achievement of organizational objectives, but others – dysfunctions – interfered with it and thus necessitated further innovations. Perfect adjustment is hardly possible because the very practices instituted to enhance adjustment in some respects often disturb it in others. Hence the stable attainment of organizational objectives depends on perpetual change in the bureaucratic structure.

Indeed, the dynamics of bureaucratic development is not confined to the emergence of new instruments for the accomplishment of specified objectives, but in the process the objectives themselves change, too. Particularly in innovating organizations, although not only there, competent officials tend to become interested in assuming new responsibilities and in expanding the jurisdiction of the agency, since this would increase their work satisfaction and benefit their careers.

This chapter, which concludes the substantive analysis, is devoted to the discussion of some principles of bureaucratic development suggested by our findings and a few of their implications.

Emergent Organizational Needs and Structural Change

Weber conceived of bureaucracy as the social mechanism that maximizes efficiency in administration and also as a form of social organization with specific characteristics.[14] Both these criteria cannot be part of the definition, since the relationship between the attributes of a social institution and its consequences is a question for empirical verification and not a matter of definition. Weber's discussion may be interpreted in one of two ways. Either he defined bureaucracy by specifying formal characteristics and hypothesized its superior operating efficiency or he intended to define it as any administrative apparatus that maximizes efficiency and advanced hypotheses about organizational attributes that would typically have this effect.[15]

In terms of the second alternative, bureaucracies can be looked upon as institutionalized strategies for the achievement of administrative objectives by the concerted effort of many officials. They are methods of organizing social conduct in order to transform exceptional problems into routine duties of experts[16] and to effect the co-ordination of specialized tasks. In different cultures, different social arrangements will prove most suitable for these purposes. When an authoritarian orientation toward social relationships prevails in the family and in the society generally and when lack of education limits the qualification of subaltern officials, as in Germany in Weber's time, strict hierarchical control may be the most efficient method of bureaucratic operation. However, when equality in social relationships is highly valued and when a much higher level of popular education has been reached, as in the United States today, permitting junior officials considerable discretion in discharging their responsibilities may be a more efficient system of administration. Similarly, in a culture in which people are oriented toward century-old traditions, bureaucratic efficiency probably requires less change in organization than it does in a young culture in which progress is a central value.

Internal as well as external forces made change a recurrent phenomenon in the two organizations studied, and efficient operations depended on such readiness to reorganize. The concept of organizational need has been helpful in the analysis of these processes of bureaucratic development, since it indicates the relationship between the consequences of established practices and the emergence of new ones. Many social patterns that served important functions for operations also had some dysfunctions, that is, they produced conditions that impeded the effective attainment of organizational objectives. These emergent needs often gave rise to new practices that met them. The introduction of statistical records in the employment agency, for instance, effected needed improvements in placement operations, but it also engendered competitiveness, which interfered with service to handicapped clients and with productivity in general. In response to these two organizational needs, social innovations developed that restored operating efficiency. First, special interviewers for handicapped clients assumed duties that obligated other interviewers to help them find jobs for their clients. Second, one group of regular interviewers devised methods for discouraging competitive tendencies, and this increased productivity, as indicated by the fact that this group was more productive than the other group of regular interviewers, in which competitive practices prevailed.

Contacts with clients furnish another illustration of adjustments that had dysfunctions necessitating further adjustments. Interviewers concerned with making many placements were frustrated by refusals of benefit clients to accept low-paying jobs. They often tried, therefore, to discourage such refusals by the more or less implicit threat that unemployment benefits would be discontinued. This practice, although adequate for its purpose, created conflicts with clients, which were particularly disturbing for these service-oriented interviewers. The resulting tensions constituted new obstacles to the effective performance of duties. In response to this emergent need, a custom developed that restored equanimity, namely, complaining and joking about clients in conversations with colleagues. This new pattern, in turn, had a dysfunction. It facilitated the interviewer's work, not by eliminating conflicts with clients, but by immunizing him against their disturbing effects, and consequently made inconsiderate treatment of clients more likely. Since this dysfunction, which did not directly interfere with operations, did not give rise to an organizational need, it persisted, to the detriment of clients.

Consultations in the federal agency reveal a different aspect of the same process of change in the structure. Agents, anxious to assure the accuracy of their decisions without exposing their difficulties to the supervisor, were in need of advice from another source. The practice of consulting colleagues met this need. It reduced the anxiety about making decisions that interfered with operations, and it generated social cohesion. However, it also produced needs that led to new patterns of interpersonal relations.

To consult peers was easier than to consult the superior in the department, but if they were approached for help too often, they ceased to be peers, and this made consulting them more difficult. As the advice of some agents was in constant demand, while others recurrently requested assistance with solving their problems, status differences emerged in the group. Agents hesitated to consult expert colleagues too frequently, lest their unofficial position suffer, just as they were reluctant to ask the supervisor too many questions for fear of endangering their official position. In either case, hierarchical relations prevented free access to consultants. The resurgent need for advice from actual peers induced most agents to establish partnerships of mutual consultation and to reserve consultations with experts for their most perplexing problems.

Peer relationships rest on reciprocity in social exchange. Unilateral services engender obligations that destroy equality of status and erect barriers to the free flow of communication. This interference with egalitarian social interaction is dysfunctional for work groups. The emerging status distinctions in Department Y not only restricted the choice of consultant but even threatened the integrated position of the less competent agents. As all were attracted to popular experts, the others felt left out of group life and experienced a need for better interpersonal relations. This need was also met by new patterns of interaction. The less competent agents tended to cultivate extensive informal relations with colleagues during the lunch period. Since this improved their popularity, it constituted an equalizing force. Although some status differences persisted, alternative mechanisms for becoming integrated in this group made it possible for most of its members to attain social acceptance among peers.

Social cohesion depends on basic equality of status. Co-operative interaction, such as the pattern of consultation, therefore affects it in two opposite ways. Co-operation is a major source of cohesion in work groups, because it unites members in the voluntary exchange of valued assistance, but it simultaneously weakens cohesion by giving rise to status distinctions, which inhibit social intercourse and thus limit feelings of fellowship. As a result of these conflicting forces, cohesiveness is not a stable condition. It requires constant effort to renew the fundamental equality that makes the members of the group fully accessible to one another and permits them to become interested in one another as distinctive persons. Treatment of associates as unique individuals rather than as social types develops primarily among peers, and such an approach is a prerequisite for social interaction that is intrinsically gratifying and thereby produces strong social ties. To perpetuate group cohesion, the orientation in interpersonal relations should disallow quantitative differentiation of status but stress qualitative differentiation of persons. This orientation toward equals whose particular qualities merit consideration is also likely to enhance identification with the purposes of the group and its standards of behavior, at least in a culture in which submission to authoritarian commands is negatively valued.

The significance of an egalitarian approach is not restricted to the internal structure of the work group but extends to the larger bureaucratic organization. Rational operations require the expeditious removal of obstructions to efficient performance. Effective communication in the hierarchy of authority, without which needed official innovations would not be made, is a necessary condition for this adjustment but not a sufficient one. No system of rules and supervision can be so finely spun that it anticipates all exigencies that may arise. Moreover, some impediments to efficiency, such as feelings of anxiety and other emotional tensions that often develop in the course of operations, cannot be eradicated by official decree. Maximum rationality in the organization, therefore, depends on the ability of operating officials to assume the initiative in establishing informal relations and instituting unofficial practices that eliminate operational difficulties as they occur. This ability, in turn, presupposes the absence of acute feelings of inequality among the members of the bureaucracy.

To be sure, the status distinctions inherent in the exercise of authority are probably necessary for the effective administration of a large organization, in which officials in central positions must be able to direct and co-ordinate the work of specialized groups. However, since bureaucratic authority rests on social consensus that issuing certain directives is just as much the duty of the superior as compliance with these directives is that of subordinates, such compliance is not experienced as subjugation, while obedience to arbitrary commands of a superior would be. Hence bureaucratic authority itself does not create profound feelings of inequality, although it involves some status differences, but it often gives rise to additional hierarchical distinctions, which are not essential for systematic administration and which destroy all feelings of equality. If subaltern officials are treated as inferiors whose sole duty is to obey detailed orders of their superior, they have neither sufficient security nor incentive to cope with problems of their work on their own initiative. To supply the confidence and motivation needed for such efforts, junior officials must be treated by administrators as colleagues in the pursuit of common professional objectives. This limited type of egalitarian treatment, which is not very dissimilar from that which actually prevailed in the federal agency, is not incompatible with the exercise of bureaucratic authority. Of course, the absence of fundamental inequalities is not the only bureaucratic condition that must be met for work groups to take the initiative in making improvements when obstructions to efficient operations arise.

Some Prerequisites of Adjustive Development

Spontaneous adjustments often occurred in the two agencies under consideration, that is, practices that solved incipient operational problems emerged among officials in the course of their work without being deliberately instituted by superiors. In previous chapters, specific instances of this process of change have been analyzed. At this point, a question on the next higher level of abstraction should be raised: What were the bureaucratic conditions that accounted for this pattern of self-adjustment, which was essential for efficiency? The exceptional cases in which organizational needs persisted without evoking innovations to meet them provide some indications of these prerequisites of adjustive development in bureaucratic organizations.

Receptionists in the employment agency, quite unconsciously, treated clients of their own skin color preferentially. Since this did not disturb the work of the members of Department X, impartial treatment of applicants was not restored. However, some organizational needs that were very disturbing also persisted. When special interviewers, fearful of risking disapproval of requests to discontinue service to psychotic clients, continued to interview these clients, they found the task most irritating. In that case, it will be remembered, a conflict between the group of officials and a top administrator prevented adjustment. Still a different factor accounts for the finding that reviewers were not relieved from cross-pressures that interfered with their work, even though they allowed agents to correct most mistakes unofficially. These temporary reviewers did not constitute a distinct group – since each one remained identified with his former departmental group – and consequently were not able effectively to defend themselves against pressure from other officials. Finally, the members of Section A in the state agency, a distinct group, did not suppress competitive practices, which were disruptive and lowered productivity. Two important differences between this situation and that in Section B, in which co-operative adjustment occurred, were that no common professional orientation had developed in Section A, and its members had felt insecure in their jobs.

These cases of enduring dysfunctions suggest five prerequisites of adjustive development: first, a minimum of employment security; second, a professional orientation toward the performance of duties; third, established work groups that command the allegiance of their members; fourth, the absence of basic conflict between work group and management; and fifth, organizational needs that are experienced as disturbing. Without assuming this list to be exhaustive, the following discussion will be confined to these five conditions, the absence of which was observed to obstruct the process of adjustment.

The ability to originate new patterns of adjustment and to adapt to those officially introduced presupposes relative job security. To be sure, the unemployed worker who feels he has nothing to lose may become a revolutionary, but insecurity in the bureaucratic situation, in which one's job hangs in the balance, breeds ritualistic adherence to the existing order. Interviewers in Section A, while on probation for their civil service appointment, were so anxious to comply with the demands of superiors that they could not afford to discourage competitive practices. The members of Section B, who already held permanent civil service positions, felt free to co-operate in disregard of official statistical records, and they thereby improved productivity. Factory workers, who can be fired any time, resist changes in the organization, and so did officials in the federal agency whose lesser competence made them insecure in a period of reductions in staff; but the majority of agents, secure in their jobs, preferred frequent change to a constant routine.

Employment security engenders the psychological freedom of action that enables individuals to initiate adjustments, but it does not guarantee that these will further the objectives of the agency. Indeed, tenure may lead to private adaptations that are detrimental to the interest of the organization. To preclude this possibility, a professional orientation must prevail among officials. This involves a common identification with professional values and norms, which makes the process of attaining professional objectives a source of satisfaction.

Civil service personnel policies enhance the chances that officials will have a professional orientation toward their work. Recruitment standards assure that only applicants with the technical training required for a job are appointed. The relative security of civil service positions and the consequent long tenure of most officials encourage loyalty to the organization and its values, particularly since the specialized qualifications acquired in many years of experience in government agencies often cannot be utilized in private industry. The expert customs inspector, for instance, can hardly find a job commensurate with his skills outside the government, and even the demand for expert employment interviewers in private industry is small. Promotions in civil service, moreover, follow explicit regulations, which enable the official to predict his promotion chances with relative accuracy, in contrast to the private employee, who is promoted at the pleasure of his employer[17] and can therefore hope for a promotion at all times.[18] The system that prevents civil servants from deriving satisfaction from hopes of spectacular advancements probably also constrains them to find gratification in their work and thus invites a professional attitude toward it.

Evaluation on the basis of results achieved rather than techniques used likewise fosters a professional orientation. If interviewers in the employment agency criticized statistical records as unprofessional, it was because they felt that the indices measured only superficial accomplishments, such as the number of placements. In the federal agency, more refined statistical criteria supplemented by qualitative evaluation of results compelled agents to strive to achieve specified objectives in their work and obviated the need for many operating rules and close supervision. This external compulsion was internalized. The periodic rating by the supervisor constrained agents to adapt to their dependent position by adopting the bureaucratic system of values and norms as their own orientation toward their tasks. Moreover, the supervisor, as a means of extending his authority over subordinates, rarely enforced operating rules but relied for control on the obligations he thereby created and on his evaluation of completed cases. This puts agents under further pressure to identify with professional objectives and with self-imposed standards of workmanship.

A professional orientation makes officials concerned with impediments to efficient operations and directs them to attempt adjustments, but it also engenders anxiety. The greater their interest in professional objectives and the fewer the external restraints on their method of achieving them, the more likely it is that they will experience anxiety. The bureaucratic officials observed found themselves in this predicament, although perhaps not to the same extent as do independent professionals. Anxieties that persevered, whether among interviewers or department heads, agents or reviewers, led to maladaptation, rigidity, and poor performance. Adaptation to the organization in general and the ability to reorganize procedures when necessary in particular depend on relatively cohesive work groups, which relieve such anxiety.

Recurrent co-operative and congenial interaction with most co-workers, and not merely with a few friends, gives officials a feeling of security in the work situation. This promotes assimilation in the bureaucratic structure and efficient performance of strenuous tasks, such as complex negotiations. The social support of the group also makes it easier for officials to adopt new practices, since it lessens their need to find emotional security in familiar routines. Social cohesion, therefore, paves the way for the development of new adjustments. In addition, it furnishes the group with instruments for instituting them.

To meet organizational needs requires group action. When agents found that reports of bribes by one of them endangered success in the future negotiations of others, any single individual was helpless in the face of the difficulty, but the group could eliminate it by collectively discouraging every agent from making such reports. When competitive practices interfered with the work of interviewers, individual efforts to check them were ineffective, but the collective enforcement of co-operation in an entire group removed this obstacle to operations. Unofficial practices that met organizational needs were most prevalent in cohesive groups, because they alone could effectively enforce informal norms.

Most members of cohesive groups value their interpersonal relations with one another, and this makes them subject to the control of the group. Unofficial sanctions are either indications by others that they have lost respect for a colleague and become less interested in associating with him or ostracism in miniature, signs of hostility in social situations that threaten an individual with ostracism. These sanctions, as well as the serious penalty of ostracism, are effective deterrents to deviant behavior only when an official's position in the group is important to him, and not otherwise. Social cohesion is the source of the group's power to exact obedience to its norms and thus of its ability to develop adjustive social patterns independent of official rules.

Social differentiation endangered cohesiveness and optimum performance of duties, unless counterforces developed that minimized it again, as previously noted in this chapter. Continuous structural modifications, changes in relative positions as well as operating practices, occurred within the larger framework of comparatively stable hierarchical positions and specified objectives. Just as a solid body consists of moving molecules, so is the bureaucratic structure composed of constantly changing elements.

Although social cohesion cannot be officially created, conditions favorable for its development can be. Job security and the explicit promotion procedure in civil service have this function. They supply most officials with the knowledge that they will neither be promoted nor lose their jobs within the next few years and thus greatly lessen their need to compete with fellow-officials. Besides, the civil service system assures that most officials remain in the same group for years, usually under conditions that give rise to a common professional orientation. Daily associations between like-minded colleagues without serious conflicts for long periods of time stimulate the emergence of social cohesion.[19]

Social cohesion enables the members of a group to institute adjustments that further their interest. These adjustments will, however, not advance the objectives of the organization if operating employees feel that their interest conflicts with that of management. This is a typical occurrence in private industry. Restriction of output among factory workers is an adjustment that is designed to protect the economic interest of workers against management and that is dysfunctional for operations. The comments and behavior of workers show that these practices are motivated by fear of losing their jobs or lowering their wages rather than by lack of professional concern with their work.[20] In contrast to those of factory workers, most unofficial practices observed in the two agencies, including some that violated official rules, contributed to operating efficiency. An important reason for this, in addition to job security, may well have been that the civil service system eliminates a basic source of conflict between operating officials and management.

Authority over personnel is split in government agencies. In private organizations, management controls employment conditions as well as operations. In government agencies, on the other hand, management controls operations but not employment conditions. Salaries and the procedures that govern promotion and discharge are determined by the civil service commission in accordance with legal statutes. Since the rating influences advancement chances, an individual's economic interest may bring him into conflict with superiors. However, the conflict between the *collective* economic interest of operating officials and the budgetary considerations of their employer finds expression in their opposition to the civil service commission and the legislature, which set the conditions of their employment. It does not affect their relationship with the administration of the agency. On the contrary, operating officials and administrators are united by their interest in legislation that benefits civil servants.

The dominant concern of employees with their jobs and incomes may submerge a common professional interest in effective performance, but this was not characteristic of the civil servants studied. Their jobs were relatively secure, and they did not feel that improvements in performance would evoke managerial action detrimental to their economic welfare, as factory workers apparently do. This situation permitted officials to become and remain interested in doing work of superior quality. Cohesive groups in which such a professional orientation prevailed readily initiated social practices that eliminated obstacles to efficient performance. This strain toward adjustive development in the organization greatly contributed to the achievement of its objectives.

Bureaucracy and Society

No unofficial adjustment will occur, even under favorable conditions, unless an organizational need is experienced as disturbing by operating officials. For example, more clients than could be served came to the employment agency, because receptionists gave too early reappointment dates to those they dismissed. Since this did not directly interfere with departmental operations, neither clerks nor interviewers, indeed, not even supervisors, were interested in finding ways to limit the flow of clients.

The hierarchical distribution of responsibility and authority is designed to produce official adjustments in such cases. The wider responsibility of superior officials constrains them to devise methods for meeting also those problems that interfere only indirectly with operations. Thus one department head regulated the flow of clients by instituting a precise procedure for screening them. Official innovations are required not only when an organizational need does not disturb operating officials but also when they are unable to make the needed adjustment. It was not until contradictory regulations in the federal agency were officially replaced by new ones that the difficulties they had created were eliminated.

The statement that disruptions precede the development of improvements in the organization requires a qualification. Agents who had fully mastered their tasks were anxious to be confronted by new problems, which made their work interesting again. When revisions of regulations were introduced, these agents welcomed the challenge of devising new methods for enforcing them and made the needed innovations without experiencing disturbances. If some kind of change itself becomes a goal, a situation of anticipatory adjustment arises. Since the absence of change is negatively valued, officials readily establish new procedures when the occasion to do so presents itself. Usually, only organizational needs that disturb officials evoke adjustive practices, but when dissatisfaction with routine has disturbed them before a need for improvement arises, the need is not experienced as disruptive, yet the improvement will be made.

If the bureaucratic organization satisfies the prerequisites of adjustive development, some of which have been discussed, necessary innovations will often evolve spontaneously. The concept of organizational spontaneity, it should be re-emphasized, refers not to the impulsive conduct of individuals but to the emergence of social patterns in the course of operations among officials without the deliberate intervention of administrative superiors.[21] Professionally oriented officials welcome opportunities to exercise their professional ingenuity by designing new operational techniques, and disturbances produce methods for meeting organizational needs in most other cases. Under these conditions it is only as a last resort that superiors must intercede to restore operating efficiency by officially instituting required innovations.

The process of bureaucratic development, conducive as it is to efficiency, may have detrimental effects on the society or segments of it. Some procedures generate no organizational need, but have dysfunctions for groups outside the organization. For instance, the practice of joking about clients immunized interviewers against being upset by conflicts with them, which improved their performance but also gave rise to less considerate treatment of clients. Since this practice did not interfere with operations, neither unofficial nor official adjustments developed to prevent its harmful consequences.[22] The persistence of bureaucratic modes of operation that disadvantage clients or other parts of the public constitutes a societal need for democratic mechanisms that constrain officials to change such practices.

An organizational need was not met by operating officials unless it or the fact that their tasks had become routine disturbed them sufficiently to interest them in making the required innovation. By the same token, external dysfunctions cannot be expected to disappear unless they are transformed into organizational needs, which means that their occurrence is so deleterious for administrators or for all officials that they are compelled to make adjustments. This raises the problem of developing democratic techniques that enable the public or its representatives to hold officials specifically accountable for the various consequences of bureaucratic operations, thus converting external dysfunctions into internal needs of the organization that disturb its personnel.[23] The difficulty of finding solutions to this problem is matched only by the urgency of doing so.

Clients are not the only segment of the population that may be adversely affected by bureaucratic operations, since change in the organization is not confined to methods but extends to its very objectives. On the lowest level of the hierarchy studied here, the succession of goals, which resulted from the interest of officials in the expansion of organizational responsibility, found expression merely in advocating new policies. On the highest hierarchical level, the same interest may lead to monopolization of markets, in the case of the corporation official, or of governmental power, in the case of the public administrator. Either tendency is dysfunctional for a democratic society. And so is the opposite tendency, that of administrators to compromise the objectives of the organization in response to pressure from special-interest groups. The corrupt public official dominated by racketeers furnishes the extreme illustration of such abuse of bureaucratic power. However, the subtle adulteration of policies introduced by honest administrators, because powerful minorities can exert greater influence on them than can the democratic majority, is probably no less detrimental to public welfare in the long run.

A Final Paradox

Bureaucracy and democracy are two fundamentally different analytical types of social organization. A bureaucracy is an organization established for the explicit purpose of achieving specific objectives, and the organizing principle is administrative efficiency, that is, an orientation to the expeditious attainment of the given objectives. A democracy is an organization established to ascertain the common objectives among men on the basis of the will of the majority or their representatives, and the organizing principle is the freedom of dissent necessary for majority opinions to form. The bureaucratic manager may have democratic convictions, but his administrative decisions are expected to be governed by the criterion of efficiency. Arriving at common agreements may be expedited by suppressing minority opinions, but this is irrelevant in terms of democratic values. While bureaucracy is not suited for deciding between alternative ends, it is better suited than democracy for implementing these decisions. Hence, the two forms of organization are complementary. Democratic values require not only that social objectives be determined by majority rule but also that they be implemented by the most effective methods available, that is, by bureaucratically rather than democratically governed executive agencies.

The co-existence of democratic and bureaucratic institutions in a society, however, poses a paradox. Bureaucracies seem to be necessary for, and simultaneously incompatible with, modern democracy. In a mass society democracy depends on bureaucratic institutions, such as a complex machinery for electing representatives and efficient productive units that make a high standard of living for all people possible. Yet, by concentrating power in the hands of a few men in business and government, bureaucracies threaten to destroy democratic institutions.

If this is a paradox, it is also a challenge. We cannot turn the clock back and return to the New England township, in which unbureaucratic democracy was possible, and would not if we could, since we value the products that modern bureaucracies supply. Our democratic institutions originated at a time when bureaucracies were in a rudimentary stage and hence are not designed to cope with their control. To extend these institutions by developing democratic methods for governing bureaucracies is, perhaps, the crucial problem of our age. In this study of bureaucracy's internal structure, it is not possible to do more than raise this problem, and this may best be done in the words of Robert S. Lynd:

> We fear "control" and evoke the dreadful specter of bureaucracy. We tend, therefore, to state the problem negatively, instead of asking in a more positive temper how planning and control can be used to enhance freedom at points critically important to human personality, by eliminating current wastes and insecurities that operate to curtail freedom ...
>
> A large culture which does not discover a way of structuring rank-and-file participation in, and responsibility for, authority, in some more active and inclusive way than our pallid American reliance upon the political ballot, invites the loss of even that important check upon authority. It is not the fact of planning and control that needs to be challenged, but its misuse. The question we face is: how much control, where, and how, in order to further the authentic ends of democratic living?[24]

Notes

1. The two quotations are taken from Max Weber, *Essays in Sociology*, trans. H. H. Gerth and C. W. Mills (New York: Oxford University Press, 1946), pp. 214 and 215–16. The term "bureaucracy" is used in this study for a certain type of administrative organization and without the negative connotations it has colloquially assumed.

2. *Ibid.*, p. 196.

3. The last seven quotations are taken from Max Weber, *The Theory of Social and Economic Organization*, trans. A. M. Henderson and T. Parsons (New York: Oxford University Press, 1947), pp. 330–34 (italics in original).

4. Chester I. Barnard, *The Functions of the Executive* (Cambridge, Mass.: Harvard University Press, 1938), pp. 115 and 123.

5. The classical example is found in F. J. Roethlisberger and William J. Dickson, *Management and the Worker* (Cambridge, Mass.: Harvard University Press, 1939).

6. Robert K. Merton, *Social Theory and Social Structure* (rev. ed.; Glencoe, Ill.: Free Press, 1957), pp. 19–84. Émile Durkheim, in 1895, was the first to set forth principles

of functional analysis in the social sciences. See *Rules of Sociological Method* (Chicago: University of Chicago Press, 1938), pp. 89–124. Although Weber explicitly rejected this approach (*op. cit.*, pp. 102–7), his discussion of bureaucracy is implicitly a functional analysis. For further formulations of this theory, parts of which are antithetical to that followed here, see Bronislaw Malinowski, "Culture," in *Encyclopaedia of the Social Sciences*, IV (1931), 621–45, and "The Group and the Individual in Functional Analysis," *American Journal of Sociology*, XLIV (1939), 939–64; A. R. Radcliffe-Brown, "On the Concept of Function in Social Science," *American Anthropologist* XXXVII (1935), 349–402, and "On Social Structure," *Journal of the Royal Anthropological Institute of Great Britain and Ireland*, LXX (1940), 1–12; Clyde Kluckhohn, *Navaho Witchcraft*, in Papers of the Peabody Museum of American Archeology and Ethnology, Harvard University, Vol. XXII, No. 2 (Cambridge, Mass.: Peabody Museum, 1944); Talcott Parsons, *Essays in Sociological Theory* (Glencoe, Ill.: Free Press, 1949), pp. 3–41; and Marion J. Levy, Jr., *The Structure of Society* (Princeton, N.J.: Princeton University Press, 1952).

7. Merton, *op. cit.*, p. 50 (italics in original).

8. See on this point Herbert A. Simon, *Administrative Behavior* (New York: Macmillan Co., 1945), p. 172 and *passim*.

9. See A. R. Radcliffe-Brown, "The Methods of Ethnology and Social Anthropology," *South African Journal of Science*, 1923, pp. 124–47, and "On the Concept . . . ," *op. cit.*

10. Merton, *op. cit.*, p. 51.

11. Often functions only reduce, and dysfunctions only intensify, social needs.

12. Conversely, changes in value orientations also produce new needs; conditions that were once considered satisfactory are defined by new objectives as necessitating improvement, Changes in value orientations in the two organizations studied are discussed in chap. xii.

13. See Merton, *op. cit.*, p. 52.

14. See the two sets of quotations from Weber at the beginning of chap. i.

15. A basic shortcoming of the ideal-type construct is that it contains both definitions of concepts and hypotheses about empirical relationships but fails to make a distinction between these two fundamentally different scientific tools. For other criticisms of Weber's ideal type see Alexander von Schelting, "Die logische Theorie der historischen Kulturwissenschaften von Max Weber und im Besondern sein Begriff des Idealtypus," *Archiv für Sozialwissenschaft und Sozialpolitik*, XLIX (1922), 623–752; Talcott Parsons, *The Structure of Social Action* (New York: McGraw-Hill Book Co., 1937), pp. 601–24; Carl J. Friedrich, "Some Observations on Weber's Analysis of Bureaucracy," in R. K. Merton *et al.* (eds.), *Reader in Bureaucracy* (Glencoe, Ill.: Free Press, 1952); and Reinhard Bendix, *Max Weber* (New York: Doubleday & Co., 60), pp. 280–82.

16. Everett C. Hughes shows that the emergencies of other people become the daily routine of professional experts. See his "Mistakes at Work," *Canadian Journal of Economics and Political Science*, XVII (1951), 320–27.

17. Except in private bureaucracies that have also adopted explicit promotion procedures.

18. None of 69 officials interviewed *aspired* to high positions in civil service within the next ten years, but 30 aspired to high positions in private industry or self-employment although only 8 *expected* to leave the government. Whether an individual directed his aspirations outside or inside civil service was not related to his work satisfaction but simply depended on whether he expressed *any high* aspirations or not. Hopeful

aspirations are not necessarily realistic, but their attainment must be conceivable, not impossible. Since officials knew that it was legally impossible for them suddenly to be promoted to, say, assistant commissioner, they either ceased to entertain hopes of this type of success or, if they wanted to indulge in wishful thinking, directed their aspirations toward careers outside the government service. One of the merits of the civil service system is that it discourages occupational aspirations that, by their very nature, must be frustrated in the majority of cases.

19. Conditions that reduce social cohesion are, of course, dysfunctional for bureaucratic operations. This seems to be an unintended dysfunction of loyalty investigations. For example, two agents, both of whom were subsequently cleared, had been investigated. This gave rise to serious dissension in the federal agency, involving many officials aside from the two directly concerned. It stirred up political differences, which had hardly been discussed before; it produced conflict between those who testified for an innocent colleague and those who disapproved of testifying for somebody under suspicion of disloyalty; it created emotional conflicts for those who were afraid to testify for a colleague they considered innocent, and disputes between them and those who regarded a refusal to bear witness in such a situation a betrayal; and it alienated from one another those who testified in support of and those who testified against the charges.

20. Donald Roy indicates that the workers he observed had a professional interest in, and derived satisfaction from, working efficiently, but they felt they must work slowly, although they did not like to do so, lest their piece rates be cut. See his "Quota Restriction and Goldbricking in a Machine Shop," *American Journal of Sociology*, LVII (1952), 427–42; see also Stanley B. Mathewson, *Restrictions of Output among Unorganized Workers* (New York: Viking Press, 1931). The same phenomenon is observed, but differently interpreted by F. J. Roethlisberger and William J. Dickson, *Management and the Worker* (Cambridge, Mass.: Harvard University Press, 1939). For a discussion of professionalization among factory workers see Nelson N. Foote, "The Professionalization of Labor in Detroit," *American Journal of Sociology*, LVIII (1953), 371–80.

21. Since these emergent social practices were not spontaneously accepted by every individual, the work group enforced conformity with them among its members through the use of sanctions.

22. Dysfunctions for the public do not evoke the concern of officials preoccupied with operations. They are also likely to fail to attract the attention of the observer focused upon studying the bureaucratic structure. This may account for the scarcity of examples of these dysfunctions.

23. Identification with clients is no substitute for such democratic checks, since it may lead to favoritism, as has been shown, and hence conflict with the collective interest of clients.

24. Robert S. Lynd, *Knowledge for What?* (Princeton, N.J.: Princeton University Press, 1946), pp. 210–11, 212.

60

The Organization Man

William H. Whyte

Introduction

This book is about the organization man. If the term is vague, it is because I can think of no other way to describe the people I am talking about. They are not the workers, nor are they the white-collar people in the usual, clerk sense of the word. These people only work for The Organization. The ones I am talking about *belong* to it as well. They are the ones of our middle class who have left home, spiritually as well as physically, to take the vows of organization life, and it is they who are the mind and soul of our great self-perpetuating institutions. Only a few are top managers or ever will be. In a system that makes such hazy terminology as 'junior executive' psychologically necessary, they are of the staff as much as the line, and most are destined to live poised in a middle area that still awaits a satisfactory euphemism. But they are the dominant members of our society nonetheless. They have not joined together into a recognizable élite – our country does not stand still long enough for that – but it is from their ranks that are coming most of the first and second echelons of our leadership, and it is their values which will set the American temper.

The corporation man is the most conspicuous example, but he is only one, for the collectivization so visible in the corporation has affected almost every field of work. Blood brother to the business trainee off to join Du Pont is the seminary student who will end up in the church hierarchy, the doctor headed for the corporate clinic, the physics Ph.D. in a government laboratory, the intellectual on the foundation-sponsored team project, the engineering graduate in the huge drafting room at Lockheed, the young apprentice in a Wall Street law factory.

They are all, as they so often put it, in the same boat. Listen to them talk to each other over the front lawns of their suburbia and you cannot help but be struck by how well they grasp the common denominators which bind them. Whatever the differences in their organization ties, it is the common problems

---

Source: William Whyte, *The Organization Man*, (Harmondsworth: Penguin, 1965).

of collective work that dominate their attentions, and when the Du Pont man talks to the research chemist or the chemist to the army man, it is these problems that are uppermost. The word *collective* most of them can't bring themselves to use – except to describe foreign countries or organizations they don't work for – but they are keenly aware of how much more deeply beholden they are to organization than were their elders. They are wry about it, to be sure; they talk of the 'treadmill', the 'rat race', of the inability to control one's direction. But they have no great sense of plight; between themselves and organization they believe they see an ultimate harmony and, more than most elders recognize, they are building an ideology that will vouchsafe this trust.

It is the growth of this ideology, and its practical effects, that is the thread I wish to follow in this book. America has paid much attention to the economic and political consequences of big organization – the concentration of power in large corporations, for example, the political power of the civil service bureaucracies, the possible emergence of a managerial hierarchy that might dominate the rest of us. These are proper concerns, but no less important is the principal impact that organization life has had on the individuals within it. A collision has been taking place – indeed, hundreds of thousands of them, and in the aggregate they have been producing what I believe is a major shift in American ideology.

Officially, we are a people who hold to the Protestant Ethic. Because of the denominational implications of the term many would deny its relevance to them, but let them eulogize the American Dream, however, and they virtually define the Protestant Ethic. Whatever the embroidery, there is almost always the thought that pursuit of individual salvation through hard work, thrift, and competitive struggle is the heart of the American achievement.

But the harsh facts of organization life simply do not jibe with these precepts. This conflict is certainly not a peculiarly American development. In their own countries such Europeans as Max Weber and Durkheim many years ago foretold the change, and though Europeans now like to see their troubles as an American export, the problems they speak of stem from a bureaucratization of society that has affected every Western country.

It is in America, however, that the contrast between the old ethic and current reality has been most apparent – and most poignant. Of all peoples it is we who have led in the public worship of individualism. One hundred years ago De Tocqueville was noting that though our special genius – and failing – lay in cooperative action, we talked more than others of personal independence and freedom. We kept on, and as late as the twenties, when big organization was long since a fact, affirmed the old faith as if nothing had really changed at all.

Today many still try, and it is the members of the kind of organization most responsible for the change, the corporation, who try the hardest. It is the corporation man whose institutional ads protest so much that Americans speak up in town meetings, that Americans are the best inventors because Americans don't care that other people scoff, that Americans are the best soldiers because they have so much initiative and native ingenuity, that the boy selling papers on the street corner is the prototype of our business society. Collectivism? He abhors it, and when he makes his ritualistic attack on Welfare Statism, it is in terms of a Protestant Ethic undefiled by change – the sacredness of property, the enervating effect of security, the virtues of thrift, of hard work and independence. Thanks be, he says, that there are some people left – e.g., businessmen – to defend the American Dream.

He is not being hypocritical, only compulsive. He honestly wants to believe he follows the tenets he extols, and if he extols them so frequently it is, perhaps, to shut out a nagging suspicion that he, too, the last defender of the faith, is no longer pure. Only by using the language of individualism to describe the collective can he stave off the thought that he himself is in a collective as pervading as any ever dreamed of by the reformers, the intellectuals, and the utopian visionaries he so regularly warns against.

The older generation may still convince themselves; the younger generation does not. When a young man says that to make a living these days you must do what somebody else wants you to do, he states it not only as a fact of life that must be accepted but as an inherently good proposition. If the American Dream deprecates this for him, it is the American Dream that is going to have to give, whatever its more elderly guardians may think. People grow restive with a mythology that is too distant from the way things actually are, and as more and more lives have been encompassed by the organization way of life, the pressures for an accompanying ideological shift have been mounting. The pressures of the group, the frustrations of individual creativity, the anonymity of achievement: are these defects to struggle against – or are they virtues in disguise? The organization man seeks a redefinition of his place on earth – a faith that will satisfy him that what he must endure has a deeper meaning than appears on the surface. He needs, in short, something that will do for him what the Protestant Ethic did once. And slowly, almost imperceptibly, a body of thought has been coalescing that does that.

*

I am going to call it a Social Ethic. With reason it could be called an organization ethic, or a bureaucratic ethic: more than anything else it rationalizes the organization's demands for fealty and gives those who offer it wholeheartedly a sense of dedication in doing so – *in extremis*, you might say, it converts what would seem in other times a bill of no rights into a restatement of individualism.

But there is a real moral imperative behind it, and whether one inclines to its beliefs or not he must acknowledge that this moral basis, not mere expediency, is the source of its power. Nor is it simply an opiate for those who must work in big organizations. The search for a secular faith that it represents can be found throughout our society – and among those who swear they would never set foot in a corporation or a government bureau. Though it has its greatest applicability to the organization man, its ideological underpinnings have been provided not by the organization man but by intellectuals he knows little of and toward whom, indeed, he tends to be rather suspicious.

Any groove of abstraction, Whitehead once remarked, is bound to be an inadequate way of describing reality, and so with the concept of the Social Ethic. It is an attempt to illustrate an underlying consistency in what in actuality is by no means an orderly system of thought. No one says, 'I believe in the social ethic', and though many would subscribe wholeheartedly to the separate ideas that make it up, these ideas have yet to be put together in the final, harmonious synthesis. But the unity is there.

In looking at what might seem dissimilar aspects of organization society, it is this unity I wish to underscore. The 'professionalization' of the manager, for example, and the drive for a more practical education are parts of the same phenomenon; just as the student now feels technique more vital than content, so the trainee believes managing an end in itself, an *expertise* relatively independent of the content of what is being managed. And the reasons are the same. So too in other sectors of our society; for all the differences in particulars, dominant is a growing accommodation to the needs of society – and a growing urge to justify it.

*

Let me now define my terms. By Social Ethic I mean that contemporary body of thought which makes morally legitimate the pressures of society against the individual. Its major propositions are three: a belief in the group as the source of creativity; a belief in 'belongingness' as the ultimate need of the individual; and a belief in the application of science to achieve the belongingness.

In subsequent chapters I will explore these ideas more thoroughly, but for the moment I think the gist can be paraphrased thus: Man exists as a unit of society. Of himself, he is isolated, meaningless; only as he collaborates with others does he become worth while, for by sublimating himself in the group, he helps produce a whole that is greater than the sum of its parts. There should be, then, no conflict between man and society. What we think are conflicts are misunderstandings, breakdowns in communication. By applying the methods of science to human relations we can eliminate these obstacles to consensus and create an equilibrium in which society's needs and the needs of the individual are one and the same.

Essentially, it is a utopian faith. Superficially, it seems dedicated to the practical problems of organization life, and its proponents often use the word *hard* (versus *soft*) to describe their approach. But it is the long-range promise that animates its followers, for it relates techniques to the vision of a finite, achievable harmony. It is quite reminiscent of the beliefs of utopian communities of the 1840s. As in the Owen communities, there is the same faith that there need be no conflict between the individual's aspirations and the community's wishes, because it is the natural order of things that the two be synonymous.

Like the utopian communities, it interprets society in a fairly narrow, immediate sense. One can believe man has a social obligation and that the individual must ultimately contribute to the community without believing that group harmony is the test of it. In the Social Ethic I am describing, however, man's obligation is in the here and now; his duty is not so much to the community in a broad sense but to the actual, physical one about him, and the idea that in isolation from it – or active rebellion against it – he might eventually discharge the greater service is little considered. In practice, those who most eagerly subscribe to the Social Ethic worry very little over the long-range problems of society. It is not that they don't care but rather that they tend to assume that the ends of the organization and morality coincide, and on such matters as social welfare they give their proxy to the organization.

*

It is possible that I am attaching too much weight to what, after all, is something of a mythology. Those more sanguine than I have argued that this faith is betrayed by reality in some key respects and that because it cannot long hide from organization man that life is still essentially competitive the faith must fall of its own weight. They also maintain that the Social Ethic is only one trend in a society which is a prolific breeder of counter-trends. The farther the pendulum swings, they believe, the more it must eventually swing back.

I am not persuaded. We are indeed a flexible people, but society is not a clock and to stake so much on counter-trends is to put a rather heavy burden on providence. Let me get ahead of my story a bit with two examples of trend v. counter-trend. One is the long-term swing to the highly vocational business-administration courses. Each year for seven years I have collected all the speeches by businessmen, educators, and others on the subject, and invariably each year the gist of them is that this particular pendulum has swung much too far and that there will shortly be a reversal. Similarly sanguine, many academic people have been announcing that they discern the beginnings of a popular swing back to the humanities. Another index is the growth of personality testing. Regularly year after year many social scientists have assured me that this bowdlerization of psychology is a contemporary aberration soon to be laughed out of court.

Meanwhile, the organization world grinds on. Each year the number of business-administration majors has increased over the last year – until, in 1954, they together made up the largest single field of undergraduate instruction outside of the field of education itself. Personality testing? Again, each year the number of people subjected to it has grown, and the criticism has served mainly to make organizations more adept in sugar-coating their purpose. No one can say whether these trends will continue to outpace the counter-trends, but neither can we trust that an equilibrium-minded providence will see to it that excesses will cancel each other out. Counter-trends there are. There always have been, and in the sweep of ideas ineffectual many have proved to be.

It is also true that the Social Ethic is something of a mythology, and there is a great difference between mythology and practice. An individualism as stringent, as selfish as that often preached in the name of the Protestant Ethic would never have been tolerated, and in reality our predecessors cooperated with one another far more skilfully than nineteenth-century oratory would suggest. Something of the obverse is true of the Social Ethic; so complete a denial of individual will won't work either, and even the most willing believers in the group harbour some secret misgivings, some latent antagonism toward the pressures they seek to deify.

But the Social Ethic is no less powerful for that, and though it can never produce the peace of mind it seems to offer, it will help shape the nature of the quest in the years to come. The old dogma of individualism betrayed reality too, yet few would argue, I dare say, that it was not an immensely powerful influence in the time of its dominance. So I argue of the Social Ethic; call it mythology, if you will, but it is becoming the dominant one.

*

In the first part of this book I wish to go into some of the ideas that have helped produce the Social Ethic. I do not intend an intellectual history; my aim is the more limited one of suggesting how deep are its roots and that it is not a temporary phenomenon triggered by the New Deal or the war or our recent prosperity.

I will then pick up the organization man in college, follow him through his initial indoctrination in organization life, and explore the impact of the group way upon him. While I will speak of the corporation man more than any other, I wish to show the universality of the Social Ethic. I will turn, accordingly, to the research laboratory and academic life and argue that the inclination to the cooperative ideal has had just as important consequences in these areas also. To illustrate further the universality of the Social Ethic, I will take up its expression in popular fiction. This will bring me finally to what I consider the best place to get a preview of the direction the Social Ethic is likely to take in the future

This is the new suburbia, the packaged villages that have become the dormitory of the new generation of organization men. They are not typical American communities, but because they provide such a cross section of young organization people we can see in bolder relief than elsewhere the kind of world organization man wants and may in time bring about. Here I will go into the tremendous effect transiency has had on the organization people and how their religious life, their politics, and the way they take to their neighbours reveal the new kind of rootedness they are looking for. And, finally, the moral of it all as they explain it to their children – the next generation of organization people.

*

While the burden of this book is reportorial, I take a position and, in fairness to the reader, I would like to make plain the assumptions on which I base it. To that end, let me first say what I am *not* talking about.

This book is not a plea for non-conformity. Such pleas have an occasional therapeutic value, but as an abstraction, non-conformity is an empty goal, and rebellion against prevailing opinion merely because it is prevailing should no more be praised than acquiescence to it. Indeed, it is often a mask for cowardice, and few are more pathetic than those who flaunt outer differences to expiate their inner surrender.

I am not, accordingly, addressing myself to the surface uniformities of U.S. life. There will be no strictures in this book against 'Mass Man' – a person the author has never met – nor will there be any strictures against ranch wagons, or television sets, or grey-flannel suits. They are irrelevant to the main problem, and, furthermore, there's no harm in them. I would not wish to go to the other extreme and suggest that these uniformities *per se* are good, but the spectacle of people following current custom for lack of will or imagination to do anything else is hardly a new failing, and I am not convinced that there has been any significant change in this respect except in the nature of the things we conform to. Unless one believes poverty ennobling, it is difficult to see the three-button suit as more of a strait jacket than overalls, or the ranch-type house than old law tenements.

And how important, really, are these uniformities to the central issue of individualism? We must not let the outward forms deceive us. If individualism involves following one's destiny as one's own conscience directs, it must for most of us be a realizable destiny, and a sensible awareness of the rules of the game can be a condition of individualism as well as a constraint upon it. The man who drives a Buick Special and lives in a ranch-type house just like hundreds of other ranch-type houses can assert himself as effectively and courageously against his particular society as the bohemian against his particular society. He usually does not, it is true, but if he does, the surface uniformities can serve quite well as protective coloration. The organization people who are best able to control their environment rather than be controlled by it are well aware that they are not too easily distinguishable from the others in the outward obeisances paid to the good opinions of others. And that is one of the reasons they do control. They disarm society.

I do not equate the Social Ethic with conformity, nor do I believe those who urge it wish it to be, for most of them believe deeply that their work will help, rather than harm, the individual. I think their ideas are out of joint with the needs of the times they invoke, but it is their ideas, and not their good will, I wish to question. As for the lackeys of organization and the charlatans, they are not worth talking about.

Neither do I intend this book as a censure of the fact of organization society. We have quite enough problems today without muddying the issue with misplaced nostalgia, and in contrasting the old ideology with the new I mean no contrast of paradise with paradise lost, an idyllic eighteenth century with a dehumanized twentieth. Whether or not our own era is worse than former ones in the climate of freedom is a matter that can be left to later historians, but for the purposes of this book I write with the optimistic premiss that individualism is as possible in our times as in others.

I speak of individualism *within* organization life. This is not the only kind, and some day it may be that the mystics and philosophers more distant from it may prove the crucial figures. But they are affected too by the centre of society, and they can be of no help unless they grasp the nature of the main stream. Intellectual scoldings based on an impossibly lofty ideal may be of some service in upbraiding organization man with his failures, but they can give him no guidance. The organization man may agree that industrialism has destroyed the moral fabric of society and that we need to return to the agrarian virtues, or that business needs to be broken up into a series of smaller organizations, or that it's government that needs to be broken up, and so on. But he will go his way with his own dilemmas left untouched.

I am going to argue that he should fight the organization. But not self-destructively. He may tell the boss to go to hell, but he is going to have another boss, and, unlike the heroes of popular fiction, he cannot find surcease by leaving the arena to be husbandman. If he chafes at the pressures of his particular organization, either he must succumb, resist them, try to change them, or move to yet another organization.

Every decision he faces on the problem of the individual versus authority is something of a dilemma. It is not a case of whether he should fight against black tyranny or blaze a new trail against patent stupidity. That would be easy – intellectually, at least. The real issue is far more subtle. For it is not the evils of organization life that puzzle him, *but its very beneficence.* He is imprisoned in brotherhood. Because his area of manoeuvre seems so small and because the trapping so mundane, his fight lacks the heroic cast, but it is for all this as tough a fight as ever his predecessors had to fight.

*

Thus to my thesis. I believe the emphasis of the Social Ethic is wrong for him. People do have to work with others, yes; the well-functioning team is a whole greater than the sum of its parts, yes all this is indeed true. But is it the truth that now needs belabouring? Precisely because it *is* an age of organization, it is the other side of the coin that needs emphasis. We do need to know how to cooperate with The Organization but, more than ever, so do we need to know how to resist it. Out of context this would be an irresponsible statement. Time and place are critical, and history has taught us that a philosophical individualism can venerate conflict too much and cooperation too little. But what is the context today? The tide has swung far enough the other way, I submit, that we need not worry that a counter-emphasis will stimulate people to an excess of individualism.

The energies Americans have devoted to the cooperative, to the social, are not to be demeaned; we would not, after all, have such a problem to discuss unless we had learned to adapt ourselves to an increasingly collective society as well as we have. An ideal of individualism which denies the obligations of man to others is manifestly impossible in a society such as ours, and it is a credit to our wisdom that while we preached it, we never fully practised it.

But in searching for that elusive middle of the road, we have gone very far afield, and in our attention to making organization work we have come close to deifying it. We are describing its defects as virtues and denying that there is – or should be – a conflict between the individual and organization. This denial is bad for the organization. It is worse for the individual. What it does, in soothing him, is to rob him of the intellectual armour he so badly needs. For the more power organization has over him, the more he needs to recognize the area where he must assert himself against it. And this, almost because we have made organization life so equable, has become excruciatingly difficult.

To say that we must recognize the dilemmas of organization society is not to be inconsistent with the hopeful premiss that organization society can be as compatible for the individual as any previous society. We are not hapless beings caught in the grip of forces we can do little about, and wholesale damnations of our society only lend a further mystique to organization. Organization has been made by man; it can be changed by man. It has not been the immutable course of history that has produced such constrictions on the individual as personality tests. It is organization man who has brought them to pass and it is he who can stop them.

The fault is not in organization, in short, it is in our worship of it. It is in our vain quest for a utopian equilibrium, which would be horrible if it ever did come to pass; it is in the soft-minded denial that there is a conflict between the individual and society. There must always be, and it is the price of being an individual that he must face these conflicts. He cannot evade them, and in seeking an ethic that offers a spurious peace of mind, thus does he tyrannize himself.

There are only a few times in organization life when he can wrench his destiny into his own hands – and if he does not fight then, he will make a surrender that will later mock him. But when is that time? Will he know the time when he sees it? By what standards is he to judge? He does feel an obligation to the group; he does sense moral constraints on his free will. If he goes against the group, is he being courageous – or just stubborn? Helpful – or selfish? Is he, as he so often wonders, right after all? It is in the resolution of a multitude of such dilemmas, I submit, that the real issue of individualism lies today.

The Decline of the Protestant Ethic

Let us go back a moment to the turn of the century. If we pick up the Protestant Ethic as it was then expressed we will find it apparently in full flower. We will also find, however, an ethic that already had been strained by reality. The country had changed. The ethic had not.

Here, in the words of banker Henry Clews as he gave some fatherly advice to Yale students in 1908, is the Protestant Ethic in purest form:

> *Survival of Fittest*: You may start in business, or the professions with your feet on the bottom rung of the ladder – it rests with you to acquire the strength to climb to the top. You can do so if you have the will and the force to back you. There is always plenty of room at the top. . . . Success comes to the man who tries to compel success to yield to him. Cassius spoke well to Brutus when he said, 'The fault is not in our stars, dear Brutus, that we are underlings, but in our natures.'

> *Thrift*: Form the habit as soon as you become a money-earner, or money-maker, of saving a part of your salary, or profits. Put away one dollar out of every ten you earn. The time will come in your lives when, if you have a little money, you can control circumstances; otherwise circumstances will control you. . . .

Note the use of such active words as *climb, force, compel, control.* As stringently as ever before, the Protestant Ethic still counselled struggle against one's environment – the kind of practical, here and now struggle that paid off in material rewards. And spiritually too. The hard-boiled part of the Protestant Ethic was incomplete, of course, without the companion assurance that such success was moral as well as practical. To continue with Mr Clews:

> Under this free system of government, whereby individuals are free to get a living or to pursue wealth as each chooses, the usual result is competition. Obviously, then, competition really means industrial freedom. Thus, anyone may choose his own trade or profession, or, if he does not like it, he may change. He is free to work hard or not; he may make his own bargains and set his price upon his labour or his products. He is free to acquire property to any extent, or to part with it. By dint of greater effort or superior skill, or by intelligence, if he can make better wages, he is free to live better, just as his neighbour is free to follow his example and to learn to excel him in turn. If anyone has a genius for

making and managing money, he is free to exercise his genius, just as another is free to handle his tools.... If an individual enjoys his money, gained by energy and successful effort, his neighbours are urged to work the harder, that they and their children may have the same enjoyment.

It was an exuberantly optimistic ethic. If everyone could believe that seeking his self-interest automatically improves the lot of all, then the application of hard work should eventually produce a heaven on earth. Some, like the garrulous Mr Clews, felt it already had.

America is the true field for the human race. It is the hope and the asylum for the oppressed and down-trodden of every clime. It is the inspiring example of America – peerless among the nations of the earth, the brightest star in the political firmament – that is leavening the hard lump of aristocracy and promoting a democratic spirit throughout the world. It is indeed the gem of the ocean to which the world may well offer homage. Here merit is the sole test. Birth is nothing. The fittest survive. Merit is the supreme and only qualification essential to success.

Intelligence rules worlds and systems of worlds. It is the dread monarch of illimitable space, and in human society, especially in America, it shines as a diadem on the foreheads of those who stand in the foremost ranks of human enterprise. Here only a natural order of nobility is recognized, and its motto, without coat of arms or boast of heraldry, is 'Intelligence and integrity'.[1]

Without this ethic capitalism would have been impossible. Whether the Protestant Ethic preceded capitalism, as Max Weber argued, or whether it grew up as a consequence, in either event it provided a degree of unity between the way people wanted to behave and the way they thought they *ought* to behave, and without this ideology, society would have been hostile to the entrepreneur. Without the comfort of the Protestant Ethic, he couldn't have gotten away with his acquisitions – not merely because other people wouldn't have allowed him, but because his own conscience would not have. But now he was fortified by the assurance that he was pursuing his obligation to God, and before long, what for centuries had been looked on as the meanest greed, a rising middle class would interpret as the earthly manifestation of God's will.

*

But the very industrial revolution which this highly serviceable ethic begot in time began to confound it. The inconsistencies were a long while in making themselves apparent. The nineteenth century inheritors of the ethic were creating an increasingly collective society but steadfastly they denied the implications of it. In current retrospect the turn of the century seems a golden age of individualism, yet by the 1880s the corporation had already shown the eventual bureaucratic direction it was going to take. As institutions grew in size and became more stratified, they made all too apparent inconsistencies which formerly could be ignored. One of the key assumptions of the Protestant Ethic had been that success was due neither to luck nor to environment but only to one's natural qualities – if men grew rich it was because they deserved to. But the big organization became a standing taunt to this dream of individual success. Quite obviously to anyone who worked in a big organization, those who survived best were not necessarily the fittest but, in more cases than not, those who by birth and personal connexions had the breaks.

*

As organizations continued to expand, the Protestant Ethic became more and more divergent from the reality The Organization was itself creating. The managers steadfastly denied the change, but they, as much as those they led, were affected by it. Today, some still deny the inconsistency or blame it on creeping socialism; for the younger generation of managers however, the inconsistencies have become importuning

Thrift, for example. How can the organization man be thrifty? Other people are thrifty *for* him. He still buys most of his own life insurance, but for the bulk of his rainy-day saving, he gives his proxy to the financial and personnel departments of his organization. In his professional capacity also thrift is becoming a little un-American. The same man who will quote from Benjamin Franklin on thrift for the house organ would be horrified if consumers took these maxims to heart and started putting more money into savings and less into instalment purchases. No longer can he afford the luxury of damning the profligacy of the public; not in public, at any rate. He not only has to persuade people to buy more but persuade them out of any guilt feelings they might have for following his advice. Few talents are more commercially sought today than the knack of describing departures from the Protestant Ethic as reaffirmations of it.[2]

In an advertisement that should go down in social history, the J. Walter Thompson agency has hit the problem of absolution head-on. It quotes Benjamin Franklin on the benefits of spending. 'Is not the hope of being one day able to purchase and enjoy luxuries a great spur to labour and industry? ... May not luxury therefore produce more than it consumes, if, without such a spur, people would be, as they are naturally enough inclined to be, lazy and indolent?' This thought, the ad says, in a meaningful aside, 'appears to be a mature afterthought, qualifying his earlier and more familiar writings on the importance of thrift.'

*

'Hard work?' What price capitalism, the question is now so frequently asked, unless we turn our productivity into more leisure, more of the good life? To the organization man this makes abundant sense, and he is as sensitive to the bogy of overwork and ulcers as his forebears were to the bogy of slothfulness. But he is split. He believes in leisure, but so does he believe in the Puritan insistence on hard, self-denying work – and there are, alas, only twenty-four hours a day. How, then, to be 'broad gauge'? The 'broad-gauge' model we hear so much about these days is the man who keeps his work separate from leisure and the rest of his life. Any organization man who managed to accomplish this feat wouldn't get very far. He still works hard, in short, but now he has to feel somewhat guilty about it.

Self-reliance? The corporation estates have been expanding so dynamically of late that until about now the management man could suppress the thought that he was a bureaucrat; bureaucrats, as every businessman knew, were those people down in Washington who preferred safety to adventure. Just when the recognition began to dawn, no one can say, but since the war the younger generation of management haven't been talking of self-reliance and adventure with quite the straight face of their elders.

That upward path toward the rainbow of achievement leads smack through the conference room. No matter what name the process is called – permissive management, multiple management, the art of administration – the committee way simply can't be equated with the 'rugged' individualism that is supposed to be the business of business. Not for lack of ambition do the younger men dream so moderately; what they lack is the illusion that they will carry on in the great entrepreneurial spirit. Although they cannot bring themselves to use the word bureaucrat, the approved term – the 'administrator' – is not signally different in its implications. The man of the future, as junior executives see him, is not the individualist but the man who works through others for others.

*

Let me pause for a moment to emphasize a necessary distinction. Within business there are still many who cling resolutely to the Protestant Ethic, and some with as much rapacity as drove any nineteenth-century buccaneer. But only rarely are they of The Organization. Save for a small, and spectacular, group of financial operators, most who adhere to the old creed are small businessmen, and to group them as part of the 'business community', while convenient, implies a degree of ideological kinship with big business that does not exist.

Out of inertia, the small business is praised as the acorn from which a great oak may grow, the shadow of one man that may lengthen into a large enterprise. Examine businesses with fifty or less employees, however, and it becomes apparent the sentimentality obscures some profound differences. You will find some entrepreneurs in the classic sense – men who develop new products, new appetites, or new systems of distribution – and some of these enterprises may mature into self-perpetuating institutions. But very few.

The great majority of small business firms cannot be placed on any continuum with the corporation. For one thing, they are rarely engaged in primary industry; for the most part they are the laundries, the insurance agencies, the restaurants, the drugstores, the bottling plants, the lumber yards, the automobile dealers. They are vital, to be sure, but essentially they service an economy; they do not create new money within their area and they are dependent ultimately on the business and agriculture that does.

In this dependency they react more as antagonists than allies with the corporation. The corporation, it has become clear, is expansionist – a force for change that is forever a threat to the economics of the small businessman. By instinct he inclines to the monopolistic and the restrictive. When the druggists got the 'Fair Trade' laws passed it was not only the manufacturers (and customers) they were rebelling against but the whole mass economy movement of the twentieth century.

The tail wagged the dog in this case and it still often does. That it can, in the face of the growing power of the corporation, illustrates again the dominance mythology can have over reality. Economically, many a small businessman is a counter-revolutionist and the revolution he is fighting is that of the corporation as much as the New or Fair Deal. But the corporation man still clings to the idea that the two are firm allies, and on some particulars, such as fair trade, he often makes policy on this basis when in fact it is against the corporation's interests to do so.

But the revolution is not to be stopped by sentiment. Many anachronisms do remain; in personal income, for example, the corporation man who runs a branch plant on which a whole town depends is lucky to make half the income of the local car dealer or the man with the Coca-Cola franchise. The economy has a way of attending to these discrepancies, however, and the local businessman can smell the future as well as anyone else. The bland young man The Organization sent to town to manage the plant is almost damnably inoffensive; he didn't rent the old place on the hill but a smaller house, he drives an Olds instead of a Caddy, and when he comes to the Thursday luncheons he listens more than he talks. But he's the future just the same.

*

I have been talking of the impact of organization on the Protestant Ethic; just as important, however, was the intellectual assault. In the great revolt against traditionalism that began around the turn of the century, William James, John Dewey, Charles Beard, Thorstein Veblen, the muckrakers, and a host of reformers brought the anachronisms of the Protestant Ethic under relentless fire, and in so doing helped lay the groundwork for the Social Ethic. It would be a long time before organization men would grasp the relevance of these new ideas, and to this day many of the most thorough-going pragmatists in business would recoil at being grouped with the intellectuals. (And *vice versa.*) But the two movements were intimately related. To what degree the intellectuals were a cause of change, or a manifestation, no one can say for certain, but more presciently than those in organization they grasped the antithesis between the old concept of the rational, unbeholden individual and the world one had to live in. They were not rebels against society; what they fought was the denial of society's power, and they provided an intellectual framework that would complement, rather than inhibit, the further growth of big organization.

It is not in the province of this book to go into a diagnosis of the ideas of Dewey and James and the other pragmatists. But there is one point of history I think very much needs making at this time. Many people still look on the decline of the Protestant Ethic as our fall from grace, a detour from Americanism for which we can blame pragmatism, ethical relativism, Freudianism, and other such developments. These movements have contributed much to the Social Ethic, and many of their presuppositions are as shaky as those they replaced. To criticize them on this score is in order; to criticize them as having subverted the American temper, however, is highly misleading.

Critics of pragmatism, and followers too, should remember the context of the times in which the pragmatists made their case. The pragmatists' emphasis on social utility may be redundant for today's needs, but when they made their case it was not a time when psychology or adjustment or social living were popular topics but at a time when the weight of conservative opinion denied that there was anything much that needed adjusting.

Quite clearly revolt was in order. The growth of the organization society did demand a recognition that man was not entirely a product of his free will; the country did need an educational plant more responsive to the need of the people. It did need a new breeze, and if there had been no James or no Dewey, some form of pragmatism would probably have been invented anyway. Nonphilosophical Americans sensed that changes were in order too; what the philosophers of pragmatism did was to give their guidance and tell them in intellectually responsible terms that they were right in feeling that way.

Pragmatism's emphasis on the social and the practical, further more, was thoroughly in the American tradition. From the beginning, Americans had always been impatient with doctrines and systems; like the Puritans, many came here because of a doctrine but what they came to was a new environment that required some powerful adapting to, and whenever the doctrine got in the way of practicality, the doctrine lost out. Few people have had such a genius for bending ideals to the demands of the times, and the construction of fundamental theory, theological or scientific has never excited Americans overmuch. Long before James, *Does it work?* was a respectable question to ask. If impatience at abstract thought was a defect, it was the defect of a virtue, and the virtue, call it what you will, has always been very close to pragmatism as Dewey and

James defined it. By defining it they gave it coherence and power at a time when it needed assertion, but the inclination to the practical antedated the philosophy; it was not the product of it.

*

Reform was everywhere in the air. By the time of the First World War the Protestant Ethic had taken a shellacking from which it would not recover, rugged individualism and hard work had done wonders for the people to whom God in his infinite wisdom, as one put it, had given control of society. But it hadn't done so well for everyone else and now they, as well as the intellectuals were all too aware of the fact.

The ground, in short, was ready, and though the conservative opinion that drew the fire of the rebels seemed entrenched, the basic temper of the country was so inclined in the other direction that emphasis on the social became the dominant current of thought. In a great outburst of curiosity, people became fascinated with the discovering of all the environmental pressures on the individual that previous philosophies had denied. As with Freud's discoveries, the findings of such inquiries were deeply disillusioning at first, but with characteristic exuberance Americans found a rainbow. Man might not be perfectible after all, but there was another dream and now at last it seemed practical: the perfectibility of *society*.

Scientism

Just how these currents of reforms congealed into an orthodoxy is a problem in intellectual history I must duck. Trying to weigh whose ideas were most responsible is in any event somewhat fruitless, for it is what people want to believe that is important and those whose ideas they so frequently misinterpret should not be whipped for the bowdlerization. Freud, for example, who once remarked that he was not a Freudian, never maintained that man was forever a hostage to childhood traumata, with resolution and intelligence, he believed, the individual could, by understanding these factors, perhaps surmount them. Nor did James or Dewey ever say that the convenience of society was the key test of morality, and they most certainly did not believe that man was totally the product of those around him.

The popular ideology I am describing is highly elastic but it has a remarkable unity nonetheless. Most believers in the many sub-branches of American organization life are still unaware of the interlocking nature of their separate credos, and it is partly for this reason they so often feel themselves missionaries in the midst of the unbelieving. Change a word here and there, however, and what many an educator is prescribing is exactly what many a personnel man is prescribing, and many a research director, and so on through the roster of our institutions.

In these next three chapters I am going to outline three principal denominators which bind them. While each is important in its own right, it is their interrelationship that I wish to illuminate. Until this unity is discerned, to attack the fallacies of technique in each separate field is as futile as hacking away at the hydra; it is the central, nourishing vision that we must address ourselves to.

*

The first denominator is scientism. This is the practical part of the Social Ethic, for it is the promise that with the same techniques that have worked in the physical sciences we can eventually create an exact science of man.[3] In one form or another, it has had a long and dismal record of achievement; even its proponents readily admit that the bugs are appalling. But this has not shaken the faith in scientism, for it is essentially a utopian rather than a technical idea.

The preamble of the believers is always the same. We are in a terrible fix and it is almost too late. We have applied science to things, and only now have we begun applying it to man himself. Already we have learned some useful social techniques; we can measure personality, can spot the obstacles to good group dynamics, and predict communication response. But these are merely the beginning; if only we provide the time and money, before long we can unwrap the whole enigma with a unified science of man.

Here, extracted from the proceedings of several conferences, is a fair composite of the message:

> If we draw into our group increasing numbers of hardheaded students, some of whom are not afraid of mathematics, and if we have faith and daring, we can build a science of man. . . . The conditions which determine human happiness are discoverable by scientific methods and are to a major extent capable of realization. . . . More than ever, the world's greatest need is a science of human relationships and an art of human engineering based upon the laws of such science. We should, to put it brutally, pay more attention, first to the scientific aspects of our problems rather than to the philosophical ones. . . . Although human relationship problems are extremely complicated, science is gradually reducing them to simple fundamentals through which these complexities are reduced to factors that respond to direct and simple treatment.

Inevitably, there is the atom-bomb analogy:

> It is trite but true to say that if social science had been given early enough the four billion dollars that have been spent on the atomic bomb and on chemical and germ warfare – say, half for research and the other

half for popular education – perhaps then the first release of atomic energy would have been for peaceful purposes.

And how very ancient it all is ! Most of the people who hearken to the vision of a unified science of man believe theirs is a fresh new vision, but in reality it is a cliché that has been kicked around for centuries.[4] Ever since Newton, scores of natural scientists have stepped out of their area of competence to suggest the possibilities of a science of man, and Erasmus's *Praise of Folly* suggests that even before this some savants had much the same idea. It was an understandable dream for a natural scientist to have. Even Descartes himself was seized with the idea that the discipline of mathematics could be extended to the affairs of man. Eventually, he thought, a 'Universal Mathematical Science' would solve the problem of society – if only there were sufficient funds and time for the job.

Later others tried the geometric tack: Thomas Hobbes worked out a complete set of algebraic equations to explain ethics. As Laurence Sterne remarked, his equations 'plussed or minussed you to heaven or hell . . . so that none but the expert mathematician would ever be able to settle his accounts with Saint Peter'. In 1725 one Francis Hutchison devised an even more elaborate mathematical calculation on morality, and without the advantages of modern technocracy, he was able to produce formulas fully as intricate as any being worked out today.

With the founding of the École Polytechnique in Paris at the end of the eighteenth century scientism was given another forward push; Saint-Simon and Auguste Comte energized a formidable school with the promise of positivism. If man would only apply the discipline of the natural sciences to the study of man, then only a sufficient expenditure of time, money, and thought would separate him from the good society.

If only . . . In a hundred variations, this promise has been phrased and rephrased. Yet one would gather from current exhortations that we are just about starting from scratch just the same. Current literature is full of dawn-of-discovery analogies – Balboa discovering the Pacific, Newton and the apple, etc. But it is precisely this figure of thought, this sense of being on the frontier that gives scientism so tremendous an appeal.

And for people in the commercial as well as the academic world. '"SECOND INDUSTRIAL REVOLUTIONARY" TO FORCE MAJOR CHANGES IN PRODUCTION, MERCHANDISING, AND SELLING' headlined *Advertising Age* (5 October 1953). E. B. Weiss, perhaps the best-known consultant in the merchandising field, explained to readers that it isn't simply that such advances as electronic calculators and automatic factories are going to make for more efficiency. A whole new science, he says, is abuilding, and with the confusion between control of the physical and control of the mental which is characteristic of believers in scientism, he proclaims that 'The Second Industrial Revolution will substitute the machine for the common, and for some fairly uncommon functions of the human *mind*. It is not his contention, he says in qualification, 'that the robot will replace *all* human endeavour'. But almost all. After initial successes, such as cutting out the personal element in retail selling, making inventory-taking automatic, the machine will advance into hitherto sacrosanct areas, and with what seems unwonted relish, he cites a scientist's prophecy that in time the machine will replace man in the realm of reasoning and logical deduction. 'NEXT WEEK: No. 2 in this series – How Cybernetic Principles Are Being and Will Be Applied in Factory, Office, and Warehouse.'

The field of public relations is particularly susceptible. Here, for example, the *Public Relations Journal* editorializes on the subject:

> Now, whether he knows it or not, every practising public-relations man is an engineer too – a *social engineer*. He develops new relationships and operations in society; designs new organizations and institutions, sets up and lubricates the human machinery for getting things done. The challenge of social engineering in our time is like the challenge of technical engineering fifty years ago. If the first half of the twentieth century was the era of the technical engineers, the second half may well be the era of the social engineers.

Dip into personnel journals, advertising trade journals, and you will find the same refrain. A lot of it is sheer malarkey, of course, but I think most of it is evidence of a genuine longing to be related to a faith.

We talk much about the alienation of the worker from the satisfaction of the whole job, but the same longing for a sense of continuity and purpose affects managerial people every bit as much. As our organizations have grown larger and more bureaucratic, they have created great layers of staff functions and the people in them often feel neither fish nor fowl – intellectuals, yet not of the intellectual world; managerial, yet without authority or prestige. Scientism, with its implications of the specialist as eventual saviour, can give the frustrated a sense of purpose that cuts across organization and occupational lines. I do not believe I read into scientism a coherence that they themselves do not feel. No matter what branch of social engineering a man is engaged in – 'mass' communication, 'the engineering of consent', public relations, advertising, personnel counselling – he can feel himself part of a larger movement.

Their good will is overpowering. Thoreau once said if you see a man approach you with the obvious intent of doing you good, you should run for your life; it is hard to restrain the impulse in talking with social engineers. Theirs is not a mere limited desire to help out a bit with the scientific method; the vision that energizes them is total – and exclusive. Science is not merely a tool, it is the only path to salvation in a world where the laymen have gone mad. There is no justification, one angry social engineer writes, 'in inflicting wounds on social scientists who might conceivably be blazing trails toward solutions of an otherwise hopeless crisis in civilization.' If the techniques are faulty, and this they admit, that is a matter of unfinished detail and insufficient funds, not principles, and no one should criticize until he offers a counter-utopia himself.

One should not fall into the trap of equating social engineering with social science. Some social scientists do believe in social engineering but a great many do not, and the claims some make in the name of social science are a serious embarrassment to them. A pretty good case could be made that the field would be more productive were it now called social *studies*. The study of man and society is quite worthy enough an occupation without being saddled with the task of hammering out a finite, embracing science, and the ultimate test of a social scientist's particular way of looking at people cannot be absolute truth; only the arrogant – or the stupid – can so aspire.

Part of the trouble lies in our new-found ability to measure more precisely, and the idea that the successes of natural science were due in large measure to the objectiveness of the phenomena studied eludes social engineers. There are, of course, aspects of man's behaviour that we can properly measure and we learn much by doing so. But how fascinating, alas, it all is! Here, it would seem, we can at last be rid of the bugbear of values. The median income level of a hundred selected families in an urban industrial universe correlates ·76 with population density – not ·78 or ·61 but ·76, and that's a fact. The next step beckons: having measured this far, it seems that there is nothing that can't be measured. We are purged of bias, and somehow by the sheer accumulation of such bias-free findings, we will have the basis of a theoretical formula that describes all. Just like physics.

In a pure example of scientism, psychologist James G. Miller has described how an institute could make this final integration.

> In constructing theory, we can employ models from the physical sciences. All psychological phenomena are essentially naturalistic – that is, ultimately they can be translated into principles of physics. . . . By having individuals from different disciplines working closely together on both theory and research, communication between disciplines can be greatly improved. . . . If there are general principles running through them all, these are more likely to be discovered by groups from different fields working together, and in close communication, than by individuals working alone. . . . Another related possibility is the use throughout all theoretical work of what Bertalanffy has called 'general system theory'. This is the contention, developing from the unity of science movement, that every system – whether it be a strictly physical system like a dry cell, or an automobile, a biological system like a single nerve cell or organ; a total organism; or a society – has certain formal characteristics which make possible comparison of it with all others. Hence, generalizations about all systems are feasible. . . . Perhaps an overall theory of behaviour is too near the end of the rainbow to be

reached; perhaps it is a will-o'-the-wisp. If so, our efforts may still be rewarded by the salvage of microtheories about limited areas.

Let us assume, for the moment, that a precise science of man is not a will-o'-the-wisp and that we are on our way to achieving it. We are left with a knotty problem. What do we do about good and evil, right and wrong? Believers in scientism confess that the question requires hard thinking. They are glad that ethical relativism has freed us from the narrow view that our own group's given values are the only correct ones. Obviously, then, a science of man could not freeze on one scheme of ethics. If we are to be governed by it, however, it would need some sort of ethics. How are we to determine just what they should be?

Social engineers have emboldened themselves to seek the final solution. Now, they say, we will *scientifically determine ethics*. This is to be done, in part, through the concept of 'equilibrium'. 'How can we hope . . . to fix with assurity a particular class of behaviour as right or good?' asks anthropologist Elliot Chapple. 'From our point of view, this can be done by the use of the concept of equilibrium . . . hence good or bad, right or wrong, are comparable to the concept of health and medicine.'

I have read definitions of many equilibrium concepts but I am still not sure just what they mean and I am not sure their creators are either; as far as can be determined, it is one of those mushy words so serviceable to obscuring contradictions. As Gunnar Myrdal, in explaining his own theoretical model in *An American Dilemma*, has pointed out, in borrowing the equilibrium notion from physics most social scientists have thought of only one kind of equilibrium, the *stable* equilibrium. This generally can lead to an acceptance of social harmony – either that of the *status quo* or some future one – and the companion terms such as disharmony, disequilibrium, maladjustment, disorganization are by implication 'bad' things.

This helps explain the bias against conflict that is so prevalent in most social-science literature. Where the by-products of harmony are the good things, the by-products of conflict – such as tension, frustration – are the bad things. Without taking the equally wrong position of saying that tension and frustration *per se* are good, one can point out that it takes a rather firm set of values to classify them as bad. Few social engineers would state categorically that they classify conflict as bad, nevertheless the practical gist of the ethics-of-equilibrium notion is that good values are values that allow groups to interact benevolently on one another and the individuals in them.

If we grant the concept of equilibrium we are still left with a formidable task in getting down to cases. How do we find what an organization's equilibrium is? If it isn't in it, how is it to be gotten there? If ethics is to be scientized, some specific people will have to do it, and some specific people are going to have to see to it the ethics are applied to society. Who, then, is to be in charge?

Being most of them democratically inclined, the new utopians take this question very seriously. If manipulating people is bad and manipulation is one of the dirtiest words in the new lexicon how can one justify the manipulation of people for good ends? At every convocation of believers the matter is dialectically treated, and the result of this soul-searching has been a new enrichment of the vocabulary. Though social engineers love to analyse semantic folly, no group has searched more arduously for the magic term which will combine manipulation with moral sanction. Thus we hear that the wielder of the new social techniques will be a 'peace planner', a 'group therapist', an 'integrative leader', a 'social diagnostician' – a person empowered to dominate society, but disciplined by a scientific code of ethics from using his knowledge in any but good ways.

In spelling this out social engineers characteristically shield themselves from the implication of their doctrine by describing how social engineering could be applied to a worthy cause. In a typical example, psychiatrist William Borberg explains how social engineering would be applied to the United Nations.

> Now, the knowledge accumulated in the social sciences and the understanding of its possible value to the United Nations must of necessity be greater among the scientists themselves than among policy-making leaders and diplomats. I therefore wonder whether the social scientists might not consider the desirability of creating themselves an organ for the purpose of that relationship.... This would be one of the means by which we may gradually introduce into the thinking of policy-making leaders more and more scientific knowledge, scientific methods, and scientific mentality, and thus gradually substitute the present, essentially emotional basis for peace by a much better and much more reliable one, the scientific view of peace.[5]

As in other such suggested projects, the scientific *élite* is not supposed to give orders. Yet there runs through all of them a clear notion that questions of policy can be made somewhat non-partisan by the application of science. There seems little recognition that the contributions of social science to policy-making can never go beyond staff work. Policy can never be scientific, and any social scientist who has risen to an administrative position has learned this quickly enough. Opinion, values, and debate are the heart of policy, and while fact can narrow down the realm of debate, it can do no more.

And what a terrible world it would be! Hell is no less hell for being antiseptic. In the 1984 of Big Brother one would at least know who the enemy was – a bunch of bad men who wanted power because they liked power. But in the other kind of 1984 one would be disarmed for not knowing who the enemy was, and when the day of reckoning came the people on the other side of the table wouldn't be Big Brother's bad henchmen; they would be a mild-looking group of therapists who, like the Grand Inquisitor, would be doing what they did to help you.

But such a spectre is not the consequence of scientism that should preoccupy us. It's not merely that social engineers have no such vision in mind – they don't; the point is that they couldn't pull it off if they did. Curiously, many who have warned most urgently of the horrors of a scientific utopia are themselves awed by scientism; their fears are based on the premise that it can work. Science-fiction writers, perhaps our most vigorous moralists, often seem to say that what would be wrong would be *too much* scientism, and even those dead set against it appear impressed with the possibility of its dominance. Some European critics of America have gone them one better. They say it has already happened. If anybody wants to see man crushed by science and mechanization, it appears he has only to take a trip to the U.S. The latest such critic, Robert Jungk, draws a picture of white-coated men around UNIVAC, and docile robots listening to piped music. *Tomorrow,* he warns, *is already here.*

That kind of tomorrow isn't here and it probably never will be. The implied choice between science and humanity is a false one. The danger is not in science dominating man, and the fears of this rest on a false personalization of the inanimate, not to mention a romantic, if retrograde, longing for a past utopia. Nor need the spectre of a scientific *élite* worry us. It need not worry us because a 'science of man' cannot work in the way its believers think it can, and in subsequent chapters I hope to demonstrate how naïve some of the current techniques are.

But the gospel of scientism is no less important for that reason. To stretch a point, the trouble is not so much that these techniques work, but that they *do not* work. Schemes that don't work can have as much effect on society as schemes that do. Machiavellian rules ask one to compromise, in this case, on one's ethics. But at least they can work, and if we sell our souls we get some satisfying sin in recompense. Scientism asks that we make a compromise, but it can't deliver anything really in return. The scientific formulas for 'mass communication', for example: using them we manage to debase our prose, assault our instincts, and insult our listeners – but never do we get that sure-fire communion promised for our surrender. A poor bargain.

What I am arguing is that the real impact of scientism is upon our values. The danger, to put it another way, is not man being dominated but man surrendering. At the present writing there is not one section of American life that has not drunk deeply of the promise of scientism. It appears in many forms – pedagogy, aptitude tests, that monstrous nonentity called 'mass communication' – and there are few readers who have not had a personal collision with it.

Belongingness

What kind of society is to be engineered? Some critics of social engineering are sure that what is being cooked up for us is a socialistic paradise, a radically new, if not brave, world, alien to every tradition of man. This is wrong. Lump together the social engineers' prescriptions for the new society and you find they are anything but radical. Boiled down, what they ask for is an environment in which everyone is tightly knit into a belongingness with one another; one in which there is no restless wandering but rather the deep emotional security that comes from total integration with the group. Radical? It is like nothing so much as the Middle Ages.

And what, some have been asking, was so wrong with the Middle Ages anyway? They had excellent human relations. The didn't have the self-consciousness about their society to make them rationalize it or the scientific approach with which to do it. But belongingness they had. They knew where they stood – peasant and noble alike. They saw the fruit of their labour, and the tiny world about them protected as well as demanded. Psychologically, they had a home.

Not that we should go back to all this, mind you. The job, to paraphrase, is to *re-create* the belongingness of the Middle Ages. What with the Enlightenment, the Industrial Revolution, and other calamities, the job is immensely more difficult than it was in those simpler days. But with new scientific techniques we can solve the problem. What we must do is to learn consciously to achieve what once came naturally. We must form an *élite* of skilled leaders who will guide men back, benevolently, to group belongingness.

An unfair paraphrase? The young men who enthuse so unqualifiedly about human relations as the last best hope would be shocked to be accused of holding so reactionary a view. The people who have been the intellectual founders of the human relations gospel, however, have not been so muddy-minded. They were not the cheery optimists their latter-day followers seem to be; they were rather pessimistic about the capacities of man, and the society they prescribed was by no means a utopia which would be all things to all men. A man would have to make sacrifices to enjoy it, and the prophets of belongingness stated this with admirable toughness of mind.

*

The father of the human-relations school is Elton Mayo. Mayo, professor of industrial research at the Harvard Business School, was concerned with the anomie, or rootlessness, of the industrial worker. Ever since he first started studying industry in Australia in 1903 he had been looking for a way to reconcile the worker's need for belongingness with the conflicting allegiances of the complex world he now finds himself in.

For Mayo, and his colleagues, the great turning point came as the result of what started to be a very modest experiment. In 1927 some of Mayo's colleagues began the now celebrated study at the Hawthorne, Illinois, plant of Western Electric.[6] The company had a challenging problem for them. For several years it had been trying to measure how much more telephone equipment the workers would produce as lighting was improved in the rooms they worked in. The researchers chose three rooms and progressively increased the illumination in each, at the same time keeping a careful record of the work output. To their surprise, there seemed no clear relation between production and better illumination. They tried a more careful experiment: this time they would use only two rooms, one a 'control' group where conditions would be left the same and the experimental room where the changes would be introduced. Again, mixed results: output went up in the experimental room – but so did it go up in the control room.

At this point the Harvard group entered the picture and collaborated with the company on a more elaborate experiment: in a 'relay assembly' test room they isolated a group of women operators from others doing the same work and one by one introduced changes – not only lighting, but changes in rest periods, hours, and economic incentives. According to the commonly accepted 'scientific management principles' earlier advanced by Frederick Taylor, these changes in physical conditions and, most particularly, incentives would make the test group more productive than the other. But they didn't. As experiment followed experiment (the research was to continue until 1932) it became abundantly clear that physical changes were not the key. As in the earlier experiments, output did shoot ahead where conditions were changed, but so did output shoot ahead where no changes had been made.

How come? The researchers came to the conclusion that output shot up in both groups because in both groups the workers' participation had been solicited and this involvement, clearly, was more important than physical perquisites. The workers were a social system; the system was informal but it was what really determined the worker's attitude toward his job. This social system could work against management, but if the managers troubled themselves to understand the system and its function for the worker, the system could work for management.

In the literature of human relations the Hawthorne experiment is customarily regarded as a discovery. In large part it was; more than any other event, it dramatized the inadequacy of the purely economic view of man. The conclusions that flowed from the experiment, however, were a good bit more than as statement of objective fact, for Mayo and his group were evangelists as well a researchers. He had come to quite similar conclusions many years before, and for him the Hawthorne experiment did not reveal so much as confirm.

The two slim books Mayo published since Hawthorne have proved to be an immensely powerful manifesto. Mayo never pretended that he was free from values and he frankly presents an argument as well as a diagnosis. In *The Social Problems of an Industrial Civilization*, he opens his case by picturing man's happiness in more primitive times. 'Historically and traditionally our fathers worked for social cooperation – and achieved it. This is true also of any primitive society. But we, for at least a century of the most amazing scientific and material progress have abandoned the effort – by inadvertence, it is true – and are now reaping the consequences.'

In the Middle Ages people had been disciplined by social codes into working well together. The Industrial Revolution, as Mayo described the consequences, had split society into a whole host of conflicting groups. Part of a man belonged to one group, part to another, and he was bewildered; no longer was there *one* group in which he could sublimate himself. The liberal philosophers, who were quite happy to see an end to feudal belongingness, interpreted this release from the group as freedom. Mayo does not see it this way. To him, the dominant urge of mankind is to belong: 'Man's desire to be continuously associated in work with his fellows', he states, 'is a strong, if not the strongest, human characteristic.'

Whether the urge to cooperate is in fact man's most dominant drive, it does not follow that the cooperation is necessarily good. What is he going to cooperate *about*? What ends is the group working toward? But these questions do not greatly interest Mayo, and he seems to feel that the sheer fact of 'spontaneous' cooperation carries its own ethic. 'For *all* of us', Mayo states, 'the feeling of security and certainty derives *always* from assured membership of a group.' (Italics mine.)

Suppose there is a conflict between the individual and the group? Mayo sees conflict primarily as a breakdown in communication. If a man is unhappy or dissatisfied in his work, it is not that there is a conflict to be resolved so much as a misunderstanding to be cleared up. The worker might not see it this way and most certainly the unions do not, but we have already been told that the individual is a non-logical animal incapable of rationally solving his own problems or, in fact, of recognizing what the problem is.

At this point the human relations doctrine comes perilously close to demanding that the individual sacrifice his own beliefs that he may belong. The only way to escape this trap would be through the notion that by the process of equilibrium, a clarification of which never seems to detain anyone very long, what's good for the group is good for the individual. In speaking of the primitive group Mayo writes: 'The situation is not simply that the society exercises a forceful compulsion on the individual; on the contrary, the social code and the desire of the individual are, for all practical purposes, identical. Every member of the group participates in all social activities because it is his chief desire to do so.'

How to get back to this idyllic state? Mayo does not recommend a return to the Middle Ages. Too much water – and damn muddy water too, if you ask Mayo – has flowed under the bridge for that. The goal must be 'an *adaptive* society' – a society in which we can once again enjoy the belongingness of primitive times but without the disadvantages of them.

This won't come about naturally. What with the mischief caused by the philosophers of individualism, most contemporary leaders are untrained in the necessary social skill to bring the adaptive society to pass. What is needed is an administrative *élite*, people trained to recognize that what man really wants most is group solidarity even if he does not realize it himself. They won't push him around; they won't even argue with him – unfettered as they will be of 'prejudice and emotion', they won't have any philosophy, other than cooperation, to argue about. They will adjust him. Through the scientific application of human relations, these neutralist technicians will guide him into satisfying solidarity with the group so skilfully and unobtrusively that he will scarcely realize how the benefaction has been accomplished.

*

When Mayo got down to cases he was entirely consistent with his philosophy. His advocacy of 'non-directive counselling' is a good case in point. In the course of their interviewing at Hawthorne, Mayo and his colleagues became impressed with the therapeutic effects the interviews had on the workers and went on to make the interview a management tool. The idea was to have a group of counsellors who would be paid by management but who would not report to management what the workers said to them when they spilled their troubles. Since the workers knew this they could feel free to talk out their problems.

Implicit in this technique is the assumption that the worker's problems can indeed be *talked out*. He is to adjust to the group rather than *vice versa*; and the alternative of actually changing reality is hardly considered. If a worker is sore at his foreman the chances are good that he is not really sore at the foreman because of some rational gripe but is merely venting on the foreman certain repressed feelings. By listening patiently, like a psychiatrist, the counsellor helps such persons understand that what they are really sore about flows from inner, subjective conflict. Characteristically, Mayo cites a woman worker who 'discovered for herself during an interview that her dislike of a certain supervisor was based upon a fancied resemblance to a detested stepfather'.

In similar cases it is possible the worker might not be maladjusted at all. The foreman might have been dividing up the work load problem badly, and maybe he had a few syndromes himself. The non-directive counselling idea, however, pooh-poohs the possibility: if there is a conflict of values that can't be talked out the interview has no provision in it for action to be taken – the set-up itself, in short, is a value judgement that adjustment, rather than change, is the desideratum.

For a number of reasons, one being the hostility of the unions to it, the non-directive counselling system as such has never taken hold of the American industry. But the basic idea has. As I hope to demonstrate in later chapters, many of the more popular techniques – such as psychological 'personality' testing, conference techniques – are all manifestations of the same principle. The rock is the group and maladjustment is disharmony with it.

Ironically, the primary target of this adjustment has become the managers themselves. While Mayo intended human relations to apply to the workers and managers both, the managers first seized on it as an excellent tool for manipulating the workers into a chronic contentment that would turn them away from the unions. But manipulation is a two-edged weapon; having learned how illogical workers were, managerial pioneers of human relations soon began to ponder the fact that their colleagues weren't so logical either. They needed to belong too – and even more than the worker, for more of their life was involved in the organization. Looking at the neuroses about him, many a progressive young organization man resolved that here, not on the shop floor, was the place that needed human relations most.

The use of psychological tests, if I may get a bit ahead of my story, is symptomatic. Originally, they were introduced by the managers as a tool for weeding out unqualified workers. As time went on, and personality tests were added to aptitude tests, the managers began using them on other managers, present and prospective, and today most personality testing is directed not at the worker, but at the organization man. If he is being hoist, it is by his own philosophy.

*

Not so long after Mayo and his colleagues documented the importance of the group at Hawthorne, a former student of Mayo's, anthropologist Lloyd Warner, began coming to remarkably similar conclusions in a study of a New England town. This study, which has had a tremendous impact on social science, was an impressively large-scale undertaking in which some twenty researchers spent three years making a study of Newburyport, Massachusetts. Every conceivable fact about Newburyport was to be dug up, and through scientific evaluations, some objective conclusions were to be arrived at.

Several years before, Warner had studied a tribe of Australian aborigines and had been immensely impressed by the way in which the tribal customs and the unwritten laws kept the individual in harmony with the group. The rituals and sanctions seemed illogical at times, but they shielded man from the kind of individual decisions which a fast-changing industrial society could overwhelm him with.

When Warner began poking around Newburyport, he discovered strong parallels. It was a venerable old New England town rich in tradition and full of people with a strong attachment to the past.[7] There were Memorial Day celebrations instead of the Nurngin totem rites, but in many ways it seemed much the same, and Warner drew the same moral. Of the many conclusions that came out of the study, by all odds the most important finding was the function of social structure in fixing the individual in a satisfying relation to the society. Newburyport did not present altogether as happy a picture of stability as a medieval or primitive society would have. Even though it had been touched by the Industrial Revolution, however, it did provide excellent grist for Warner's argument that the happiness of man depended on the rootedness in a stable group. Like several other old communities, it had lost the economic basis of its early prosperity and thus was frozen somewhat in the mould of previous times.

Warner saw, and charted, seven class divisions in Newburyport, and from these generalized a concept of class and status for the country as a whole. The concept has long since been subjected to a thorough-going critical analysis by many social scientists; suffice it to say here that Warner's description carried with it a strong note of advocacy. Warner did believe that there should be some mobility between classes and he thought it healthy that a number of people could move up from, say, the upper-middle to the lower-upper. But not *too* many. The class structure would become meaningless in that case, and people would become bewildered for lack of a firm group to relate themselves to.

Conflict, change, fluidity – these are the evils from which man should be insulated. To Warner, the unconscious yearning for belongingness was all-important. During the time he and his associates were at Newburyport, the workers in the shoe factory there went on strike. Ostensibly, the strike was over economic matters; the workers thought they wanted more money. But Warner and his colleagues saw it another way. They saw so many other factors that they produced a book on the subject (called, somewhat flatly, *The Social System of the Modern Factory*). The real cause of the strike, the book implies, was not so much the economic plight of the workers as the social one. Back in the eighteen-hundreds they had enjoyed the status that comes from a firm hierarchy of skills and there had been the steadying hand of the paternal local capitalists. But now increased mechanization, while not rampant in the shoe industry, had downgraded the old high-status jobs; equally unfortunate, the absentee ownership of 'Big City capitalism' had supplanted the local oligarchy. Whether they knew it or not, in short, the workers struck because the cohesive society of old had broken down.

Some day someone is going to create a stir by proposing a radical new tool for the study of people. It will be called the face-value technique. It will be based on the premiss that people often do what they do for the reasons they think they do. The use of this technique would lead to many pitfalls, for it is undeniably true that people do not always act logically or say what they mean. But I wonder if it would produce findings any more unscientific than the opposite course.

That strike at Newburyport, for example. Warner did devote a couple of sentences to the logical, economic factors, but it's clear in reading the other three hundred pages that he feels that the real cause lay in the fact that there was no longer any 'hierarchy of skills' that used to give workers a sense of satisfaction and status. Well, maybe so, but most of the workers who struck didn't happen to have been around to remember the idyllic days of old described by Warner, and it is somewhat debatable if they would have liked them quite as much as Warner seems to believe they would. As far as I can gather from a careful reading of Warner's account of it, the workers acted with eminent logic. They wanted more money; the employers didn't want to give it to them; the workers banded together in strike, and the employers gave in. Is it so very naïve, then, to explain this strike as very much of an economic matter? Any more naïve than to attribute it to a nostalgia for ancient paternalism? Who has the nostalgia?

In fairness to Warner, it should be pointed out that he has subsequently been coming to the view that there is more mobility than Newburyport would suggest. His followers, however, have not been so flexible, and the Warner thesis, for all the defections of its author, remains a very powerful force. Among educators in particular it is one of the principal ideological bases for the belief that only a segment of society should be schooled in the humanities. The majority, goes the idea, should be taught lesser skills; rather than tantalize themselves with aspirations, they should adjust to the fact of a fairly fixed social system.

*

Neither Warner nor Mayo had much enthusiasm for the union as a social group; in Mayo's case it split loyalties in the factory scheme of things; in Warner's case it split the loyalties of the stable, fixed, small community. It could be argued, however, that if workers needed an embracing group the union had as much right to be it as any other group. Which brings us to the third variation on belongingness – the proposition of Frank Tannenbaum. Unlike Mayo, he is the father of no school; he is an historian rather than a labour leader. But his views are well worth examining all the same; they may not be symptomatic of labour thought but they are symptomatic of the growing quest for belongingness.

In the opening pages of Tannenbaum's *A Philosophy of Labor* (New York, Knopf, 1951) there is the customary salute to the Middle Ages.

> Membership in a guild, manorial estate, or village protected man throughout his life and gave him the peace and serenity from which could flow the medieval art and craft. The life of man was a nearly unified whole. Being a member of an integrated society protected and raised the dignity of the individual and gave each person his own special role. Each man, each act, was part of a total life drama, the plot of which was known and in which the part allotted to each was prescribed. No one was isolated or abandoned. His individuality and his ambitions were fulfilled within the customary law that ruled the community to which he belonged.

Then came the Industrial Revolution and paradise lost.

> The Industrial Revolution destroyed the solid moorings of an older way of life and cast the helpless workers adrift in a strange and difficult world. The peasant who had been reared in the intimacy of a small age . . . now found himself isolated and bewildered in a city crowded with strangers and indifferent to a common rule. The symbolic universe that had patterned the ways of men across the ages in village, manor, or guild had disappeared. This is the great moral tragedy of the industrial system.

To make matters worse, Tannenbaum continues, the philosophers of the enlightenment rationalized this breakdown of the old society in terms of individualism. 'This doctrine gave the social disintegration then taking place a moral purpose. . . . In its extreme form the theory seemed to advance the idea that the best society was that in which organized human relations and responsibilities were least.'

As Tannenbaum rightly points out, this doctrine of self-sufficiency was all very fine for the *bourgeoisie*, but for the workers, self-sufficiency was an illusion. In learning this, however, the workers were taking the first steps to re-creating a community. In making them recognize their individual helplessness, the employers made them recognize their common strength, 'The trade union', as Tannenbaum says, 'was the visible evidence that man is not a commodity, and that he is not sufficient unto himself.'

The kind of sufficiency Tannenbaum is most concerned with is social rather than economic, and thus to him the real promise of the unions lay in their potential as a social unit. But the workers, no less affected by the Protestant Ethic than their employers, had too pressing an agenda to be diverted from bread-and-butter economic matters. Thus, in fighting the unions, the employers were diverting the unions' energies from the ultimate goal. And the employers didn't do it just to save money; they resisted unionization 'because a society tends to become an all-embracing way of life'.

Now, however, Tannenbaum argues that the unions are at last in a position to become instruments of 'governance' rather than instruments of war. 'Only when the battle for recognition is finished can the institutional role come into its own. If the trade union could not fulfil its larger responsibilities, it would have no reason for existence, would not be a true society, would have no moral role, and would disintegrate.' The true end, then, is for a society in which the worker, like his ancestors in the Middle Ages, will be firmly rooted in a group with customs, laws, and guides. He will lose his mobility: – not for him the upward – and individual – path to the managerial world; the 'fluidity', both geographic and social, that we will see in suburbia is precisely the thing Tannenbaum wants to insulate man from. And the trend away from fluidity is not to be denied. 'Institutionally the trade union movement is an unconscious effort to harness the drift of our time and reorganize it around the cohesive identity that men working together always achieve. That is why the trade union is a repudiation of the individualism of the French Revolution and the liberalism of English utilitarian philosophers.'

Tannenbaum seems to be working the other side of the street from Mayo and Warner. But while they are truer to the medieval spirit in wanting the nobility rather than the serfs to be in charge, the outlook is the same. Any dispute is merely jurisdictional; they don't agree on *which* group should do the embracing but they are all of a piece on the idea the embracing should be done – although not by the state, for that would be totalitarian.

I do not mean to deprecate study of the function of groups. One can study something without deifying it, and a recognition that a society can be all-embracing doesn't require belief that it should be. The most vigorous criticism of the human-relations doctrine has come from social scientists, and most of them have by no means been uninterested in the power of the group or its value. However one differs with the findings of particular studies, the point at issue should be the findings, not the fact of the studies. An obvious point perhaps, but there does seem too little middle ground between the near-evangelical acceptance of social-science research on the one hand, and the damnation of it as the improper study of mankind because its particulars are found wanting.

Nor do values mar it; the point is to recognize the values that we may judge them. Mayo made his quite explicit, and in fairness to him and the other pioneers of human relations, we must remember the prevailing climate of opinion at the time; as John Dewey was to authoritarian education, so they were to authoritarian industry. Mayo emphasized group cohesiveness and administrative social skill so much because he felt – with considerable justification – that Americans had been slighting these matters. At a time when the people in charge of big organizations clung to the mechanistic views of the efficiency experts, Mayo brought a badly needed shift in perspective, he helped sensitize a steady stream of influential management people to the importance of the whole vast informal network beneath them and the necessity of comprehending it. One does not have to go along with Mayo's philosophy of the adaptive society to recognize the benefits in better management that he helped bring about.

But what was once counter-cyclical is now orthodoxy. Already human relations is a standard part of the curriculum of the business schools and it will not be very long before it is standard in the high schools too. Human relations can mean a lot of things – as one critic defines it, it is any study called human relations to escape the discipline of established theory in the appropriate field. But, generally speaking, most human-relations doctrine is pointed toward the vision of Mayo, and this reinforces what many people are already very well prepared to believe.

Particularly, the organization man. Who is the hero in human relations? In the older ideology, it was the top leader who was venerated. In human relations it is the organization man, and thus the quasi-religious overtones with which he gratefully endows it The older ideology provided an unsatisfactory view of the system for the large and growing bureaucratic slice of management. The human-relations doctrine, however, not only tells them that they are important, but that they are the key figures. As sociologist Reinhard Bendix has observed, in the new managerial ideology, it is not the leaders of industry that are idealized – if anything, they are scolded – but the lieutenants. The people that the workers are to cooperate with are not the top employers but enlightened bureaucrats.

At times it almost seems that human relations is a revolutionary tool the organization man is to use *against* the bosses. Listen to an unreconstructed boss give a speech castigating unreconstructed bosses for not being more enlightened about human relations, and you get the feeling the speech is a subtle form of revenge on the part of the harried underling who wrote it. For reasons of protocol, organization men publicly extol human relations for the beneficial effects it casts downward, but privately they spend most of their time talking about using it upward. Whenever there is responsible criticism of human relations, there is a hurt response from middle management staff people, and, invariably, the complaint boils down to something like this: Why, why hurt us? Many of the criticisms are true all right – some people have gone haywire on this – but we progressives have a tough enough fight converting the reactionaries on top, and any criticism at this time only gives aid and comfort to them.

It is not an easy complaint to answer – many older executives are indeed reactionary and many are against human relations for strange reasons. What makes the complaint particularly tough to answer, however, is the trusting way organization men assume that only techniques are subject for criticism and that surely the goals must be non-controversial. They thought that battle was won long ago. So it was. If I do not dwell more in this book on the beneficial aspects of human relations, it is because they have been reiterated quite enough already.

In practice, of course, corporations have not changed their ways quite so much as their self-congratulations on human relations suggest, and many a highly publicized programme is only a sugar-coating of the mixture as before. Because there remains a divergence between precept and practice, however, does not mean that the precept is any the less important. While older men may appropriate the vocabulary of human relations without the underlying philosophy, the younger men believe. They have had an indoctrination their superiors did not, and though experience may disillusion them somewhat they view the day of their ascension with genuine missionary zeal.

*

The point I am trying to make is not that the corporation, or any other specific kind of organization, is going to be *the* citadel of belongingness. The union of Frank Tannenbaum, the community of Lloyd Warner, the corporation of Elton

Mayo – each is in conflict as to which group is going to furnish the vital belongingness, and these three by no means exhaust the roster of groups proposed. Spokesmen in other areas have similarly bewailed the lack of an encompassing, integrated life, and in an excess of good will have asked that their group take over the whole messy job. Many a contemporary prescription for utopia can be summarized if you cross out the name of one group and substitute another in the following charge: Society has broken down; the family, the church, the community, the schools, business – each has failed to give the individual the belongingness he needs and thus it is now the task of – group to do the job. It is fortunate there are so many groups; with such competition for the individual psyche it is difficult for any one of them to land the franchise.

But ideologically these pleas do not cancel each other out. For there is always the common thread that a man must belong and that he must be unhappy if he does not belong rather completely. The idea that conflicting allegiances safeguard him as well as abrade him is sloughed over, and for the people who must endure the tensions of independence there is no condolence; only the message that the tensions are sickness – either in themselves or in society. It does not make any difference whether the Good Society is to be represented by a union or by a corporation or by a church; it is to be a society unified and purged of conflict.

To turn about and preach that conflicting allegiances are absolute virtues is not justified either. But at this particular time the function they perform in the maintenance of individual freedom is worthy of more respect. Clark Kerr, Chancellor of the University of California, at Berkeley, has put it well:

> The danger is not that loyalties are divided today but that they may be undivided tomorrow. . . . I would urge each individual to avoid total involvement in any organization; to seek to whatever extent lies within his power to limit each group to the minimum control necessary for performance of essential functions; to struggle against the effort to absorb; to lend his energies to many organizations and give himself completely to none; to teach children, in the home and in the school, 'to be laws to themselves and to depend on themselves', as Walt Whitman urged us many years ago – for that is the well source of the independent spirit.

Notes

1. Henry Clews, *Fifty Years in Wall Street*, New York (Irving Publishing Company), 1908.
2. Helping in this task is what a good part of 'motivation research' is all about. Motivation researcher Dr Ernest Dichter, in a bulletin to business, says, 'We are now

confronted with the problem of permitting the average American to feel moral even when he is flirting, even when he is spending, even when he is not saving, even when he is taking two vacations a year and buying a second or third car. One of the basic problems of this prosperity, then, is to give people the sanction and justification to enjoy it and to demonstrate that the hedonistic approach to his life is a moral, not an immoral one.'

3. N.B.: This is a very rough definition, and most people who have used the term have a different way of analysing its bases. Hayek describes it as based on three fallacies: objectivism, collectivism, and historicism. By this he means the attempt to dispense with subjective knowledge; to treat abstract wholes – such as 'society' – as definite objectives, like biological organisms; the attempt to make history a science, and the only one of social phenomena. (F. A. Hayek, *The Counter-Revolution of Science: Studies on the Abuse of Reason*, Glencoe Illinois (The Free Press), 1952.) Another critic of scientism, Eric Voegelin, also divides scientism into three components: '(1) the assumption that the mathematized science of natural phenomena is a model science to which all other sciences ought to conform; (2) that all realms of being are accessible to the methods of the sciences of phenomena; and (3) that all reality which is not accessible to sciences of phenomena is either irrelevant or, in the more radical form of the dogma, illusionary.' (*Social Research*, December 1948.)

4. For an excellent summary of early attempts at scientism see 'The Invention of the Ethical Calculus', by Louis I. Bredvold in *The Seventeenth Century: Studies in the History of English Thought and Literature from Bacon to Pope*, Richard F. Jones *et al.*, Stanford University Press, 1951.

5. William Borberg, 'On Methods of the Social Sciences in Their Approach to International Problems,' *American Journal of Psychiatry*, Vol. 107, No. 9, March 1951.

6. For a full account of this experiment, see *Management and the Worker*, by F. S. Roethlisberger and William J. Dickson, Cambridge, Massachusetts (Harvard University Press), 1939. A good summary is to be found in Stuart Chase's *The Proper Study of Mankind*, New York (Harper and Brothers), 1948.

7. It was also the home town of J. P. Marquand, a fact which was later to produce *Point of No Return* and some sharp passages about anthropologists studying a venerable old New England town.

61

The Power Elite

C. Wright Mills

Except for the unsuccessful Civil War, changes in the power system of the United States have not involved important challenges to its basic legitimations. Even when they have been decisive enough to be called 'revolutions,' they have not involved the 'resort to the guns of a cruiser, the dispersal of an elected assembly by bayonets, or the mechanisms of a police state.'[1] Nor have they involved, in any decisive way, any ideological struggle to control masses. Changes in the American structure of power have generally come about by institutional shifts in the relative positions of the political, the economic, and the military orders. From this point of view, and broadly speaking, the American power elite has gone through four epochs, and is now well into a fifth.

1

I.

During the first – roughly from the Revolution through the administration of John Adams – the social and economic, the political and the military institutions were more or less unified in a simple and direct way: the individual men of these several elites moved easily from one role to another at the top of each of the major institutional orders. Many of them were many-sided men who could take the part of legislator and merchant, frontiersman and soldier, scholar and surveyor.[2]

Until the downfall of the Congressional caucus of 1824, political institutions seemed quite central; political decisions, of great importance; many politicians, considered national statesmen of note. 'Society, as I first remember it,' Henry Cabot Lodge once said, speaking of the Boston of his early boyhood, 'was based on the old families; Doctor Holmes defines them in the "Autocrat" as the families which had held high position in the colony, the province and during the Revolution and the early decades of the United States.

Source: C. Wright Mills, *The Power Elite*, (New York: Oxford University Press, 1959).

They represented several generations of education and standing in the community.... They had ancestors who had filled the pulpits, sat upon the bench, and taken part in the government under the crown; who had fought in the Revolution, helped to make the State and National constitutions and served in the army or navy; who had been members of the House or Senate in the early days of the Republic, and who had won success as merchants, manufacturers, lawyers, or men of letters.'[3]

Such men of affairs, who – as I have noted – were the backbone of Mrs. John Jay's social list of 1787, definitely included political figures of note. The important fact about these early days is that social life, economic institutions, military establishment, and political order coincided, and men who were high politicians also played key roles in the economy and, with their families, were among those of the reputable who made up local society. In fact, this first period is marked by the leadership of men whose status does not rest exclusively upon their political position, although their political activities are important and the prestige of politicians high. And this prestige seems attached to the men who occupy Congressional position as well as the cabinet. The elite are political men of education and of administrative experience, and, as Lord Bryce noted, possess a certain 'largeness of view and dignity of character.'[4]

II.

During the early nineteenth century – which followed Jefferson's political philosophy, but, in due course, Hamilton's economic principles – the economic and political and military orders fitted loosely into the great scatter of the American social structure. The broadening of the economic order which came to be seated in the individual property owner was dramatized by Jefferson's purchase of the Louisiana Territory and by the formation of the Democratic-Republican party as successor to the Federalists.

In this society, the 'elite' became a plurality of top groups, each in turn quite loosely made up. They overlapped to be sure, but again quite loosely so. One definite key to the period, and certainly to our images of it, is the fact that the Jacksonian Revolution was much more of a status revolution than either an economic or a political one. The metropolitan 400 could not truly flourish in the face of the status tides of Jacksonian democracy; alongside it was a political elite in charge of the new party system. No set of men controlled centralized means of power; no small clique dominated economic, much less political, affairs. The economic order was ascendant over both social status and political power; within the economic order, a quite sizeable proportion of all the economic men were among those who decided. For this was the period – roughly from Jefferson to Lincoln – when the elite was at most a loose coalition. The period ended, of course, with the decisive split of southern and northern types.

Official commentators like to contrast the ascendancy in totalitarian countries of a tightly organized clique with the American system of power. Such comments, however, are easier to sustain if one compares mid-twentieth-century Russia with mid-nineteenth century America, which is what is often done by Tocqueville-quoting Americans making the contrast. But that was an America of a century ago, and in the century that has passed, the American elite have not remained as patrioteer essayists have described them to us. The 'loose cliques' now head institutions of a scale and power not then existing and, especially since World War I, the loose cliques have tightened up. We are well beyond the era of romantic pluralism.

III.

The supremacy of corporate economic power began, in a formal way, with the Congressional elections of 1866, and was consolidated by the Supreme Court decision of 1886 which declared that the Fourteenth Amendment protected the corporation. That period witnessed the transfer of the center of initiative from government to corporation. Until the First World War (which gave us an advanced showing of certain features of our own period) this was an age of raids on the government by the economic elite, an age of simple corruption, when Senators and judges were simply bought up. Here, once upon a time, in the era of McKinley and Morgan, far removed from the undocumented complexities of our own time, many now believe, was the golden era of the American ruling class.[5]

The military order of this period, as in the second, was subordinate to the political, which in turn was subordinate to the economic. The military was thus off to the side of the main driving forces of United States history. Political institutions in the United States have never formed a centralized and autonomous domain of power; they have been enlarged and centralized only reluctantly in slow response to the public consequence of the corporate economy.

In the post-Civil-War era, that economy was the dynamic; the 'trusts' – as policies and events make amply clear – could readily use the relatively weak governmental apparatus for their own ends. That both state and federal governments were decisively limited in their power to regulate, in fact meant that they were themselves regulatable by the larger moneyed interests. Their powers were scattered and unorganized; the powers of the industrial and financial corporations concentrated and interlocked. The Morgan interests alone held 341 directorships in 112 corporations with an aggregate capitalization of over $22 billion – over three times the assessed value of all real and personal property in New England.[6] With revenues greater and employees more numerous than those of many states, corporations controlled parties, bought laws, and kept Congressmen of the 'neutral' state. And as private economic power overshadowed public political power, so the economic elite overshadowed the political.

Yet even between 1896 and 1919, events of importance tended to assume a political form, foreshadowing the shape of power which after the partial boom of the 'twenties was to prevail in the New Deal. Perhaps there has never been any period in American history so politically transparent as the Progressive era of President-makers and Muckrakers.

IV.

The New Deal did *not* reverse the political and economic relations of the third era, but it did create within the political arena, as well as in the corporate world itself, competing centers of power that challenged those of the corporate directors. As the New Deal directorate gained political power, the economic elite, which in the third period had fought against the growth of 'government' while raiding it for crafty privileges, belatedly attempted to join it on the higher levels. When they did so they found themselves confronting other interests and men, for the places of decision were crowded. In due course, they did come to control and to use for their own purposes the New Deal institutions whose creation they had so bitterly denounced.

But during the 'thirties, the political order was still an instrument of small propertied farmers and businessmen, although they were weakened, having lost their last chance for real ascendancy in the Progressive era. The struggle between big and small property flared up again, however, in the political realm of the New Deal era, and to this struggle there was added, as we have seen, the new struggle of organized labor and the unorganized unemployed. This new force flourished under political tutelage, but nevertheless, for the first time in United States history, social legislation and lower-class issues became important features of the reform movement.

In the decade of the 'thirties, a set of shifting balances involving newly instituted farm measures and newly organized labor unions – along with big business – made up the political and administrative drama of power. These farm, labor, and business groups, moreover, were more or less contained within the framework of an enlarging governmental structure, whose political directorship made decisions in a definitely political manner. These groups pressured, and in pressuring against one another and against the governmental and party system, they helped to shape it. But it could not be said that any of them for any considerable length of time used that government unilaterally as their instrument. That is why the 'thirties was a *political* decade: the power of business was not replaced, but it was contested and supplemented: it became one major power within a structure of power that was chiefly run by political men, and not by economic or military men turned political.

The earlier and middle Roosevelt administrations can best be understood as a desperate search for ways and means, within the existing capitalist system, of reducing the staggering and ominous army of the unemployed. In these years, the New Deal as a system of power was essentially a balance of pressure groups and interest blocs. The political top adjusted many conflicts, gave way to this demand, sidetracked that one, was the unilateral servant of none, and so evened it all out into such going policy line as prevailed from one minor crisis to another. Policies were the result of a political act of balance at the top. Of course, the balancing act that Roosevelt performed did not affect the fundamental institutions of capitalism as a type of economy. By his policies, he subsidized the defaults of the capitalist economy, which had simply broken down; and by his rhetoric, he balanced its political disgrace, putting 'economic royalists' in the political doghouse.

The 'welfare state,' created to sustain the balance and to carry out the subsidy, differed from the 'laissez-faire' state: 'If the state was believed neutral in the days of T.R. because its leaders claimed to sanction favors for no one,' Richard Hofstadter has remarked, 'the state under F.D.R. could be called neutral only in the sense that it offered favors to everyone.'[7] The new state of the corporate commissars differs from the old welfare state. In fact, the later Roosevelt years – beginning with the entrance of the United States into overt acts of war and preparations for World War II – cannot be understood entirely in terms of an adroit equipoise of political power.

2

We study history, it has been said, to rid ourselves of it, and the history of the power elite is a clear case for which this maxim is correct. Like the tempo of American life in general, the longterm trends of the power structure have been greatly speeded up since World War II, and certain newer trends within and between the dominant institutions have also set the shape of the power elite and given historically specific meaning to its fifth epoch:

I.

In so far as the structural clue to the power elite today lies in the political order, that clue is the decline of politics as genuine and public debate of alternative decisions – with nationally responsible and policy-coherent parties and with autonomous organizations connecting the lower and middle levels of power with the top levels of decision. America is now in considerable part more a formal political democracy than a democratic social structure, and even the formal political mechanics are weak.

The long-time tendency of business and government to become more intricately and deeply involved with each other has, in the fifth epoch, reached a new point of explicitness. The two cannot now be seen clearly as two distinct worlds. It is in terms of the executive agencies of the state that the rapprochement has proceeded most decisively. The growth of the executive branch of the government, with its agencies that patrol the complex economy, does not mean merely the 'enlargement of government' as some sort of autonomous bureaucracy: it has meant the ascendancy of the corporation's man as a political eminence.

During the New Deal the corporate chieftains joined the political directorate; as of World War II they have come to dominate it. Long interlocked with government, now they have moved into quite full direction of the economy of the war effort and of the postwar era. This shift of the corporation executives into the political directorate has accelerated the long-term relegation of the professional politicians in the Congress to the middle levels of power.

II.

In so far as the structural clue to the power elite today lies in the enlarged and military state, that clue becomes evident in the military ascendancy. The warlords have gained decisive political relevance, and the military structure of America is now in considerable part a political structure. The seemingly permanent military threat places a premium on the military and upon their control of men, materiel, money, and power; virtually all political and economic actions are now judged in terms of military definitions of reality: the higher warlords have ascended to a firm position within the power elite of the fifth epoch.

In part at least this has resulted from one simple historical fact, pivotal for the years since 1939: the focus of elite attention has been shifted from domestic problems, centered in the 'thirties around slump, to international problems, centered in the 'forties and 'fifties around war. Since the governing apparatus of the United States has by long historic usage been adapted to and shaped by domestic clash and balance, it has not, from any angle, had suitable agencies and traditions for the handling of international problems. Such formal democratic mechanics as had arisen in the century and a half of national development prior to 1941, had not been extended to the American handling of international affairs. It is, in considerable part, in this vacuum that the power elite has grown.

III.

In so far as the structural clue to the power elite today lies in the economic order, that clue is the fact that the economy is at once a permanent-war economy and a private-corporation economy. American capitalism is now in considerable part a military capitalism, and the most important relation of the big corporation to the state rests on the coincidence of interests between military and corporate needs, as defined by warlords and corporate rich. Within the elite as a whole, this coincidence of interest between the high military and the corporate chieftains strengthens both of them and further subordinates the role of the merely political men. Not politicians, but corporate executives, sit with the military and plan the organization of war effort.

The shape and meaning of the power elite today can be understood only when these three sets of structural trends are seen at their point of coincidence: the military capitalism of private corporations exists in a weakened and formal democratic system containing a military order already quite political in outlook and demeanour. Accordingly, at the top of this structure, the power elite has been shaped by the coincidence of interest between those who control the major means of production and those who control the newly enlarged means of violence; from the decline of the professional politician and the rise to explicit political command of the corporate chieftains and the professional warlords; from the absence of any genuine civil service of skill and integrity, independent of vested interests.

The power elite is composed of political, economic, and military men, but this instituted elite is frequently in some tension: it comes together only on certain coinciding points and only on certain occasions of 'crisis.' In the long peace of the nineteenth century, the military were not in the high councils of state, not of the political directorate, and neither were the economic men – they made raids upon the state but they did not join its directorate. During the 'thirties, the political man was ascendant. Now the military and the corporate men are in top positions.

Of the three types of circle that compose the power elite today, it is the military that has benefited the most in its enhanced power, although the corporate circles have also become more explicitly intrenched in the more public decision-making circles. It is the professional politician that has lost the most, so much that in examining the events and decisions, one is tempted to speak of a political vacuum in which the corporate rich and the high warlord, in their coinciding interests, rule.

It should not be said that the three 'take turns' in carrying the initiative, for the mechanics of the power elite are not often as deliberate as that would imply. At times, of course, it is – as when political men, thinking they can borrow the prestige of generals, find that they must pay for it, or, as when during big slumps, economic men feel the need of a politician at once safe and possessing vote appeal. Today all three are involved in virtually all widely ramifying decisions. Which of the three types seems to lead depends upon 'the tasks of the period' as they, the elite, define them. Just now, these tasks center upon 'defense' and international affairs. Accordingly, as we have seen, the military are ascendant in two senses: as personnel and as justifying ideology. That is why, just now, we can most easily specify the unity and the shape of the power elite in terms of the military ascendancy.

But we must always be historically specific and open to complexities. The simple Marxian view makes the big economic man the *real* holder of power; the simple liberal view makes the big political man the chief of the power system; and there are some who would view the warlords as virtual dictators. Each of these is an oversimplified view. It is to avoid them that we use the term 'power elite' rather than, for example, 'ruling class.'[8]

In so far as the power elite has come to wide public attention, it has done so in terms of the 'military clique.' The power elite does, in fact, take its current shape from the decisive entrance into it of the military. Their presence and their ideology are its major legitimations, whenever the power elite feels the need to provide any. But what is called the 'Washington military clique' is not composed merely of military men, and it does not prevail merely in Washington. Its members exist all over the country, and it is a coalition of generals in the roles of corporation executives, of politicians masquerading as admirals, of corporation executives acting like politicians, of civil servants who become majors, office-admirals who are also the assistants to a cabinet officer, who is himself, by the way, really a member of the managerial elite.

Neither the idea of a 'ruling class' nor of a simple monolithic rise of 'bureaucratic politicians' nor of a 'military clique' is adequate. The power elite today involves the often uneasy coincidence of economic, military, and political power.

3

Even if our understanding were limited to these structural trends, we should have grounds for believing the power elite a useful, indeed indispensable, concept for the interpretation of what is going on at the topside of modern American society. But we are not, of course, so limited: our conception of the power elite does not need to rest only upon the correspondence of the institutional hierarchies involved, or upon the many points at which their shifting interests coincide. The power elite, as we conceive it, also rests upon the similarity of its personnel, and their personal and official relations with one another, upon their social and psychological affinities. In order to grasp the personal and social basis of the power elite's unity, we have first to remind ourselves of the facts of origin, career, and style of life of each of the types of circle whose members compose the power elite.

The power elite is *not* an aristocracy, which is to say that it is not a political ruling group based upon a nobility of hereditary origin. It has no compact basis in a small circle of great families whose members can and do consistently occupy the top positions in the several higher circles which overlap as the power elite. But such nobility is only one possible basis of common origin. That it does not exist for the American elite does not mean that members of this elite derive socially from the full range of strata composing American society. They derive in substantial proportions from the upper classes, both new and old, of local society and the metropolitan 400. The bulk of the very rich, the corporate executives, the political outsiders, the high military, derive from, at most, the upper third of the income and occupational pyramids. Their fathers were at least of the professional and business strata, and very frequently higher than that. They are native-born Americans of native parents, primarily from urban areas, and, with the exceptions of the politicians among them, overwhelmingly from the East. They are mainly Protestants, especially Episcopalian or Presbyterian. In general, the higher the position, the greater the proportion of men within it who have derived from and who maintain connections with the upper classes. The generally similar origins of the members of the power elite are underlined and carried further by the fact of their increasingly common educational routine. Overwhelmingly college graduates, substantial proportions have attended Ivy League colleges, although the education of the higher military, of course, differs from that of other members of the power elite.

But what do these apparently simple facts about the social composition of the higher circles really mean? In particular, what do they mean for any attempt to understand the degree of unity, and the direction of policy and interest that may prevail among these several circles? Perhaps it is best to put this question in a deceptively simple way: in terms of origin and career, who or what do these men at the top represent?

Of course, if they are elected politicians, they are supposed to represent those who elected them; and, if they are appointed, they are supposed to represent, indirectly, those who elected their appointers. But this is recognized as something of an abstraction, as a rhetorical formula by which all men of power in almost all systems of government nowadays justify their power of decision. At times it may be true, both in the sense of their motives and in the sense of who benefits from their decisions. Yet it would not be wise in any power system merely to assume it.

The fact that members of the power elite come from near the top of the nation's class and status levels does not mean that they are necessarily 'representative' of the top levels only. And if they were, as social types, representative of a cross-section of the population, that would not mean that a balanced democracy of interest and power would automatically be the going political fact.

We cannot infer the direction of policy merely from the social origins and careers of the policy-makers. The social and economic backgrounds of the men of power do not tell us all that we need to know in order to understand the distribution of social power. For: (1) Men from high places may be ideological representatives of the poor and humble. (2) Men of humble origin, brightly self-made, may energetically serve the most vested and inherited interests. Moreover (3), not all men who effectively represent the interests of a stratum need in any way belong to it or personally benefit by policies that further its interests. Among the politicians, in short, there are sympathetic *agents* of given groups, conscious and unconscious, paid and unpaid. Finally (4), among the top decision-makers we find men who have been chosen for their positions because of their 'expert knowledge.' These are some of the obvious reasons why the social origins and careers of the power elite do not enable us to infer the class interests and policy directions of a modern system of power.

Do the high social origin and careers of the top men mean nothing, then, about the distribution of power? By no means. They simply remind us that we must be careful of any simple and direct inference from origin and career to political character and policy, not that we must ignore them in our attempt at political understanding. They simply mean that we must analyze the political psychology and the actual decisions of the political directorate as well as its social composition. And they mean, above all, that we should control, as we have done here, any inference we make from the origin and careers of the political actors by close understanding of the institutional landscape in which they act out their drama. Otherwise we should be guilty of a rather simpleminded biographical theory of society and history.

Just as we cannot rest the notion of the power elite solely upon the institutional mechanics that lead to its formation, so we cannot rest the notion solely upon the facts of the origin and career of its personnel. We need both, and we have both – as well as other bases, among them that of the status intermingling.

But it is not only the similarities of social origin, religious affiliation, nativity, and education that are important to the psychological and social affinities of the members of the power elite. Even if their recruitment and formal training were more heterogeneous than they are, these men would still be of quite homogeneous social type. For the most important set of facts about a circle of men is the criteria of admission, of praise, of honor, of promotion that prevails among them; if these are similar within a circle, then they will tend as personalities to become similar. The circles that compose the power elite do tend to have such codes and criteria in common. The co-optation of the social types to which these common values lead is often more important than any statistics of common origin and career that we might have at hand.

There is a kind of reciprocal attraction among the fraternity of the successful – not between each and every member of the circles of the high and mighty, but between enough of them to insure a certain unity. On the slight side, it is a sort of tacit, mutual admiration; in the strongest tie-ins, it proceeds by intermarriage. And there are all grades and types of connection between these extremes. Some overlaps certainly occur by means of cliques and clubs, churches and schools.

If social origin and formal education in common tend to make the members of the power elite more readily understood and trusted by one another, their continued association further cements what they feel they have in common. Members of the several higher circles know one another as personal friends and even as neighbors; they mingle with one another on the golf course, in the gentleman's clubs, at resorts, on transcontinental airplanes, and on ocean liners. They meet at the estates of mutual friends, face each other in front of the TV camera, or serve on the same philanthropic committee; and many are sure to cross one another's path in the columns of newspapers, if not in the exact cafes from which many of these columns originate. As we have seen, of 'The New 400' of cafe society, one chronicler has named forty-one members of the very rich, ninety-three political leaders, and seventy-nine chief executives of corporations.

'I did not know, I could not have dreamed,' Whittaker Chambers has written, 'of the immense scope and power of Hiss' political alliances and his social connections, which cut across all party lines and ran from the Supreme Court to the Religious Society of Friends, from governors of states and instructors in college faculties to the staff members of liberal magazines. In the decade since I had last seen him, he had used his career, and, in particular, his identification with the cause of peace through his part in organizing the United Nations, to put down roots that made him one with the matted forest floor of American upper class, enlightened middle class, liberal and official life. His roots could not be disturbed without disturbing all the roots on all sides of him.'[9]

The sphere of status has reflected the epochs of the power elite. In the third epoch, for example, who could compete with big money? And in the fourth, with big politicians, or even the bright young men of the New Deal? And in the fifth, who can compete with the generals and the admirals and the corporate officials now so sympathetically portrayed on the stage, in the novel, and on the screen? Can one imagine *Executive Suite* as a successful motion picture in 1935? Or *The Caine Mutiny*?

The multiplicity of high-prestige organizations to which the elite usually belong is revealed by even casual examination of the obituaries of the big businessman, the high-prestige lawyer, the top general and admiral, the key senator: usually, high-prestige church, business associations, plus high-prestige clubs, and often plus military rank. In the course of their lifetimes, the university president, the New York Stock Exchange chairman, the head of the bank, the old West Pointer – mingle in the status sphere, within which they easily renew old friendships and draw upon them in an effort to understand through the experience of trusted others those contexts of power and decision in which they have not personally moved.

In these diverse contexts, prestige accumulates in each of the higher circles, and the members of each borrow status from one another. Their self-images are fed by these accumulations and these borrowings, and accordingly, however segmental a given man's role may seem, he comes to feel himself a 'diffuse' or 'generalized' man of the higher circles; a 'broad-gauge' man. Perhaps such inside experience is one feature of what is meant by 'judgment.'

The key organizations, perhaps, are the major corporations themselves, for on the boards of directors we find a heavy overlapping among the members of these several elites. On the lighter side, again in the summer and winter resorts, we find that, in an intricate series of overlapping circles; in the course of time, each meets each or knows somebody who knows somebody who knows that one.

The higher members of the military, economic, and political orders are able readily to take over one another's point of view, always in a sympathetic way, and often in a knowledgeable way as well. They define one another as among those who count, and who, accordingly, must be taken into account. Each of them as a member of the power elite comes to incorporate into his own integrity, his own honor, his own conscience, the viewpoint, the expectations, the values of the others. If there are no common ideals and standards among them that are based upon an explicitly aristocratic culture, that does not mean that they do not feel responsibility to one another.

All the structural coincidence of their interests as well as the intricate, psychological facts of their origins and their education, their careers and their associations make possible the psychological affinities that prevail among them, affinities that make it possible for them to say of one another: He is, of course, one of us. And all this points to the basic, psychological meaning of class consciousness. Nowhere in America is there as great a 'class consciousness' as among the elite; nowhere is it organized as effectively as among the power elite. For by class consciousness, as a psychological fact, one means that the individual member of a 'class' accepts only those accepted by his circle as among those who are significant to his own image of self.

Within the higher circles of the power elite, factions do exist; there are conflicts of policy; individual ambitions do clash. There are still enough divisions of importance within the Republican party, and even between Republicans and Democrats, to make for different methods of operation. But more powerful than these divisions are the internal discipline and the community of interests that bind the power elite together, even across the boundaries of nations at war.[10]

4

Yet we must give due weight to the other side of the case which may not question the facts but only our interpretation of them. There is a set of objections that will inevitably be made to our whole conception of the power elite, but which has essentially to do with only the psychology of its members. It might well be put by liberals or by conservatives in some such way as this:

'To talk of a power elite – isn't this to characterize men by their origins and associations? Isn't such characterization both unfair and untrue? Don't men modify themselves, especially Americans such as these, as they rise in stature to meet the demands of their jobs? Don't they arrive at a view and a line of policy that represents, so far as they in their human weaknesses can know, the interests of the nation as a whole? Aren't they merely honorable men who are doing their duty?'

What are we to reply to these objections?

I.

We are sure that they are honorable men. But what is honor? Honor can only mean living up to a code that one believes to be honorable. There is no one code upon which we are all agreed. That is why, if we are civilized men, we do not kill off all of those with whom we disagree. The question is not: are these honorable men? The question is: what are their codes of honor? The answer to that question is that they are the codes of their circles, of those to whose opinions they defer. How could it be otherwise? That is one meaning of the important truism that all men are human and that all men are social creatures. As for sincerity, it can only be disproved, never proved.

II.

To the question of their adaptability – which means their capacity to transcend the codes of conduct which, in their life's work and experience, they have acquired – we must answer: simply no, they cannot, at least not in the handful of years most of them have left. To expect that is to assume that they are indeed strange and expedient: such flexibility would in fact involve a violation of what we may rightly call their character and their integrity. By the way, may it not be precisely because of the lack of such character and integrity that earlier types of American politicians have not represented as great a threat as do these men of character?

It would be an insult to the effective training of the military, and to their indoctrination as well, to suppose that military officials shed their military character and outlook upon changing from uniform to mufti. This background is more important perhaps in the military case than in that of the corporate executives, for the training of the career is deeper and more total.

'Lack of imagination,' Gerald W. Johnson has noted, 'is not to be confused with lack of principle. On the contrary, an unimaginative man is often a man of the highest principles. The trouble is that his principles conform to Cornford's famous definition: "A principle is a rule of inaction giving valid general reasons for not doing in a specific instance what to unprincipled instinct would seem to be right."'[11]

Would it not be ridiculous, for example, to believe seriously that, in psychological fact, Charles Erwin Wilson represented anyone or any interest other than those of the corporate world? This is not because he is dishonest; on the contrary, it is because he is probably a man of solid integrity – as sound as a dollar. He is what he is and he cannot very well be anything else. He is a member of the professional corporation elite, just as are his colleagues, in the government and out of it; he represents the wealth of the higher corporate world; he represents its power; and he believes sincerely in his oft-quoted remark that 'what is good for the United States is good for the General Motors Corporation and vice versa.'

The revealing point about the pitiful hearings on the confirmation of such men for political posts is not the cynicism toward the law and toward the lawmakers on the middle levels of power which they display, nor their reluctance to dispose of their personal stock.[12] The interesting point is how impossible it is for such men to divest themselves of their engagement with the corporate world in general and with their own corporations in particular. Not only their money, but their friends, their interests, their training – their lives in short – are deeply involved in this world. The disposal of stock is, of course, merely a purifying ritual. The point is not so much financial or personal interests in a given corporation, but identification with the corporate world. To ask a man suddenly to divest himself of these interests and sensibilities is almost like asking a man to become a woman.

III.

To the question of their patriotism, of their desire to serve the nation as a whole, we must answer first that, like codes of honor, feelings of patriotism and views of what is to the whole nation's good, are not ultimate facts but matters upon which there exists a great variety of opinion. Furthermore, patriotic opinions too are rooted in and are sustained by what a man has become by virtue of how and with whom he has lived. This is no simple mechanical determination of individual character by social conditions; it is an intricate process, well established in the major tradition of modern social study. One can only wonder why more social scientists do not use it systematically in speculating about politics.

IV.

The elite cannot be truly thought of as men who are merely doing their duty. They are the ones who determine their duty, as well as the duties of those beneath them. They are not merely following orders: they give the orders. They are not merely 'bureaucrats': they command bureaucracies. They may try to disguise these facts from others and from themselves by appeals to traditions of which they imagine themselves the instruments, but there are many traditions, and they must choose which ones they will serve. They face decisions for which there simply are no traditions.

Now, to what do these several answers add up? To the fact that we cannot reason about public events and historical trends merely from knowledge about the motives and character of the men or the small groups who sit in the seats of the high and mighty. This fact, in turn, does not mean that we should be intimidated by accusations that in taking up our problem in the way we have, we are impugning the honor, the integrity, or the ability of those who are in high office. For it is not, in the first instance, a question of individual character; and if, in further instances, we find that it is, we should not hesitate to say so plainly. In the meantime, we must judge men of power by the standards of power, by what they do as decision-makers, and not by who they are or what they may do in private life. Our interest is not in that: we are interested in their policies and in the *consequences* of their conduct of office. We must remember that these men of the power elite now occupy the strategic places in the structure of American society; that they command the dominant institutions of a dominant nation; that, as a set of men, they are in a position to make decisions with terrible consequences for the underlying populations of the world.

5

Despite their social similarity and psychological affinities, the members of the power elite do not constitute a club having a permanent membership with fixed and formal boundaries. It is of the nature of the power elite that within it there is a good deal of shifting about, and that it thus does not consist of one small set of the same men in the same positions in the same hierarchies. Because men know each other personally does not mean that among them there is a unity of policy; and because they do not know each other personally does not mean that among them there is a disunity. The conception of the power elite does not rest, as I have repeatedly said, primarily upon personal friendship.

As the requirements of the top places in each of the major hierarchies become similar, the types of men occupying these roles at the top – by selection and by training in the jobs – become similar. This is no mere deduction from structure to personnel. That it is a fact is revealed by the heavy traffic that has been going on between the three structures, often in very intricate patterns. The chief executives, the warlords, and selected politicians came into contact with one another in an intimate, working way during World War II; after that war ended, they continued their associations, out of common beliefs, social congeniality, and coinciding interests. Noticeable proportions of top men from the military, the economic, and the political worlds have during the last fifteen years occupied positions in one or both of the other worlds: between these higher circles there is an interchangeability of position, based formally upon the supposed transferability of 'executive ability,' based in substance upon the co-optation by cliques of insiders. As members of a power elite, many of those busy in this traffic have come to look upon 'the government' as an umbrella under whose authority they do their work.

As the business between the big three increases in volume and importance, so does the traffic in personnel. The very criteria for selecting men who will rise come to embody this fact. The corporate commissar, dealing with the state and its military, is wiser to choose a young man who has experienced the state and its military than one who has not. The political director, often dependent for his own political success upon corporate decisions and corporations, is also wiser to choose a man with corporate experience. Thus, by virtue of the very criterion of success, the interchange of personnel and the unity of the power elite is increased.

Given the formal similarity of the three hierarchies in which the several members of the elite spend their working lives, given the ramifications of the decisions made in each upon the others, given the coincidence of interest that prevails among them at many points, and given the administrative vacuum of the American civilian state along with its enlargement of tasks – given these trends of structure, and adding to them the psychological affinities we have noted – we should indeed be surprised were we to find that men said to be skilled in administrative contacts and full of organizing ability would fail to do more than get in touch with one another. They have, of course, done much more than that: increasingly, they assume positions in one another's domains.

The unity revealed by the interchangeability of top roles rests upon the parallel development of the top jobs in each of the big three domains. The interchange occurs most frequently at the points of their coinciding interest, as between regulatory agency and the regulated industry; contracting agency and contractor. And, as we shall see, it leads to co-ordinations that are more explicit, and even formal.

The inner core of the power elite consists, first, of those who interchange commanding roles at the top of one dominant institutional order with those in another: the admiral who is also a banker and a lawyer and who heads up an important federal commission; the corporation executive whose company was one of the two or three leading war materiel producers who is now the Secretary of Defense; the wartime general who dons civilian clothes to sit on the political directorate and then becomes a member of the board of directors of a leading economic corporation.

Although the executive who becomes a general, the general who becomes a statesman, the statesman who becomes a banker, see much more than ordinary men in their ordinary environments, still the perspectives of even such men often remain tied to their dominant locales. In their very career, however, they interchange roles within the big three and thus readily transcend the particularity of interest in any one of these institutional milieux. By their very careers and activities, they lace the three types of milieux together. They are, accordingly, the core members of the power elite.

These men are not necessarily familiar with every major arena of power. We refer to one man who moves in and between perhaps two circles – say the industrial and the military – and to another man who moves in the military and the political, and to a third who moves in the political as well as among opinion-makers. These inbetween types most closely display our image of the power elite's structure and operation, even of behind-the-scenes operations. To the extent that there is any 'invisible elite,' these advisory and liaison types are its core. Even if – as I believe to be very likely – many of them are, at least in the first part of their careers, 'agents' of the various elites rather than themselves elite, it is they who are most active in organizing the several top milieux into a structure of power and maintaining it.

The inner core of the power elite also includes men of the higher legal and financial type from the great law factories and investment firms, who are almost professional go-betweens of economic, political and military affairs, and who thus act to unify the power elite. The corporation lawyer and the investment banker perform the functions of the 'go-between' effectively and powerfully. By the nature of their work, they transcend the narrower milieu of any one industry, and accordingly are in a position to speak and act for the corporate world or at least sizable sectors of it. The corporation lawyer is a key link between the economic and military and political areas; the investment banker is a key organizer and unifier of the corporate world and a person well versed in spending the huge amounts of money the American military establishment now ponders. When you get a lawyer who handles the legal work of investment bankers you get a key member of the power elite.

During the Democratic era, one link between private corporate organizations and governmental institutions was the investment house of Dillon, Read. From it came such men as James Forrestal and Charles F. Detmar, Jr.; Ferdinand Eberstadt had once been a partner in it before he branched out into his own investment house from which came other men to political and military circles. Republican administrations seem to favor the investment firm of Kuhn, Loeb and the advertising firm of Batten, Barton, Durstine and Osborn.

Regardless of administrations, there is always the law firm of Sullivan and Cromwell. Mid-West investment banker Cyrus Eaton has said that 'Arthur H. Dean, a senior partner of Sullivan & Cromwell of No. 48 Wall Street, was one of those who assisted in the drafting of the Securities Act of 1933, the first of the series of bills passed to regulate the capital markets. He and his firm, which is reputed to be the largest in the United States, have maintained close relations with the SEC since its creation, and theirs is the dominating influence on the Commission.'[13]

There is also the third largest bank in the United States: the Chase National Bank of New York (now Chase-Manhattan). Regardless of political administration, executives of this bank and those of the International Bank of Reconstruction and Development have changed positions: John J. McCloy, who became Chairman of the Chase National in 1953, is a former president of the World Bank; and his successor to the presidency of the World Bank was a former senior vice-president of the Chase National Bank.[14] And in 1953, the president of the Chase National Bank, Winthrop W. Aldrich, had left to become Ambassador to Great Britain.

The outermost fringes of the power elite – which change more than its core – consist of 'those who count' even though they may not be 'in' on given decisions of consequence nor in their career move between the hierarchies. Each member of the power elite need not be a man who personally decides every decision that is to be ascribed to the power elite. Each member, in the decisions that he does make, takes the others seriously into account. They not only make decisions in the several major areas of war and peace; they are the men who, in decisions in which they take no direct part, are taken into decisive account by those who are directly in charge.

On the fringes and below them, somewhat to the side of the lower echelons, the power elite fades off into the middle levels of power, into the rank and file of the Congress, the pressure groups that are not vested in the power elite itself, as well as a multiplicity of regional and state and local interests. If all the men on the middle levels are not among those who count, they sometimes must be taken into account, handled, cajoled, broken or raised to higher circles.

When the power elite find that in order to get things done they must reach below their own realms – as is the case when it is necessary to get bills passed through Congress – they themselves must exert some pressure. But among the power elite, the name for such high-level lobbying is 'liaison work.' There are 'liaison' military men with Congress, with certain wayward sections of industry, with practically every important element not directly concerned with the power elite. The two men on the White House staff who are *named* 'liaison' men are both experienced in military matters; one of them is a former investment banker and lawyer as well as a general.

Not the trade associations but the higher cliques of lawyers and investment bankers are the active political heads of the corporate rich and the members of the power elite. 'While it is generally assumed that the national associations carry tremendous weight in formulating public opinion and directing the course of national policy, there is some evidence to indicate that interaction between associations on a formal level is not a very tight-knit affair. The general tendency within associations seems to be to stimulate activities around the specific interests of the organization, and more effort is made to educate its members rather than to spend much time in trying to influence other associations on the issue at hand. . . . As media for stating and re-stating the over-all value structure of the nation they (the trade associations) are important. . . . But when issues are firmly drawn, individuals related to the larger corporate interests are called upon to exert pressure in the proper places at the strategic time. The national associations may act as media for co-ordinating such pressures, but a great volume of intercommunication between members at the apex of power of the larger corporate interests seems to be the decisive factor in final policy determination.'[15]

Conventional 'lobbying,' carried on by trade associations, still exists, although it usually concerns the middle levels of power – usually being targeted at Congress and, of course, its own rank and file members. The important function of the National Association of Manufacturers, for example, is less directly to influence policy than to reveal to small businessmen that their interests are the same as those of larger businesses. But there is also 'high level lobbying.' All over the country the corporate leaders are drawn into the circle of the high military and political through personal friendship, trade and professional associations and their various subcommittees, prestige clubs, open political affiliation, and customer relationships. 'There is . . . an awareness among these power leaders,' one first-hand investigator of such executive cliques has asserted, 'of many of the current major policy issues before the nation such as keeping taxes down, turning all productive operations over to private enterprises, increasing foreign trade, keeping governmental welfare and other domestic activities to a minimum, and strengthening and maintaining the hold of the current party in power nationally.'[16]

There are, in fact, cliques of corporate executives who are more important as informal opinion leaders in the top echelons of corporate, military, and political power than as actual participants in military and political organizations. Inside military circles and inside political circles and 'on the sidelines' in the economic area, these circles and cliques of corporation executives are in on most all major decisions regardless of topic. And what is important about all this high-level lobbying is that it is done within the confines of that elite.

6

The conception of the power elite and of its unity rests upon the corresponding developments and the coincidence of interests among economic, political, and military organizations. It also rests upon the similarity of origin and outlook, and the social and personal intermingling of the top circles from each of these dominant hierarchies. This conjunction of institutional and psychological forces, in turn, is revealed by the heavy personnel traffic within and between the big three institutional orders, as well as by the rise of go-betweens as in the high-level lobbying. The conception of the power elite, accordingly, does *not* rest upon the assumption that American history since the origins of World War II must be understood as a secret plot, or as a great and co-ordinated conspiracy of the members of this elite. The conception rests upon quite impersonal grounds.

There is, however, little doubt that the American power elite – which contains, we are told, some of 'the greatest organizers in the world' – has also planned and has plotted. The rise of the elite, as we have already made clear, was not and could not have been caused by a plot; and the tenability of the conception does not rest upon the existence of any secret or any publicly known organization. But, once the conjunction of structural trend and of the personal will to utilize it gave rise to the power elite, then plans and programs did occur to its members and indeed it is not possible to interpret many events and official policies of the fifth epoch without reference to the power elite. 'There is a great difference,' Richard Hofstadter has remarked, 'between locating conspiracies *in* history and saying that history *is*, in effect, a conspiracy. . . .'[17]

The structural trends of institutions become defined as opportunities by those who occupy their command posts. Once such opportunities are recognized, men may avail themselves of them. Certain types of men from each of the dominant institutional areas, more far-sighted than others, have actively promoted the liaison before it took its truly modern shape. They have often done so for reasons not shared by their partners, although not objected to by them either; and often the outcome of their liaison has had consequences which none of them foresaw, much less shaped, and which only later in the course of development came under explicit control. Only after it was well under way did most of its members find themselves part of it and become gladdened, although sometimes also worried, by this fact. But once the co-ordination is a going concern, new men come readily into it and assume its existence without question.

So far as explicit organization – conspiratorial or not – is concerned, the power elite, by its very nature, is more likely to use existing organizations, working within and between them, than to set up explicit organizations whose membership is strictly limited to its own members. But if there is no machinery in existence to ensure, for example, that military and political factors will be balanced in decisions made, they will invent such machinery and use it, as with the National Security Council. Moreover, in a formally democratic polity, the aims and the powers of the various elements of this elite are further supported by an aspect of the permanent war economy: the assumption that the security of the nation supposedly rests upon great secrecy of plan and intent. Many higher events that would reveal the working of the power elite can be withheld from public knowledge under the guise of secrecy. With the wide secrecy covering their operations and decisions, the power elite can mask their intentions, operations, and further consolidation. Any secrecy that is imposed upon those in positions to observe high decision-makers clearly works for and not against the operations of the power elite.

There is accordingly reason to suspect – but by the nature of the case, no proof – that the power elite is not altogether 'surfaced.' There is nothing hidden about it, although its activities are not publicized. As an elite, it is not organized, although its members often know one another, seem quite naturally to work together, and share many organizations in common. There is nothing conspiratorial about it, although its decisions are often publicly unknown and its mode of operation manipulative rather than explicit.

It is not that the elite 'believe in' a compact elite behind the scenes and a mass down below. It is not put in that language. It is just that the people are of necessity confused and must, like trusting children, place all the new world of foreign policy and strategy and executive action in the hands of experts. It is just that everyone knows somebody has got to run the show, and that somebody usually does. Others do not really care anyway, and besides, they do not know how. So the gap between the two types gets wider.

When crises are defined as total, and as seemingly permanent, the consequences of decision become total, and the decisions in each major area of life come to be integrated and total. Up to a point, these consequences for other institutional orders can be assessed; beyond such points, chances have to be taken. It is then that the felt scarcity of trained and imaginative judgment leads to plaintive feelings among executives about the shortage of qualified successors in political, military, and economic life. This feeling, in turn, leads to an increasing concern with the training of successors who could take over as older men of power retire.[18] In each area, there slowly arises a new generation which has grown up in an age of co-ordinated decisions.

In each of the elite circles, we have noticed this concern to recruit and to train successors as 'broad-gauge' men, that is, as men capable of making decisions that involve institutional areas other than their own. The chief executives have set up formal recruitment and training programs to man the corporate world as virtually a state within a state. Recruitment and training for the military elite has long been rigidly professionalized, but has now come to include educational routines of a sort which the remnants of older generals and admirals consider quite nonsensical.

Only the political order, with its absence of a genuine civil service, has lagged behind, creating an administrative vacuum into which military bureaucrats and corporate outsiders have been drawn. But even in this domain, since World War II, there have been repeated attempts, by elite men of such vision as the late James Forrestal's, to inaugurate a career service that would include periods in the corporate world as well as in the governmental.[19]

What is lacking is a truly common elite program of recruitment and training; for the prep school, Ivy League College, and law school sequence of the metropolitan 400 is not up to the demands now made upon members of the power elite.[20] Britishers, such as Field Marshall Viscount Montgomery, well aware of this lack, recently urged the adoption of a system 'under which a minority of high-caliber young students could be separated from the mediocre and given the best education possible to supply the country with leadership.' His proposal is echoed, in various forms, by many who accept his criticism of 'the American theory of public education on the ground that it is ill-suited to produce the "elite" group of leaders . . . this country needs to fulfill its obligations of world leadership.'[21]

In part these demands reject the unstated need to transcend recruitment on the sole basis of economic success, especially since it is suspect as often involving the higher immorality; in part it reflects the stated need to have men who, as Viscount Montgomery says, know 'the meaning of discipline.' But above all these demands reflect the at least vague consciousness on the part of the power elite themselves that the age of co-ordinated decisions, entailing a newly enormous range of consequences, requires a power elite that is of a new caliber. In so far as the sweep of matters which go into the making of decisions is vast and interrelated, the information needed for judgments complex and requiring particularized knowledge,[22] the men in charge will not only call upon one another; they will try to train their successors for the work at hand. These new men will grow up as men of power within the co-ordination of economic and political and military decision.

7

The idea of the power elite rests upon and enables us to make sense of (1) the decisive institutional trends that characterize the structure of our epoch, in particular, the military ascendancy in a privately incorporated economy, and more broadly, the several coincidences of objective interests between economic, military, and political institutions; (2) the social similarities and the psychological affinities of the men who occupy the command posts of these structures, in particular the increased interchangeability of the top positions in each of them and the increased traffic between these orders in the careers of men of power; (3) the ramifications, to the point of virtual totality, of the kind of decisions that are made at the top, and the rise to power of a set of men who, by training and bent, are professional organizers of considerable force and who are unrestrained by democratic party training.

Negatively, the formation of the power elite rests upon (1) the relegation of the professional party politician to the middle levels of power, (2) the semi-organized stalemate of the interests of sovereign localities into which the legislative function has fallen, (3) the virtually complete absence of a civil service that constitutes a politically neutral, but politically relevant, depository of brainpower and executive skill, and (4) the increased official secrecy behind which great decisions are made without benefit of public or even Congressional debate.

As a result, the political directorate, the corporate rich, and the ascendant military have come together as the power elite, and the expanded and centralized hierarchies which they head have encroached upon the old balances and have now relegated them to the middle levels of power. Now the balancing society is a conception that pertains accurately to the middle levels, and on that level the balance has become more often an affair of intrenched provincial and nationally irresponsible forces and demands than a center of power and national decision.

But how about the bottom? As all these trends have become visible at the top and on the middle, what has been happening to the great American public? If the top is unprecedentedly powerful and increasingly unified and willful; if the middle zones are increasingly a semi-organized stalemate – in what shape is the bottom, in what condition is the public at large? The rise of the power elite, we shall now see, rests upon, and in some ways is part of, the transformation of the publics of America into a mass society.

Notes

1. Cf. Elmer Davis, *But We Were Born Free* (Indianapolis: BobbsMerrill, 1953), p. 187.

2. For points used to characterize the first and second of these phases I have drawn from Robert Lamb, 'Political Elites and the Process of Economic Development,' *The Progress of Underdeveloped Areas* (Edited by Bert Hoselitz) (Chicago: The University of Chicago Press, 1952).

3. Henry Cabot Lodge, *Early Memoirs*, cited by Dixon Wecter, *The Saga of American Society* (New York: Scribner's, 1937), p. 206.

4. Lord James Bryce, *The American Commonwealth* (New York: Macmillan, 1918), vol. I, pp. 84–5. In pre-revolutionary America, regional differences were of course important; but see: William E. Dodd *The Cotton Kingdom* (Volume 27 of the Chronicles of

America Series, edited by Allen Johnson) (New Haven: Yale University Press, 1919), p. 41; Louis B. Wright, *The First Gentlemen of Virginia* (Huntington Library, 1940), Chapter 12; Samuel Morison and Henry S. Commager, *The Growth of the American Republic* (New York: Oxford University Press, 1950), pp. 177–8; James T. Adams, *Provincial Society, 1690–1763* (New York: Macmillan, 1927), p. 83.

5. Cf., for example, David Riesman, in collaboration with Reuel Denney and Nathan Glazer, *The Lonely Crowd* (New Haven: Yale University Press, 1950).

6. See the Hearings of the Pujo Committee, quoted in Richard Hofstadter, *The Age of Reform* (New York: Knopf, 1955), p. 230; and Louis D. Brandeis, *Other People's Money* (New York: Stokes, 1932), pp. 22–3.

7. Richard Hofstadter, op. cit., p. 305.

8. 'Ruling class' is a badly loaded phrase. 'Class' is an economic term; 'rule' a political one. the phrase 'ruling class,' thus contains the theory that an economic class rules politically. That short-cut theory may or may not at times be true, but we do not want to carry that one rather simple theory about in the terms that we use to define our problems; we wish to state the theories explicitly, using terms of more precise and unilateral meaning. Specifically, the phrase 'ruling class,' in its common political connotations, does not allow enough autonomy to the political order and its agents, and it says nothing about the military as such. It should be clear to the reader by now that we do not accept as adequate the simple view that high economic men unilaterally make all the decisions of national consequence. We hold that such a simple view of 'economic determinism' must be elaborated by 'political determinism' and 'military determinism'; that the higher agents of each of these three domains now often have a noticeable degree of autonomy; and that only in the often intricate ways of coalition do they make up and carry through the most important decisions. Those are the major reasons we prefer 'power elite' to ruling class' as a characterizing phrase for the higher circles when we consider them in terms of power.

9. Whittaker Chambers, *Witness* (New York: Random House, 1952), p. 550.

10. For an excellent introduction to the international unity of corporate interests, see James Stewart Martin, *All Honorable Men* (Boston: Little Brown, 1950).

11. Gerald W. Johnson, 'The Superficial Aspect,' *New Republic*, 25 October 1954, p. 7.

12. See the Hearings before the Committee on Armed Services, United States Senate, Eighty-third Congress, First Session, On Nominees Designate Charles E. Wilson, Roger M. Keyes, Robert T. Stevens, Robert B. Anderson, and Harold E. Talbott, 15, 16, and 23 January 1953 (Washington, D.C.: U.S. Government Printing Office, 1953).

13. Hearings before the Subcommittee on Study of Monopoly Power of the Committee on the Judiciary, House of Representatives, Eight-first Congress, First Session, Serial No. 14, Part 2-A (Washington, D.C.: U.S. Government Printing Office, 1950), p. 468.

14. Cf. *The New York Times*, 6 December 1952, p. 1.

15. Floyd Hunter, 'Pilot Study of National Power and Policy Structures.' Institute for Research in Social Science, University of North Carolina, Research Previews, vol. 2, No. 2, March 1954 (mimeo), p. 8.

16. Ibid. p. 9.

17. Richard Hofstadter, op. cit., pp. 71–2.

18. Cf. Gerth and Mills, *Character and Social Structure* (New York: Harcourt, Brace, 1953).

19. Cf. Mills, 'The Conscription of America,' *Common Sense*, April 1945, pp. 15 ff.
20. Cf. 'Twelve of the Best American Schools,' *Fortune*, January 1936, p. 48.
21. Speech of Field Marshall Viscount Montgomery at Columbia University as reported in *The New York Times*, 24 November 1954, p. 25.
22. Cf. Dean Acheson, 'What a Secretary of State Really Does,' *Harper's*, December 1954, p. 48.

62

C. Wright Mills

Ralph Miliband

I mourn the death of C. Wright Mills, bitterly and personally. We had, in the last five years of his life, become close friends. I am not minded to write a detached appraisal of his work and thought. But I think I can write about the man he was, and what he was about.

Mills was forty-five years old when he died of a second heart attack last March, at his home in West Nyack, near New York. He had by then long established himself as the most interesting and controversial sociologist writing in the United States. With books like *White Collar, The Power Elite*, and *The Sociological Imagination*, he had succeeded in proving to a new generation of students what most of their teachers had managed to conceal from them: that social analysis could be probing, tough-minded, critical, relevant, and scholarly; that ideas need not be handled as undertakers handle bodies, with care but without passion; that commitment need not be dogmatic; and that radicalism need not be a substitute for hard thinking. With what he called "pamphlets," like *The Causes of World War III* and *Listen, Yankee*, he had wanted, and managed, to reach a wider public, in the hope of doing what one man could against the brainwashing and intimidation to which his fellow Americans were, and are, exposed from all sides, day in and day out.

Mills was as American as could be. He was born in Texas, and liked to recall that his grandfather, in the old days of one man one gun, had died, shot in the back. However, he not only fled from the intellectual desert of Texas as soon as he had graduated from its University: let his enemies make of it what they will, he also came to feel a deep alienation from America, its ethos, its politics, its way of life. His was not the snob dislike which some Americans feel for a country incapable of matching the hierarchical graces of Europe, nor the alienation which often accompanies the romantic vision of vanished America, rural, small-town, face-to-face. Mills' interest in Europe was strictly sociological. Nor did he feel the need to look for radical inspiration outside America: the Wobblies would do quite well. And he was not, as some critics alleged, an *égaré* Jeffersonian, hankering for a pre-industrial age:

Source: G. William Domhoff and Hoyt B. Ballard (eds.), *C. Wright Mills and the Power Elite*, (Boston: Beacon Press, 1968).

he liked stainless steel, efficient heating systems, fast motorcycles. He was an excellent mechanic and professional with a camera. He would have made a first-class engineer. What he loathed about America was not its industrial strength, but the mess which a profit-oriented society has made, and cannot but make, of its human and material powers; not America's cars, but their built-in shoddiness, not television, but its commercialized misuse. *Caveat Emptor* did not strike him as the last word in social wisdom.

Enters *The Power Elite*. It is easy but dishonest to attribute the corruption of a society to its people. Rousseau was right: the people is never corrupt. But it is often corrupted – by those whom it pays to corrupt, by those who have the power to do it. In *White Collar*, which he thought his best book, he had analyzed the various kinds of corruption which had affected the middle layers of American society. In *The Power Elite*, he went on to locate the corrupters-in-chief, the men of the "higher immorality," and found them in three interlocking groups: the corporate rich and the "warlords" (those whom an unexpected disciple, Eisenhower by name, has called the "industrial–military complex") and the political directorate.

The Power Elite is a rich and intricate book, written, like all that Mills wrote, in a compelling style – intense, muscular, alive. It is one of the very few books to glitter among the grey mass of what, in the United States, passed for social analysis in the frightened fifties. There is room for debate about much of its detail. But I don't think there is much room for serious debate about the book's general thesis, namely, that in America some men have enormous power denied to everyone else; that these men are, increasingly, a self-perpetuating elite; that their power is, increasingly, unchecked and irresponsible; and that their decision-making, based on an increasingly "military definition of reality" and on "crackpot realism," is oriented to immoral ends.

Mills was an angry man, with the disciplined, directed anger of the humanist in an irrational society – for what is humanism if not anger with unreason? His fiercest anger, however, was not with the Power Elite: for they were merely acting out the role cast for them by the social setting in which they were allowed to wield power; nor with American labor leaders, the men whom he had, in one of his first books, hopefully called the "New Men of Power." True, they had failed to form an effective counterweight to the Power Elite; worse, they had adopted its ethos and its purposes. But then, Mills had long given up (mistakenly, I think) the belief that organized labor could ever, in an advanced capitalist society, be the maker of radical history – the "labor metaphysic," he called that belief. It was not the Power Elite, Labor, or White Collar which angered him most, but defaulting academics and intellectuals.

To an extraordinary degree, Mills had something which is not very common among academics and intellectuals: an intense respect for the intellectual craft; for the world of ideas, knowledge, and scholarship; for the intellectual as the high priest of reason and truth. He really liked only two kinds of people: those who were good with their hands, a carpenter, a mechanic, a gunsmith;

and those who were possessed by the intellectual passion, as he was himself. He never made the vulgar mistake of taking seriously only those who shared his view of the world. Unlike many radicals (not to speak of anti-radicals), he was an intensely listening man. The basic requirement was not shared opinions, but honesty and knowledge, scholarship and relevance. Every working day (and every day was a working day), he was engaged, through books, essays, articles, newspapers, in a silent but active debate with fellow writers, anywhere. I have never seen anyone read as creatively as Mills did. He couldn't even read a detective story without pencil in hand.

"All social scientists," he wrote, "by the fact of their existence, are involved in the struggle between enlightenment and obscurantism." But he knew that there was an "ought" missing from that proposition, that many social scientists, in the struggle between enlightenment and obscurantism, are on the wrong side, or refuse to be involved, which comes to the same. This is what roused him to indignation – conformist unthinking, reason at the eager service of unreasonable kings, sophisticated apologetics for the inexcusable, social scientists as shields of orthodoxy and bellboys of authority.

It is from that indignation that stemmed *The Sociological Imagination*. That book was both a denunciation and a plea: a denunciation of social science as abstracted triviality, as windy pretension allied to timid respectability, of the uses of social science for the purpose, not of challenge, but of adjustment; and a plea – for the big probe, for a social science "of direct relevance to urgent public issues and insistent human trouble," for the social scientist as a man fired with the will "to make a difference in the quality of human life in our time."

The trouble with Mills was that he never managed to emancipate himself from a view of the intellectual as the free man, in duty bound to help make others free. Such a romantic, naive belief is inconvenient; it poses a threat. No wonder he made enemies in the academic fraternity.

It was only in 1956 that Mills, on leave from Columbia University, first came to Europe. He had, until then, been very America-oriented. In April 1957 he came to a weekend seminar in Surrey, organized by the Students' Union of the London School of Economics. He was a big man, who looked bigger, reserved but intensely alert, deliberate in speech and coolly appraising, unassumingly at ease with the students, whom he bowled over, quite unselfconsciously. Shortly after, in July, he and I went to Poland, where Adam Schaff as the philosopher of official Poland, and Leszek Kolakowski as the most acute of the young Polish "revisionists," showed us two parts of an equation, to which neither had the complete answer, nor could have.

Until then, Mills had generally shared the outlook of that particular stream of American radicalism which views the Soviet regime as inherently evil, and present-day Communism as the frozen caricature of a uniquely penetrating body of thought. For the record, I might as well add here that the label "Texas Trotskyite" which some people stupidly tried to pin on him was doubly inaccurate: he was born in Texas but he was not a Texan; nor did he ever identify himself with any of the fifty-seven varieties of American Trotskyism. He simply thought Trotsky one of the most remarkable minds of the Marxist tradition – who but a fool or an ignoramus does not? His visit to Poland, two subsequent visits to Russia, in 1960 and 1961, and much talk and debate with intellectuals in the Communist bloc, left him intensely interested and pondering, "ambiguous," as he put it, about much of Soviet society, better aware of its problems, its evils, *and* its promise. Unlike the dogmatic anti-Communists of the American Left, whom he now saw as "members of the old futilitarians of the dead Left," Mills did not react to the Soviet bloc as if he had a vested intellectual and political interest in the perpetuation of all that was evil in it: *his* world would not be shattered by the humanization of Soviet society and by the unfreezing of its Stalinist mold. Some of his friends thought and said that he had "gone soft" on the Stalinists. It was an absurd charge which deeply distressed him, more than any other attack from any other quarter ever distressed him. He was the last man to surrender his judgment and his perception to the dogmatists of either camp. He was still "working on" Communism and the Soviet bloc when he died: his last book, *The Marxists*, published shortly after his death, is the last testimony to the rare honesty he brought to that effort. One of his unfinished manuscripts was a *Letter to a Russian Intellectual*, a book in which he hoped to enter into a thorough examination of the problems, common and dissimilar, which intellectuals of East and West confront, or ought to confront.

Some men are pamphleteers by vocation. Mills was not. He became one in the late fifties, reluctantly, out of a deeply felt need to present, to as wide an audience as could be reached, alternatives to the military definition of reality which he believed to be at the center of his country's foreign policies. What he was concerned with, he wrote about. By the late fifties, he had come to be haunted (as only idiots are not) by the fear that East and West were trapped in a terrible dialectic, which would ultimately turn the planet into a thermonuclear crematorium.

The detailed analysis and prescriptions of *The Causes of World War III* matter less here than its insistence on "the wholesale cultural and political default of NATO intellectuals during the past decade and a half" as one of the causes of World War III. He had no illusions as to the likelihood of his proposals being acted upon "this week by the power elite of the United States," the more so since, from their standpoint, these proposals "were indeed utopian, expensive, idealistic, unsound and, for all I know, traitorous." Mills was speaking above all to intellectuals, "scientists and artists, ministers and scholars . . . those who represent the human intellect . . . who are part of the great discourse of inquiry and reason, of sensibility and imagination." I don't know how many were persuaded, but I know that many listened, and drew strength from what they heard. He had, in those last years, become a voice and was becoming the spokesman of a movement, "the big daddy of the New Left," as someone sneered. He did not relish the role. For all his intensity and impatience, he was a singularly modest, unpretentious man. He was embarrassed by the fan mail which poured into his letter box, and he hated being distracted from the big books he wanted to write. But there was no surcease. For suddenly, there was Cuba.

As Mills wrote in *Listen, Yankee*, he had not thought much about Cuba until the summer of 1960 – eighteen months after Fidel Castro took power in Havana. Cuba was forced upon his attention by visits to Brazil in the autumn of 1959 and to Mexico in the spring of 1960. "In both Rio de Janeiro and Mexico City," he recalled, "Cuba was of course a major topic of discussion. But I did not know what was happening there, much less what I might think about it, and I was then busy with other studies." He decided to "look into" Cuba: by the time he went there in the late summer of 1960, he had set up one of his beloved "files" and had read voraciously on Cuba and Latin America. The book which came out of that trip was written in six weeks, at white heat, the way Tom Paine must have written *Common Sense*, for another revolution.

Mills was rather detached about his previous books: the next ones would be *much* better. But he was proud of *Listen, Yankee*, and with good reason. For it is a good and brave book, in which one Yankee tried to explain, well and bravely, through the fog of misrepresentation with which the American press had shrouded the island, why the Cuban Revolution was by far the best and most decent thing that had ever happened in and to Latin America. Mills did not go into Cuba gooey-eyed, nor did he come out of Cuba gooey-eyed. As he wrote, "I am for the Cuban Revolution. I do not worry about it. I worry for it and with it." He did believe that Castro, having been his own Kerensky and Lenin, could avoid becoming his own Stalin as well. His desperate anxiety to persuade his countrymen that the Cuban Revolution should be helped stemmed from his conviction that nothing was more likely to make the moustache and not the beard the symbol of the revolution than the United States' attempt to destroy it. Long before it happened, he had come to believe that the United States *would* attempt to destroy the Revolution by force. It filled him with bitter, helpless shame. In fact, it broke his heart. It was in December 1960 that he suffered his first major heart attack. It was altogether fitting that, when Mills died fifteen months later, Fidel Castro should have sent a wreath to the funeral. For Mills was a casualty of the Cuban Revolution, and of the revolution of our times.

C. Wright Mills cannot be neatly labeled and cataloged. He never belonged to any party or faction; he did not think of himself as a "Marxist"; he had the most profound contempt for orthodox Social Democrats and for closed minds in the Communist world. He detested smug liberals and the kind of radical whose response to urgent and uncomfortable choices is hand wringing. He was a man on his own, with both the strength and also the weakness which go with that solitude. He was on the Left, but not of the Left, a deliberately lone guerrilla, not a regular soldier. He was highly organized, but unwilling to *be* organized, with self-discipline the only discipline he could tolerate. He had friends rather than comrades. Despite all this, perhaps because of it, he occupied a unique position in American radicalism. He was desperately needed by socialists everywhere, and his death leaves a gaping void. In a trapped and inhumane world, he taught what it means to be a free and humane intellect. "Get on with it," he used to say. "Work." So, in his spirit, let us.

Note

Ralph Miliband teaches political sociology at the London School of Economics. He is the author of *Parliamentary Socialism* and co-editor of three volumes of *The Socialist Register*. This article appeared first in the *New Left Review*, May–June, 1962, and then in the *Monthly Review*, September, 1962.

63

The Sociology of C. Wright Mills

Eugene V. Schneider

Men of sensibility, as Mills would say, may agree on the nature of present-day society, and yet disagree on the process by which this society was brought into being and in what direction it will develop. And if there is such disagreement, then it is virtually certain that there will be disagreement on what must be done, on what *can* be done, by those who wish to change the drift of things. The aim of this article is not to offer a critique of Mills – that would be quite impossible in the space of a few pages – but to present in highly condensed form the main features of his beliefs about modern society.

Theoretical Approach

Mills was above all a social scientist, that is, he believed that society could be made the object of rational inquiry. It is important to keep this in mind precisely because Mills leveled such bitter attacks on present-day social science, whether of the academic or "Marxist" varieties. Those who doubt that society can be studied scientifically are going to be disappointed in Mills, no matter how much they may enjoy his attacks on current social sciences.

But he was a social scientist of his own kind. He rejected most academic social science on two grounds. First, he scornfully rejected that social science which lacks historical perspective of any kind, which views society as essentially an equilibrium, maintained by a set of functioning institutions. For such social science there are no internal contradictions, only deviance; there are no long-term forces of social change, only variations about equilibrium; there is no succession of historically unique societies, only variations of "society." Second, he rejected academic social science because it refused to take a moral stand on what it was studying. For Mills this was not only a moral fault, it was a sin against science, for it confined the social sciences to studying things as they are, without ever coming to grips with things as they might be. Yet the potentialities in any given situation are also real. By failing to recognize this

---

Source: G. William Domhoff and Hoyt B. Ballard (eds.), *C. Wright Mills and the Power Elite*, (Boston: Beacon Press, 1968).

fact, academic social science doomed itself to a static view of society, to the trivial, the obvious, the half-baked. Even worse, it seemed to justify the present, with all its absurdity, inhumanity, and danger, as somehow necessary or even right.

It might seem that this position must lead Mills to the acceptance of Marxism as the only possible valid social science. And in a certain sense, it did; Mills explicitly labeled himself a "plain Marxist." But it is necessary to understand what Mills meant by this term.

For Mills, Marxism was three things: an approach to social phenomena, a method for studying them, and a system of values by which to judge societies and to formulate programs of action. The Marxist approach to the study of society was an historical and a functional one. It held that all societies were constantly changing, by evolution or by revolution, into new forms. Each form was marked by specific types of social structure, human personalities, processes of change and resistance to change, and specific functional relationships between all of these. Each society, then, was governed by "laws" specific to itself. As a method, Marxism demanded that once a model of any specific society was constructed, deductions be made from this model which could be used to predict the course of events, but only until such time as the model would be rendered obsolete by evolution or revolution. As a philosophy, Marxism judged each society in terms of its capacity to provide the basic elements of a truly human condition, by which Marx meant not only material necessities, but the widest possible opportunity for the exercise of reason and freedom.

Marxism, in Mills' view, did *not* mean that one set of "laws," deducted from one master model, was applicable to all types and stages of capitalist society, let alone other types of society. The trouble with almost all the existing varieties of Marxism was that they sought to use a model which Marx derived largely from one form of capitalist society to analyze quite different types of society. Because these models are obsolete, the predictions derived from them about the course of modern history have been fallacious. Thus they have led to what Mills regarded as fallacious predictions about the increasing alienation and pauperization of the working class, the constant worsening of economic crises and ultimate stagnation, the ever constant and sharpening class struggle, and the outbreak of revolutions in advanced capitalist societies.

Mills believed that underlying these fallacies is a false model of modern society. Thus he denies that in our time men are dominated by their relationships to the means of production. He asks, can the behavior of blue-collar workers, white-collar workers, capitalists, managers, generals, Negroes, be understood in these terms? He denies that the "superstructure" of society – the prevailing ideas and institutions – is always the reflection of the economic base. Is it true, for instance, that the state has always been the servant of the capitalist class, that it is never able to restrain its capitalists? He denies that, today, social being always determines consciousness. How, he asks, can one account for "false consciousness"? What about the ability of the mass media to *create* consciousness in relation to certain issues and objects? He denies that men in our time can make history only within the limits set by changes in the economic base of society. This, he argues, is gravely to underestimate the role of leaders and men of power in the making of modern history. Mills did not deny that all of these assumptions of the classical Marxist model may have been valid in another period; but he held that they are not eternal principles of society and that they certainly do not adequately describe our own times.

At this time the reader may be left wondering in what sense Mills was a Marxist. Perhaps instead of calling himself a "plain Marxist," Mills should have said along with Marx and in the precise sense that Marx meant it: "I, at least, am not a Marxist."

Society

Using what he considered to be the Marxian approach, method, and philosophy, Mills set about constructing what he thought was a more adequate model of advanced industrial society. It is possible here only to indicate briefly some of the major elements in this model. It will be found described in detail in his trilogy, *New Men of Power, White Collar,* and *The Power Elite.*

First, it must be understood that Mills believed that all advanced industrial societies, capitalist or non-capitalist, are subject to many of the same dynamic forces. Above all, modern society is marked by a process of rationalization (which is not the same thing as ordinary rationality). Rationalization is manifest in the growth of large-scale bureaucracies, revolutions in technology, developing techniques for the manipulation of people, the great growth of science. In the economic sphere, the result has been the bureaucratization and concentration of many phases of production. In the military sphere, the result has been the modern military machine – vast, bureaucratized, armed with the weapons of mass destruction. In the political sphere, there has appeared the state bureaucracy and the mass media as a means of manipulating people. Only society as a whole, at least in the capitalist countries, has resisted this process of rationalization.

From these central conditions of advanced industrial society flows a train of consequences, of which the most fateful are (1) the rise of an elite of powerful men who are in control of the means of death, production, and political power; and (2) below them an unorganized "mass" ruled over and controlled by this elite to an extent unique in human history.

The power elite are those who control the great organizations; they are the men at the head of the great corporations, the armed forces, the state, the mass media of communication. They are the men who make the "big decisions" – whether to go to war, to drop a bomb, to make peace, to join an alliance, to adopt a new economic policy. And they have the power to make sure that the rest of society accepts their decisions, if, indeed, they bother to secure assent at all. Their appearance is inevitable in advanced industrial society, but in the

United States their position is, for a variety of reasons, peculiarly invulnerable: there is the absence of competing elites, the lack of a civil service, the sudden rise of America to a position of world power without the traditions or institutions to play such a role.

The power elite is *not* an economic class, based on ownership of property. Those who control the military forces have no property rights in their organization, and the same is true of the political directorate. Nor does the capitalist class simply control the giant economic bureaucracies. It is more accurate to say that the corporations have reorganized the capitalist class; its wealth is now largely corporate wealth. It is the interests and programs of the corporate elite which dominate the capitalist class more than the other way about. But who are the members of this elite? Some of them, to be sure, are drawn from the capitalist class; their wealth and connections have been their tickets of admission to the world of corporate power. Some of them have come up through their own organizations. Some have come in from other giant organizations, particularly the military. This shift of power from the capitalist class to the economic elite is reflected in the declining prestige of the "very rich," the legendary families, the "400's." For members of these declining elites to wield power, they must enter the corporate world, or one of the other great organizations.

Yet to some degree this power elite does form a unified group, with a similarity of outlook, programs, and values. They have similar interests, first of all in maintaining themselves in power and then in substantive matters of policy. Thus a permanent war economy reflects the interests of the economic elite in an assured and profitable market; at the same time it guarantees the position of the military elite, and provides the state with the necessary leverage for conducting foreign policy. Unity is also based on the similarity of the types of men who make up the elite. As heads of large-scale organizations, they have a great deal of experience in common. They have had similar educational and occupational careers. They tend to come from the same religious, ethnic, and occupational backgrounds. Because they are the same type of men, and because their interests coincide at many points, they find it easy and profitable to interchange positions, and this serves to unify them further. Probably they are not formally organized; their unity is achieved by go-betweens, through informal associations, through the interchange of positions.

The state plays a peculiar role in Mills' model. The state is, of course, one of the great organizations of advanced industrial society, and as such it forms a major source of power in society. But the state has now spawned an independent elite. There is no civil service, independent of passing administrations, on the level of policy decisions. Most professional politicians operate on the middle levels of power. Rather, the political elite is composed of a mixture of top-level politicians and members of the military and economic elites. Yet this does not mean that the state is merely the tool of the economic-military elite, much less of the capitalist class. No matter what the source of the political elite, the state remains, to some degree, an independent source of power and policy. There is certainly much coincidence of interest and outlook between the political directorage and the other elites; but this does not mean that the political elite is not able to initiate and pursue a policy of its own.

Forming a sort of penumbra to the power elite are the go-betweens, the advisers and consultants of the elite, powerful politicians, local and regional upper classes, and celebrities whose faces are known to the general public. On occasion members of these groups may be raised into the power elite.

Below this elite of powerful men are the middle levels of power where various special interest groups struggle among themselves for advantage and position. Occasionally the powerful may intervene in their struggles for tactical reasons and, of course, the power elite will brook no opposition from that quarter. But within these limits, the middle levels are quite free to carry on their struggles. It is here that are found the labor unions, the farm organizations, the Congress, and all the myriad of special local or regional interests that it represents. These groups have readily abdicated from making the big decisions; they have traded national power for immediate advantage and, from this point of view, many of them have done well.

Below these top and middle levels of power is the "mass society." It includes all those who have little or no power over the decision-makers at the top, those who receive from the top orders, information, interpretations of events, sometimes in recognizable form, sometimes not. On the one hand, the mass is more or less firmly controlled, depending on the needs of the power elite, by various institutions such as education, religion, unions, the press, the movies, radio, and TV. On the other hand, the mass lacks its own organizations, leadership, or ideology. As a result, the mass can be manipulated by the top for whatever purposes it chooses: to secure assent for a decision . . . a market . . . a source of military manpower, or for whatever other reason.

It should be noted that by a "mass society" Mills does not necessarily mean a homogeneous society. There may be plenty of distinctions within a mass society; distinctions of age, sex, race, occupation, religion, even class. The point is that in a mass society these distinctions do not and cannot serve as a basis for organization to counter the power of the elite.

The mass society, like the power elite, has risen from forces lying deeply imbedded within the social structure. First, mass society is the obverse of the power elite; as power has been concentrated at the top, the mass has been denuded of it. But, second, mass society is the outcome of certain changes in the class structure. The old middle class of small property and wealth, which at one time supported populist or even anti-capitalist movements, has decreased in numbers and largely lost whatever organization and influence it once possessed. In its place has appeared a very numerous and growing class of white-collar workers, clinging frantically to the prestige of the older middle class, but without even its economic base. This class has no traditions, no organizations, no unity. It is probably the most easily controlled group in society; given a small amount of status, the opportunity to remain distinct from the working class, even a vague hope of "rising," it will remain quiescent.

What has happened to the working class, the class upon which Marxists everywhere have placed their hopes, and which Mills himself at one time (in *The New Men of Power*) considered the only bar to slump and war? Organized labor has, of course, entered the middle levels of power; it has become bureaucratized and its leaders quite happily abdicate any claims to positions within the power elite in return for freedom of action within their own little spheres. Organized labor has, in fact, become one of the institutions of mass society; its function there is to control the working class in behalf of the power elite. At the same time, the rank and file of the working class has lost much of whatever unity and militancy (which was never very much, in Mills' estimate) it once possessed. In numbers, it is a declining class; it is split by ethnic and racial divisions; those sections which are employed and organized are smug, those which are neither shattered; it has accepted the values of the "mass society" and yearns vaguely for the white collar for itself or its children, for a home in the suburbs. It possesses virtually no organizations outside of its unions, and it has lost control even of them.

The institutions of society have lost or abdicated whatever position they once had as centers of rational thought, freedom, and initiative. The schools long ago abandoned any opposition to the Establishment. Religion has traded its concern with the freedom and development of the human soul for a mess of comfort and respectability. The universities have been lulled or forced into quietude by liberal grants for research in behalf of the interests of the power elite, by the rise of the academic bureaucrat, by a relentless war against their independent teachers. Science has become a machine in the service of the power elite.

Mills' Program of Action

Who then, according to Mills, has the will and the capacity to oppose the power elite, the mass society, the inexorable drift toward slump and war? Mills argues that the only group in society with at least the will, if not the power, is the intelligentsia. Intellectuals are defined as all those whose concern is with discovering and articulating the meaning and development of societal forces, and in relating these forces to the personal problems that people face; intellectuals are those who offer alternatives for the development of society and thus for the self, and who suggest programs of action for attaining these alternatives. Insofar as intellectuals function as intellectuals, they cannot help but realize and oppose the role of the power elite in this society and the drift toward slump and war that it has set in motion. By the same token, the intellectuals cannot help but oppose the mass society, with its denial of rationality and freedom to all but a very few, with the limited and distorted selves that it produces. The mere dealers in ideas – those who have become technicians in the service of the Establishment, or those who have, through disgust or disillusionment, ceased to face these problems – are not intellectuals; they have forfeited their right to that name.

Note

Eugene V. Schneider is a professor of sociology at Bryn Mawr College. He is the author of *Industrial Sociology*. This paper, which appeared in the *Monthly Review*, February, 1963, has been retitled and the first and last sections condensed (with the permission of the author) because they were addressed only to political leftists, telling them that Mills had many ideas not shared by the traditional Left about which they would have to make up their minds.

64

The End of Ideology in the West

Daniel Bell

> Men commit the error of not knowing when to limit their hopes.
> – Machiavelli

There have been few periods in history when man felt his world to be durable, suspended surely, as in Christian allegory, between chaos and heaven. In an Egyptian papyrus of more than four thousand years ago, one finds: ". . . impudence is rife . . . the country is spinning round and round like a potters wheel . . . the masses are like timid sheep without a shepherd . . . one who yesterday was indigent is now wealthy and the sometime rich overwhelm him with adulation." The Hellenistic period as described by Gilbert Murray was one of a "failure of nerve"; there was "the rise of pessimism, a loss of self-confidence, of hope in this life and of faith in normal human effort." And the old scoundrel Talleyrand claimed that only those who lived before 1789 could have tasted life in all its sweetness.[1]

This age, too, can add appropriate citations – made all the more wry and bitter by the long period of bright hope that preceded it – for the two decades between 1930 and 1950 have an intensity peculiar in written history: worldwide economic depression and sharp class struggles; the rise of fascism and racial imperialism in a country that had stood at an advanced stage of human culture; the tragic self-immolation of a revolutionary generation that had proclaimed the finer ideals of man; destructive war of a breadth and scale hitherto unknown; the bureaucratised murder of millions in concentration camps and death chambers.

For the radical intellectual who had articulated the revolutionary impulses of the past century and a half, all this has meant an end to chiliastic hopes, to millenarianism, to apocalyptic thinking – and to ideology. For ideology, which once was a road to action, has come to be a dead end.

Whatever its origins among the French *philosophes*, ideology as a way of translating ideas into action was given its sharpest phrasing by the left Hegelians, by Feuerbach and by Marx. For them, the function of philosophy was to be

---

Source: Daniel Bell, *The End of Ideology: On the Exhaustion of Political Ideas in the Fifties*, (Glencoe, Ill.: Free Press, 1960).

critical, to rid the present of the past. ("The tradition of all the dead generations weighs like a nightmare on the brain of the living," wrote Marx.) Feuerbach, the most radical of all the left Hegelians, called himself Luther II. Man would be free, he said, if we could demythologize religion. The history of all thought was a history of progressive disenchantment, and if finally, in Christianity, God had been transformed from a parochial deity to a universal abstraction, the function of criticism – using the radical tool of alienation, or self-estrangement – was to replace theology by anthropology, to substitute Man for God. Philosophy was to be directed at life, man was to be liberated from the "specter of abstractions" and extricated from the bind of the supernatural. Religion was capable only of creating "false consciousness." Philosophy would reveal "true consciousness." And by placing Man, rather than God, at the center of consciousness, Feuerbach sought to bring the "infinite into the finite."[2]

If Feuerbach "descended into the world," Marx sought to transform it. And where Feuerbach proclaimed anthropology, Marx, reclaiming a root insight of Hegel, emphasized History and historical contexts. The world was not generic Man, but men; and of men, classes of men. Men differed because of their class position. And truths were class truths. All truths, thus, were masks, or partial truths, but the real truth was the revolutionary truth. And this real truth was rational.

Thus a dynamic was introduced into the analysis of ideology, and into the creation of a new ideology. By demythologizing religion, one recovered (from God and sin) the potential in man. By the unfolding of history, rationality was revealed. In the struggle of classes, true consciousness, rather than false consciousness, could be achieved. But if truth lay in action, one must act. The left Hegelians, said Marx, were only *littérateurs*. (For them a magazine was "practice.") For Marx, the only real action was in politics. But action, revolutionary action as Marx conceived it, was not mere social change. It was, in its way, the resumption of all the old millenarian, chiliastic ideas of the Anabaptists. It was, in its new vision, a new ideology.

The analysis of ideology belongs properly in the discussion of the intelligentsia. One can say that what the priest is to religion, the intellectual is to ideology. This in itself gives us a clue to the dimensions of the word and the reason for its multivariate functions. The word *ideology* was coined by the French philosopher Destutt de Tracy, at the end of the 18th century. Together with other Enlightenment philosophers, notably such materialists as Helvetius and Holbach, de Tracy was trying to define a way of discovering "truth" other than through faith and authority, the traditional methods encouraged by Church and State. And, equally, under the influence of Francis Bacon, these men were seeking some way to eliminate the accidents of bias, the distortions of prejudice, the idiosyncracies of upbringing, the interventions of self-interest or the simple will to believe, all of which, like shadows in Plato's cave, created illusions of truth.[3] Their aim was to "purify" ideas in order to achieve "objective" truth and "correct" thought. Some of them, Helvetius, for example, believed that one had to go back to the origin and development of ideas in order to see how distortions entered. De Tracy believed that one "purified" ideas by reducing them to sense perceptions – a belated French variant of British empiricism with a barely concealed anti-religious bias – and this new science of ideas he called "ideology."

The negative connotations of the term arose with Napoleon. Having consolidated his power, he forbade the teaching of moral and political science at the Institut National and denounced the "ideologues" as irresponsible speculators who were subverting morality and patriotism. As a republican, Napoleon had been sympathetic to the ideas of the philosophers; as Emperor, he recognized the importance of religious orthodoxy for the maintenance of the State.

But it was with Marx that the word "ideology" went through some curiously different transmutations. For Marx, as in his work *The German Ideology*, ideology was linked to philosophical idealism, or the conception that ideas are autonomous, and that ideas, independently, have the power to reveal truth and consciousness. For Marx, as a materialist, this was false since "existence determined consciousness" rather than vice versa; any attempt to draw a picture of reality from ideas alone could produce only "false consciousness."

Thus, for example, in following Feuerbach – from whom Marx drew most of his analysis of ideology and alienation – he considered religion to be a false consciousness: Gods are the creation of men's minds and they only appear to exist independently and determine man's fate; religion therefore is an ideology.

But Marx went one step further. Ideologies, he said, are not only false ideas, but they mask particular interests. Ideologies claim to be truth, but reflect the needs of specific groups. In his early essays on *The Jewish Question*, one of the few places where he dealt specifically with the philosophical problems of State and Society, Marx sharply attacked the concept of "natural rights" as it appeared in the French Revolution's Declaration of the Rights of Man, and as these rights were specified in the State constitutions of Pennsylvania and New Hampshire. The presumption of "natural rights" – the freedom to worship or the freedom to own property – was that they were "absolute" or "transcendant" rights; for Marx, they were only "bourgeois rights," historically achieved, which made false claim to universal validity. The function of the State, Marx pointed out, was to create some basis for the "general will." In the "civil society" which the bourgeoisie had created, the State presumably was to be negative or neutral. Each man would pursue his own self-interest, and a social harmony would prevail. But in fact, he argued, the State was used to enforce the rights of particular groups. Thus the claim of "natural rights" simply masked the demand of the bourgeoisie to be able to use property to their own advantage. Marx believed that the individualism of "natural rights" was a false individualism, since man could only "realize" himself in community, and that true freedom was not freedom *of* property or freedom of religion, but freedom *from* property and freedom *from* religion – in short, from ideology.

The attempt, therefore, to claim universal validity for what was in fact a class interest, was ideology.

Marx differed from Bentham, and other utilitarians, in recognizing that individuals were not always motivated by direct self-interest. (This was "vulgar hedonism.") Ideology, he said, was a meaningful force. "One must not form the narrow-minded idea," he wrote in *The Eighteenth Brumaire*, "that the petty-bourgeoisie wants on principle to enforce an egoistic class interest. It believes, rather, that the *special* conditions of its emancipation are the *general* conditions through which alone modern society can be saved and the class struggle avoided." The "unmasking" of ideology, thus, is to reveal the "objective" interest behind the idea, and to see what function the ideology serves.[4]

The implications of all this are quite direct. For one, a rationalistic analysis of politics alone is inadequate. What people say they believe cannot always be taken at face value, and one must search for the structure of interests beneath the ideas; one looks not at the *content* of ideas, but their *function*. A second, more radical conclusion is that if ideas mask material interests, then the "test of truth" of a doctrine is to see what class interests it serves. In short, truth is "class truth." Thus, there is no objective philosophy, but only "bourgeois philosophy" and "proletarian philosophy"; no objective sociology but only "bourgeois sociology" and "proletarian sociology." But Marxism is not, simply, a relativistic doctrine: there is an "objective" ordering of the social universe, which is revealed through "history." History, for Marx as for Hegel, is a progressive unfolding reason, in which society, through man's conquest of nature and the destruction of all mythologies and superstitions, moves on to "higher stages." The "truth" of doctrine, therefore, is to be determined by its "closeness of fit" to the development of history; and in practice, it has meant that "truth" was determined by whether or not it contributed to he advancement of revolution.

There are many difficulties to the theory of the "social determination of ideas." One is the role of science. Marx did not speak of the natural sciences as ideologies. Yet a number of Marxists, particularly in the Soviet Union in the 1930's, did claim that there was a "bourgeois science" and a "bourgeois physics" and a "proletarian science" and a "proletarian physics." Thus, the relativity theories of Albert Einstein were attacked as "idealistic." And while today in the Soviet Union, there is hardly any talk of "bourgeois physics," the theories of Sigmund Freud are officially condemned as "idealistic." Yet if science is not class-bound, is this equally true of the social sciences? The question of the autonomy of science is one that has never been satisfactorily resolved in Marxian thought.

A second difficulty is the deterministic presumption that there is a *one-to-one* correspondence between a set of ideas and some "class" purpose. Yet this is rarely the case. Empiricism is usually associated with liberal inquiry. Yet David Hume, the most "radical" empiricist, was a Tory, and Edmund Burke, who had argued the most vigorously against rationalist efforts to blueprint a new society, was conservative. Hobbes, one of the most profound of materialists, was a royalist, and T. H. Green, one of the leaders of the idealist revival in Great Britain, a liberal.

And the third difficulty is the definition of class. For Marx (though class was never rigorously defined in his work) the key social divisions in society arose out of the distribution of property. Yet in a politico-technological world, property has increasingly lost its force as a determinant of power, and sometimes, even, of wealth. In almost all modern societies, technical skill becomes more important than inheritance as a determinant of occupation, and political power takes precedence over economic. What then is the meaning of class?

And yet, one cannot wholly discount the force of the proposition that "styles of thought" are related to historic class groups and their interests, or that ideas emerge as a consequence of the different world-views, or perspectives, of different groups in the society. The problem is how to specify the relationships between the existential base and the "mental production." Max Weber, the sociologist, argued, for example, that there is an "elective affinity" between ideas and interests. The social origin of an idea, or of a theorist, or a revolutionist, is less relevant than the fact that certain ideas become "selected out," so to speak, by social groups that find them congenial and thus espouse them. This was the basis for the theory of the "Protestant Ethic," in which he argued that certain features of Calvinistic thought, and the kind of personality that such a doctrine sanctioned, became necessary, and causal, in the development of capitalism, despite the other-worldly foundation of these ideas. Karl Mannheim, another sociologist, sought to divide social thought into two fundamental styles, which he called "ideological" and "utopian." He accepted the proposition, derived from Marx, that ideas are "time-bound," but insisted that Marx's ideas, as those of all socialists, came within the same stricture. Since all ideas serve interests, those which defended the existing order he called "ideological" and those which sought to change the social order he called "utopian." But was all effort, then, at objective truth hopeless? Was Bacon's quest therefore a mirage? Mannheim felt that one social group could be relatively objective – the intellectuals. Since the intelligentsia were a "floating stratum" in society, and therefore were less bound than other class groups, they could achieve multi-perspectives that transcended the parochial limits of the other social groups.

In the development of the social sciences, the problem raised by Bacon, de Tracy, Marx and others – the clarification of the role of ideas in social change – has become part of a technical field known as the "sociology of knowledge." (For a clear discussion of these issues, see the chapter by Robert K. Merton in his *Social Theory and Social Structure*.) But in popular usage the word *ideology* remains as a vague term where it seems to denote a world-view or belief-system or creeds held by a social group about the social arrangements in society, which is morally justified as being right. People then talk of the "ideology of the small businessman," or of liberalism, or fascism, as an "ideology." Or some writer will talk of "the dream-world of ideology (in which) Americans see their country as a place where every child is born to 'equality of opportunity,' where every man is essentially as good as every other man if not better." In this sense, ideology connotes a "myth" rather than just a set of values.

Clearly, such usages, by mixing together many things, create only confusion. Some distinctions, therefore, are in order.

We can, perhaps, borrow a distinction from Mannheim, and distinguish between what he called "the *particular* conception of ideology," and "the *total* conception of ideology." In the first sense, we can say that individuals who profess certain values do have interests as well, and we can better understand the meaning of these values or beliefs, or the reasons why they come forth where they have, by linking them up with the interests they have – though the interests may not always be economic; they may be status interests (such as an ethnic group that wants higher standing or social approval in a society), political interests, such as representation, and the like. It is in this sense that we can talk of the *ideology* of business, or of labor, or the like. (When Charles E. Wilson, the Secretary of Defense in the Eisenhower Administration and one-time president of General Motors, said, "What is good for the United States is good for General Motors, and vice-versa," he was expressing ideology – i.e., the view that economic policy should be geared to the needs of the business community, since the welfare of the country depended on the health of business.) A *total* ideology is an all-inclusive system of comprehensive reality, it is a set of beliefs, infused with passion, and seeks to transform the whole of a way of life. This commitment to ideology – the yearning for a "cause," or the satisfaction of deep moral feelings – is not necessarily the reflection of interests in the shape of ideas. Ideology, in this sense, and in the sense that we use it here, is a secular religion.

Ideology is the conversion of ideas into social levers. Without irony, Max Lerner once entitled a book "Ideas Are Weapons." This is the language of ideology. It is more. It is the commitment to the consequences of ideas. When Vissarion Belinsky, the father of Russian criticism, first read Hegel and became convinced of the philosophical correctness of the formula "what is, is what ought to be," he became a supporter of the Russian autocracy. But when it was shown to him that Hegel's thought contained the contrary tendency, that dialectically the "is" evolves into a different form, he became a revolutionary overnight. "Belinsky's conversion," comments Rufus W. Mathewson, Jr., "illustrates an attitude toward ideas which is both passionate and myopic, which responds to them on the basis of their immediate relevances alone, and inevitably reduces them to tools."[5]

What gives ideology its force is its passion. Abstract philosophical inquiry has always sought to eliminate passion, and the person, to rationalize all ideas. For the ideologue, truth arises in action, and meaning is given to experience by the "transforming moment." He comes alive not in contemplation, but in "the deed." One might say, in fact, that the most important, latent, function of ideology is to tap emotion. Other than religion (and war and nationalism), there have been few forms of channelizing emotional energy. Religion symbolized, drained away, dispersed emotional energy from the world onto the litany, the liturgy, the sacraments, the edifices, the arts. Ideology fuses these energies and channels them into politics.

But religion, at its most effective, was more. It was a way for people to cope with the problem of death. The fear of death — forceful and inevitable — and more, the fear of violent death, shatters the glittering, imposing, momentary dream of man's power. The fear of death, as Hobbes pointed out, is the source of conscience; the effort to avoid violent death is the source of law. When it was possible to believe, really believe, in heaven and hell, then some of the fear of death could be tempered or controlled; without such belief, there is only the total annihilation of the self.[6]

It may well be that with the decline in religious *faith* in the last century and more, this fear of death as total annihilation, unconsciously expressed, has probably increased. One may hypothesize, in fact, that here is a cause of the breakthrough of the irrational, which is such a marked feature of the changed moral temper of our time. Fanaticism, violence, and cruelty are not, of course, unique in human history. But there was a time when such frenzies and mass emotions could be displaced, symbolized, drained away, and dispersed through religious devotion and practice. Now there is only this life, and the assertion of self becomes possible — for some even necessary — in the domination over others.[7] One can challenge death by emphasizing the omnipotence of a movement (as in the "inevitable" victory of communism), or overcome death (as did the "immortality" of Captain Ahab) by bending others to one's will. Both paths are taken, but politics, because it can institutionalize power, in the way that religion once did, becomes the ready avenue for domination. The modern effort to transform the world chiefly or solely through politics (as meant that all other religious transformation of the self) has meant that all other institutional ways of mobilizing emotional energy would necessarily atrophy. In effect, sect and church became party and social movement.

A social movement can rouse people when it can do three things: simplify ideas, establish a claim to truth, and, in the union of the two, demand a commitment to action. Thus, not only does ideology transform ideas, it transforms people as well. The nineteenth-century ideologies, by emphasizing inevitability and by infusing passion into their followers, could compete with religion. By identifying inevitability with progress, they linked up with the positive values of science. But more important, these ideologies were linked, too, with the rising class of intellectuals, which was seeking to assert a place in society.

The differences between the intellectual and the scholar, without being invidious, are important to understand. The scholar has a bounded field of knowledge, a tradition, and seeks to find his place in it, adding to the accumulated, tested knowledge of the past as to a mosaic. The scholar, qua scholar, is less involved with his "self." The intellectual begins with *his* experience, *his* individual perceptions of the world, *his* privileges and deprivations, and judges the world by these sensibilities. Since his own status is of high value, his judgements of the society reflect the treatment accorded him. In a business civilization, the intellectual felt that the wrong values were being honored, and rejected the society. Thus there was a "built-in" compulsion for the free-floating intellectual to become political. The ideologies, therefore, which emerged from the nineteenth century had the force of the intellectuals behind them. They embarked upon what William James called "the faith ladder," which in its vision of the future cannot distinguish possibilities from probabilities, and converts the latter into certainties.

Today, these ideologies are exhausted. The events behind this important sociological change are complex and varied. Such calamities as the Moscow Trials, the Nazi-Soviet pact, the concentration camps, the suppression of the Hungarian workers, form one chain; such social changes as the modification of capitalism, the rise of the Welfare State, another. In philosophy, one can trace the decline of simplistic, rationalistic beliefs and the emergence of new stoic-theological images of man, e.g. Freud, Tillich, Jaspers, etc. This is not to say that such ideologies as communism in France and Italy do not have a political weight, or a driving momentum from other sources. But out of all this history, one simple fact emerges: for the radical intelligentsia, the old ideologies have lost their "truth" and their power to persuade.

Few serious minds believe any longer that one can set down "blueprints" and through "social engineering" bring about a new utopia of social harmony. At the same time, the older "counter-beliefs" have lost their intellectual force as well. Few "classic" liberals insist that the State should play no role in the economy, and few serious conservatives, at least in England and on the Continent, believe that the Welfare State is "the road to serfdom." In the Western world, therefore, there is today a rough consensus among intellectuals on political issues: the acceptance of a Welfare State, the desirability of decentralized power; a system of mixed economy and of political pluralism. In that sense, too, the ideological age has ended.

And yet, the extraordinary fact is that while the old nineteenth-century ideologies and intellectual debates have become exhausted, the rising states of Asia and Africa are fashioning new ideologies with a different appeal for their own people. These are the ideologies of industrialization, modernization, Pan-Arabism, color, and nationalism. In the distinctive difference between the two kinds of ideologies lies the great political and social problems of the second half of the twentieth century. The ideologies of the nineteenth century were universalistic, humanistic, and fashioned by intellectuals. The mass ideologies of Asia and Africa are parochial, instrumental, and created by political leaders. The driving forces of the old ideologies were social equality and, in the largest sense, freedom. The impulsions of the new ideologies are economic development and national power.

And in this appeal, Russia and China have become models. The fascination these countries exert is no longer the old idea of the free society, but the new one of economic growth. And if this involves the wholesale coercion of the population and the rise of new elites to drive the people, the new repressions are justified on the ground that without such coercions economic advance cannot take place rapidly enough. And even for some of the liberals of the West, "economic development" has become a new ideology that washes away the memory of old disillusionments.

It is hard to quarrel with an appeal for rapid economic growth and modernization, and few can dispute the goal, as few could ever dispute an appeal for equality and freedom. But in this powerful surge – and its swiftness is amazing – any movement that instates such goals risks the sacrifice of the present generation for a future that may see only a new exploitation by a new elite. For the newly-risen countries, the debate is not over the merits of Communism – the content of that doctrine has long been forgotten by friends and foes alike. The question is an older one: whether new societies can grow by building democratic institutions and allowing people to make choices – and sacrifices – voluntarily, or whether the new elites, heady with power, will impose totalitarian means to transform their countries. Certainly in these traditional and old colonial societies where the masses are apathetic and easily manipulated, the answer lies with the intellectual classes and their conceptions of the future.

Thus one finds, at the end of the fifties, a disconcerting caesura. In the West, among the intellectuals, the old passions are spent. The new generation, with no meaningful memory of these old debates, and no secure tradition to build upon, finds itself seeking new purposes within a framework of political society that has rejected, intellectually speaking, the old apocalyptic and chiliastic visions. In the search for a "cause," there is a deep, desperate, almost pathetic anger. The theme runs through a remarkable book, *Convictions*, by a dozen of the sharpest young Left Wing intellectuals in Britain. They cannot define the content of the "cause" they seek, but the yearning is clear. In the U.S. too there is a restless search for a new intellectual radicalism. Richard Chase, in his thoughtful assessment of American society, *The Democratic Vista*, insists that the greatness of nineteenth-century America for the rest of the world consisted in its radical vision of man (such a vision as Whitman's), and calls for a new radical criticism today. But the problem is that the old politico-economic radicalism (pre-occupied with such matters as the socialization of industry) has lost its meaning, while the stultifying aspects of contemporary culture (e.g., television) cannot be redressed in political terms. At the same time, American culture has almost completely accepted the avant-garde, particularly in art, and the older academic styles have been driven out completely. The irony, further, for those who seek "causes" is that the workers, whose grievances were once the driving energy for social change, are more satisfied with the society than the intellectuals. The workers have not achieved utopia, but their expectations were less than those of the intellectuals, and the gains correspondingly larger.

The young intellectual is unhappy because the "middle way" is for the middle-aged, not for him; it is without passion and is deadening.[8] Ideology, which by its nature is an all-or-none affair, and temperamentally the thing he wants, is intellectually devitalized, and few issues can be formulated any more, intellectually, in ideological terms. The emotional energies – and needs – exist, and the question of how one mobilizes these energies is a difficult one. Politics offers little excitement. Some of the younger intellectuals have found an outlet in science or university pursuits, but often at the expense of narrowing their talent into mere technique; others have sought self-expression in the arts, but in the wasteland the lack of content has meant, too, the lack of the necessary tension that creates new forms and styles.

Whether the intellectuals in the West can find passions outside of politics is moot. Unfortunately, social reform does not have any unifying appeal, nor does it give a younger generation the outlet for "self-expression" and "self-definition" that it wants. The trajectory of enthusiasm has curved East, where, in the new ecstasies for economic utopia, the "future" is all that counts.

The end of ideology is not – should not be – the end of utopia as well. If anything, one can begin anew the discussion of utopia only by being aware of the trap of ideology. The point is that ideologists are "terrible simplifiers." Ideology makes it unnecessary for people to confront individual issues on their individual merits. One simply turns to the ideological vending machine, and out comes the prepared formulae. And when these beliefs are suffused by apocalyptic fervor, ideas become weapons, and with dreadful results.

There is now, more than ever, some need for utopia, in the sense that men need – as they have always needed – some vision of their potential, some manner of fusing passion with intelligence. Yet the ladder to the City of Heaven can no longer be a "faith ladder," but an empirical one: a utopia has to specify *where* one wants to go, *how* to get there, the costs of the enterprise, and some realization of, and justification for the determination of *who* is to pay.

The end of ideology closes the book, intellectually speaking, on an era, the one of easy "left" formulae for social change. But to close the book is not to turn one's back upon it. This is all the more important now when a "new Left," with few memories of the past, is emerging. This "new Left" has passion and energy, but little definition of the future. Its outriders exult that it is "on the move." But where it is going, what it means by Socialism, how to guard against bureaucratization, what one means by democratic planning or workers' control – any of the questions that require hard thought, are only answered by bravura phrases.

It is in attitudes towards Cuba and the new States in Africa that the meaning of intellectual maturity, and of the end of ideology, will be tested. For among the "new Left," there is an alarming readiness to create a *tabula rasa*, to accept the word "Revolution" as an absolution for outrages, to justify the suppression of civil rights and opposition – in short, to erase the lessons of the last forty years with an emotional alacrity that is astounding. The fact that many of these emerging social movements are justified in their demands for freedom, for the right to control their own political and economic destinies, does not mean they have a right to a blank check for everything they choose to do in the name of their emancipation. Nor does the fact that such movements take power in the name of freedom guarantee that they will not turn out to be as imperialist, as grandeur-concerned (in the name of Pan-Africanism or some other ideology), as demanding their turn on the stage of History, as the States they have displaced.

If the end of ideology has any meaning, it is to ask for the end of rhetoric, and rhetoricians, of "revolution" of the day when the young French anarchist Vaillant tossed a bomb into the Chamber of Deputies, and the literary critic Laurent Tailhade declared in his defense: "What do a few human lives matter; it was a *beau geste.*" (*A beau geste* that ended, one might say, in a mirthless jest: two years later, Tailhade lost an eye when a bomb was thrown into a restaurant.) Today, in Cuba, as George Sherman, reporting for the London Observer summed it up: "The Revolution is law today although nobody has said clearly what that law is. You are expected to be simply for or against it and judge and be judged accordingly. Hatred and intolerance are wiping out whatever middle ground may have existed."

The problems which confront us at home and in the world are resistant to the old terms of ideological debate between "left" and "right," and if "ideology" by now, and with good reason, is an irretrievably fallen word, it is not necessary that "utopia" suffer the same fate. But it will if those who now call loudest for new utopias begin to justify degrading *means* in the name of some Utopian or revolutionary *end*, and forget the simple lessons that if the old debates are meaningless, some old verities are not – the verities of free speech, free press, the right of opposition and of free inquiry.

And if the intellectual history of the past hundred years has any meaning – and lesson – it is to reassert Jefferson's wisdom (aimed at removing the dead hand of the past, but which can serve as a warning against the heavy hand of the future as well), that "the present belongs to the living." This is the wisdom that revolutionists, old and new, who are sensitive to the fate of their fellow men, rediscover in every generation. "I will never believe," says a protagonist in a poignant dialogue written by the gallant Polish philosopher Leszek Kolakowski, "that the moral and intellectual life of mankind follows the law of economics, that is by saying today we can have more tomorrow; that we should use lives now so that truth will triumph or that we should profit by crime to pave the way for nobility."

And these words, written during the Polish "thaw," when the intellectuals had asserted, from their experience with the "future," the claims of humanism, echo the protest of the Russian writer Alexander Herzen, who, in a dialogue a hundred years ago, reproached an earlier revolutionist who would sacrifice the present mankind for a promised tomorrow: "Do you truly wish to condemn all human beings alive today to the sad role of caryatids . . . supporting a floor for others some day to dance on? . . . This alone should serve as a warning to people: an end that is infinitely remote is not an end, but, if you like, a trap; an end must be nearer — it ought to be, at the very least, the labourer's wage or pleasure in the work done. Each age, each generation, each life has its own fullness...."9

Notes

1. Karl Jaspers has assembled a fascinating collection of laments by philosophers of each age who see their own time as crisis and the past as a golden age. These — and the quotations from the Egyptian papyri as well as the remark of Talleyrand — can be found in his *Man in the Modern Age* (rev. ed., London, 1951), Chapter II. The quotation from Gilbert Murray is from *Five Stages of Greek Religion* (2d ed.; New York, 1930), Chapter IV.

2. The citation from Marx from the celebrated opening passages of *The Eighteenth Brumaire of Louis Napoleon* has a general discussion of alienation, but I have followed here with profit the discussion by Hans Sepia in his *Social Order and the Risks of War* (New York, 1952), Chapter XI.

3. Francis Bacon in the *Novum Organum* sought to release Reason from the "imperfections of the mind" by positing different kinds of distortion. These he called The *Idols of the Tribe; the Idols of the Cave* ("everyone ... has a cave or den of his own, which refracts and discolors the light of nature; owing ... to his education and conversation with others; or to the reading of books, and the authority of those he esteems and admires ..."); *The Idols of the Market-Place; and The Idols of the Theatre* ("because in my judgement all the received systems [of philosophy] are but so many stage-plays representing worlds of their own creation after an unreal and scenic fashion"). For a discussion of the history of the idea of bias in the social sciences in relation to ideology, see Reinhard Bendix's *Social Science and the Distrust of Reason* (University of California Press, 1951).

4. To this extent, the "unmasking of ideology" is somewhat akin to the theory of "rationalization" in the Freudian system. A rationalization hides an underlying motive. This does not mean it is necessarily false. In fact to function effectively, a rationalization has to have some "close fit" with reality. Yet an ulterior or underlying motive exists as well, and analysis seeks to point this out.

5. Rufus W. Mathewson, Jr., *The Positive Hero in Russian Literature* (New York, 1958), p. 6.

6. See Leo Strauss, *The Political Philosophy of Hobbes* (Chicago, 1952), pp. 14–29.

7. The Marquis de Sade, who, more than any man, explored the limits of self-assertion, once wrote: "'there is not a single man who doesn't want to be a despot when he is excited ... he would like to be alone in the world .. any sort of equality would destroy the despotism he enjoys then." de Sade proposed, therefore, to canalize these impulses into sexual activity by opening universal brothels which could serve to drain away these emotions. de Sade, it should be pointed out, was a bitter enemy of religion, but he understood well the latent function of religion in mobilizing emotions.

8. Raymond Aron, *The Opium of the Intellectuals* (New York, 1958); Edward Shils, "Ideology and Civility," *Sewanee Review*, Vol. LXVI, No. 3, Summer, 1958, and "The Intellectuals and the Powers," in *Comparative Studies in Society and History*, Vol. I, No. 1, October, 1958.

9. To see history as changes in sensibilities and style or, more, how different classes or people mobilized their emotional energies and adopted different moral postures is relatively novel; yet the history of moral temper is, I feel, one of the most important ways of understanding social change, and particularly the irrational forces at work in men. The great model for a cultural period is J. H. Huizinga's *The Waning of the Middle Ages*, with its discussion of changing attitudes toward death, cruelty, and love. Lucien Febvre, the great French historian, long ago urged the writing of history in terms of different sensibilities, and his study of Rabelais and the problem of covert belief (*Le problème de l'incroyance du XVIème siècle*) is one of the great landmarks of this approach. Most historians of social movements have been excessively "intellectualistic" in that the emphasis has been on doctrine or on organizational technique, and less on emotional styles. Nathan Leites' *A Study of Bolshevism* may be more important, ultimately, for its treatment of the changing moral temper of the Russian intelligentsia than for the formal study of Bolshevik behavior. Arthur Koestler's novels and autobiography are a brilliant mirror of the changes in belief of the European intellectual. Herbert Leuthy's study of the playwright Bert Brecht (*Encounter*, July, 1956) is a jewel in its subtle analysis of the changes in moral judgement created by the acceptance of the image of "the Bolshevik." The career of Georg Lukacs, the Hungarian Marxist, is instructive regarding an intellectual who has accepted the soldierly discipline of the Communist ethic; other than some penetrating but brief remarks by Franz Borkenau (see his *World Communism* [New York, 1939], pp. 172–75), and the articles by Morris Watnick (*Soviet Survey* [London, 1958], Nos. 23–25), very little has been written about this extraordinary man. Ignazio Silone's "The Choice of Comrades" (reprinted in *Voices of Dissent* [New York, 1959]) is a sensitive reflection of the positive experiences of radicalism. An interesting history of the millenarian and chiliastic movements is Norman Cohn's *The Pursuit of the Millennium*. From a Catholic viewpoint, Father Ronald Knox's study *Enthusiasm*, deals with the "ecstatic" movements in Christian history.

65

Two Views of Mass Society

William Kornhauser

The theory of mass society has two major intellectual sources, one in the nineteenth century reaction to the revolutionary changes in European (especially French) society, and the other in the twentieth century reaction to the rise of totalitarianism, especially in Russia and Germany. The first and major source may be termed the *aristocratic* criticism of mass society; the second, the *democratic* criticism of mass society. The first centers in the intellectual defense of elite values against the rise of mass participation. The second centers in the intellectual defense of democratic values against the rise of elites bent on total domination. The defensive posture of the aristocrats has been adopted by democrats who, having won the nineteenth century war of ideas and institutions with the former, now seek to preserve their values against the totalitarian challenge.

Not all intellectual rejections of revolutionary change have been based on the idea of mass society. Criticisms of nineteenth century trends that may properly be termed theories of mass society found the decisive social process to be *the loss of exclusiveness of elites and the rise of mass participation in cultural and political life.* Burckhardt (1955) and Gustave Le Bon (1947) were among the leading aristocratic critics of mass tendencies in the nineteenth century; Ortega y Gasset (1932), and Karl Mannheim (1940, pp. 79–96), in his discussions of elites, are twentieth century representatives of this approach.[1]

Similarly, not all democratic criticisms of totalitarianism are based on a theory of mass society. Those which may properly be termed theories of mass society find the decisive social process to be *the loss of insulation of non-elites and the rise of elites bent on total mobilization of a population.* Emil Lederer (1940) and Hannah Arendt (1951) are leading representatives of this conception of the nature of mass society.[2]

Paradoxical as it may appear to be, these democratic critics have come to rely heavily on the intellectual weapons employed by aristocratic thinkers against the rising flood of democratic ideologists during the nineteenth century. The central idea taken over by these democratic theorists from their

Source: William Kornhauser, *The Politics of Mass Society*, (London: Routledge & Kegan Paul, 1960).

aristocratic critics is that *the preservation of critical values (especially freedom) requires the social insulation of those segments of society that embody them.* Aristocratic and democratic critics of mass society agree on this, even as they disagree on the content of the values to be preserved – especially the nature of freedom – and, correspondingly, on the segments of society that embody them.

The aristocratic notion of freedom emphasizes the conditions that permit men to act as they *ought* to act, that is, in accordance with standards of right conduct. Mannheim has noted that this idea of freedom is counterposed to an egalitarian conception: "Men, . . . [the aristocratic theorists] claimed are essentially *unequal,* unequal in their gifts and abilities, and unequal to the very core of their beings" (1953, p. 106). Standards of right conduct are most highly developed in the upper reaches of society, and therefore the "true bearers," the "true subjects" of liberty are the "organic communities" of aristocratic elites. "The 'liberty' of the different estates under feudalism which meant their 'privileges,' and the distinctly qualitative and non-egalitarian flavour which was contained in the medieval concept, is here revived once more" (Mannheim, 1953, p. 107). The traditional order based on moral law insulates aristocratic elites and thereby preserves liberty.

The democratic notion of freedom, on the other hand, implies the minimizing of social control (including that of the traditional order), that is, the removal of as many external constraints on the individual as is consistent with the freedom of his fellows. Freedom so conceived is dependent on *equality of rights.* This value is embodied in the whole community. Therefore, it is the independent group life of the non-elite which functions to preserve liberty, as independent groups insulate people from domination by elites.

In sum, these two versions of the mass society differ in their conception of freedom and the social foundations of freedom. One sees mass society as a set of conditions under which elites are exposed to mass pressures. The other conceives of mass society as a set of conditions under which non-elites are exposed to elite pressures. Nevertheless, they share a common image of mass society as the *naked society,* where the direct exposure of social units to outside forces makes freedom precarious. We shall attempt to formulate a general theory of mass society that incorporates elements from both the aristocratic and democratic criticism. This is our objective in Part I of the present study.

But to reach this goal, it is necessary to explicate partial and polemical versions of the theory. Therefore, we consider first the major argument of the aristocratic criticism of mass society, and then we analyze the democratic criticism of mass society. First a word about the bases for distinguishing these two views.

Our interest is in analyzing the theoretical basis of each approach, rather than in examining the value orientation typically associated with each of them. The two approaches have been distinguished according to whether the condition of elites or the condition of non-elites is identified as the basic criterion of "mass society." This means that any theory that locates the decisive feature of mass society in the exposure of accessible elites to mass intervention is classified as "aristocratic," while any theory that locates the essential feature of mass society in the exposure of atomized non-elites to elite domination is classified as "democratic." The choice of the terms "aristocratic" and "democratic" to describe these two theories should not obscure the fact that the classification is based on an *analytical* rather than a value distinction. However, there is an affinity between each of these theoretical positions and each value orientation. Most writers on mass society whose *theories* have focused on the loss of insulation of elites have also advocated aristocratic *values*, while most of those whose theories have focused on the loss of insulation of non-elites have also advocated democratic values. Nevertheless, there are some exceptions, for some writers hold values of the one type and expound theories of the other. When this occurs, the contributions are classified according to the theoretical, not the value, position of the writer. This explains why Mannheim, for example, is cited as a representative of the "aristocratic" approach; though committed to the preservation of democratic *values*, his *theory* of mass society tends to stress the way in which mass participation undermines elite functions.[3]

There is a second point, relating to the theoretical nature of the classification (rather than its value relevance), that should be borne in mind. Our interest is in the logic of each argument, rather than in the work of particular theorists. A separate series of logically connected propositions about the nature of mass society is related to the major premise of each approach. A particular theorist may well incorporate aspects of both arguments in his writings, without thereby providing a clear outline of either argument or a general and systematic statement of the theory of mass society. It may sometimes happen, therefore, that the same writer is at one time cited in support of a proposition embodied in the aristocratic approach, and at another time cited in support of a proposition embodied in the democratic approach. This will occasion no confusion if it is recalled that *ideas, not men, are the objects of classification.* On the whole, it is true that those who adopt the major premise of one school tend to ignore the social processes central to the major premise of the other school. Yet there are some exceptions, particularly De Tocqueville, who analyzed not only the need for insulation of elites, but also the role played by multiple autonomous groups in the insulation of non-elites.

What follows is not an historical reconstruction of ideas on mass society, but a logical reconstruction of two major intellectual traditions that are intermingled in the literature on mass society. *Our integrated statement of mass-society theory is based on elements drawn from both traditions. At the same time, it accepts the democratic concern with the identification of conditions favorable to the preservation of democratic values.*

The Loss of Authority in Mass Society

During the nineteenth century, aristocratic critics of bourgeois society spun a rhetoric of pessimism concerning the value-standards men live by in an age of increasing materialism and equalitarianism. Le Bon crystallized this theme in sociological terms when he depicted the times as an "era of crowds," and spoke bitingly of crowds as vehicles in the downfall of civilization: "the populace is sovereign, and the tide of barbarism mounts" (1947, pp. 14, 207). Ortega popularized this thesis as the "revolt of the masses," a situation which leads to the "sovereignty of the unqualified" (1932, p. 25). Such present-day critics as T. S. Eliot (1948) use the term "mass society" in this pejorative sense to designate the alleged destructiveness of popular pressures on traditional values and elites.

Aristocratic theorists believe that liberty and equality are incompatible: "The spread of democratic equal rights facilitates, as Nietzsche prophesied, the equal violation of rights" (Viereck, 1955, p. 96). The paradigmatic experiences underlying this imagery were the French Revolution and the 1848 revolutions against the ancient regimes. The heart of the imagery itself is the *equalitarian society*, without excellence, distinction, style, meaning. Such a (mass) society is viewed as lacking the moral basis for resisting Caesarism, for preventing political tyranny as well as cultural decay.

Thus De Tocqueville has written:

I believe that it is easier to establish an absolute and despotic government among a people in which the conditions of society are equal than among any other; and I think that if such a government were once established among such a people, it not only would oppress men, but would eventually strip each of them of several of the highest qualities of humanity. (1945, v. II, p. 322)

Thus Burckhardt has written:

So long as the masses can bring pressure on their leaders, one value after another must be sacrificed: position, property, religion, distinguished tradition, higher learning. (Quoted by Viereck, 1956, p. 159)

Thus Mannheim has written:

The open character of democratic mass society, together with its growth in size and the tendency towards general public participation, not only produces far too many elites but also deprives these elites of the exclusiveness which they need [to perform their functions]. . . . The lack of leadership in late liberal mass society can . . . be . . . diagnosed as the result of the change for the worse in selecting the elite. We must recognize further that it is this general lack of direction in modern mass society that gives the opportunity to groups with dictatorial ambitions. (1940, pp. 86–7)

Thus Lippmann has written:

> Where mass opinion dominates the government, there is a morbid derangement of the true functions of power. The derangement brings about the enfeeblement, verging on paralysis, of the capacity to govern. (1956, p. 19)

The conception of mass society contained in such writings as these includes three major terms: (a) growing equalitarianism (loss of traditional authority); (b) widespread readiness to support anti-aristocratic forms of rule (quest for popular authority); (c) rule by the masses (domination by pseudo-authority). In this universe of discourse, "mass society" is the opposite of aristocratic order. Mass society is the condition under which rule by the masses – either directly or through the popularly supported demagogue – displaces aristocratic rule. This condition is equality of voice in the determination of social policy. Therefore, mass society is the equalitarian society, in which the masses seek to raise up leaders in their own image. As a result, it produces rule by the incompetent.

However, the incompetence of the many is not what distinguishes mass society, according to the aristocratic criticism. Mass society is new, whereas there always has been widespread ignorance in society.[4] Mannheim observes in this connection that the student of such changes as the loss of distinctive art styles, the increasing intellectual indecisiveness, or the decline of leadership, "if he is not used to noticing the social mechanisms at work behind the immediate concrete events is inclined to believe ... that human beings are today less talented and less creative and have less initiative than in earlier periods" (1940, p. 87). What has changed is the structural relationship between the many and the few. In the mass society, there is a marked increase in opportunities for the many to intervene in areas previously reserved to the few. These opportunities invite the determination of social policies and cultural standards by large numbers who are not competent to make such decisions.

Mass society from this standpoint is the society in which there is a *loss of exclusiveness of elites*:[5] it is a social structure possessing high access to governing groups. High access to elites results from such procedures as direct popular elections and the shared expectation that public opinion is sovereign. When elites are easily accessible, the masses pressure them to conform to the transitory general will: "the voice of the masses [is] preponderant" (Le Bon, 1947, p. 15).[6] Therefore, loss of authority on the part of institutional elites results from widespread opportunities to participate in the formation of major social policies.

A system in which there is high access to elites generates popular pressures on the elites that prevent them from performing their creative and value-sustaining functions. People are not expected to have particular qualifications to make different kinds of decisions. Public opinion, viewed as the transitory general will, is regarded as the *immediate* as well as ultimate arbiter of all matters of policy and taste. Therefore, *anyone* is qualified; anyone may feel justified in judging or trying to influence any decision. As a result, the aristocratic critics claim, it is not simply that a large number of individuals is unqualified, but rather, it is the very *system* that is unqualified. For the system makes no provision for separating the qualified from the unqualified; and therefore excellence (whether in governing, in art, or in any other sphere) can neither be discovered, developed, nor protected.[7] It is a situation in which elites cannot be creative nor can they deeply influence society. But only elites can perform these functions: "Civilizations as yet have only been created and directed by a small intellectual aristocracy, never by crowds. Crowds are only powerful for destruction" (Le Bon, 1947, p. 18).

Insofar as popular participation cannot be controlled, it destroys liberty as well as authority. Equalitarianism is judged to be incompatible with individual liberty, for "liberty is preserved not by mass-will nor by counting noses but by tiny, heroic natural-aristocracies and by the majesty – beyond mob majorities – of moral law" (Viereck, 1955, p. 104).

But is it the mere quantitative fact of widespread participation in the setting of social policy which destroys elite functions and thereby liberty? Aristocratic critics would not deny that if people intervened only at certain points in the decision-making process, and in a manner regulated and controlled according to set rules, then elites would be protected from undue interference and could fulfill their critical functions. They assume, however, that popular participation will not be of this kind. Thus Le Bon (1947) uses such terms as suggestible, unconscious, impulsive, capricious, and the like, to characterize popular participation where elites are accessible. And Ortega (1932) speaks of the indocility of the masses in a similar vein. These aristocratic critics are arguing that when people intervene in decision-making processes in an excitable and intractable manner, liberty is threatened.

We must ask the aristocratic critics how *equality* of opportunity to participate leads to *unrestrained* intervention, as in political strikes. We may agree that high access to elites is a permissive condition for recurrent mass behavior of this sort. But it is not a sufficient condition, since *non-elites may be restrained on their side, by means of their own groups and values.* That is, those members of society who identify themselves with the central values of a constitutional order are not likely to exploit opportunities to subvert elites. On the other hand, people who are *alienated* from society may express their resentment by using the most accessible instruments of action to impose their will. In short, the source of mass behavior cannot be located *only* in the structure of elites. It also must be found in the structure of non-elites, in a set of conditions close to the personal environment of the people who engage in mass behavior. Open elites can provide the "pull" for unrestrained participation in the vital centers of society, but not the "push." Since the democratic criticism specifies a set of conditions under which people will be propelled into mass actions, the aristocratic view of mass society may be strengthened by taking these additional conditions into account.[8]

The Loss of Community in Mass Society

From the democratic viewpoint, the threat posed by mass society is less how elites may be protected from the masses and more how non-elites may be shielded from domination by elites. This difference is part of the larger difference dividing the two approaches: concern with opportunities for and functions of the few, on the one hand, versus concern with widespread opportunities for large numbers of people to participate in the collective life, on the other hand. The aristocratic position judges the formulation of broad social policy to be the responsibility and capability of the few, whereas the democratic position implies that potentially all members of society share in this responsibility.

Aristocratic critics attribute loss of liberty to the rise of popular participation in areas previously limited to the specially qualified: mass society is a condition under which there is too much control by the many over the few. Democratic critics, in their turn, attribute loss of liberty to the rise of mass manipulation and mobilization in areas previously left to the privacy of the individual and the group: mass society is a condition under which there is too much control by the few over the many. In short, one conception views mass society as unlimited democracy ("hyperdemocracy" in Ortega's terms), the other as unlimited tyranny.

Now, of course, these two states could be intimately related. In fact, one student of the problem has stated the belief that "a whole literature on mass behavior and mass psychology [has] demonstrated and popularized the wisdom, so familiar to the ancients, of the affinity between democracy and dictatorship, between mob rule and tyranny" (Arendt, 1951, pp. 309–10). It is the thesis of this study that such an affinity is caught by the concept of mass society; but the fact remains that unlimited democracy is not unlimited tyranny, even though it may become so. Therefore, it remains to be clarified how a theory of mass society may specify this relationship.

Another difference between the two approaches to mass society concerns the consequences of equalitarianism. The democratic criticism does not find equality of condition inherently inimical to liberty, nor does it look only to elites for the defense of liberty. From this point of view, the chief characteristic of the mass is not brutality and backwardness, as the aristocratic criticism implies, but isolation and amorphous social relations. Furthermore, *mass behavior may characterize people in high status positions as well as those from lower classes*; "highly cultured people were particularly attracted to mass movements [in post-war Europe]" (Arendt, 1951, p. 310).

What concerns the democratic critics is the possible emergence of another elite modeled after those thrown up by the Nazi and Bolshevik revolutions, with the consequent destruction of political democracy. The core of this imagery is the *atomized society*. Mass society is a situation in which an aggregate of individuals are related to one another only by way of their relation to a common authority, especially the state. That is, individuals are not directly related to one another in a variety of independent groups. A population in this condition is not insulated in any way from the ruling group, nor yet from elements within itself. For insulation requires a multiplicity of independent and often conflicting forms of association, each of which is strong enough to ward off threats to the autonomy of the individual. But it is precisely the weakness or absence of such social groups, *rather than their equality*, which distinguishes the mass society, according to these theorists. In their absence, people lack the resources to restrain their own behavior as well as that of others. Social atomization engenders strong feelings of alienation and anxiety, and therefore the disposition to engage in extreme behavior to escape from these tensions. In a mass society there is a heightened readiness to form hyper-attachments to symbols and leaders. "Such loyalty can be expected only from the completely isolated human being who, without any other social ties . . . derives his sense of having a place in the world only from his belonging to a movement" (Arendt, 1951, pp. 316–17). Total loyalty, in turn, is the psychological basis for total domination, i.e., totalitarianism.

There are three major terms implied in the democratic criticism of mass society: (a) growing atomization (loss of community); (b) widespread readiness to embrace new ideologies (quest for community); (c) totalitarianism (total domination by pseudo-community). In this universe of discourse, mass society is a condition in which elite domination replaces democratic rule. Mass society is objectively the *atomized* society, and subjectively the *alienated* population. Therefore, mass society is a system in which there is *high availability of a population for mobilization by elites.*

People become available for mobilization by elites when they lack or lose an independent group life. The term *masses* applies "only where we deal with people who . . . cannot be integrated into any organization based on common interest, into political parties or municipal governments or professional organizations or trade unions" (Arendt, 1951, p. 305). The lack of autonomous relations generates widespread social alienation. Alienation heightens responsiveness to the appeal of mass movements because they provide occasions for expressing resentment against what is, as well as promises of a totally different world. In short, *people who are atomized readily become mobilized.* Since totalitarianism is a state of total mobilization, mass society is highly vulnerable to totalitarian movements and regimes.

We must ask the democratic critics at this point whether mass society is totalitarian, or only may become so. Democratic critics tend to construe totalitarianism as mass society, because elite domination based on a mobilized population is the central meaning of their conception of totalitarianism. However, they also tend to designate societies that are vulnerable to totalitarianism as mass society. For example, both Weimar Germany and Nazi Germany have been called mass societies. This obscures the problem of developmental patterns, since factors which encourage totalitarian movements in political democracies are not necessarily the same as those which *sustain* totalitarian regimes once they are in power. It is necessary, therefore, to distinguish between a mass society and a totalitarian society.

We must next inquire whether an available population constitutes by itself a condition sufficient to result in numerous mass movements, as the democratic theorists imply. There are at least three reasons why high access to elites must also be present. In the first place, it is apparent that in order for available masses to become mobilized at all, agents of mobilization – for example, Communist spokesmen and organizations – must have opportunities to contact and appeal to large numbers of people. This requires readily accessible channels of communication. Moreover, if the paths to power were not open, there would be little incentive to mobilize and incite masses. In this sense, an accessible elite can serve as a magnet, both to would-be totalitarian leaders and to discontented masses. People in the mass (i.e., an undifferentiated and amorphous collectivity) are highly susceptible to total mobilization; but unless there is access to the means of communication and power, counter-elites (such as Communist leaders) will not be able to seize the opportunity provided by the mass for the conquest of total power.

Secondly, the success of totalitarian movements is contingent upon the vulnerability of existing elites. An accessible elite should not be equated with a vulnerable elite for the strength or weakness of elites depends upon a host of factors other than their degree of accessibility. Nevertheless, an accessible elite is more vulnerable than one which is not accessible, other things being equal. When access is low, elites are relatively immune to popular pressures, so that mass movements peter out without overturning elites or infiltrating elite positions. Accessible elites more easily succumb to the attacks of totalitarian movements.

There is yet a third reason for suggesting that an available population does not automatically call forth elite domination. Totalitarian regimes are installed by new elites who have successfully mobilized an available population. But if this were in fact the sole condition required for the seizure of total power by new elites, how is it that the old elites, favored by this very same condition (i.e., an atomized population available for mobilization), have not themselves absorbed total power? Evidently *elites may be restrained on their side by means of their own relations and values.* Old elites generally lack the will and capacity to mobilize a large population. The one major exception is when the very existence of the social order is believed to be threatened, as in war or revolution. That is, mobilized movements led by representatives of existing institutions tend to be military ventures against external or internal enemies. Such mass movements may be developed in response to the mobilization of forces by another nation or by a revolutionary group, or in response to the expectation of such an enemy mobilization. It is under these conditions that a mass society may move toward totalitarianism under the direction of institutional rather than anti-institutional leadership. The model of the "garrison state" (Lasswell, 1941) is precisely such a state of mobilization by established elites in the name of national security.

The "garrison state" undoubtedly is a possible course along which mass society can move. But there are a number of factors which militate against mobilization of large numbers by existing elites (except under conditions of total war). In the first place, these elites are part of a going concern, and this alone makes for an essentially mundane orientation. Activism entails a readiness to reject routine modes of activity, and therefore tends to be eschewed by groups whose very power is bound to established routines. It usually requires a new elite devoid of the restraints incident upon institutional participation to mobilize widespread activism As a form of charismatic leadership, the totalitarian elite is "outside the realm of everyday routine" and is "foreign to all rules" (Weber, 1947, p. 361).

Another reason why existing elites infrequently set in motion a large population is the presence of leadership rivalries. These conflicts between leaders operate as checks on the power of each, including any attempts to expand power by mobilizing masses.

In addition, existing elites may be restrained by their value commitments. They ordinarily have a strong stake in preserving the social order, for their own positions are legitimated by established values. Those who are successful are often more amenable to abiding by the rules of the game. Further, the achievement of high position may reflect or induce a heightened sense of responsibility for and awareness of institutional values.

Thus it is that popular mobilization generally is the work of counter-elites, since they are not inhibited by commitments to the social order, nor by constraints resulting from participation in a balance of power.[9] These counter-elites are pushed towards making allies among the masses, since this is the only way to gain total power in mass society. Finally, established elites in a mass society not only lack the capacity to mobilize a large population; they also are ill-equipped to protect their organizations from penetration by counter-elites bent on destroying an existing order. This point will be developed in detail when we analyze the origins of mass movements in Part II.

We may therefore conclude that high vulnerability to the *development* of totalitarianism presupposes accessible elites as well as available non-elites. A rising totalitarian movement finds its prey not only in an exposed mass but also in an exposed elite. The penetration of an existing elite by a successful totalitarian movement (as the Nazis penetrated the Weimar government) is *prima facie* evidence of its accessibility. On the other hand, the maintenance of a population in a state of mobilization by a given (totalitarian) elite requires low access to elites; otherwise the ruling group would not be able to maintain its power.

Thus, the concept of mass society, in order to be useful for a theory of the transformation of democratic into totalitarian society, *necessarily* presupposes accessible elites. *The democratic criticism of mass society requires for its completion the notion of accessible elites provided by aristocratic critics.* It now may be shown that the negative consequences of accessible elites envisioned by aristocratic critics are greatly increased when non-elites are available by virtue of the loss of community.

Aristocratic theorists assume that whenever people are given the opportunity to participate in the shaping of social policies, they will do so in a destructive manner. But the opportunity for widespread participation in society does not automatically call forth mass action unrestrained by social relations and cultural norms. Not all members of a society, but only *people in the mass* are disposed to seize the opportunity provided by accessible elites to impress mass standards on all spheres of society, and to do so in an unrestrained manner. This is true for two reasons. First, when large numbers of people are interrelated only as members of a mass, they are more likely to pressure elites to provide satisfactions previously supplied by a plurality of more proximate groups. Second, they are likely to do so in a direct and unmediated way, because there is a paucity of intervening groups to channelize and filter popular participation in the larger society. As a result, mass participation tends to be irrational and unrestrained, since there are few points at which it may be checked by personal experience and the experience of others. Where people are not securely related to a plurality of independent groups, they are available for all kinds of adventures and "activist modes of intervention" in the larger society. It is one thing for a population to participate at specified times and in institutional ways for defined interests – for example, through trade associations and trade unions, or in elections. It is quite another to create *ad hoc* methods of direct pressure on critical centers of society, such as the "invasion" of a state legislature, street political gangs, etc. (Selznick, 1952, p. 294). It is the latter form of collective activity that the aristocratic theorists fear, but they err in assuming that equal access to elites is sufficient to produce it: widespread availability attendant upon social atomization also must exist.

Thus, each conception of mass society requires the other for its completion. Together they provide the basis for a general theory of mass society.

Notes

1. Catholic critics of nineteenth century society, like Bonald and De Maistre share certain views with aristocratic critics. So do such aesthetic critics as Arnold. In the most general sense, all anti-bourgeois intellectuals of the nineteenth century shared certain ideas which were congenial to a theory of mass society. For a brief review of conservative ideas since the French Revolution, see Viereck (1956).

2. Arendt's recent discussion (1956) of authority closely follows the aristocratic criticism of mass society.

3. Critics of the theory of mass society generally fail to differentiate between the aristocratic and democratic versions of that theory. A recent example is Daniel Bell's critique (1956).

4. Thus Ortega remarks that mass society is "entirely new in the history of our modern civilization" (1932, p. 21).

5. The term "elite" as used in this study refers to a relatively small circle of people who claim and are charged with the responsibility for framing and sustaining fundamental values and policies in their area of competence.

6. Ortega also speaks of "the predominance ... of the mass" (1932, p. 16).

7. Cf. Selznick (1952, p. 278) and Mannheim (1940, pp. 82 ff.).

8. Several aristocratic thinkers also have been concerned with this problem, and have influenced the formulations of later democratic theorists. But it has remained for the latter to provide a basic understanding of sources of mass behavior in the transformation of community. Thus, a present-day conservative thinker has written: "I think that one of the principal errors of conservatively-inclined men has been their neglect of the need for true community" (Kirk, 1956, p. 129).

9. A recent review of the literature on community conflict in the United States (Coleman, 1957, p. 13) notes that "both community organizations and community leaders are faced with constraints when a dispute arises; the formation of a combat group to carry on the controversy and the emergence of a previous unknown as the combat leader are in part results of the *immobility of responsible organizations and leaders*. Both the new leader and the new organization are freed from some of the usual shackles of community norms and internal cross-pressures which make pre-existing organizations and leaders tend to soften the dispute."

References

Arendt, Hannah. *The Origins of Totalitarianism.* New York: Harcourt, Brace, 1951.,
Burckhardt, Jacob. *Force and Freedom.* New York: Meridian Books 1955.
Eliot, T. S. *Notes Towards the Definition of Culture.* London: Faber and Faber, 1948.
Lasswell, Harold D. "The Garrison State," *The American Journal of Sociology*, XLVI (1941), 455–68.
Le Bon, Gustave. *The Crowd.* London: Ernest Bonn Ltd., 1947.
Lederer, Emil. *State of the Masses.* New York: W. W. Norton, 1940.
Lippmann, Walter. *The Public Philosophy.* New York: Mentor Books, 1956.
Mannheim, Karl. *Man and Society in an Age of Reconstruction.* London: Kegan Paul, 1940.
Mannheim, Karl. *Essays on Sociology and Social Psychology.* New York: Oxford University Press, 1953.
Ortega y Gasset, José. *The Revolt of the Masses.* New York: W. W. Norton, 1932.
Selznick, Philip. *The Organizational Weapon.* New York: McGrawHill, 1952.
De Tocqueville, Alexis. *Democracy in America.* 2 vols. New York: Knopf, 1945.
Viereck, Peter. "The Revolt Against the Elite," in *The New American Right*, ed. Daniel Bell. New York: Criterion Books, 1955.
Viereck, Peter. *Conservatism from John Adams to Churchill.* New York: D. Van Nostrand, 1956.
Weber, Max. *The Theory of Social and Economic Organization.* New York: Oxford University Press, 1947.

AMERICAN SOCIOLOGY IN THE TWENTIETH CENTURY

RECENT TRENDS IN SOCIOLOGICAL THEORY

66

Social Differentiation and Organic Solidarity: The *Division of Labor* Revisited

Hans-Peter Müller[1]

Introduction

It might seem strange to open the celebration of the centennial anniversary of Emile Durkheim's *De la division du travail social* (1893) with an odd question: Is Durkheim's work a sociological classic? If so what is it that allows his work to live up to seminal, even sacred books like Marx's *Capital*, Weber's *Protestant Ethic*, or Simmel's *Philosophy of Money*? Or is *Division of Labor* just the promising doctoral dissertation of a talented young professor who later happened to become the father of institutionalized French sociology? Is it a dissertation that is well done but incomplete, full of logical as well empirical inconsistencies, which reads in large parts like a reprise of Spencer's arguments on this topic with modifications as to the frame of reference, that is to say from individualistic utilitarianism to collectivistic moralism?

That we convene for celebration makes the "classicity" of the *Division of Labor* self-evident. Yet it is not without irony that some luminaries in the discipline met Durkheim's first book with reservation. Without going into the details of the history of reception (cf. Müller and Schmid, 1988), a brief illustration: For his French contemporaries the dissertation expressed the new spirit of positivism and the unfortunate promise of secular, i.e., laicistic religion, which could haunt and divide the Third Republic in the years to come. His German contemporaries were more sympathetic but not without serious objections: Gustav Schmoller (1894), though greeting the elective affinity of thinking, criticized the speculative character of his arguments, which are high above the facts of empirical reality. Ferdinand Tönnies (1929) detected the parallels of mechanical and organic solidarity with "Gemeinschaft" and "Gesellschaft" but regarded organic solidarity as a concept that is ill-conceived. Later on, Talcott Parsons, in his *Structure of Social Action* (1937/1968), referred to Durkheim in a double sense: he saw him on the verge of a voluntaristic theory of action and he welcomed his idea of the "non-contractual elements of contract" as a path-breaking critique of utilitarianism. Yet he paid not much attention to *Division of Labor* because of its unstable positivistic position and its many inherent flaws. And to close this brief list of reviews, Peter A. Corning (1982) recently demonstrated convincingly the Spencerian nature of Durkheim's line of reasoning. Contrary to the highly critical attitude toward Spencer, Corning argues, Durkheim drew heavily upon his work – so much so that the *Division of Labor* appears as a copy of Spencer's theory of differentiation and evolution.

Perhaps we should wait another two years to celebrate the positivistic (or better: rationalistic) manifesto of the Durkheim school – *Les règles de la méthode sociologique* (*The Rules of Sociological Method*; 1895); or to make doubly sure, we should meet in four years to think of a sociological classic beyond doubt – *Le Suicide* (*Suicide*; 1897)?

Despite the multifolded criticisms of Durkheim's first book, I would like to argue for the classical character of the *Division of Labor* (cf. Bellah, 1973). In my view, there are at least four lines of reasoning or dimensions that lend Durkheim's first work classical status. These dimensions are

1. the problem dimension,
2. the diagnostical dimension,
3. the methodical dimension, and
4. the substantial dimension.

First, a brief comment upon the first three.

The Problem Dimension

Emile Durkheim addresses the age-old problem of social order but he does so in a truly sociological vein. He transforms the problem into a question: How is a social order possible that allows for individual autonomy? Or, in his own words (closely resembling Simmel's problem): "How does it come about that the individual, whilst becoming more autonomous, depends ever more closely upon society? How can he become at the same time more of an individual and yet more linked to society? For it is indisputable that these two movements, however contradictory they appear to be, are carried out in tandem" (Durkheim, 1978: XLIII; tr. 1984: XXX).

The Diagnostical Dimension

Durkheim gives a sociological diagnosis of the time. Starting from the uneasiness in contemporary European society and culture, he denotes a crisis of anomie, much like Sigmund Freud. Where does the anomie come from? Anticipating Ogburn's cultural-lag thesis, he discovers the unequal rhythm of structural and cultural domain. Social differentiation and social change develop so fast that new social and moral rules do not have the time to emerge and regulate the newly constituted social structure. The result is crisis.

The Methodical Dimension

Division of Labor is the prototype of a sociological explanation. According to Durkheim's (1895) *Rules*, to understand a sociological phenomenon like the division of labor, three kinds of propositions are necessary: first, its functional relationship; second, its causal emergence; and third, its normal or pathological consequences. These are the three parts of a complete sociological explanation. The three books the *Division of Labor* are divided to reflect this pattern: Book I treats the functioning, Book II the causes and conditions, and Book III the abnormal forms of the division of labor.

The Substantial Dimension

Durkheim addresses the problem of order by looking at the relationships of differentiation and integration. How – under what circumstances and with which effects – does the division of labor lead to organic solidarity? This is the major problem he sets out to tackle in the *Division of Labor*, and this is what formed his lifelong central preoccupation (cf. Müller, 1983).

The *Division of Labor*, then, is a classic; consider the innovative way of viewing the compatibility of social order and individual autonomy; his sensitive perception of uneasiness with regards to the crisis of anomie; the lucid sociological account, especially the tripartite explanation of the division of labor in terms of its functioning, emergence, and consequences; and the conceptualization of the problem of order, i.e., the relationship of differentiation and integration – that is, of the division of labor and organic solidarity. It is my general thesis that these four dimensions express the classicity of Durkheim's first book. To be sure, "classical" does not mean original nor without flaws. Rather, it denotes a configuration in which a problem or a set of problems is given such a paradigmatic form that the scientific community of a discipline in their ongoing research cannot ignore.

Here we will examine the fourth dimension – the relationship of differentiation and integration. How does Durkheim conceptualize the division of labor and organic solidarity? First, we will locate the debate on the division of labor in the history of social thought; second, we examine mechanical and organic solidarity; and third, we discuss the problems "inside organic solidarity" (Pope and Johnson, 1983).

The Division of Labor in the History of 18th- and 19th-Century Thought

With his first study Durkeim does not take up an entirely new topic but enters a well-established field of investigation. In the social theory of the 18th and 19th century the division of labor is regarded as the crucial structural principle that helps explain the transition from traditional agrarian society to modern industrial society. In elucidating "the great transformation" (Polanyi, 1978) three distinct traditions of thought emerge that highlight different aspects of the division of labor. These are the British tradition of utilitarian individualism, the German tradition of Marxian collectivism, and the French tradition of communal associationalism.

The *utilitarian-individualistic* tradition of classical political economy draws the picture of a peaceful market society. Adam Smith (1723–1790), who codifies the discourse on the division of labor in the *Wealth of Nations* (1776/1937), starts from the natural "propensity to trade, barter and change" (13) and distinguishes between three forms of the division of labor. Each of them increases the productivity and therefore the "wealth of nations" as well as the individual welfare. Adopting the utilitarian frame of reference, Herbert Spencer (1820–1903) enriches the economic explanation by additional structural prerequisites of the division of labor and claims the transition from bellicose military society to peaceable industrial society. Industrious activities upon the organizational basis of voluntary associations trigger the economic growth and the progress of these societies.

The *collecivistic-socialistic* tradition deeply criticizes this optimistic view. Marx concedes the revolutionary character of capitalist technology and the progress of economic wealth but this progress implies unevenly distributed costs: the expropriation of workers from their means of production, the emergence of antagonistic class relationship, and the exploitation, alienation, and pauperization of the working class. Capitalist society, in short, exhibits an ambivalent pattern of development: an increase of wealth on the one hand, a pauperization of the populace on the other hand. The revolutionary transformation of capitalist into socialist society according to Marx is the only viable way of overcoming this ambivalence. It is interesting to note that this pessimistic view on the division of labor – the dilemma of increased productivity and enhanced exploitation – dominates the German discussion under the label of the "social question." Gustav Schmoller, a "socialist of the chair" in the "Verein für Sozialpolitik," for instance, welcomes the division of labor as the decisive achievement of modern civilization but underlines the dark side of this process as well. And Ferdinand Tönnies, whose *Gemeinschaft und Gesellschaft* (1887) perceptively conceptualizes the transition from tradition to modernity, associates society with excessive division of labor, warlike competition, the atomization of the individual, and the breakdown of solidarity and cohesion. In this sense, he resembles Marx so much so that Durkheim – in his review of *Gemeinschaft und Gesellschaft* (1889) – has the impression that Tönnies paints society in the somber colors of Marx and Lassalle.

The French socialistic tradition that I called "communal associationalism" argues differently and is internally divided. Saint-Simon (1760–1825) welcomes emphatically the new industry: in fact, he coins the term "industrial society" to denote a new type of society. And it is the innovative spirit of engineers and technicians that drives the static aristocratic society into a dynamic industrialism with technological progress, division of labor, and productivity. His disciple Auguste Comte (1799–1857) is more ambivalent. He argues that the division of labor entails fragmentation, and as a consequence, imperils the cohesion of society. Since the economy alone is unable to generate consensus – as Comte coins the social bond – it is the duty of a strong state to produce cohesion by the help of a new common religion.

This is the spectrum of positions that exists when Durkheim enters the field. In trying to develop a genuine *sociological* account on the division of labor – its problems and prospects – he takes two central decisions: (1) He follows the French tradition and tries to theorize the social bond. This implies the question: Is the division of labor the new social bond? Once this question is posed it becomes clear why the relationship between division of labor and organic solidarity forms the theoretical core of his book and why Durkheim's interest is exclusively on the moral value of the division of labor. (2) Given this affiliation toward the French tradition Durkheim has to refute the British and the German tradition – utilitarian individualism and Marxian socialism. This is why Marcel Mauss (1958) tells us that Durkheim's original problem of his dissertation was the relationship between individualism and socialism. Division of labor does not entail a peaceful market society implying wealth of nations and individual welfare. Quite to the contrary, there is much strife, struggle for existence, and *anomie*. Nor does capitalistic division of labor automatically lead to exploitation, alienation, and pauperization. Quite to the contrary, it entails differentiation, specialization, and economic productivity under certain circumstances.

These two decisions, in fact, are switchmen for the entire makeup of Durkheim's argumentation. Why? Since Durkheim is a "à la recherche d'une solution sociologique de la division du travail social" to clothe it in Proustean language, he tries to win a "middle way" between individualism and socialism. This is why many parts of the book read like an ongoing conversation and confrontation with Spencer – as well as with Comte – and pace Tönnies with Marx. And this middle way prescribes what he can argue and what not. Furthermore, he is willing to defend the division of labor as a benevolent structural principle of modern society. It is this self-imposed constraint toward sociological originality and his apologetic attitude (cf. Bouglé, 1903: 142) that counts for many of the inconsistencies and contradictions that run through the overall argument on division of labor and organic solidarity. How does Durkheim conceptualize this relationship?

Mechanical and Organic Solidarity

Since we are all familiar with this sociological classic by now I will deliver the basic line of argument in broad strokes. In order to construct his thesis concerning the division of labor and solidarity, Durkheim lays three foundations: conceptually, a definition of solidarity; methodically, a comparative argument; and substantially, a supposed relationship between solidarity, law, and integration.

Contrary to the commonsense understanding of solidarity (cf. Bourgois, 1897: Hayward, 1959), Durkheim uses this term in a specific sense. In the opening lecture of his course in sociology (1888/1970: 257), he says that the initial problems of sociology are the social bonds. Solidarity, therefore, aims at "the general forms of sociability and their laws." In his view social bonds, or relationships, vary according to the type of society and to the modes of solidarity, respectively. Durkheim conceives of solidarity in a relational mode. For him, solidarity is a form of sociability that designates the relationship of the structure and functioning of society: its social organization on the one hand and its system of values – its morality – on the other. A high degree of adaptive cohesion or solidarity will be produced if social organization and morality smoothly correspond; where this coordination is absent there are no social bonds, and hence, society plunges into *anomie*. The first to have elucidated this relational usage of solidarity that is the relationship of organization and morality or social structure and cultural rules was Harry Alpert (1941, 1961).

The relational character of the concept of solidarity becomes immediately clear if we look at his comparative argument. Durkheim distinguishes between two types of solidarity that prevail in different kinds of society. Since operationalization of solidarity is by law, he ends up with two types of law. And regarding integration, he is driven to suggest two forms of integration. Given this kind of modeling, he ends up with the line of distinction that we all are familiar with: Archaic societies consist of small, segmentally differentiated units, in which a strong collective conscience creates solidarity out of similarities between members. This *mechanical solidarity directly* integrates the individual within the community. Modern societies, by contrast, consist of large, functionally differentiated spheres of life. The division of labor creates a network of interdependencies. *Organic solidarity* thus consists of differences, and binds the individual *indirectly* to society by integrating him into whatever fields of activity he is involved in. Differentiation and specialization favor the development of the individual personality because different special activities require different abilities. As the individualization of the members of society advances, they can no longer be integrated within one single collective conscience. Instead, the collective conscience itself also becomes differentiated into a plentitude of function-specific codes of norms, which nevertheless retain their moral character. There is, consequently, a link between the division of labor, solidarity, and morality: "In short, since the division of labor becomes the predominant source of social solidarity, at the same time it becomes the foundation of the moral order" (Durkheim, 1978: 396; tr. 1984: 333).

But the precise link between the division of labor and organic solidarity is notoriously unclear (Luhmann, 1977: 17–34; Lukes, 1973: 137–178; Müller,

1983: 128ff.; Parsons, 1967: 166–191; Pizzorno, 1963: 1–36; Poggi, 1972: 165ff.; Pope and Johnson, 1983: 681–692; Sirianni, 1984: 449–70; Tyrell, 1985: 181–250). Ironically only in the brief third book of *The Division of Labor* in Society, on the *abnormal* forms of the division of labor, does one learn about the *normal* emergence of organic solidarity and hence the alleged relationship between solidarity, law, and integration. Durkheim distinguished three pathological forms: the anomic, the enforced division of labor, as well as "another abnormal form," which might be termed lack of internal organizational coordination. *Anomie*, which is expressed in economic crises the antagonism between capital and labor, and anarchy in science – arises at times of rapid change, during which new organs and functions develop without a corresponding development of rules of cooperation, and therefore of social ties. *Normally*, Durkheim assumes, rules develop *spontaneously* in the course of social intercourse, as part of a gradual process of *habitualization* in which the exchange is first regulated provisionally, then as a habit, and last of all legally. This hypothesis of the self-regulation of social life therefore relies on the factors of "time" and "continuous contact" between the various bodies concerned. In the long term, organic solidarity "normally," but mysteriously, arises form functional interdependencies. *Anomie* – the lack of regulation or deregulation of social life – is the result of rapid and radical social change. But anomie does not mean a fundamental *crisis of the system,* but rather a *crisis of adapation*; continuous contact will eventually produce new rules and a new functional equilibrium between the divided functions, thus assuring social integration.

Though *anomie* can be eliminated by the gradual development of new rules, in the case of the *enforced division of labor*, it is "these very rules that are the cause of evil" (Durkheim, 1978: 367; tr. 1984: 310). Rules come to be felt as oppressive and unjust when they represent a social order that no longer corresponds to the developed moral conscience and can therefore only be maintained by force. Class conflict and anger over unjust contracts are products of the discrepancy between traditional social structure and the feeling of social justice. The traditional allocation of status according to the privileges of birth flies in the face of the natural distribution of talents and is antithetical to modern professional society, which must assign status according to performance, not social origin. Durkheim therefore champions formal equality of opportunity – freedom to choose a profession. Force points to a crisis in the system – a constitutive defect in a society's system of rules – which can only be eliminated by radical changes in the rules themselves and can by no means be left to the healing power of time. Revolutionary change of this kind would necessarily have to alter property rights, control over the means of production, and the distribution mechanism for scarce goods and resources, which is to say a radical transformation of the social order such as Marx had foreseen.

Anomie therefore indicates a *transitional* state of absence of rules; *force* indicates an illegitimate order, whose unjust rules *systematically* create an asymmetrical division of power that favors a small elite at the expense of the mass of society. The type of crisis held to be dominant is of decisive importance both in regard to the theory of society in general, and political sociology in particular (Horton, 1964: 283–300; Lukes, 1967: 134–156; Rüschemeyer, 195). Marx traces the origins of the enforced division of labor to the laws of capitalist production, leading to exploitation and alienation. In so doing he provides the premise of the German tradition, according to which the division of labor is always seen in the context of the development of classes. For Durkheim, on the other hand, the anomic division of labor is the dominant fact. He regards force as a temporary phenomenon, associated with anomie, which disappears when new rules for the coordination of functions and the cooperation of groups have been institutionalized.

According to Durkheim's diagnosis, modern societies are in a state of transitional anomic crisis. Though not a fundamental crisis of the system, the "cure" lies not in a radical transformation, but in subjecting social relations to planned social change. In this respect, Durkheim is a typical representative of the French tradition, which stresses the "moral value of the division of labor":

> Thus it is wrong to oppose a society that derives from a community of beliefs to one whose foundation is co-operation, by granting only the first a moral character and seeing in the latter only an economic grouping. In reality, co-operation has also its intrinsic morality. (1978: 208; tr. 1984: 173ff.)

The Dilemma of Organic Solidarity

Yet Durkheim was not able to spell out the relationship of division of labor and organic solidarity – hence the morality of cooperation. He claimed it without substantiation. Why did he fail to do so? The reasons for his failure become visible when we turn to conceptual and theoretical difficulties inherent in his model.

The conceptual problems affect his major terms *solidarity, integration,* and *collective consciousness.* First of all, solidarity has two contradictory meanings: in mechanical solidarity it denotes similarity; in organic solidarity it is coexistent with difference (Parsons, 1967). Since in primitive society mechanical solidarity implies that every individual is formed as a prototype of the collective consciousness, it is based upon equality; whereas organic solidarity entails the differentiation of functions and specialization of individuals, these differences in terms of functions and individuals create inequality and heterogeneity. Second, solidarity exhibits two different ways in which it works. Mechanical solidarity contributes to the direct integration of individual into society. In other words, it is *social integration* by the appeal to a common collective consciousness. Organic solidarity, however, leads to indirect integration through the web of interdependencies it creates. It is *system integration* to employ the distinction by David Lockwood (1956, 1964) because the focus is on the differentiated parts and their integration into society. Third, Durkheim evokes the impression that the collective consciousness as the engine of solidarity is gradually replaced by the division of labor. In the language of theoretical modeling a value variable is replaced by a structural variable in short, he seems to switch from culture to structure.

The conceptual ambiguities in the key terms of solidarity – integration and collective consciousness – are mirrored in three theoretical problems. They exist because the connection between the division of labor and organic solidarity ultimately remains unexplained. These problems are as follows:

1. The role of *collective actors*: Since Durkheim based his argument largely on the antithesis between the individual and society, the carriers of organic solidarity are not dealt with in detail. Who are the bearers of this type of solidarity? The answer is given in the second foreword: the occupational groups.
2. The role of the *State*: Durkheim's appraisal in the *Division of Labor* is ambiguous. Against Comte's collectivist appeal for a strong state, he suggests that the modern state itself is only a by-product of social differentiation. His objection to Spencer's liberal "nightwatchman" state is that the state has already become a central regulation body. What, then, is the proper role of the modern state?
3. The role of the *modern collective conscience*: On the one hand, he gives the impression that the division of labor is taking the place formerly held by the collective conscience as the source of solidarity, and that the collective representations are being diluted by the "cult of the individual." On the other hand, he considers the cult of the individual to be the ultimate and supreme collective ideal of modern times. What is the fate of moral individualism?

These unsolved problems from the *Division of Labor* are the subject of Durkheim's political writings. In the *Leçons de sociologie*, he (1969; tr. 1991 and 1992) discusses the role of professional groups as the vehicles of organic solidarity, the functions of the state and democracy, and the significance of "moral individualism" as a modern collective ideal. He reasons that if it is possible through institutional reforms to achieve smooth coordination between professional groups, the democratic State, and the individualistic ideal, then the division of labor will create organic solidarity and ensure social integration. In *Leçons de sociologie*, he therefore outlines the *nomos* of a functionally differentiated society and sketches a normative picture of a dynamic and just social order (cf. Müller, 1991).

Yet it is interesting to note how he tacitly alters major terms in his concept of a well-ordered society. Occupational groups may function as bearers of social solidarity but only by connecting mechanical and organic solidarity:

internally, binding the individual to the group they operate on a mechanical basis; *externally*, in competition and cooperation with other groups, they operate on an organical basis in order to fill a position in the web of interdependencies.

The modern state is not just a by-product of social differentiation, nor a central organ as the organical analogy would suggest. Rather, the democratic state sets the general framework as the arena for pluralistic group struggle and is the guardian of the "cult of the individual."

This "cult of the individual," finally, is just the crucial point of reference to which specific codes of morality have to pay respect. Yet this normative picture of a good society that Durkheim paints, reaches far beyond the relationship between division of labor and organic solidarity but it may very well provide an answer to the problem of order and individual autonomy.

Resumé: The Enduring Importance of Durkheim's Problem

As the criticisms have shown, Durkheim cannot demonstrate the alleged benevolent relationship between division of labor and organic solidarity without inconsistencies and additional considerations. With an unshakable conviction, he paves his sociological way in the debate on differentiation and develops a strong pleading in defense of the progressive nature of the division of labor. A true heir of Saint-Simon, Durkheim welcomes the "great transformation" and the three revolutions that accompany this transition with evolutionary optimism. In the Industrial Revolution and the emergence of a capitalist economy, in the political revolution and the institutionalization of democracy, and in the ethical revolution and the emergence of moral individualism, he sees the outline of a "new framework." Interestingly enough, neither Spencer's liberal market society nor Marx's socialist society have become an institutional reality in Western industrial nations. But the mixed economy, the modern welfare state, and the "cult of individual" are now the main characteristic elements Durkheim had foreseen in his political writings as the "new framework."

Apart from this vision that is already present in Durkheim's *Division of Labor*, three moments mark the lasting importance of his first book: (1) the dangers of *anomie* and the necessity of social solidarity, (2) the constitutive relationship of differentiation and integration in modern society, and (3) the moral concept of a well-ordered society in the sense described above. These are the thematic, theoretical, and substantive moments that demonstrate the actuality of the problems Durkheim addressed.

If we look at the massive problems East European societies in transition are faced with, if we turn our attention to current theoretical debate from Parsons to Luhmann, Habermas and Giddens – and if we take up the moral issues discussed in communitarianism, we get an impression as to the vitality of Durkheim's *Division of Labor*.

Acknowledgements

I would like to thank Edward A. Tiryakian, the members of the panel, and Lewis A. Coser for helpful comments.

Note

1. Department of Social Sciences, Institute of Sociology, Humboldt University to Berlin, Germany.

References

Alexander, Jeffrey C., 1982, *Theoretical Logic in Sociology*, vol. 2: *The Antinomies of Classical Thought: Marx and Durkheim*. London, Melbourne and Henley: Routledge & Kegan Paul.
Alpert, Harry, 1941, "Emile Durkheim and the theory of social integration." *Journal of Social Philosophy* 6: 172–184.
Alpert, Harry, 1961, *Emile Durkheim and His Sociology*, 2nd ed. New York.
Bellah, Robert N., 1973, "Introduction." In R. N. Bellah (ed.), *Emile Durkheim. On Morality and Society*: IX–LV. Chicago: Chicago University Press.
Blau, Peter M., 1977, *Inequality and Heterogeneity. A Primitive Theory of Social Structure*. New York: The Free Press.
Bottomore, Tom, 1981, "A Marxist consideration of Durkheim." *Social Forces* 59(4): 902–917.
Bouglé, Celestin, 1903, "Revue générale des théories récentes sur la division du travail." *Année sociologique* 6: 73–122.
Bourgois, Leon, 1897, *La solidarité*. Paris: Alcan.
Bücher, Karl, 1968, "Arbeitsteilung und soziale Kassenbildung." (1893) In B. Seidel and S. Jenkner (eds.), *Klassenbildung und Sozialschichlung*: 70–101. Darmstadt: Wissenschaftliche Buchgesellschaft.
Corning, Peter A., 1982, "Spencer and Durkheim." *British Journal of Sociology* 33(3): 359–382.
Durkheim, Emile, 1970, "Cours de sciences sociales. Leçon d'ouverture." (1888) In *La science sociale et l'action*. Introduction et présentation de J. C. Filloux: 77–110. Paris: Presses Universitaires de France.
Durkheim, Emile, 1975, "Tönnies Ferdinand, Gemeinschaft und Gesellschaft. Abhandlung des Communismus und des Socialismus als empirische Culturformen. Leipzig 1887." (1889) In V. Karady (ed.), *Emile Durkheim, Textes*, vol. 1: 383–390. Paris: Minuit.
Durkheim, Emile, 1893, *De la division du travail social*. Paris: Alcan.
Durkheim, Emile, 1895, *Les règles de la méthode sociologique*. Paris: Alcan.
Durkheim, Emile, 1897, *Le Suicide*. Paris: Alcan.
Durkheim, Emile, 1984, *The Division of Labor in Society*, 2nd. ed. (1902) W. D. Halls, tr., with introduction by Lewis A. Coser. New York: The Free Press.
Durkheim, Emile, 1928, *Le Socialisme. La definition, ses débuts, la doctrine saint-simonienne*. Paris: Presses Universitaires de France.
Durkheim, Emile, 1969, *Leçons de Sociologie. Physique des moeurs et du droit*. Paris: PUF. (Tr. by C. Brookfield, with a new preface by B. S. Turner 1992. *Professional Ethics and Civil*

Morals. London: Routledge; tr. into German by M. Bischoff, ed., with an afterword by H. P. Müller 1991. *Physik der Sitten und des Rechts.* Frankfurt/M.: Suhrkamp.)

Filloux, Jean Claude, 1970, "Introduction." In *Emile Durkheim, La science sociale et l'action*: 5–68. Paris: Presses Universitaires de France.

Friedmann, George, 1956, "Emile Durkheim und die modernen Formen der Arbeitsteilung." *Kölner Zeitschrift für Soziologie und Sozialpsychologie* 8: 12–25.

Giddens, Anthony, 1978, *Durkheim.* Hassocks: The Harvester Press.

Gouldner, Alvin W., 1958, "Introduction" to E. Durkheim, *Socialism and Saint-Simon*: V–XXVI. Yellow Springs: The Antioch Press.

Hayward, J. E. S., 1959, "Solidarity: The social history of an idea in nineteenth century France." *International Review of Social History* 4: 261–284.

Horton, John, 1964, "The dehumanization of anomie and alienation." *British Journal of Sociology* 15: 283–300.

Jarring, H., 1979, "A rational reconstruction of Durkheim's thesis concerning the division of labour in society." *Mens en Maatschappij* 54: 171–210.

Kemper, Theodor D., 1972, "The division of labor: A post Durkheimian analytical view." *American Sociological Review* 37: 739–753.

König, René, 1976, "Emile Durkheim. Der Soziologe als Moralist." In D. Käsler (ed.), *Klassiker des soziologischen Denkens,* vol. 1: 312–364. München: Beck.

Krause, E. A., 1982, *Division of Labor. A Political Perspective.* Westport and London: Greenwood Press.

Lockwood, David, 1956, "The social system." *British Journal of Sociology* 7: 134–146.

Lockwood, David, 1964, "Social integration and system integration." In George K. Zollschan and Waller Hirsch (eds.), *Explorations in Social Change*: 244–257. London.

Luhmann, Niklas, ed., 1985, *Soziale Differenzierung. Zur Geschichte einer Idee,* Opladen: Westdeutscher Verlag.

Lukes, Steven, 1967, "Alienation and Anomie." In P. Laslett and W. G. Runciman (eds.), *Philosophy, Politics and Society,* vol. 3. Oxford.

Lukes, Steven, 1973, *Emile Durkheim. His Life and Work. A Historical and Critical Study.* Harmondsworth: Penguin Books.

Mauss, Marel, 1958, "Introduction to the first edition." In E. Durkheim, *Socialism and Saint Simon*: 1–4. Yellow Springs: The Antioch Press.

Merton, Robert K., 1965, "Durkheim's 'Division of Labor in Society.'" In R. Nisbet (ed.), *Emile Durkheim*: 105–112. Englewood Cliffs, NJ: Prentice-Hall.

Müller, Hans-Peter, 1983, *Wertkrise und Gesellschaftsreform. Emile Dukheims Schriften zur Politik.* Stuttgart: Enke.

Müller, Hans-Peter, 1987, "Social structure and Civil Religion. Legitimation crisis in a later Durkheimian perspective." In J. C. Alexander (ed.), *Durkheimian Sociology*: 220–256. Cambridge: Cambridge University Press.

Müller, Hans-Peter, 1991, "Die Moralökologie moderner Gesellschaften." Afterword to E. Durkheim, *Physik der Sitten und des Rechts.* Vorlesungen zur Soziologie der Moral: 307–341. Frankfurt/M.: Suhrkamp.

Müller, Hans-Peter and Michael Schmid, 1988, "Arbeitsteilung Solidarität und Moral." Afterword to E. Durkheim, *Über soziale Arbeitsteilung,* 2nd ed.: 481–532. Frankfurt/M.

O'Connor, James, 1980, "The division of labor in society." *Insurgent Sociologist* 10: 60–68.

Parsons, Talcott, 1967, "Durkheim's Contribution to the Theory of Integration of Social Systems." In his *Sociological Theory and Modern Society*: 3–34. New York and London: The Free Press.

Parsons, Talcott, 1968, *The Structure of Social Action. A Study in Social Theory with Special Reference to a Group of Recent European Writers*, vol. 2. (1937) New York: The Free Press.

Pizzorno, Alessandro, 1963, "Lecture actuelle de Durkheim." *Europäisches Archiv für Soziologie* 4: 1–36.

Poggi, Gianfranco, 1972, *Images of Society. Essays on the Sociological Theories of Tocqueville, Marx and Durkheim.* Stanford, CA: Stanford University Press.

Polanyi, Karl, 1978, *The Great Transformation.* Frankfurt/M.: Suhrkamp.

Rüschemeyer, Dietrich, 1982, "On Durkheim's explanation of the division of labor." *American Journal of Sociology* 88: 579–589.

Rüschemeyer, Dietrich, 1985, *Power and the Division of Labor.* London: Polity Press.

Schmid, Michael, 1989, "Arbeitsteilung und Solidarität." *Kölner Zeitschrift für Soziologie und Sozialpsychologie* 41: 619–643.

Schmoller, Gustav, 1894, "Besprechung von Emile Durkheim, 'De la division du travail social.'" *Jahrbuch für Gesetzgebung, Verwaltung und Volkswirtschaft im Deutschen Reich* 18: 286–289.

Smith, Adam, 1937, *An Inquiry into the Nature and Causes of the Wealth of Nations.* (1776) New York.

Tiryakian, Edward A., 1981, "Emile Durkheim." In T. Bottomore and R. Nisbet (eds.), *A History of Sociological Analysis*: 187–236. New York: Basic Books.

Tönnies, Ferdinand, 1929, *Soziologische Studien und Kritiken, Dritte Sammlung.* Jena: Gustav Fischer.

Turner, Jonathan H., 1981, "Emile Durkheim's theory of integration in differentiated social systems." *Political Science Review* 24: 379–391.

Tyrell, Hartmann, 1985, "Emile Durkheim. Das Dilemma Der organischen Solidarität." In N. Luhmann (ed.), *Soziale Differenzierung. Zur Geschichte einer Idee*: 181–250. Opladen: Westdeutscher Verlag.

67

Social Theory and Talcott Parsons in the 1980s

David Sciulli and Dean Gerstein

Introduction

For a number of years, the mark of sophistication on the subject of action theory has been to ask: "Who now reads Parsons?" (Bryant 1983). The old structure-functional schema with its cargo of concepts finally disappeared over the horizon, it seems, its sails filled by the critical blasts of many theorists such as Gouldner (1970) and Giddens (1968, 1976). Booklists and journals harbor vital discussion of hermeneutics, networks, rational expectations, and structuralism, while the abandoned theory of action glides unread toward its wreckage in the rocky straits between Introduction to Theory and The History of Social Thought.

In this idyll, the appearance of a Parsonian revival in the 1980s must rank as a major surprise to many in the discipline, catching unaware even one as accomplished at sounding theoretical tides as Mullins (1983). The year 1980 was a significant turning point. Shortly after Parsons' death in 1979, new critical readings of Parsons began to appear with increasing prominence, led by Münch (1981b, 1982a) and Alexander (1982a, b, 1983a, b). The distinctive mark of this new commentary and debate is an attempt to account for and derive theoretical insights from Parsons' entire fifty-year project rather than to focus narrowly on single works or isolated dimensions of Parsonian thought.

The decline of structure-functionalism was to a substantial degree self-inflicted. As initiated by Parsons and associates in *Toward a General Theory of Action* (Parsons & Shils 1951) and *The Social System* (Parsons 1951), structure-functionalism degraded much too readily from the supple framework of analytical concepts in *The Structure of Social Action* (Parsons 1937) into an "ideal type" approach that Parsons himself had attacked and laid the basis for transcending in that earlier work. This defect manifested itself in hardening of the categories: a tendency to convert sound theoretical insights into elaborate typologies and to treat ongoing empirical research mostly as a question of properly assigning events or structures to the "correct" categories.

In large part because Parsons strove toward logical completeness, his major works of the early 1950s were long on formal distinctions and short on interesting research findings. Parsons was unable to let these conceptual schemes rest, so that the immense effort of concentration and study demanded by the 1951 volumes was repaid by Parsons revising their most complex conceptual machinery following new theoretical "breakthroughs", e.g. Parsons' (1960) response to Dubin's (1960) analysis of the pattern-variable scheme. The potential for accumulation, parsimony, and clarity tended to vanish in these formal complexities; and with it vanished the possibility that most readers of *The Social System* (such as Mills 1959) might ever again willingly venture to read anything Parsons wrote.

The movement toward a more sophisticated analytical theory began in *Economy and Society* (Parsons & Smelser 1956) and continued over the next quarter of a century.[1] But many of the empirical researchers (e.g. Levy 1952, Apter 1965, Almond & Powell 1966) – and their readers – who took the categories in *The Social System* literally in good faith could credibly claim that Parsons had misled them with many implied propositions about empirical social life that turned out to be unsupportable. Having built his work into a dominant influence on the discipline during the 1940s, Parsons in *The Social System* simply did not deliver the anticipated goods. By the time he recovered from the excesses of the middle period and regained the intellectual momentum of the earlier phase, enough devastating broadsides had landed against *The Social System* that virtually the whole sociological audience had lost any further interest in action theory.

In spite of the defects of the early 1950s, action theory overall – across Parsons' 50 years of publications – has a major strength which becomes clear when Parsons' overall project is compared with other major projects in theory-building: comprehensiveness on an analytical level. The appeal of Parsons in Germany today (exemplified by Münch 1982b and documented by Alexander 1984b) is largely due to his rigorous pursuit of a logically complete and integrated system of concepts that can mediate, accumulate, and transmit knowledge from every branch and sub-branch of the social and behavioral sciences as well as closely allied humanities and natural sciences.

The scope of his project – ranging from biology to theology – was in fact too comprehensive to permit him or any other individual theorist, even in 50 years, to personally invent every component it called for. But the framework was suggestive enough for him to recognize when theoretical work in specialized fields, even by those working completely outside the language of action theory, was moving in close approximation to the outlines of Parsons' thinking. On this basis he openly embraced, for example, the work of Freud, Keynes, Schumpeter, Alfred Emerson, James Olds, Ernst Mayr, Jean Piaget, Lon Fuller, Gunther Stent (as outlined in his autobiographical reflection, Parsons 1970; for some accounts of personal collaboration with Parsons, see Smelser 1981, Platt 1981, and Gerstein 1981a).

Through the 1950s, 1960s, and 1970s, Parsons was repeatedly called upon to defend and interpret his work – inevitably his old work – in the face of criticism. There were rumblings that this situation of dealing with Parsons' work piecemeal could not be expected to last but must give way to assessments based on all of Parsons' texts.[2] With Parsons' death in Munich in 1979, the opportunity to evaluate action theory in terms of its texts alone, and independently of the direct influence of its principal architect, moved from possibility to necessity.

The Turning Point: Action Theory in the 1980s

Two events best symbolize the recent revival of interest in Parsons' theories: The *American Journal of Sociology*'s translation and publication of Münch's "Talcott Parsons and the Theory of Action," (1981b, 1982a: these are chapters one and two of Münch 1982b): and the publication of Alexander's four-volume *Theoretical Logic in Sociology* (1982a, 1982b, 1983a, 1983b). In retrospect, however, three important contributions helped to prepare the ground for these events: (a) Habermas's (1981a) critical commentary on Parsons at the 1980 meeting of the German Sociological Association, flanked by his discussion of Parsons in the second volume of *The Theory of Communicative Action* (Habermas 1981b), his comparison of Weber, Parsons, and Luhmann in *Legitimation Crisis* (1973) and his (1977) comparison of Parsons and Arendt: (b) Alexander's 1978 essay on formal and substantive voluntarism in the *American Sociological Review*; and especially (c) Bershady's (1973) masterful criticism, a clear advance beyond the preceding 25 years of debate on Parsons' work.

Bershady, Münch, and Alexander express sharp dissatisfaction with the quality of earlier commentaries. In fact, they find little of worth in the critiques of Parsons still most frequently cited in sociological journals, monographs, and especially textbooks. All four – Habermas included – attempt to account for Parsons' social theory overall, rather than limiting their critique to a particular phase or a particular set of concepts. Each of the four commentators, whatever his opinion on the ultimate merits of Parsons' social theory, raises penetrating questions that go beyond Parsons to address the enterprise of social theory as such. Alternative theories, such as those offered by Habermas, Luhmann, Gouldner, and Giddens, must face the same issues and questions, and the breadth of this new debate is precisely what is elevating the status of Parsons' work in the 1980s.

The contemporary revived interest in Parsons therefore represents a watershed, differing substantially from the debates surrounding his work from the 1950s to the mid-1970s. Nevertheless, the earlier, piecemeal debates form a considerable literature, and we expect that sociologists unfamiliar with Alexander, Münch, Bershady, and Habermas, or unwilling to address Parsons' work in methodical fashion, will fall back on these older arguments out of convenience: conflict vs consensus theory (Lockwood 1956, Dahrendorf 1959, Giddens 1968); distortion of the classics (Cohen, Hazelrigg & Pope 1975, Giddens 1976); conservative or status quo ideological bias (Hacker 1961, Gouldner 1970); functionalism as an oversocialized or collectivized conception of man (Wrong 1961, Homans 1964); functionalism's unacceptable teleology (e.g. Black 1961; but see the counter arguments of Piccone 1968 and Wright 1983); or the reductionist sociology of knowledge focusing on Parsons' family background, position at Harvard during the Depression, and American or WASP ethnocentrism (e.g. Gouldner 1970). This literature defines the conventional wisdom of the discipline and has unfortunately been repeated endlessly in sociology survey texts.

Against this received wisdom, the Münch translation was eventful because it dramatically illustrated to American sociologists that regardless of the waning influence of Parsons in the US (and the conventional American attacks are well known in Germany), action theory, when subjected to close reading, is being found to suffer from fewer manifest self-contradictions or unsupportable assumptions than do Parsons' classical or contemporary alternatives. For all the legitimate questions that can be raised about Parsons' works — and we see no reason why these should be dismissed or ignored — Parsons' social theory has attracted commentary because it offers the possibility of standing up better in the face of rigorous questioning than Marx's, Weber's, or Durkheim's social theories, or the alternatives offered by neo-Marxism, the first generation of the Frankfurt school, or contemporaries like Giddens and Collins.

Alexander's four volumes were significant because they recast fundamental questions of social theory construction that Parsons had posed and then turned those same questions to Parsons' works themselves. Initial critical reviews of Alexander have not stopped to consider that any work in social theory is as important for the avenues of theory construction that it closes off, or prevents from being unreflectively pursued, as for the new avenues it immediately establishes. Alexander successfully forecloses both the casual adoption of ideal-type approaches and the possibility that Parsons' future critics, exegetes, or followers can legitimately return to the earlier literature or earlier ways of bringing Parsons' theories to empirical research. Any commentator attempting to return cannot escape dealing first and systematically with Alexander's *Theoretical Logic* (1982a, 1982b, 1983a, 1983b). In our view, Alexander's conclusion, that Parsons' social theory succumbs ultimately to idealistic determinism, is somewhat over-stated. Nevertheless, we consider *Theoretical Logic in Sociology* the most challenging single contribution to the enterprise of social theory by an American author since Parsons' *The Structure of Social Action* (1937) and Merton's *Social Theory and Structure* (1957).

The frameworks for reading Parsons that have been proposed by Alexander, Münch, Habermas, and Bershady differ markedly from each other, as will become clear below. This suggests that the interpretation of Parsons' work as a whole has only begun to be established. It also suggests a major reason why fruitful uses of Parsons' social theory in detailed empirical research have to date been greatly delayed. This needs to be put bluntly: The discipline of American sociology is only today beginning to understand the project of the most methodical and comprehensive American theorist. The pointed critiques of Parsons made by Bershady (1973) and Habermas (1973, 1977, 1981a) moved the debate beyond its earlier limits by explicating specific standards against which any social theory must be evaluated and applying these standards to Parsons.

Bershady (1973) persistently raised the charge against Parsons of overgenerality: Parsons' analytical framework of concepts may well overarch all individual societies and therefore escape the empirical relativism of ideal-type approaches to social theory, but Parsons' framework "cannot reproduce the features of any single society." Given this problem of separation between theory and empirical specificity, Bershady moved to a more fundamental issue: By what standard should we, or can we, evaluate the merits of Parsons' social theory relative to competing concepts and categories? Bershady insisted that it is meaningless to criticize Parsons' social theory for being "inherently conservative" or incorporating a narrow vision of human creativity or freedom. Bershady notes that Parsons' intention was to distinguish human social action from non-human behavior as such, just as Chomsky's (1965) syntactics was intended to distinguish grammatical sentence construction. Each theorist provides a fundamental intersubjective framework that allows and requires human creativity, providing both participants and observers with the possibility of recognizing and understanding in common what human creativity is. Bershady sees Parsons and Chomsky as employing the Kantian approach of basing their theories on the irreducible components of social interaction. This is why Bershady says that Parsons' social theory is "an epistemology of intersubjectivity" and not an epistemology of causality. Bershady's thesis is that we can therefore only criticize Parsons' social theory by showing *either* that his analytical framework is not generalizable and comprehensive (but, rather, succumbs to the relativism of time and place, and/or fails to present methodically all possible analytical components of any possible social action), or that Parsons' analytical framework cannot overcome its over generality so as to inform empirical research or normative debate, i.e. "that Parsons' rules are too meager or faulty to comprehend historical diversity and possible future social worlds, adequately specified."

Turning to Parsons' functionalism to illustrate this problem of overgenerality, Bershady says that Parsons' AGIL schema, the four functional subsystems of adaptation, goal-attainment, integration, and latent pattern maintenance, can only inform empirical research if all four sets of symbolic media of social interchange (in order: money, power, influence, and value commitments) "are perfectly understood." However, the media of influence and value commitments in particular "are conceptually unclear at the macroscopic range, and this vagueness is not merely an imperfect fit between system problems and institutions." For Bershady, Parsons' definitions of the media are ambiguous, the definitions of the boundaries of the functional subsystems are not sharp enough to precisely differentiate functions from dysfunctions, and the interchanges between subsystems are too vague to account in any specific empirical instance for the proposition that I and L are "higher" than A and G rather than vice versa.

Bershady's critique still poses the most fundamental and important challenge to the revitalization of Parsons' social theory. Bershady views the challenge as unanswered by Parsons, though not, in principle, unanswerable by those using Parsons' theoretical framework.

Although not referring directly to Bershady, Habermas (1981b) in essence brings out the implications of the charge of overgenerality. Unlike Bershady, however, he insists that overgenerality is an inherent and irremediable characteristic of Parsons' theory, so that it cannot inform either empirical research or social practice, no matter how it is employed or reworked. Habermas argues that Parsons' early concept of voluntarism is based on "isolated individuals," so that social order for Parsons is a matter of the pure contingency of individual decisionmaking within some larger framework of social values and norms. According to Habermas, as Parsons' theory construction evolved into the 1960s and 1970s, this autonomous individual-based contingency was smothered by "systems theory": extra-individual functional imperatives not only overcome the resistance of recalcitrant individuals but undermine the integrity of any and all resistant cultural patterns. Habermas refers to Menzies (1977) and uses Lockwood's (1956) early distinction between "system integration" and "social integration" to document his reading of Parsons as a systems theorist.

Having read Parsons in this way, Habermas raises three very specific interrelated challenges to any analyst of advanced societies, but especially to "Parsons' students." Neither Münch nor Alexander nor any other Parsons commentator has directly responded to Habermas, three challenges. In our view, any theorist, Parsonian or otherwise, seeking to demonstrate the potential empirical richness and specificity of a theoretical framework must respond.

First, the challenge of grounding reasoned protection of cultural integrity against the corrosive effects of money and power: Habermas asks whether a theory can identify any barriers strictly within the realm of social values and norms that can resist changes induced by the instrumental adaptation of social systems that characterizes late capitalism. Habermas' thesis is that Parsons' theoretical framework lacks the concepts to explain why any distinctive cultural patterns might be resilient in the face of functional systemic imperatives of "capitalistically rationalized" modernization.

Second, the challenge of a grounded criticism of modernity: Habermas says that "Parsons cannot discern the costs or pathologies of modernization" (e.g. urban decay, the overbureaucratization and thus intellectual impoverishment of higher education) as could Marx, Weber, and Durkheim. For Habermas, misdirected systemic complexity (or misdirected functional differentiation) can be detected only through its pathological effects at the *Lebenswelt* or life-world level, the interpersonal and everyday meanings and experiences of actors. Because Habermas sees Parsons analyzing systemic and functional change with the same categories he uses to analyze instrumental rationalization in the actors' life-worlds, Habermas says that Parsons has no conceptual basis for criticizing modern social change. For Habermas this explains why Parsons' work conveys a sense of harmony rather than a sense of pathos about modern social life.

Third, the challenge of a grounded basis for reasoned, practical reforms: Habermas acknowledges that some of Parsons' students – particularly Rainer Baum (1976b) – attempt to respond to the difficulties in Parsons' work by treating manifest pathologies of modernization as the underdevelopment of the "higher" symbolic media of social interchange, that is, influence and value-commitments. This underdevelopment leads to the "misuse" of the lower-level media of money and power by participants in decisionmaking. However, Habermas counters that the theory of symbolic media of interchange can only be used critically, to locate or reform such pathologies, if "one can assign direct normative significance to well-defined equilibria." He adds: "Whoever starts on this road should not hesitate to take up the task of constructing a theory of value implementation or value realization that can be normatively understood from the perspective of the participants," (Habermas 1981a). It is the participants, after all, who must implement or realize values by acting in concert, and the social theory must account for how they can come to a common recognition and understanding of the problem and then agree on, initiate, and maintain reform. Habermas is "highly doubtful that the normative implications of such an endeavor could be compatible with the character of Parsons' theory" (Habermas: 1981a: 195).

Münch (1981b, 1982a) is less interested in the practical ends or empirical uses of action theory than in the integrity or rigor of Parsons' philosophical foundations, a task presented by the German debate in sociology: he therefore does Bershady's or Habermas' challenges. Münch, like Habermas, was trained as a philosopher, and again like Habermas, came to a reading of Parsons through a reading of Luhmann's (1976, 1981) structural or systems theory. Münch's thesis is that "a Kantian core" informs all of Parsons' works as a deep structure, regardless of Parsons' own surface- or self-understanding of his social theory. Thus, Münch does not see Parsons' theory becoming skewed into a one-sided systems theory but, rather, sees it as recapitulating the logical form of Kant's *Critique of Pure Reason* and Kant's epistemological and substantive dualisms, e.g. fact/value, objective/subjective, theory/practical experience. For Münch, Parsons' general action theory and theory of the social system are "exactly parallel, in structure and method, to Kant's critical philosophy," and "*The Structure of Social Action* must be read as the sociological equivalent of Kant's moral philosophy."

Parsons' Kantian dualism is best illustrated, according to Münch, by the relationship between institutionalization of norms at the societal level and internalization of norms at the personality level. For Münch, each process for Parsons transcends the dichotomy of external coercion vs individual calculation of utility; it represents the "interpenetration" of the conditional and the normative. Münch sees Parsons employing the Kantian dualisms and transcending them through "the theorem of interpenetration" by posing and answering the following question: "Given that social order exists, what conditions constitute the framework within which social action necessarily takes place"? Münch says that Parsons' answer is that there must be "a limit on [actors'] arbitrariness of action *determined solely by subjective considerations*" (emphasis in original).

For Kant, subjective choices can only be limited either by moral standards or by calculation of self-interest (in Kantian terms, categorical vs hypothetical principles). Only the first kind of principle "can produce a consistency of choice of actions and, therefore, can account for social order." What Parsons calls a norm, Münch tells us, is a categorical rule in Kant's sense, which must be held valid for all actors rather than merely being based on expectations of (hypothetical) profit or loss. Thus, Münch says, "the paramount question for [any] sociological theory is how is this categorical obligation possible?" For Münch, the key is "interpenetration" which "replaces the old doctrine of differentiation." The interpenetration of each side of the dualism by the other side "elevates the tension" inherent in the dualism "so that unity [social order] can be maintained."

This emphasis on the interpenetration of rational calculation and subjectively acceptable moral limits on self-interestedness provides Münch with the basis to make several assertions regarding Parsons' project: First, not only Parsons but all the classic sociologists came eventually to the theorem of interpenetration to overcome dualism, but "nowhere else in sociology has this basic idea been elaborated as lucidly as in the writings of Parsons." Second, Parsons' Kantian approach has more in common methodologically with common law adjudication, which applies precedents but holds out the possibility of reversals or challenges by local level action, than with "the scientific method" of deduction and causality. Third, Parsons (1937) defined voluntarism as the irreducible free will or freedom of the individual in a two-term framework (goal-rational or instrumental action vs categorical-normative obligation), but beginning in 1951 this "was replaced" by the three-term schema (cultural, social, personality systems, subsequently adding the behavioral system) and "the analysis explicitly revolves around their interpenetration" to explain both social action and social order. Finally, because Münch emphasizes the interpenetration of internalization and institutionalization, he contends that the integrative or societal community subsystem in Parsons' later writings was really "the highest level of control", standing above the latent pattern-maintenance subsystem rather than below it, as Parsons maintained. For Münch, the latter provides too little control over the options of calculating, self-interested actors, whereas the integrative subsystem is the locus of obligations that are both "self-evident" (i.e. internalized and institutionalized) and "imposed" (by the same processes). These subjectively accepted duties control actors' options and thus establish and maintain social order.

Alexander's treatment of Parsons is the longest and most detailed yet to appear. Following a generalized introduction to "theoretical logic" (Alexander 1982a), he discusses four major social theorists – Marx and Durkheim in volume two (Alexander 1982b), Weber in volume three (Alexander 1983a), and Parsons in volume four (1983b) – within an overall exploration of *conflation* (or *conflationary error*) and *multidimensionality* in social theory. Conflationary error involves the collapse of essential analytical distinctions between theoretical levels, particularly the levels of general presuppositions, ideological orientations, empirical propositions, and methodological assumptions. Multidimensionality means the consistently wellbalanced treatment, mainly at the general presuppositional level, of ideal and empirical factors in social life.

For each author, Alexander first presents the strands of multidimensionality in the relevant works. Then he locates where and why each theorist succumbed to a specific type of conflationary error, reifying or overrelying on one or another level of theory construction, and as a result tilted the balance of his theory irretrievably toward either ideal or material factors. In short, Alexander offers the following standard against which any theorist's works may be evaluated: The work must escape conflation and must maintain a multidimensional approach to the study of society, particularly in regard to the two "decisive questions" at the presuppositional level: how are social *action* and social *order* possible? Alexander adopts Parsons' early criterion for the ultimate success of analytical or methodical social theory: ecumenicism, or success in providing a framework of concepts that can render social science knowledge cumulative by making research findings mutually understandable across disciplines, research interests, and levels of analysis.

In the first half of volume four, Alexander argues that Parsons' analytical AGIL interchange model and social change theory marked a clear advance beyond the three classical sociologists in the development of multidimensional social theory. Parsons did not give "epistemological priority" to social norms and values, did not in this sense overemphasize cultural or ideal factors, but rather exposed their interrelationships with material factors and utilitarian calculations of cost and benefit. Nevertheless, the second half of Alexander's volume four builds the case that "Parsons overlays his multidimensional analysis with a reductionistic and highly damaging form of sociological idealism" (Alexander 1983b, p. 152).

In Alexander's view, Parsons' theory, like those of Marx, Weber, and Durkheim, suffers fundamentally from "central equivocations in the theory itself." As a result, Parsons, like his predecessors, was ultimately unable to "resist any presuppositional bias, to maintain an objective, multidimensional orientation . . ." (Alexander 1983b, p. 151). Parsons increasingly attempted to generate action theory strictly by deduction from first principles, thereby reifying his theory and turning it into an arid formalism. Even though Parsons' analytical framework of concepts is epistemologically sophisticated, anticipating the work of Thomas Kuhn and contemporary postpositivist philosophy of science, Alexander sees Parsons as having a commitment to empiricist principles regarding the status of "facts", a commitment he never consistently reconciled with his analytical sophistication. "He believes that his analytic discoveries are, in fact, concrete" (Alexander 1983b, p. 153). Thus Parsons could never overcome his "ambivalence about the relationship between theory and fact" (p. 153). Parsons ultimately held "a positivist faith in the conjunction of theory and fact," not a Kantian view that facts are inherently formed and given pattern by categories. Parsons' "neopositivist formalism" can be found "in every piece of his later work, in every book, every essay, every discussion that utilizes interchange to engage in more specific empirical argumentation" (p. 162). By the 1960s, "each of the interchange model's key terms [. . . is . . .] presented as if it were derived from some inherent logic of systems rather than from Parsons's efforts to model his analytic synthesis of instrumental and normative order" (p. 171).

Alexander's second charge is that Parsons conflates the problems of action and order. According to Alexander, Parsons treats rational action as inherently individualistic, that is, based on actors' narrow calculation of material self-interest. Therefore, collective order is necessarily the product of "supraindividual external force" that is normative rather than instrumental. "Parsons repeatedly defines normative order as the preferable – if not the only – reference point for collectivist theorizing" (Alexander 1983b, p. 218). The possibility that collective order may be based on instrumental calculation is eliminated as a collective or an empirical possibility. "Collective instrumental order becomes a residual category: it is no longer among the central axioms of Parsons' theoretical logic" (Alexander 1983b, p. 214).

New Developments in Action Theory

Bershady and Habermas concur that the major targets of opportunity for empirical research and theoretical specification in action theory are the "higher order" social media, influence, and value-commitments, and their bases in the societal community and fiduciary subsystems. Probably the most exciting recent efforts by action theorists have focused precisely on these areas. Alongside this process of empirical and analytical specification, the effort to establish a broadly accepted understanding of Parsons' project can be expected to continue because the readings of Parsons offered by Alexander, Münch, Habermas, and Bershady differ in fundamental respects.

Luhmann (1976, 1981) has played a major role in these efforts, as recently outlined by Alexander (1984b). Each of the German social theorists, including

Habermas and Münch (and one may add Rainer Baum), who reads Parsons does so through the eyes or under the influence of the theories of Luhmann, who has emphasized the problem of action in terms of contingency, uncertainty, risk, and complexity. He identifies structures, rather than functions, as being primary in accounting for order in social systems. The generalized media, in his view, are specialized mechanisms or ways of managing the expansion and reduction of complexity and contingency. Luhmann also replaces the Parsonian media of influence and commitment with rather differently conceived media of love and trust, opening here as elsewhere rich veins of theoretical discussion that have stimulated many action theorists (e.g. Loubser 1976, Baum 1976a, 1976b, Münch 1981a, 1982b).

Research being undertaken by many action theorists now reflects the need to specify empirically the most important analytical components of the societal community and fiduciary system as these interact with other social structures, Alexander (1980) theorizes that multiethnic societies (whether in the West or the Third World) revolve around a "core group" bearing ascriptive qualities and common internalized substantive beliefs, and that this core presents an insuperable barrier even to successfully assimilated "outside" groups, who cannot feel subjectively as comfortable with their place in society as the core group does. Alexander (1984a) is also carrying out a study of the symbolic and affective implications of the Watergate crisis. Münch (private communication) has just completed a two-volume study on the substantive belief systems of four advanced Western societies: Germany, France, Britain and the United States. Lidz (1979a, 1985) has begun publishing works from a study of cultural secularization and socio-political change in the United States in the twentieth century. Colomy (1985) analyzes the uneven rates at which mass-based political parties developed (differentiated) from older patterns of deference and class relations in antebellum American states. Gould (private communication) has applied macroanalytic methods that he earlier (Gould 1976) adapted from Keynesian theory to the English revolution. Wallace (1985) explores the differences between Parsons' and Luhman's approach to religion and pattern-maintenance, focusing on Parsons' greater openness to the implications of religious pluralism.

Baum (1976b, 1981), Baum & Lechner (1981), and Lechner (1985) grapple with the most radical and pathological vehicle of the discontents of modernity: fascism, and particularly German National Socialism. Their approach is to undertake detailed historical studies of the Nazi period with a strong theory on the "loss of societal steering mechanisms" mediated especially by elites; their aim is to elaborate a general theory of fascist movements that will have predictive and explanatory utility and be able to address normative questions of a sort that are highly pertinent in the aftermath of National Socialism and the Holocaust in modern Germany (Baum 1978). Moral authority and influence based on various solidarities, cultural value-patterns, and legal norms may restrain the modern state from its enormous potential for external and internal barbarism. But historically observable conditions that foster fundamentalist attempts to revitalize a dedifferentiated "core" value-pattern and a national ethnic identity clearly permit alignments of state power and bureaucratic efficiency that override commitments to moral decency.

Another line of work here involves value implementation in science. Loubser (1976) used evolutionary AGIL concepts to study the history of American social sciences and the alternations between emphasis on external (general societal) and internal (scientific-cognitive) value-commitments – a dimensional variation sometimes reified in the ideal types of value-relevance vs "value-freedom." Mayhew (1976) locates this dimension as an enduring functional tension within a broader set of such tensions that are inherent in the methodology of social science precisely because congruent tensions are "inherent in the nature of social life itself." Lidz (1981) provides a cogent framework for identifying the methodological and substantive significance of the approaches to the problem of value-relevance taken by Parsons, Weber, Simmel, and Dilthey.

One of the present authors, Sciulli (1984, 1985, 1986), proposes that Parsons increasingly accounted for both action and order in modern societies by turning to procedural norms, collegial forms of organization, and symbolic media of interchange, which orient collective action in the face of the great pluralism of actors' beliefs and motivations. Parsons, in short, purposely and consistently separated "normative motivations," that are internalized substantive beliefs, from "normative orientations," that at least in part involve what Parsons called procedural institutions. Sciulli (1985, 1986) sees Parsons' (1978a) appropriation of Lon Fuller's (1964, 1969) principles of "procedural legality" as central to understanding Parsons' social theory. On the basis of this procedural turn, Sciulli specifies the institutions that must be present in modern society if arbitrary political and/or socioeconomic power is to be restrained, a complex he calls "societal constitutionalism." Sciulli (1985) thereby poses a challenge to Habermas's students, contending that Habermas cannot possibly bring his own procedural communication theory to political practice, above the level of serial interpersonal relations, unless he links his theory to societal constitutionalism or an equivalent.

A second broad line of Parsonian action theory is at the general action level, which treats the social system on an analytical par with personality, culture, and behavioral systems. The accusations that the individual in action theory tends to be "oversocialized" and a "cultural dope" derived in large part from Parsons' difficulties in separating cognitive processes from biological ones and thereby in creating a firm theoretical foundation for individual cognitive autonomy (Warner 1978). Parsons' original concept of the "behavioral organism" (Parsons & Shils 1951) was the least well bounded or defined of the four general action systems, covering an extensive range of biological organizing processes. The organic part of the connection, the heritage of genetic endowment, could not be effectively integrated with the symbolic character of personality, social systems, and cultural systems, and left insufficient room for a concept of individual schemes and or processes of independent thought or rationality. The problem of finding a nonreductionist accommodation between society and biology is by no means restricted to action theory but is a very broad issue.

This problem came under forceful assault by Lidz & Lidz (1976), leading to a complete reformulation that Parsons accepted (1978b). Instead of a behavioral organism, they present a fully developed "behavioral system whose content is as symbolic as the personality, but in a fundamentally cognitive vein. The rechristened "behavioral system" operates much in the mold of Piaget's concepts of cognitive structures and operations, though without commitment to Piaget's rigid developmental states. Behavioral processes generate intelligence as a broad resource for social, cultural, and personal action, while structures of perceptual, interpretive, expectational, and formal-categorical knowledge – the AGIL of the behavioral system – constitute intelligent action.

A second innovation in general action theory was to develop relatively middle-range theories of general action "complexes" in empirical case analysis, as suggested by the "cognitive complex" developed in the analysis of the American university by Parsons & Platt (1973). Lidz (1979b) has suggested a "moral matrix" in the analysis of law. An example that has had extended empirical investigation is the "addiction complex", a construct that involves all four general action systems, and builds especially on the Durkheimian aspects of action theory. Walker & Lidz (Gould et al 1974, Lidz & Walker 1978, 1980, Walker & Lidz 1983) develop a comprehensive description and explanation of the manner in which the ideology and politics of the "drug abuse crisis" at the national, state, and local levels, including the microdynamic action of clinical and street life, arose as a systematic working through of a fundamental conflict of moral schemas: instrumental activism vs expressive passivism, in the sharpest formulation. This problem has also been addressed by one of the present authors: Attewell & Gerstein (1979) analyze the effects of ideological and moral conflict on the formation and implementation of methadone maintenance policies; Parsons & Gerstein (1977) explore the theoretical congruence between addiction to heroin and addiction to power; and Gerstein specifies the major social (1976) and cultural (1981b) components of the heroin complex and integrates these within a broader Durkheimian reinterpretation of the general action scheme (1983, 1986).

A final general action reformulation that has come about in the recent period is to emphasize the centrality of language and linguistic processes for meaningful action. Lidz (1976) outlined the idea that the elementary structure of social action was fundamentally congruent to the elementary structure of syntax, and that the composition of complex social structure was continuous with the problem of composing and decoding meaningful sentences. Edelson (1976) and Turner (1976) carried out the most elaborate expressions of the "linguistic drift' in action theory. Edelson applied a notion derived from generative-transformational linguistics to the personality system, relying especially on the notion that the relations between deep structure and surface structure in the analysis of speech can be applied to the relation between wishes and dreams in psychoanalysis. Turner developed a case that familial units express in socialization the deep structure of intergenerational kinship. Hayes (1981) has criticized both these efforts for insufficient rigor in using linguistic concepts, though he calls for continued exploration of the semiotics of specialized media languages, a perspective that seems increasingly appropriate to the nature of analytical action systems.

Conclusion

The book on Talcott Parsons has been reopened in the 1980s, and it is not possible to predict where this may lead. The major characteristic of the new work is its explicit attention to the full range of Parsons' published works in contrast to the piecemeal analyses that characterized earlier criticism. Bershady, Habermas, Münch, and Alexander provide an interpretive opening to explore the longer term merits of Parsons' social theory – but only an opening.

Bershady and Habermas concur that Parsons' theory has been overgeneral, and they elaborate specific problems that must be faced in any effort to bring theory – whether Parsonian, neo-Marxian, or any other kind – to bear on empirical problems. Habermas and Bershady disagree about whether Parsons' framework is inherently insufficient to examine the restraints and possibilities of modern societies. In our view, analyses framed entirely within Parsons' theory can be addressed with great specificity to each of Habermas' three questions – questions which strike us as fair, judicious, and central in importance. We concede, with Habermas, that neither Parsons nor his students – nor the students of any theoretical tradition – have as yet given satisfactory responses to these questions.

Münch's elaboration and development of Bershady's insights into the neo-Kantian foundations of Parsons' theory is an important contribution. But a caution must be observed in reading Parsons through the lens of Luhmann and continental, especially German, traditions of social philosophy. As important as the German tradition is for Parsons, his work has also absorbed and been shaped throughout by traditional Anglo-American concerns with pragmatic and procedural restraints on arbitrary power. These concerns are not easily grasped within a strictly Kantian – or, for that matter, Hegelian – interpretation.

Alexander has made a thorough, long overdue, assessment of Parsons' distinctive combination of analytic strength, methodological complexity, and rejection of materialist reduction. At the same time, we are not persuaded that Alexander's case for the presence of strongly neopositivistic and idealistic strands is substantiated by Parsons' work. Alexander's logic is strongly propelled by assertions that Parsons conflated analytic distinctions with concrete observations. We think that Parsons' concepts must, as a rule, be read as analytic except when he explicitly said otherwise. Alexander departs often from this rule, and these departures are the main base on which his case for Parsons' methodological neopositivism and presuppositional idealism are constructed.

The significance of the interpretive analysis of Parsons' work is twofold, in Europe, and particularly in Germany, the rigor and breadth of Parsons' analytical framework, and consequently its value for considering the existential and philosophical problems of modernity, are sufficient to sustain interest in Parsonian theory. But the major indicator for the future acceptance of Parsons' theory in American sociology will be the quality and quantity of empirical work inspired by it. The citations here represent a reopening in this empirical direction following a period of quiescence – but only an opening.

Notes

1. Parsons revised or reversed key formulations of *The Social System* in a variety of later texts; for explicit examples, see Parsons 1961, pp. 331–2; 1969a, p. 395n; 1969b, p. 486n; 1971, pp. 383–5; 1978b, p. 367n. More subtle or less explicitly acknowledged departures from *The Social System* are pervasive (see, e.g., Parsons 1967, pp. 15, 28; 1970, pp. 844ff).

2. See, for example, the treatments by Mitchell (1967), Gouldner (1970), Bershady (1973), Rocher (1975), Adriaansens (1976), Loubser et al (1976), Menzies (1977), Bourricaud (1977), and Alexander (1978).

In addition to the published texts, a large body of unpublished material still awaits analysis (V. M. Lidz, private communication); some of this unpublished corpus may be expected to appear over the next several years, particularly (a) a long essay written in 1940–41 entitled "Actor, situation, and normative pattern," which is intermediate between the theoretical formulations in Parsons (1937) and Parsons (1951); (b) a long empirical and theoretical analysis of social science as a national resource, written by Parsons in 1947 to influence the formation of the National Science Foundation (Klausner & Lidz, 1985); (c) the key chapters on American values from a book manuscript written with Winston White between 1958 to 1962, entitled *American Society*: and (d) Parsons' last book, in nearly final draft (800 ms pp) at his death, called *The American Societal Community*.

References

Adriaansens, H. P. M. 1976. Transl. 1980. *Talcott Parsons and the Conceptual Dilemma*. London: Routledge. 1980.

Alexander, J. C. 1978. "Formal and Substantive Voluntarism". *Am. Sociol. Rev.* 13: 177–98.

Alexander, J. C. 1980. "Core Solidarity, Ethnic Outgroup, and Social Differentiation: A Multidimensional Model of Inclusion in Modern Societies". In *National and Ethnic Movements*, ed. J. Dofny, A. Akiwowo, pp. 5–28. Beverly Hills: Sage.

Alexander, J. C. 1981. "The Mass News Media in Systemic, Historical, and Comparative Perspective". In *Mass Media and Social Change*, ed. E. Katz and T. Szecsko, pp. 17–52. Beverly Hills: Sage.
Alexander, J. C. 1982a. *Theoretical Logic in Sociology*, Volume 1, *Positivism. Presuppositions, And Current Controversies*. Berkeley: Univ. of Calif. 234 pp.
Alexander, J. C. 1982b. *Theoretical Logic in Sociology*, Volume 2, *The Antinomies Of Classical Thought: Marx and Durkheim*. Berkeley: Univ. of Calif. 564 pp.
Alexander, J. C. 1983a. *Theoretical Logic in Sociology*, Volume 3, *The Classical Attempt At Theoretical Synthesis: Max Weber*. Berkeley: Univ. of Calif. 240 pp.
Alexander, J. C. 1983b. *Theoretical Logic in Sociology*, Volume 4, *The Modern Reconstruction of Classical Thought: Talcott Parsons*.
Alexander, J. C. 1984a. "Watergate and the Crisis of Civil Society". In *Sociological Theory*, 1984, ed. R. Collins, pp. 290–314. San Francisco: Jossey-Bass.
Alexander, J. C. 1984b. "The Parsons revival in Germany". In *Sociological Theory*, 1984, ed. R. Collins, pp. 394–412. San Francisco: Jossey-Bass.
Almond, G. A., Powell, G. B. 1966. *Comparative Politics: A Developmental Approach*. Boston: Little, Brown.
Apter, D. E. 1965. *The Politics of Modernization*. Chicago: Univ. of Chicago. 481 pp.
Attewell, P., Gerstein, D. 1979. "Government Policy and Local Practice: The Case of Methodone Maintenance". *Am. Sociol. Rev.* 44: 311–327.
Baum, R. C. 1976a. "Communication and Media". See Loubser et al. 1976, pp 533–556.
Baum, R. C. 1976b. "On Societal Media Dynamics". See Loubser et al. 1976, pp. 579–608.
Baum, R. C. 1978. "The Holocaust – Anomic Hobbesian 'state of nature'". *Zeitschrift für Soziologie* 7: 303–26.
Baum, R. C. 1981. *The Holocaust and the German Elite: Genocide and National Suicide in Germany, 1871–1945*. Totowa, NJ: Rowman & Littlefield. 374 pp.
Baum, R. C., Lechner, F. J. 1981. "National Socialism: Towards an Actional-Theoretical Interpretation". *Sociol. Inq.* 51: 281–308.
Bershady, H. J. 1973. *Ideology and Social Knowledge*. New York: Wiley.
Bourricaud, F. 1977. (tr. 1981) *The Sociology of Talcott Parsons*. Chicago: Univ. of Chicago. 326 pp.
Black, M. 1961. "Some Questions about Parsons' Theories". In *The Social Theories of Talcott Parsons*, ed. M. Black, pp. 268–88. Carbondale: Southern Ill. Univ. Press.
Bryant, C. G. A. 1983. "Review Article: Who Now Reads Parsons?" *Sociol. Rev.* 31: 337–49.
Chomsky, N. 1965. *Aspects of the Theory of Syntax*, Cambridge: M.I.T. Press.
Cohen, J., Hazelrigg, L. D., Pope, W. 1975. "De-Parsonizing Weber: A Critique of Parsons' Interpretation of Weber's Sociology". *Am. Sociol. Rev.* 40: 229–41.
Colomy, P. 1985. "Uneven Differentiation: Towards Comparative Theory". In *NeoFunctionalism*, ed. J. Alexander. Beverly Hills: Sage. In press.
Dahrendorf, R. 1959. *Class and Class Conflict in Industrial Society*. Stanford: Stanford Univ. Press. 336 pp.
Dubin, R. 1960. "Parsons' Actors: Continuities on Social Theory". *Am. Sociol. Rev.* 25: 457–66.
Edelson, M. 1976. "Toward a Study of Interpretation in Psychoanalysis". See Loubser et al 1976, pp. 151–181.
Fuller, L. L. 1964. *The Morality of Law*. New Haven: Yale Univ. Press.
Fuller, L. L. 1969. *Anatomy of the Law*. New York: Praeger.

Gerstein, D. R. 1975. "A Note on the Continuity of Parsonian Action Theory". *Sociol. Inq.* 45 (4): 11–15.

Gerstein, D. R. 1976. "The Structure of Heroin Communities" (in relation to methodone maintenance). *Am. J. Drug & Alcohol Abuse.*

Gerstein, D. R. 1981a. "A Reminiscence of Talcott Parsons, September 1970 to April 1979". *Sociol. Inq.* 51: 166–70.

Gerstein, D. R. 1981b. "Cultural Action and Heroin Addiction". *Sociol. Inq.* 51: 355–70.

Gerstein, D. R. 1983. "Durkheim's Paradigm: Reconstructing a Social Theory". In *Sociological Theory* 1983, ed. R. Collins, pp. 234–258. San Francisco: Jossey-Bass.

Gerstein, D. R. 1986. "A Theory of the Addiction Complex". In *Micro and Macro Levels in Sociological Theory*, ed. J. C. Alexander, H. Haferkamp, R. Münch, N. J. Smelser. Berkeley: Univ. of Calif. Press. In press.

Giddens, A. 1968. "'Power' in the Recent Writings of Talcott Parsons". *Sociology* 2: 257–272.

Giddens, A. 1976. "Classical Social Theory and the Origins of Modern Sociology". *Am. J. Sociol.* 81: 703–729.

Gould, C. C., Walker, A. L., Crane, L. E., Lidz, C. W. 1974. "Connections: Notes from the Heroin World". New Haven: Yale Univ. Press. 736 pp.

Gould, M. 1976. "System Analysis, Macrosociology, and the Generalized Media of Social Action". See Loubser et al. 1976. pp. 470–506.

Gouldner, A. W. 1970. *The Coming Crisis of Western Sociology.* New York: Basic.

Habermas, J. 1973. *Legitimation Crisis.* Boston: Beacon.

Habermas, J. 1977. "Hannah Arendt's Communications Concept of Power". *Soc. Res.* 41: 3–24.

Habermas, J. 1981a. "Talcott Parsons: Problems of Theory Construction". *Sociol. Inq.* 51 (3/4): 173–96.

Habermas, J. 1981b. *Theorie des Kommunikativen Handelns.* Frankfurt: Suhrkamp.

Hacker, A. 1961. "Sociology and Ideology". In *The Social Theories of Talcott Parsons*, ed. M. Black, pp. 289–310. Carbondale: Southern Ill. Univ.

Hayes, A. C. 1981. "Structure and Creativity: The Use of Transformational-Generative Models in Action Theory". *Sociol. Inq.* 51 (3/4): 219–39.

Homans, G. 1964. "Bringing Men Back In". *Am. Sociol. Rev.* 79: 808–18.

Klausner, S., Lidz, V. W. 1985. *Social Science: A Basic National Resource.* Philadelphia: Univ. Penn. Press. In press.

Lechner, 1985. "Modernity and its Discontents: Revitalization Syndromes in Action-Theoretical Perspectives". In *NeoFunctionalism.* ed. J. Alexander. Beverly Hills: Sage.

Levy, M. 1957. *The Structure of Society.* Princeton: Princeton Univ. Press.

Lidz, C. W., Lidz, V. M. 1976. "Piaget's Psychology of Intelligence and the Theory of Action". See Loubser et al 1976, pp. 195–239.

Lidz, C. W., Walker, A. L. 1978. "Therapeutic Control of Heroin: Dedifferentiating Legal and Psychiatric Controls". *Social System And Legal Process.* ed. H. M. Johnson, pp. 294–321. San Francisco: Jossey-Bass.

Lidz, C. W., Walker, A. L. 1980. *Heroin, Deviance, and Morality* Beverly Hills: Sage. 269 pp.

Lidz, V. M. 1976. "Introduction to Part II: General Action Analysis". See Loubser et al 1976, pp. 124–150.

Lidz, V. M. 1979a. "Secularization, Ethical Life and Religion in Modern Societies". In *Religious Change and Continuity. Sociological Perspectives*, ed. H. M. Johnson, pp. 191–217. San Francisco: Jossey-Bass.

Lidz, V. M. 1979b. "The Law as Index, Phenomenon, and Element – Conceptual Steps Toward a General Sociology of Law". *Sociol. Inq.* 49 (1): 5–26.

Lidz, V. M. 1981. "Conceptions of Value-Relevance and the Theory of Action". *Sociol. Inq.* 51: 371–408.

Lidz, V. M. 1985. "Television and the Moral Order in a Secular Age". In *Interpreting Television*, ed. W. D. Rowland, Jr., B. Watkins. Beverly Hills: Sage.

Lockwood, D. 1956. "Some Remarks on *The Social System*". *Br. J. Sociol.* 7: 134–46.

Loubser, J. J., Baum, R. C., Effrat, A., Lidz, V. M. 1976. *Explorations in General Theory in Social Science: Volumes 1 and 2.* New York: Free. 909 pp.

Loubser, J. J. 1976. "The Values Problem in Social Science in Developmental Perspective". See Loubser et al 1976, pp. 75–89.

Luhmann, N. 1976. "Generalized Media and the Problem of Contingency." See Loubser et al 1976, pp. 507–32.

Luhmann, N. 1981. *The Differentiation of Society.* New York: Columbia Univ. Press.

Mayhew, L. 1976. "Methodological Dilemmas in Social Science". See Loubser et al 1976, pp. 59–74.

Menzies, K. 1977. *Talcott Parsons and the Social Image of Man.* London: Routledge. 197 pp.

Merton, R. K. 1957. *Social Theory and Social Structure.* Revised and enlarged edition. New York: Free Press.

Mills, C. W. 1959. In *The Sociological Imagination.* London/New York: Oxford Univ. Press.

Mitchell, W. C. 1967. *Sociological Analysis and Politics: The Theories of Talcott Parsons.* Englewood Cliffs, N.J.: Prentice-Hall. 222 pp.

Mullins, N. C. 1983. *Theories and theory groups revisited.* In *Sociological Theory* 1983. ed. R. Collins, pp. 319–38. San Francisco: Jossey-Bass.

Münch, R. 1981a. "Socialization and Personality Development from the Point of View of Action Theory, the Legacy of Emile Durkheim". *Sociol. Inq.* 51 (3/4): 331–54.

Münch, R. 1981b. "Talcott Parsons and the Theory of Action. I. The Structure of the Kantian Core". *Am. J. Sociol.* 86: 709–39.

Münch, R. 1982a. "Talcott Parsons and the Theory of Action. II. The Continuity of the Development". *Am. J. Sociol.* 87: 771–826.

Münch, R. 1982b. *Theorie des Handelns – Zur Rekonstruktion der Beitrage, von Talcott Parsons, Emile Durkheim, und Max Weber.* Frankfurt: Suhrkamp. 693 pp.

Parsons, T. 1937. *The Structure of Social Action: A Study in Social Theory with Special Reference to a Group of Recent European Writers.* New York: Macmillan. 817 pp.

Parsons, T. 1951. *The Social System.* Glencoe, Ill.: Free Press.

Parsons, T. 1960. "Pattern Variables Revisited: A Response to Robert Dubin". *Am. Sociol. Rev.* 25: 466–84.

Parsons, T. 1961. "The Point of View of the Author". In *The Social Theories of Talcott Parsons: A Critical Examination.* ed. M. Black, pp. 311–363. Carbondale: Southern Ill. Univ. Press.

Parsons, T. 1967. "Durkheim's Contribution to the Theory of Integration of Social Systems". In *Sociological Theory and Modern Society*, pp. 3–34. New York: Free Press.

Parsons, T. 1969a. "On the Concept of Political Power". In *Politics and Social Structure*, pp. 35–404. New York: Free Press.

Parsons, T. 1969b. "Polity and Society: Some General Considerations". In *Politics and Social Structure*, pp. 473–522. New York: Free Press.

Parsons, T. 1970. "On Building Social Systems Theory: A Personal History". *Dædalus* 99: 826–81.
Parsons, T. 1971. "Commentary". In *Institutions and Social Exchange: The Sociologies of Talcott Parsons and George C. Homans*. ed. H. Turk, R. L. Simpson. Indianapolis: Bobbs-Merrill.
Parsons, T. 1978a. "Law as an Intellectual Stepchild". In *Social System and Legal Process.* ed. H. M. Johnson, pp. 11–58. San Francisco: Jossey-Bass.
Parsons, T. 1978b. "A Paradigm of the Human Condition". In *Action Theory and the Human Condition.* ed. T. Parsons, pp. 352–433. New York: Free Press.
Parsons, T., Gerstein, D. R. 1977. "The Case of Social Deviance: Addiction to Heroin, Addiction to Power". In *Deviance and Social Change*, ed. E. Sagarin, pp. 19–57. Beverly Hills: Sage.
Parsons, T., Platt, P. 1973. *The American University.* Cambridge: Harvard Univ. Press.
Parsons, T., Shils, E. A. 1951. *Toward a General Theory of Action: Theoretical Foundations for the Social Sciences.* Cambridge: Harvard Univ. Press. 506 pp.
Parsons, T., Smelser, N. J. 1956. *Economy and Society.* New York: Free Press. 322 pp.
Piccone, P. 1968. "Functionalism, Teleology and Objectivity", *Monist* 52: 408–23.
Platt, G. M. 1981. "The American University: Collaboration with Talcott Parsons". *Sociol. Inq.* 51: 155–65.
Rocher, G. 1975. *Talcott Parsons and American Sociology.* New York: Harper & Row.
Sciulli, D. 1984. "Parsons' Analytical Critique of Marxism's Concept of Alienation". *Am. J. Sociol.* 90: 514–40.
Sciulli, D. 1985. "The Practical Groundwork for Critical Theory: Bringing Habermas to Parsons (and vice versa)". In *NeoFunctionalism*, ed. J. C. Alexander. Beverly Hills: Sage. In press.
Sciulli, D. 1986. "Political Differentiation and Collegiality". In *Differentiation Theory: Problems and Prospects*, ed. J. C. Alexander, P. Colomy. Berkeley: Univ. of Calif. In press.
Smelser, N. J. 1959. *Social Change in the Industrial Revolution.* Chicago: Univ. of Chicago Press.
Smelser, N. J. 1981. "On Collaborating with Talcott Parsons: Some Intellectual and Personal Notes". *Sociol. Inq.* 51: 113–51.
Turner, T. S. 1976. "Family Structure and Socialization". See Loubser et al 1976, pp. 415–46.
Walker, C. W., Lidz, A. L. 1983. "Commonalities in Troublesome Habitual Behaviors: A Cultural Approach". In *Commonalities in Substance Abuse and Habitual Behavior.* ed. P. K. Levison, D. R. Gerstein, D. R. Maloff., pp. 29–44. Lexington: Heath.
Wallace, R. A. 1985. "Religion, Privatization, and Maladaptation". *Sociol. Anal.* In press.
Warner, R. S. 1978. "Toward a Redefinition of Action Theory: Paying the Cognitive Element its Due". *Am. J. Sociol.* 83 (6): 1317–19.
Wright, E. O. 1983. "Is Marxism Really Functionalist, Class Reductionist, and Teleological?" *Am. J. Sociol.* 89: 152–59.
Wrong, D. 1961. "The Oversocialized Conception of Man in Modern Sociology". *Am. Sociol. Rev.* 6: 183–93.

68

The Role of Efficiency and Power in Explanations of Division of Labour

Dietrich Rueschemeyer

We now turn to our main concern – the explanation of division of labour and the role power plays in its development. The preceding discussion of the results of division of labour has, paradoxically, already introduced us to major notions of causal explanation. This is due to the particular prevailing mode of analyzing division of labour.

The most common explanation of division of labour is its efficiency. The overall advances of division of labour, as well as the specific forms it takes, are seen as coming about because the more differentiated roles and organizations 'function more effectively in the new historical circumstances' (Smelser, 1963: 34; see also 1959: 2). This is a functionalist explanation: division of labour occurs, advances and takes specific forms because its consequences are 'functional' for a broader system.

This explanation is pervasive in current sociology and current social thought in general, even though it is rarely stated in fully developed form. In fact, it is perhaps more accurate to say that this explanation is rarely made explicit *because* it is so much taken for granted. The formulation just quoted, for instance, is part of Smelser's *definition* of structural differentiation; technically, then, any assertion about more specialized roles being more efficient becomes a tautology since greater efficiency has been made part of the very concept of structural differentiation. In recent structural functional theories of evolution and modernization (Parsons, 1966 and 1971; Smelser, 1959 and 1963), structural differentiation holds a central place, but it is often not directly explained. It mainly serves merely to identify the social changes studied, while the analysis focuses on the interrelations between different components of these processes (between differentiation and integration, for example) and on some of their consequences, rather than on their own explanation. However, structural differentiation is in these theories so closely associated with higher productivity,

---

Source: Dietrich Rueschemeyer, *Power and the Division of Labor* (Cambridge: Polity Press, 1986).

improved efficiency and greater 'adaptive capacity' that an efficiency explanation suggests itself – is, in fact, implied.

In his attempt to construct a theory of occupational prestige Donald Treiman (1977: 6) flatly states this implication: 'The basic factor promoting the division of labor is its efficiency. Relative to unspecialized labor, specialized labor is far more efficient.' Treiman then proceeds to give some reasons for expecting greater productivity from division of labour, but he does not bother to explain how the latter is caused by the former – how, to put it drastically, the child, greater productivity, gives birth to its mother, specialization.

The Functionalist Mode of Analysis

The structural-functionalist conception of society is not the only theoretical position that views division of labour as propelled and steered by efficiency gains. Similar ideas are found commonly in classical and neoclassical economics as well as in different varieties of Marxian thought.[1] It will be useful to take a closer look at the logic of functionalist analysis. This provides a counterfoil against which we can give our conception of the role of power in processes of division of labour and differentiation a more sharply defined profile.

Functional explanations do involve intricate problems, though these are not as insurmountable as the simile of child and mother, used above, suggests. Functional analysis takes off from the observation that, under varying circumstances and in spite of apparent obstacles, a social goal is repeatedly realized, a social formation remains stable, a pattern of change keeps its direction. It then asks which mechanisms are responsible for these persistent outcomes – even under adverse conditions. It asks how the political economy of capitalism gains its astounding staying power, why the upbringing of the young is a success in the overwhelming number of cases or in what way conflicts are kept from escalating into a violence that ruptures the social fabric. So far there is nothing specially problematic about this approach. It identifies important issues for investigation.

The problems begin when the existence and social reproduction of the functional patterns themselves are explained by the 'function they serve' – when stratification is explained by the part it plays in insuring that the work of society gets done, the incest taboo by its role in the protection of parental authority, division of labour by its contribution to greater productivity. It plainly will not do just to make the *assumption* that what is functionally important will, therefore, somehow come into existence and continue to play an active part under varied and adverse conditions – whether the functional 'need' is that of a society or of a dominant class. 'If wishes were horses, beggars would ride.' Rather what is necessary, if the functionalist approach is to be extended from a fruitful problem formulation to a comprehensive explanation, is an account of how the development and maintenance of the functional mechanisms come about and how their own causation and reproduction are linked to their functional contributions.

A functional analysis that is also able to provide a comprehensive causal explanation, then, consists of a set of interlinked causal propositions. To return to the efficiency explanation of division of labour, it has to theoretically specify and empirically demonstrate that division of labour makes for greater efficiency and how mechanisms related to this outcome activate processes which, in turn, bring about division of labour, its general advance, and the specific forms it takes. Each component of this agenda is problematic. The efficiency outcomes of specialization cannot be taken for granted; the 'feedback mechanisms' tying effects of division of labour back to its conditions are far from clear; and, as we shall see, even the very meaning of efficiency becomes, on closer examination, a Pandora's box of unresolved questions.

Although it has been taken as established beyond doubt since the beginnings of modern economic and social thought, the proposition that specialization makes for greater efficiency cannot be taken for granted.[2] It does rest on a number of plausible hypotheses, yet for each of these there are variable conditions favouring or inhibiting the predicted outcome that are not at all well understood. Furthermore, the relative importance of the different factors remains rather obscure. Finally, and most important, division of labour has effects other than those listed in the typical discussion of its productivity advantages – effects which counterbalance those commonly singled out. Such 'costs' of differentiation arise, for instance, from the need to coordinate and integrate the specialized parts, or from problems of morale and motivation created by job fragmentation. The balance of costs and gains in regard to efficiency may be positive or negative, depending on the specific patterns of specialization and on complex social and cultural conditions. What ultimately counts, of course, is the net effect; it is not a foregone conclusion that it will be positive.

The question of how new forms of specialization come about *because* of their positive results for productivity may seem at first sight simpler. If a convincing answer can be found to that question, it promises to solve with the same stroke the knotty problem just discussed, because it would be only the positively functional forms of division of labour that would be so encouraged, that is, those which enhance productivity. The selective advance of functional forms of division of labour is intuitively plausible on two grounds. First, with something as desirable and important as getting work done efficiently people will, so it seems, know or eventually learn about cause and effect and act accordingly. Second, this plausible subjective response would be reinforced and complemented by objective constraints. Social selection would, in analogy to natural selection, eliminate inefficient forms. Parasites with a precarious life cycle involving different host organisms 'need' to produce masses of eggs for the species to survive in a given environment. The varieties which did not develop this or an equivalent adaptation did not survive. Similarly, the forms of division of labour are exposed to constant selective pressures; in comparison to others, those which are wasteful are shown up as impossibly costly by these pressures. This similarity would seem no less relevant, if the variety of forms on which this selective pressure works does not come about by random variation, as do genetic mutations, but also involves rational anticipation and evaluative assessment of events after the fact.

Both of these ideas have been used in the analysis of division of labour, though different theories give more weight to one or the other.[3] I shall briefly describe and comment on two theoretical accounts – those of Neil Smelser and Talcott Parsons – before I turn to a closer analysis of the concepts of efficiency and productivity, which will bring out radical problems for a functionalist understanding of social differentiation.

Two Functionalist Accounts of Division of Labour

Neil Smelser (1959) applies a theoretical paradigm of structural differentiation to changes in the Lancashire cotton industry from 1770 to 1840. In his theoretical scheme – and it, rather than the details of its application to the historical data, is of interest here – he posits seven phases of change. These begin with dissatisfaction about the status quo, which may give rise to disturbances and utopian schemes; these then are subjected to social control; experimental attempts at solutions follow, which are assessed in terms of reasserted societal values; eventually, selected new forms of social organization are established and routinized (Smelser, 1959: 15f. and 404). Not all phases occur necessarily in each instance of social change, says Smelser, nor are the phases neatly separated from each other in the flow of historical events. There also can be a return to earlier phases. Yet the end result is a more differentiated organization of production, and of working-class family life, that is also more productive. The overall process represents a collective response to felt problems and dissatisfactions which is steered by common values. Shot through with irrational disturbances and groping trial and error, differentiation is seen as a fundamentally rational adaptation of collective organization to changed circumstances.

Smelser's approach interestingly combines rational and nonrational moments in social change and yet it can, by using collective values as a reference point, see the final outcome as collectively rational after turbulences are subdued. Smelser offers little argument as to why we should expect exactly this combination of moments in the process of differentiation – why non-rational responses should subside or be subdued; why more productive and more specialized arrangements should be the final outcome. These questions point to important unresolved theoretical problems. Foremost is one mentioned earlier. The outcome of increased division of labour is never really in question because improved efficiency is made part of the concept of differentiation, and because differentiation is conceived as an overall process within which different specific causal factors find their place rather than as a phenomenon which itself needs explanation. Dedifferentiation, different forms of division of labour that are not necessarily more specialized or even the maintenance of the status quo, however tension-ridden, are not even contemplated as potential outcomes. Nor is it asked whether such alternatives are possibly of similar or perhaps greater efficiency. Here I take issue not so much with Smelser's historical interpretation, but with an analytic paradigm that does not even raise these questions.

In view of twentieth-century functionalism's debts to Durkheim it is ironic that Smelser's approach, with its focus on an ultimately rational pursuit of productivity gains, is also open to the criticism Durkheim leveled against the utilitarian analysis of division of labour (provided Smelser's approach is extended to that long-term advance of division of labour which primarily interested Durkheim). Needs and wants, as well as common values, change historically. Hence, Durkheim argued, they cannot provide a long-term reference point for changes in a division of labour steered by efficiency gains:

> If [our ancestors] were so greatly tormented by the desire to increase the productive power of work, it was not to achieve goods without value to them. To appreciate these goods, they would have had to contract tastes and habits they did not have, which is to say, to change their nature. That is indeed what they have done, as the history of the transformations through which humanity has passed shows. For the need of greater happiness to account for the development of the division of labor, it would then be necessary for it also to be the cause of the changes progressively wrought in human nature, and for men to have changed in order to become happier (Durkheim, 1893/1964: 240).

I should repeat that Durkheim's criticism does not directly apply to Smelser's argument since Smelser begins his analysis with felt dissatisfaction. It does, however, raise serious questions about efficiency advantages as the reference point for a long-term functional explanation of differentiation. In particular, Durkheim's argument also seems to be at odds with any conception of functional requisites of societal life determinate enough to allow clear-cut explanations of social differentiation. All societies have to deal with problems of scarcity; all have to educate the young; all have to contain conflicts; all have to keep the motivation of sufficient numbers of people sufficiently alive; and all have to bring these various concerns under 'one roof' – arrange for coping with them more or less simultaneously.[4] But the question is whether there are not a very large number of options for doing so. If that is the case, even a definitive list of functional requirements of human social life would not be determinate enough to constitute a satisfactory reference point for a functional explanation of division of labour. Human needs and wants and social values would *variably* give more specific meaning to such bare-bone 'functional requisites' in different cultures and societies.

Needs, wants, values and the functional requirements for realizing or approximating them are, in the conception of human history which this interpretation ascribes to Durkheim, shaped by social and cultural forces. Among other factors, the very pattern of division of labour whose explanation is to be furthered by references to these culturally variable needs, wants and values is responsible for changes in the latter. We will take up these ideas of Durkheim again when we look more closely below at the meaning of 'efficiency' and 'productivity'.

In *Societies: evolutionary and comparative perspectives* (1966), Talcott Parsons develops his 'paradigm of evolutionary change', a conceptual framework for tracing the ramifications of specific 'developmental breakthroughs' throughout the functional subsystems of a society.[5] Parsons's discussion is even less concerned than Smelser's with a causal explanation of social differentiation. There are fewer directly explanatory ideas and Parsons's paradigm is more open-ended. His arguments, nevertheless, have a number of interesting implications for problems of causation. A first is that evaluative assessment of past experience and rational anticipation move into the background as we turn from families and economic enterprises to whole societies as units of analysis. In Parsons's account of societal evolution the main 'feedback mechanism' linking the outcomes of evolutionary advances to their conditions is competitive pressure, though imitation and borrowing also play a role. However, the outcomes of competitive pressure have a far from clear-cut relationship to specific 'developmental breakthroughs'. They do not simply give a premium to developments that are, other things equal, an enhancement of efficient functioning in dealing with one aspect of a given environment. One reason for this is that competitive advantage results from a balance of many factors and a given innovation may be outweighed by other factors. Certain societies 'may, indeed, be so beset with internal conflicts or other handicaps that they can hardly maintain themselves, or will even deteriorate. But among these may be . . . some of the most creative societies from the viewpoint of originating components of great long-run importance' (Parsons, 1966: 23).

The creative decadence of what Parsons calls 'seedbed societies' is not the only element that blurs the correspondence between competitive advantage and innovations that enhance efficiency. The following broad statement by Parsons (1966: 23–4) indicates quite a few alternatives to selective survival of the most efficient forms of social organization – and only of those:

> A [developmental] breakthrough endows its society with a new level of adaptive capacity in some vital respect, thereby changing the terms of its competitive relations with other societies in the system. Broadly, this kind of situation opens four possibilities for societies not immediately sharing the innovation. The innovation can simply be destroyed by more powerful, even if less advanced rivals. If the innovation is cultural, though, it is difficult to destroy completely, and may assume great importance even after its society of origin has been destroyed. Second, the terms of competition may be evened through adoption of the

innovations. The present drive to 'modernisation' among underdeveloped societies is an obvious and important case in point. A third alternative is the establishment of an insulated niche in which a society can continue to maintain its old structure, relatively undisturbed. The final possibility is the loss of societal identity through disintegration or absorption by some larger societal system. These possibilities are type concepts, and many complex combinations and shadings of them may occur.

The 'feedback' from efficiency outcomes of social differentiation to the conditions which account for its advances – the link of crucial importance in the explanatory chain of a functional efficiency explanation of division of labour – is thus beset by many problems and ambiguities. Rational assessment and understanding, differential survival of competing arrangements, and diffusion from one organization or society to another are all relevant and important here; but they are all subject to severe qualifications, which vary in unknown ways with changing circumstances. Evaluative assessment and anticipatory planning are never fully rational; they are the more limited the larger the social unit in question and the more complex its functioning. Competitive pressures may select against important innovations and let ineffective patterns survive in relative isolation. And diffusion, often based on less than thorough understanding, may or may not result in successful transplants and recombinations of elements in the overall sociocultural pattern of the host society. The circumstances under which these 'feedback' mechanisms work with different degrees of imprecision, and the ways in which they influence each other, are problems that remain rather obscure.

The Concept of Efficiency

There is a still more far-reaching problem that stands in the way of successful functionalist explanations of division of labour based on increased efficiency or 'adaptive capacity'. This concerns the meaning of efficiency. Any judgement about efficiency – the economical use of means in the pursuit of specific goals – hinges on a ranking of goals and on an evaluation of the cost of alternative means to reach these goals – cost being equal to the value of goals forgone by using the means chosen. What is an efficient use of means by one preference structure informing such ranking and evaluation may clearly be wasteful in terms of another.

It is at this point that we return to 'Durkheim's problem'. Insisting that people acquire different needs and wants – in effect, change their nature in 'the transformations through which humanity has passed' – Durkheim objected to a utilitarian explanation of division of labour as driven by a search for greater happiness. The same insight, when applied to divisions of experience, interests and values *within* a society at one time, turns into an objection to reasoning in terms of efficiency advantages for a whole society.

Not only different cultures, but lord and serf, entrepreneur and worker, executive and employee, as well as many other groups and social categories, differ fundamentally in their evaluations of the price paid and the advantage gained with a new arrangement of their social relations; and if their preferences and cost-benefit calculi vary, the meaning of efficiency, determined by varied interests and value commitments, also differs. In addition, we have seen in the previous chapter that division of labour has multiple consequences, contradictory in nature even when evaluated by a single set of standards of desirability and uneven in their impact on different groups. Once the formal character of the concept of efficiency is recognized, the question of which – or better, *whose* – preferences and interests are determinant in shaping social processes cannot be avoided. A functional explanation of division of labour in terms of efficiency gains as such becomes meaningless except in the borderline case of a society with virtually complete consensus about needs, wants and values.[6] It is for these reasons that I argue for including power systematically into the explanatory paradigm.

Before I discuss the implications of such a focus on power for explaining division of labour, however, I have to return to an issue briefly touched earlier in chapter 2 (Rueschemeyer, 1986). Is the problem of contradictory preferences not solved by the market? Classical and neoclassical economics argue that the market overcomes the divergence and contradiction among individual preferences by assigning an economy-wide value to all costs and products. Market prices – for materials, capital, labour as well as goods produced and services rendered – aggregate individual patterns of evaluation and represent a collective preference structure. This solution of the problem, it is argued, does not require shared values nor the exercise of power. It relies solely on the autonomous interaction of the participants in economic exchange.

The market represents indeed an instrument of coordination and integration of the greatest significance; one not sufficiently appreciated and studied by much of sociological analysis. However, the market does not provide a solution to our problem. Most obviously the market argument does not apply to non-marketed activities, to household work no more than to tax collection. Even for goods and services that are contractually exchanged the proposition that the market's integration of individual choices into a collective preference pattern does not involve power and bypasses issues of value consensus and divergence depends on unrealistic assumptions.

It presupposes completely free access to all markets so that market participation itself is not a privilege. It requires perfect competition within markets so that no one of the competitors can influence the price through decisions about supply or demand. It assumes an equal distribution of financial resources with which to turn needs and wants into effective demand. And it has to make the assumption that costs and benefits which do not enter the market calculus – from parental love and public defence to pollution and health hazards – do not give one set of people advantages over another. If these conditions were met, the outcome of the market's operation might still not conform to a particular conception of humane work and just distribution, but it would indeed represent a collective pattern of choice that is independent of shared or contested values and not the result of imposition by power.

Yet each of these assumptions is unrealistic. The very institutional infrastructure needed for the market's functioning, the legal regulation of property, contract, association and incorporation, is never neutral *vis-à-vis* the interests of different economic actors; yet it is guaranteed by the coercion machinery of the state.[7] Access to markets is often limited by custom and law as well as by capital and skill requirements. Perfect competition exists, in a literal sense, only in the economists' imagination; though it is true that many of its effects (such as the spur to pursue one's advantage assiduously) are retained in less than perfectly competitive markets, any deviation from the model implies power inequalities among the competitors and between those who buy and those who supply a particular good or service. Income is always unevenly distributed; so much so in most societies that the needs and wants of the poor, however urgent, do not affect the market choices as much as even superficial whims of the wealthy. Finally which resources – from roads and aircraft carriers to education and health maintenance – are made available outside the market and which are left to the play of supply and demand is to a large extent a matter of politics and of the role of the state in the political economy; so is the issue of whether dirty air becomes a priced cost of industrial production. Each of these qualifications underscores the role of power even in market exchange. Rather than representing an alternative to a power solution of the problem of divergent preferences, the market is in fact one of the mechanisms through which power is acquired and imposed.[8]

Focusing on Power

How does a focus on power help us deal with the problem of multiple and divergent interests? Disproportionate power, power concentrated in the hands of individuals and groups with similar interests and preferences, means that a certain type of cost-benefit calculus gains a disproportionate influence. The interests and reactions of the most powerful are thus a point of great leverage for any analysis of division of labour. In fact they actually are treated in such a manner in many studies, but the strategy typically remains implicit and does not receive adequate theoretical recognition. As we have seen, Smelser (1959) makes 'dissatisfaction' the first of several phases in a development of structural differentiation, but he does not specify theoretically whose dissatisfaction is relevant. In the empirical application of the theoretical framework this turns out to be the dissatisfaction of the early entrepreneurs and shop-owners. Eisenstadt, in his comparative analysis of pre-modern bureaucratization (1963), comes close to the position advocated here. He emphasizes in his explanation the interests of the ruler and, secondarily, those of the aristocracy and of urban groups, who gain importance and power with the advance of market exchange and bureaucratic rule.

If we focus on the interests of the powerful, the structure of theoretical reasoning may very well, though not necessarily, remain functional in character, taking off from efficiency gains and other consequences of division of labour and then seeking to identify links between these consequences and conditions favourable or unfavourable for processes of differentiation. The points of reference in the analysis, however, are strategically altered by focusing on the powerful. The preference structures relative to which the consequences of division of labour are analysed become more amenable to investigation. The unmanageable complexity of an endless variety of preference structures is reduced to a few. Furthermore, the behaviour and even the attitudes and sentiments of the more powerful are better documented in the historical record than the behaviour and attitudes of common people, an obvious advantage for any investigation of long-term social change (which almost by necessity must make use of historical sources).

Of similar if not greater theoretical interest is the fact that it appears possible to predict some of the interests pursued by the powerful. Clearly, this would very much increase the explanatory power of the analysis. It seems reasonable to assume (though this need not remain an untested assumption) that those in positions of power will seek to maintain their advantage and under certain conditions even attempt to increase it. It has been argued against this proposition that the assumed tendency depends on the total balance of benefits and costs experienced by incumbents of power positions as compared to their life chances when out of power, and that this balance varies with different circumstances in ways not easily predictable.[9] No doubt the proposition can and must be further refined and specified as to varying conditions. Yet as a rough generalization it seems established that greater power is not only often attractive in itself but tends to be associated with privilege and advantages of many kinds, even though these prizes need not always be so great as to invite fratricidal succession fights as they did, to cite one of the more famous examples, after the death of King David (1 Kings, chapters 1 and 2).

In addition, those in power will often think and act in terms of positional – in contrast to, and in addition to, personal – interests, strengthening a concern with maintaining their power resources. The interest in power is then transformed from a personal inclination into something owed to one's lineage, corporation or public office. Finally, for analyses involving large numbers of powerful individuals and groups one can advance the statistical argument that the proportion of those who seek to maintain and extend their advantage will be increased by virtue of the fact that they have a better chance of remaining in power positions than those who make no such efforts. This argument merely presupposes that power can vanish if it is not safeguarded, and that attempts to husband and extend power resources have some effect in the intended direction. Clearly, the powerful will pursue other interests as well; concern with maintaining their power resources is inevitably only one of several interests. However, to identify even one substantive interest that is relatively stable and relevant for policy and large-scale change is an important theoretical gain. We may speak, then, of a *raison du pouvoir* as an orientation of action that will typically be found among the powerful in all but the least complex societies.

The study of the 'causal loops' or 'feedback mechanisms' linking the consequences of division of labour to its conditions is also aided by a focus on power. Not only are the intentional reactions to perceived consequences stronger if they are those of the powerful; we can also exclude a number of effects from the analysis because in many instances the powerful will not suffer, and thus count as 'costs' some of the consequences of their policies. Increased monotony of work or heightened job insecurity, for instance, have been of little concern to entrepreneurs unless worker morale or the politics of labour relations seemed affected. Moreover, one can at least speculate that there is a correlation between holding positions of power and tending towards rational action – that is, action based on a review of goals and means in the light of one's basic preferences and the best information available about the consequences of alternative courses. Rational action in this sense is not independent of privilege; in fact it could be considered part of the standard package of social advantage except that privilege on occasion removes the spurs of ambition and necessity and dulls the urgency of goal-seeking. Rational action represents a causal loop linking consequences and conditions of division of labour to each other that is probably the more important the more we focus on power elites in command of a staff of domination.

It is not only the power of the most powerful – of political elites, of dominant classes, of the owners or executives controlling economic enterprises – that needs attention. Their counterparts, even if subordinate, also wield some power. The impact of interests and values different from those of the most powerful groups on processes of division of labour depends similarly on its backing by countervailing power of varying strength, and on similar issues concerning the translation of interests into assiduously pursued goals. For most subordinate groups the problem of how disparate actors can be brought together for collective action is especially grave. The problem is not absent in the case of aggregates of separately powerful actors with similar interests, but the many have greater difficulty to join forces for concerted action than the few; 'the masters,' as Adam Smith observed, 'being fewer in number, can combine much more easily' than workers or countrymen (Smith, 1776/1937: 66). Still, subordinate groups do not completely lack power, even without inclusive organization; and under favourable conditions they can also acquire the advantages that derive from attaining a capacity for effective collective action (Marx, 1847/n.d.: 145–6; Dahrendorf, 1959; Olson, 1965). Not only dominant power concentrations, but also the countervailing strength of subordinate groups, as well as the ensuing conflicts and their outcomes, must be taken into account in analyses of division of labour.

Formally, this can be represented in a simple model of a modified functional analysis, which Arthur Stinchcombe (1968: 93–8) has called 'Marxian functionalism'. The consequences of a given structural arrangement for different interests elicit responses in terms of these interests which are backed up by different amounts of power. The resulting balance of forces determines the maintenance of, or change in, the social structure in question, be it the institutions of representative democracy, the factory organization of work or a certain degree of job fragmentation. This model neglects a great many theoretical issues, including the problems of rational assessment and anticipation of facts and options, the difficulties of organizing for collective action, and the fact that even overwhelming power is not equivalent to social causation. It does, however, identify an important part of the agenda for an explanation of division of labour that focuses on power and retains the functional format of analysis.

Thus, focusing on phenomena of power in the study of division of labour and social differentiation leads out of the impasse that results for the prevailing functionalist efficiency explanations from the formal character of the concept of efficiency. It identifies more clearly the reference points for a modified functional analysis; it spells out more plausible 'causal loops' linking outcomes of division of labour to factors which, in turn, modify the patterns of specialization and differentiation; and it simplifies the empirical investigations required.

We can push the contrasting analysis of a functional explanation of division of labour, which uses shared values in a society as the ultimate reference point, and an explanation focusing on power one step further. Durkheim insisted that division of labour always presupposes a unity of the social whole within which division of labour takes place:

> The division of labor can . . . be produced only in the midst of a pre-existing society. By that we do not mean simply that individuals must adhere materially, but it is still necessary that there be moral links between them.

This insistence is related to his critique of utilitarian social theory (as he understood it), especially of Herbert Spencer's theory:

> If this important truth has been disregarded by the utilitarians, it is an error rooted in the manner in which they conceive of the genesis of society. They suppose originally isolated and independent individuals, who, consequently, enter into relationships only to cooperate, for they have no other reason to clear the space between them and to associate. But this theory, so widely held, postulates a veritable *creatio ex nihilo*.
>
> . . . Collective life is not born from individual life, but it is, on the contrary, the second which is born from the first (Durkheim, 1893/1964: 276–7 and 279).

This thesis — that division of labour can take place only within a moral community because collective life has analytic priority over individual life — led Durkheim to crucial insights. It was the foundation of his argument that contract cannot function without non-contractual institutional underpinnings and, more generally, that the institutions necessary for social life of a certain kind cannot be created at will by contracting individuals. At the same time, this thesis can hardly be maintained in a literal sense. Durkheim's own inconclusive discussion of international trade and international division of labour attests to this.[10]

Durkheim's conception of society as an overarching moral community has been of tremendous influence in twentieth-century functionalist social theory. It contains ideas worth preserving, even if one is critical of a consensus model of society which assumes fundamental agreement on values throughout society and which often implies this agreement is spontaneous. We have just seen that an analysis of social power (and of division of labour in terms of power) must be able to understand how mere aggregates of individuals and groups can acquire a broader collective identity that makes collective action possible. Any functional explanation of division of labour involves collective interests as reference points, be they those of an organization, a class, or a society. Thus, any contribution to an 'integration theory' that can help us understand the emergence of collective identities should be welcome to a wide variety of theoretical positions. Such contributions need not assume that individual and group allegiances to a wider collectivity are spontaneous, nor that they explain the integration of whole societies; they may well explain the coherence of classes and class fragments or even only of associations and organizations, rather than that of whole societies.

The exercise of power is one of the most important ways through which the inclination of rational members of large groups to opt for a 'free ride' may be counteracted and through which people can be made to support the common good of a collectivity (cf. Olson, 1965); coercive taxation in support of state action is only the most obvious, if not the least important, example. This is not to deny other bases of collective identity and collective action, including attachments to others, hostility to outgroups, identification with collective symbols and value commitments. A focus on power is, in fact, not in the least excluded by recognizing these factors.

It is important to state with great emphasis (though I will not elaborate it much here) that explanations of division of labour which focus on power *need not* be part of a larger theoretical argument of the functionalist kind. The substance of power interests and the distribution of power resources can more simply be analysed as causal determinants of social changes connected with division of labour and social differentiation. The approach I am proposing is very much concerned with a *process analysis* of division of labour. Power interests, differential power resources and the balance of power among different contestants are likely to be prominent among the causes of specific processes of specialization and differentiation, as well as among the causal conditions of blockages and reversals of differentiation. The promise that power variables hold for a better understanding of *processes* of division of labour is thus another important reason why a focus on power in the study of division of labour recommends itself.

Efficiency, productivity, individual and social welfare – these concepts may be considered 'essentially contested concepts' (Gallie, 1955–6), much like justice or democracy, exploitation or alienation. Insisting on the formal character of the concept of efficiency and arguing that what is good for some people may be bad for others, I have sought to bypass a contest about the substance of efficiency and welfare, individual or collective. Opting for the power approach to the analysis of division of labour and social differentiation means, then, that at this point in the argument empirical–theoretical and moral–evaluative analyses part ways. The powerful interests which steer and promote division of labour need not be good or just, nor must we think of them as unjust and evil merely because they are powerful. The moral–evaluative judgement, even if based on more complex grounds, is suspended. However, if this formulation is permitted, moral–evaluative arguments are merely differentiated from empirical–theoretical analysis (in the usual hope that the latter can be improved by pursing it more single-mindedly); the two modes of analysis are not absolutely and forever severed from each other. Even though their integration is not the main concern of this book, I will comment on some problems relating to this in the final chapter.

In the following chapters the thesis that power is a critical element in any adequate account of division of labour is further explored and put to the test. We will investigate in different contexts to what extent division of labour is shaped by the most powerful interests as well as by the struggle between groups with opposing interests and different power resources, and we will explore how much a focus on power can contribute to a better understanding of the actual processes of change in division of labour. I shall not begin at the most obvious point, the development of division of labour in industrial work, but consider first problems of dividing authority, problems that are of utmost importance in understanding secular change in organizational forms.

Notes

1. On the role of functionalist reasoning in Marxist thought see Elster (1982) and the ensuing discussion in *Theory and Society*. The specific issues related to an efficiency explanation in conjunction with assumptions about competitive market pressure, a common pattern in all three traditions, will be discussed below. It might be noted that in the *Wealth of Nations* Adam Smith made a clear distinction between the increase on the productive power of labour due to specialization – the subject of his first chapter – and the 'Principle which gives Occasion to the Division of labour', as he titled the second chapter. Smith saw division of labour ultimately grounded in the 'propensity to truck,

barter and exchange' (1776/1937: 13), a propensity he viewed as characteristic of human nature and probably related to reason and speech. ('Whether this propensity be one of those original principles of human nature, of which no further account can be given; or whether, as seems more probable, it be the necessary consequence of the facilities of reason and speech, it belongs not to our present subject to enquire. It is common to all men, and to be found in no other race of animals . . .' – ibid.) Smith specifically insisted that division of labour 'is not originally the effect of any human wisdom, which foresees and intends that general opulence to which it gives occasion', contrasting it to the propensity to exchange, 'which has in view no such extensive utility' (ibid.). While this is of some interest to our discussion below of the functionalist logic of efficiency explanations of division of labour, it is not unreasonable to view this argument of Smith's as limited to the *origins* of division of labour and to see him grant a greater role to foresight and planning at various later stages of human history.

2. Even Emile Durkheim, who challenged major premises of the utilitarian analysis of division of labour, accepted without question the proposition that division of labour increases productivity. Since, as we shall see, he rejected the idea that division of labour advances *because* of these productivity effects, he had to develop awkward arguments designed to explain the higher level of consumption which corresponds to greater productivity. He invoked greater fatigue, refined needs corresponding to a greater use of intelligence in work, the fact that new products can activate latent wants, and the attraction of novelty as explanations.

3. Wilbert Moore (1968: 373) contends that the idea of selective adaptation has been neglected in recent sociological system theory and argues for its adoption:

> In Darwinian evolutionary theory, structural differentiation derives from selective adaptation of organisms to their environment. Since environments differ both cross-sectionally and temporally, the idea of selective adaptation provides a way of accounting both for the observed diversity in structural forms and for continuing change. It is surprising that so little use has been made of this conceptual scheme in the theory of social systems, where it appears equally applicable.

This observation is roughly correct in regard to recent social theory; otherwise, it neglects the work of Bucher (1893/1901) and especially Max Weber (1922/68), who never loses sight of 'natural selection' as a force shaping the prevalent institutional patterns in different environments. As we will see below from Talcott Parsons's analysis, there are some good reasons why selective adaptation does not necessarily lead to determinate results.

4. For the best-known attempt to compose a catalogue of functional requisites see Aberle et al. (1950). An important set of unresolved issues, which I do not discuss in the text but which strengthens my sceptical conclusion, pertains to the necessary quality of the solution: how productive does an economy have to be for a society to 'get by', that is, maintain itself over generations? How much violence can be absorbed? How much lethargy and withdrawal is 'too much'?

5. To the four broad functional problems any social system has to deal with – in Parsons's abstract formulation: adaptation, goal attainment, integration and pattern maintenance – correspond four interrelated processes of evolutionary significance: adaptive upgrading, structural differentiation, integration, and a value generalization

which can make meaningful and steer diverse activities and patterns by inclusive conceptions of what is desirable.

6. Durkheim did not pose these questions, even though they are suggested by what I called 'Durkheim's problem' – the issues raised by the historical variability of needs, wants and values and their structuring by social and cultural forces. He did not apply his insight to division within a society, probably because he was inclined – mistakenly, I submit – to conceive of needs and wants as being fairly uniformly determined by society and its *conscience collective* at any one time. Structured variation of needs and wants pertained for him to intercultural and interepochal differences rather than to divisions within a society. The strategy in social theory argued by Talcott Parsons since *The Structure of Social Action* (1937) (looking for shared goals and standards of evaluation emerging in systems involving a plurality of actors) has not succeeded in solving the basic problem. The most general thrust of Parsons's strategy is widely accepted. What has remained a bone of contention is that value consensus should be the main mechanism that provides for such an integration of preferences and evaluations. The critiques have been particularly insistent, as well as convincing, when value consensus is understood as spontaneous agreement rather than as the result (in significant part, at least) of indoctrination, deceit, manipulation and coercion. Another focus of criticism has been Parsons's inclination to think of such integration as characteristic of societies, rather than only of less inclusive 'pluralities of actors'. The integration theory of social systems has not been able to dispose of these critiques.

7. To cite but one dramatic example, in *The Transformation of American Law, 1780 to 1860* (1977) Morton Horwitz details the ways in which the English legal tradition was adapted to the emerging commercial and industrial capitalism in America. He shows how the law of property, contracts, negotiable instruments, liability and employment (to name only a few areas) was transformed through judicial decision in such a manner as to favour entrepreneurial interests and in effect subsidize them at the expense of consumers, workers and farmers.

8. The position taken in the text is not particularly original. 'Money prices', argues Max Weber (1922/68: I, 108) who more than most social theorists sought to integrate economic analysis into his theoretical framework, 'are the product of conflicts of interest and of compromise; they thus result from power constellations'. The context for this remark is a discussion of the substantive conditions of formal rationality in a money economy. Weber considers three such conditions: (1) market struggle among at least relatively autonomous units; (2) capital accounting, the highest form of formal economic rationality, requires thorough market freedom; and (3) effective demand is always contingent on income distribution. In each of his brief commentaries on the three main propositions the role of power is highlighted. Our initial quote elaborates the first proposition. The second is rounded out by a critically important observation on the employment relationship: 'Strict capital accounting is further associated with the social phenomena of "shop discipline" and appropriation of the means of production, and that means: with the existence of a "system of domination" (*Herrschaftsverhältnis*)' (ibid.). Weber, in other words, recognizes as much as Marx that division of labour in the workshop, under the domination of owners or managers, is constitutive of full-fledged capitalism – the closest approximation of formal economic rationality in human history. The third proposition points itself to the economic power inherent in the distribution of wealth. Weber concludes with the comment that formal economic rationality, the subject-matter of most economic analysis, is quite different from the various

substantive rationalities that are informed by the ideals and interests of diverse groups: 'Formal and substantive rationality, no matter by what standard the latter is measured, are always in principle separate things, no matter that in many (and under certain very artificial assumptions even all) cases they may coincide empirically' (ibid.).

9. George C. Homans raised this objection when an earlier version of these ideas was presented to a colloquium at Harvard University in 1974. I am grateful for having been pressed to make my underlying arguments explicit.

10. See Durkheim (1893/1964: 280–2). As I have argued elsewhere (Rueschemeyer, 1982), while Durkheim's meta-theoretical critique of utilitarian social theory as he saw it (not necessarily as it actually existed – see Camic, 1979) is still persuasive, his causal explanation of division of labour is questionable wherever it modifies the earlier body of thought. Ironically, it was his metatheoretical concerns critical of utilitarian social theory that flawed his specific contributions to a causal explanation of social differentiation.

The explanation which Durkheim sought to modify argued that division of labour requires a large population in which – and this is the decisive factor – interaction is dense. Durkheim insisted that exchange and division of labour always presuppose an overarching moral community, which utilitarian analyses had neglected, and he rejected what classical economists had suggested as the link between increasing social density (expanding markets) and specialization – the efficiency gains that result from division of labour. Durkheim proposed instead, in a mistaken analogy to Darwin's theory which viewed the struggle for survival as the more intense the more similar the competing organisms are to each other, that increasing size and density would intensify competition to which specialization is an avoidance response. He overlooked the fact that Darwin spoke of a specialization of demands made on the resources in a given environment – of a specialization of consumption, as it were – while division of labour refers to the specialization of *production*. It is not at all clear why an increase in the consuming population or an expansion of markets should make competition among producers more intense and threaten their 'survival'; it seems more plausible to expect that under these conditions even marginal producers can still operate with a profit, that is, 'survive' more easily than with less demand and more circumscribed markets.

The relation between population density and changes in the division of labour is in fact rather complex. Increasing population density which preceded the Black Death in thirteenth-century Europe did not lead uniformly to notable advances in the division of labour. By contrast, the plague, which reduced the population drastically, may well have been a factor in subsequent advances of division of labour and technology. Gottfried (1983: 161) concludes from his study of *The Black Death*: 'Most survivors became richer. Western European peasants were, for the most part, freed from their customary bonds, and Europeans in general were spared the relentless pauperization that unbridled population growth caused in other areas of the Old World.'

References

Aberle, David F., Cohen, Albert K., Davis, A. K., Levy, Marion J. and Sutton, Francis X. 1950: The functional requisites of a society. *Ethics*, 9, 100–11.

Bucher, Karl 1893/1901: *Industrial Evolution*. New York: Holt; first German publication 1893.

Camic, Charles 1979: The utilitarians revisited. *American Journal of Sociology*, 85, 516–50.

Dahrendorf, Ralf 1959: *Class and Class Conflict in Industrial Society.* Stanford, Cal.: Stanford University Press.
Durkheim, Emile 1893/1964: *The Division of Labor.* New York: Free Press; first French publication 1893.
Eisenstadt, S. N. 1963: *The Political System of Empires.* New York: Free Press.
Elster, Jon 1982: Marxism, functionalism and game theory. *Theory and Society,* 11, 453–82.
Gallie, W. B. 1955–56: Essentially contested concepts. *Proceedings of the Aristotelian Society,* 56, 167–98.
Gottfried, Robert S. 1983: *The Black Death: natural and human disaster in medieval Europe.* New York: Free Press.
Horwitz, Morton J. 1977: *The Transformation of American Law, 1780–1860.* Cambridge, Mass.: Harvard University Press.
Marx, Karl 1847/n.d.: *The Poverty of Philosophy.* New York: International Publishers; first published in 1847.
Moore, Wilbert E. 1968: Social change. In Sills, D. L. (ed.), *International Encyclopaedia of the Social Sciences,* vol. 14. New York: Macmillan and Free Press.
Olson, Mancur 1965: *The Logic of Collective Action: public goods and the theory of groups.* Cambridge, Mass.: Harvard University Press.
Parsons, Talcott 1937: *The Structure of Social Action.* New York: McGraw-Hill.
Parsons, Talcott 1966: *Societies: evolutionary and comparative perspectives.* Englewood Cliffs, N.J.: Prentice-Hall.
Parsons, Talcott 1971: *The System of Modern Societies.* Englewood Cliffs, N.J.: Prentice-Hall.
Rueschemeyer, Dietrich 1982: On Durkheim's explanation of division of labor. *American Journal of Sociology,* 88, 579–89.
Rueschemeyer, Dietrich 1986: *Power and the Division of Labor.* Cambridge: Polity Press.
Smelser, Neil J. 1959: *Social Change in the Industrial Revolution.* Chicago: University of Chicago Press.
Smelser, Neil J. 1963: Mechanisms of change and adjustments to change. In Hoselitz, B. F. and Moore, W. E. (eds), *Industrialization and Society.* The Hague: UNESCO and Mouton, 32–54.
Smith, Adam 1776/1937: *An Inquiry into the Nature and Causes of the Wealth of Nations* (Cannan edition). New York: Random House Modern Library.
Stinchcombe, Arthur L. 1968: *Constructing Social Theories.* New York: Harcourt, Brace and World.
Treiman, Donald J. 1977: *Occupational Prestige in Comparative Perspective.* New York: Academic Press.
Weber, Max 1922/68: *Economy and Society,* 2 vols. New York: Bedminster Press; second printing Berkeley: University of California Press, 1978; translation of *Wirtschaft und Gesellschaft,* 4th edn. Tübingen: J. C. B. Mohr (Paul Siebeck), 1956; first published 1922.

69

Evaluating the Model of Structural Differentiation in Relation to Educational Change in the Nineteenth Century

Neil J. Smelser

In keeping with the spirit of this volume, my objectives in this chapter are to criticize and revise one of the major ideas associated with the tradition of functional analysis: the idea of structural differentiation as a principle of change in the process of economic, political, and social development. I will illustrate the general points made by reference to the forces that appear to have been most important in shaping the development of primary education in Great Britain and the United States in the nineteenth century.

The Rise of Formal Education as a Process of Differentiation

One historical feature of the process of education (this central term will be defined more formally a little later on) is that it has often taken place in the context of some kind of social structure that may not have education as its primary functional significance. A great deal of education and training has taken place historically in the family; the passing on of agricultural knowledge and skills in a peasant family is an example. The institution of apprenticeship (sometimes also in a family context) is education in the context of a productive economic organization (even though this may be as simple as a cobbler's shop or as complicated as a large newspaper's composing room). Education in a monastery occurs in the context of an organization dedicated primarily to various kinds of religious works. The educational ingredients of "basic training" are imparted in the context of a military organization.

The institutionalization of education on a *formal* basis implies a different kind of social structure. It implies an organization that is dedicated primarily to the process of education *as such* (even though, as I will stress throughout, it maintains linkages with other structural settings in society). It most often is an

---

Source: Jeffrey C. Alexander (ed.), *Neofunctionalism*, (Beverly Hills: Sage, 1985).

organization that is formally separated from familial, economic, military, religious, and other educational contexts. It also suggests that its governance and policymaking will also take place in a structure that is in some degree autonomous, that is, not directly controlled by these other kinds of interests, even though it may be influenced by them. It suggests, finally, that specific roles – teacher and student – are defined primarily in their own terms, rather than in the context of some other kind of roles (father–son, journeyman–apprentice, etc.). In short, the one major defining characteristic of formal education is that of *structural differentiation* from other social-structural and organizational forms.

One of the striking features of the "modernization" of the West, as well as the "modernization" of advanced non-Western countries (Soviet Union, Japan) and the aspiring Third-World countries, is that a structurally differentiated system of formal education is part of the package of "modernization." All advanced Western and non-Western nations have developed systems of mass primary and secondary education, even though they have taken very different paths and trajectories and distinctive national differences in educational systems persist. All developing countries envision not only economic, political, and administrative development, but also mass educational development as part of the package that constitutes entry into the company of advanced nations. Standard explanations of this regularity are that education is a kind of institutional contrivance, or even invention, sparked by new demands in other sectors of the society – in particular, by the demands of industrialization, which calls for qualitatively new and higher levels of technical knowledge and skills in the labor force (Halsey, 1973), and mass suffrage in a democratizing society, which appears to call for a more informed and responsible citizenry.

Another aspect of these kinds of explanations are that educational activities that are embedded in traditional familial, community, religious, and economic contexts tend to be less flexible and effective than formal educational systems, presumably because of special constraints imposed by these contexts. The family, for example, is not a very effective formal educational institution because of its limited resources and its commitments to other kinds of functions and activities. Religious organizations are not very effective because of their sectarian commitments, which tie its educational activities to specific religious-moral concerns, likely to produce educational results that are noninstrumental from an economic point of view and divisive from a point of view of generating and sustaining a commitment to societywide integration and consensus. Formal educational arrangements, according to this view, are more effective because they are better able to generate more generalized and flexible knowledge, skills, and commitments that are consonant with industrial and/or democratic societies.

Although the model of differentiation possesses some continuing validity in accounting for the rise of more specialized educational systems, the power of the model appears to be limited, largely because it envisions the main variation in outcome as "less differentiated" or "more differentiated," whereas in fact there are many different variations in educational systems that we might wish to explain that cannot be assimilated to that particular distinction. I will specify some of these lines of variation throughout this chapter. In addition, I will examine a number of the special assumptions associated with the idea of differentiation (including the assumption of "greater effectiveness") as well as a model of how this process comes about. I will now lay some further groundwork for these tasks by developing some ideas about the nature of education in society.

Education as a Special Kind of Societal Resource

As a process education must be regarded as a part of and continuous with the socialization process in general. I conceive socialization, moreover, as a process that can be conceptualized simultaneously at the individual, social, and cultural levels From the standpoint of the *individual*, socialization involves the acquisition of values, ideals, identifications, motivational commitments, interpersonal skills and style, and various kinds of cognitive skills and information. From the standpoint of society, the products of socialization are seen as resources that can be allocated to the various activities, roles, and institutional structures that constitute organized social life. And from the *cultural* standpoint socialization is one of the main mechanisms by which values, meanings, and group identity is transmitted from generation to generation, thereby assuring the continuity of a society's cultural heritage.

This series of definitions should not be taken to imply any level of orderliness or neatness of fit among the three levels. At the individual level, the process of socialization sometimes fails, is rebelled against, or otherwise varies. At the social level, the products of socialization may not fit the role and individual demands generated by the social structure, particularly if that social structure has been undergoing rapid change. And at the cultural level, the dynamics of cultural conflict and change in society suggest that the sets of values, ideals, and so forth that are transmitted to one generation may be inappropriate to the next, which may generate its own, different ones. Nevertheless, from the standpoint of the primary intention of the socializers, the process is geared to stress reproduction and continuity at the individual, social, and cultural levels.

According to conventional usage, education is that part of the socialization process that gives primary emphasis to imparting and developing information, knowledge, cognitive skills, and critical skills. Although valid in a general way, this view should not obscure the fact that education as a process is variable in its relation to the more inclusive process of socialization. That is to say, education as a process can never be a purely cognitive process, but it also inevitably involves the exposure to cultural values, ideals, heroes, and villains, as well as normative expectations relating to matters such as personal ambition, attitudes and behavior toward authorities, cooperative behavior, and so on.

The view of education and socialization here advanced is consistent with the formulations of Durkheim (1956). One particular point made by Durkheim is that education is historically variable, reflecting the particular ideals of the home civilization, whether these be values of military valor, religious asceticism, or aristocratic gentlemanliness. To press this view further, it should be acknowledged that – historically, particularly in times of change – for any given society there is no single, integrated set of cultural ideals to be transmitted, but, rather, several sets of ideals in competition with one another. In addition, insofar as society has developed specialized institutional structures – economic, legal, political, etc. – these structures will, to varying extents, have been the structural bases for precipitating groups (classes, estates, ethnic groups, etc.) that are politically significant in the competition over the values, symbols, and ideologies that are consistent with or legitimize their own claims on resources. Because socialization in general and education in particular specialize in the generation and reproduction of these kinds of cultural items, it follows that the content, style, and mode of transmitting them will be items on the social agenda that generate group conflict. Furthermore, because the educational process – like the family process and the religious process – is involved in the transmission of systems of morality from generation to generation, it also follows that conflicts over educational issues are likely to take the form of conflicts over principles, or even conflicts over the definition of the sacred.

Although education, like socialization in general, must properly be regarded as a process that occurs in some degree throughout the life cycle, the educational process in the younger years of the life cycle is particularly significant because of the extreme plasticity of the human organism in its early years and its subsequent long period of maturity. The educational process during these years typically involves the generation of motivational commitments through mechanisms such as imitation and identification, then the inculcation of general skills (for example, literacy and numeracy), and finally the development of more abstract and specialized knowledge and skills. Although a great deal of variation in such a progression is to be expected, the point to be underscored is that, in the early years of education, children are, in their social significance, *generalized* resources; that is to say, they have the potential of being channeled in many different directions with respect to the cultivation of values, outlooks, skills, and information. In fact, education can be seen as an investment in the shaping of these human resources. They are shaped, moreover, with an eye to the future commitment and contribution to different societal exigencies by the recipients of that education. Thus education can be used as a potential military resource if ideas of value, bravery, and martial skills are inculcated; it can be used as an economic resource if scientific and technical skills are given priority; it can be used as a resource for the generation of symbols of national and/or local solidarity, identification, and integration; it can be used as an avenue for generating religious commitment, and in this way as a resource for organized religion; it can be used as a resource to reinforce inequality in society (for example, by conferring status or by cultivating values of deference); it can be used as a means to encourage social mobility; or it can be, and usually is, used to generate resources relative to a variety of mixtures of these purposes.

The fact that education is a generalized resource and can be directed to diverse purposes implies that education can mean or promise different things to different groups and interests in society. The young are thus "fair game" for those sectors and groups in society who are pushing their own interests and values both for themselves and for future generations. Much educational conflict, in fact, will be among the competing demands for the young as a resource, and debate among those groups and classes that have different demands for that resource – business groups, military groups, ruling groups, "intellectual" groups, class groups, ethnic groups, and so on.

Extending the Model of Structural Differentiation

The model of structural differentiation as developed and applied by Parsons, Bales, myself, and others is in my current estimation based on a model of society as an instrumentally oriented, going concern – a problem-solving entity – though that image was not always explicit in the minds of those who worked with the model.[1] Furthermore, the model appears to posit that at the beginning of a sequence of differentiation, things are not working satisfactorily (as evidenced by dissatisfaction) and at the end of the sequence, things are working better (because of new, more differentiated structural arrangements that have been invented after a process of disturbance, handling and channeling, searching, and adaptation).

With respect to the actual initiation of structural change and the typical sequence of events leading to that change, the model was stated – with respect to industrial differentiation – as follows:

> Industrial differentiation implies that under certain market, value, and other conditions, the existing industrial structure becomes inadequate to meet productive requirements. A sequence enters its first stage when elements in the population express dissatisfaction with industrial productivity. This dissatisfaction appears in the form of complaints concerning the misuse of resources, or both. In either case the dissatisfaction is legitimized by reference to the dominant value-system of the time. The immediate responses to dissatisfaction are undirected or misdirected symptoms of disturbance. Initially these disturbances are "brought into line" by a series of holding operations which prevent the outbursts from reaching explosive proportions. Simultaneously there is a reiteration of established values and an encouragement of ideas which promise to carry the implications of these values into practice. These ideas are implemented by inventions and experiments with methods of

production. Finally, entrepreneurs turn these suggestions into action to overhaul the productive system. If successful, the entrepreneurial attempts produce a new industrial structure and an extraordinary growth of production, capitalization, and profits. (Smelser, 1959, pp. 2–3)

In my own analysis of social change during the Industrial Revolution in Britain, I attempted to apply the essentials of this model to several different sequences of social change with reference to industrial production and family life. In principle, this kind of model could be applied further to the analysis of the rise of mass systems of formal education.

Out of years of reflecting on the subject of social change and, more particularly, this kind of model of change, and out of years of research on the emergence of the systems of primary mass education in Britain and the United States during the first three-quarters of the nineteenth century, I have concluded that several of the ingredients in this model are problematical and in need of reformulation and extension.

"Dominant value-system of the time." In my empirical work on the Industrial Revolution, for purposes of heuristic assumption, I assumed a dominant value system that remained constant throughout an episode of change and in the light of which various institutional arrangements and situations were judged to be performing more or less adequately or inadequately (Smelser, 1959, p 16). It is evident that this assumption should be relaxed, so that it is possible to envision a number of value-positions, one of which might indeed be dominant, but which stand in competition or conflict with one another as bases for legitimizing the expression of dissatisfaction. Furthermore, these diverse value-positions may change over time. This means that, for any given set of institutional arrangements or social "facts," there may be a lack of consensus – indeed, disagreement – as to whether these should be regarded as unsatisfactory. It also means that we should expect to find conflict and competition over the definition of the situation itself, that is, whether an unsatisfactory state of affairs actually exists.

With respect to British society around the turn of the nineteenth century, the dominant value system could be summarized, following Perkin, as "an open aristocracy based on property and patronage":

> A hierarchical society in which men took their places in an accepted order of precedence, a pyramid stretching down from a tiny minority of the rich and powerful through ever larger and wider layers of lesser wealth and power to the great mass of the poor and powerless. (Perkin, 1969, p. 17)

It was a society based on responsibility on the part of the wealthy and ruling classes, answered by deference on the part of the lesser classes. Furthermore, the dominant values of the day legitimized a fusion of status (the aristocracy), power (the governing classes), wealth (mainly landed, but also commercial and mercantile), and religious authority (the established Church of England) at the top. At the same time this dominant value system was being challenged on various fronts: by the utilitarian value system, which envisioned among other things, a rational society based on principles of free exchange, not status and obligations; by political radicalism, which envisioned democratic participation rather than benevolent paternalism; and by religious Dissent, which argued for religious freedom, toleration, and denominationalism rather than religious Establishment. With respect to American society, in the early days of the republic the dominant values could be said to be those of activist Protestantism republican virtue and democracy (Cremin, 1980), but within these, tensions between democratic and aristocratic tendencies took different forms in different parts of the country and among numerous, different religious denominations and sects.

"Elements in the population." In my earlier work I did not specify which elements in the population were expressing the dissatisfaction, nor did I explore the possibility that other "elements" might not be expressing dissatisfaction or that they might be positively satisfied with the social arrangements in question and therefore disposed to challenge or oppose those who were expressing dissatisfaction. One of the points made by a critic, George Homans (1964), was that the "elements" in the population were "men" (mostly men engaged in making and selling cotton cloth), but he did not carry his objection much further than that. But in any event, it seems advantageous to make the assumption about "elements" more specific and to identify not only different value-bases for legitimizing the expression of dissatisfaction (and pressure to change) but also the specific social categories and groups that express dissatisfaction.

What are the bases on which such groups are best identified? With respect to the interest in primary education in both the United States and Great Britain in the nineteenth century, two bases seem paramount: primordial and functional. British society was made up of a diversity of primordial religious (Church of England, Nonconformist, Wesleyan, Catholic, Jewish) and regional-ethnic (Irish, Scottish, Welsh, and English; and within the English, various regional specifications, e.g., Cornish) groupings; in addition, that society was characterized by an increasingly complex functional (occupational and class) grouping, which tended to be assimilated into the hierarchical ordering of British society in multiple layers. American life was likewise characterized by distinctions along religious (denominational), ethnic (for example, Scotch-Irish, Pennsylvania German), racial (white, black, and Indian), and regional (Northeast, Middle Atlantic, South, Midwest, with regional divisions within each of these and within each state) lines, as well as burgeoning functional groupings (merchants, planters, free farmers, working men, etc.). It was the vocal leaders of these kinds of groups that expressed satisfaction and dissatisfaction about states of affairs, speaking simultaneously for their groups and toward some higher legitimizing principle. For both countries it appears that primordial and functional groupings overlapped and were in some degree correlated with one another (for example, aristocracy with the established church and Nonconformism with much of middle-class England; Quakers with urban commerce and Germans with independent farming in Pennsylvania), but in many other instances they were cross-cutting (e.g., German independent farmers and Scotch-Irish independent farmers in Pennsylvania) and independent from one another. In general, then, it does not seem justified to regard different primordially based voices only as disguised voices of functional (especially class) groupings. The two sets of groupings had independent significance as bases of group aspirations, group interests, and group conflicts.

In the actual debates over educational proposals, these primordial and functional groups served as a kind of political maze through which proposed reforms, legislation, and expenditures affecting primary education would pass, with the various groups – insofar as they were politically organized and articulate – ultimately taking political stands according to their perceived values and interests.

"Handling and channeling." In the original model a distinction was made between groups involved in protests of various sorts on the one hand and the authority structure that "reacted to" these protests on the other. This distinction should be broken down because, in fact, "the authorities" (political parties, vested interests in governments, etc.) themselves became involved as partisans in defining whether or not a state of affairs is unsatisfactory and in the fashioning of new, presumably more satisfactory states of affairs. In the early nineteenth century in Britain, for example, the Tories and the more moderate elements of the ruling aristocracy were divided on the issue of whether education was even desirable for the poorer classes, the former believing that education fomented dangerous ideas and the latter believing that education made the lower orders more docile, respectable, and responsible. As another example, in the middle of the nineteenth century Tories and middle-class politicians came into bitter conflict over the seriousness of the plight of children and related educational issues. And in a number of American states Whigs and Democrats struggled over public education as a partisan political issue. Educational debates, in short, involved political struggles, as well as the management of protest, among partisan groups inside and outside of government.

"Function more effectively in the new historical circumstances." This assessment of the difference between less differentiated and more differentiated structures lies at the heart of the vision of a society or one of its subsystems as a goal-oriented, purposive entity. That specific formulation of "more effectively" also implies that "effectiveness" is the motivating force behind the impulse to develop more differentiated arrangements, that is, a motivating force to make a going concern

perform better than it is. The "more effective" functioning, moreover, is assumed to provide the basis for a diminution of dissatisfaction with the previous state of affairs and a motive for establishing a new set of arrangements on a more or less routine basis.

Certainly the effectiveness of the functioning of educational or other arrangements is one basis for expressing dissatisfaction and for initiating change. For example, the infant-school movement in various Eastern cities in the United States in the 1820s and 1830s was based on a diagnosis of the inadequate functioning of workers' families with respect to the care of children; the decision to provide government-matching grants to religious bodies in Britain in 1833 was made in part because it was felt that the efforts of these voluntary groups were not effective enough in providing schools, particularly for the urban masses and in isolated rural districts; and in the mid-nineteenth century the Newcastle Commission was created mainly in response to complaints that Britain's primary education for the poor was costing too much and was not educating the young efficiently; the "payment by results" was adopted in part as a way of making that education more efficient (Sturt, 1967, pp. 239-249).

But educational change cannot be regarded solely as an instrumental problem-solving process by which less effective arrangements are replaced by more effective arrangements. Given what has been said about competing systems of legitimization and competing primordial and functional groups, it follows that the creation of new educational structures is *also* a political victory, compromise, or defeat (or all three) worked out in the context of group conflict. A new structure (educational or other) is, among other things, a commitment of resources to certain social arrangements from which a certain group or groups may benefit (or *believe* they benefit) in relation to their pretensions or interests and aspirations while other groups harbor feelings of resentment or defeat. Thus new educational arrangements may or may not be more "effective" according to some performance criterion, but at the same time it may be assessed as being "effective" or "ineffective" in accommodating the demands or pretensions of concerned groups.

There are many examples illustrating this. The initial decision of political authorities in New York City to establish generally philanthropic schools and their later decision to secularize public schools and not to establish religious schools (Baptist and Catholic) was based in part on their desire to avoid a competitive scramble among religious groups for public funds (Ravitch, 1974). The decision taken by the British Parliament in 1833 to provide matching funds to voluntary religious groupings interested in establishing schools was a kind of minimalist compromise taken after a long Parliamentary battle in which more ambitious plans for governmental intervention in education had been shot down by various primordial (mainly religious) groups (Craik, 1896). (These more ambitious plans, it might be argued, might have been more "effective" in the sense of increasing the literacy of the poor, but would not have been very "effective" politically because they promised to set off a long season of sectarian squabbling and subversion of the new arrangements.) The decision on the part of various American states in the 1830s and 1840s to provide state educational funds to districts on a voluntary, matching basis was a strategy that avoided a political confrontation that would have resulted if the state had attempted to coerce localities to tax themselves for education. The "shape" of the resulting educational arrangements in each of these examples reflected the presence of actual or potential group conflicts in the process of making these arrangements.

A somewhat different model of change thus emerges from these considerations. According to the "instrumental" model, the new structure, being more effective, renders the old structure obsolete; the latter is dismantled accordingly with varying degrees of pain and resistance. An industrial instance of this would be the obsolescence and ultimate disappearance of craft production in light of continuous technological advances and new forms of productive organization. The contrasting model of change often involves the segmentation and differentiation of new structures, but in the context of conflicting group interests. As the new arrangement is "invented" and "consolidated" in the context of competition among political groups, it may not necessarily be more "efficient" than prior arrangements, but is, rather, patched for reasons of accommodation to politically significant groups. This is no reason to assume, either, that the new arrangements will necessarily displace the old ones because they are less "effective." Particularly if old arrangements are thought to serve other groups' interests, there may be active pressure not to dismantle the old. The model of change that emerges, therefore, is not one of "more efficient arrangements replacing less efficient arrangements," but, rather, is a model of "proliferation" of new arrangements around a core of vested interests, analogous to "blistering" onto an existing core, which may remain relatively undisturbed despite the appearance of the new arrangements. (In debates over the bill that was to become the Education Act of 1870, W. E. Forster described the projected establishment of state schools as intended to "fill up gaps," that is, to leave undisturbed the existing system of state-supported, voluntary, denominational schooling [Parliamentary Papers, 1870, Col. 44.]) The ultimate "fate" of the emerging structural arrangements, therefore, depends only in part on their relative "effectiveness"; it depends on the kinds and levels of resources that continue to be made available to it and on the relative position and strength of the contending political groupings whose interests are accommodated (and those whose interests are not) by the new structural arrangements. Thus a principle of differentiation along "interest" lines is invoked in addition to a principle of differentiation along "performance" lines. This principle promises to yield a more comprehensive and detailed account of the shape of emerging educational arrangements.[2]

"If successful." To carry forth the reasoning just developed, the criteria for "success" of an institutional innovation are somewhat different than previously

noted. Rather than simply positing some level of "satisfaction" with the innovation, note should be taken of the level of "accommodation" that is generated by the innovation and the level of residual "dissatisfaction" that continues to be registered on the part of those groups that remain less than completely satisfied with the innovation, if not actually "defeated." Second, note should be taken of the fact that any new structural innovation itself generates a number of new roles (in the case of education these roles might be "teacher," "master," "student," "pupil-teacher," "parents of students," "inspectors," "school-board member," etc.), *each* of which itself constitutes a basis for the formation of groups that may themselves become political constituencies and part of the very political process that gave rise to the structural innovation. Another part of the definition of "successful," when applied to a new institution, then, must refer to the efforts on the part of new vested interests generated by that institution to perpetuate it and to protect or advance its interests.

The Structural Differentiation of Society as a Source of Obstacles and Opportunities for Educational Development

One fundamental feature underlying the aforementioned view of the rise of primary education in Great Britain and the United States is that in each case the new educational institutions were grafted onto an existing (and changing) society in which the cultural, political, social, and economic institutions constituted a distinctive combination of obstacles and opportunities; the "shape" of the emerging educational arrangements can be largely understood as reflecting these obstacles and opportunities.

The following broad, comparative structural differences between Great Britain and the United States (as of the first quarter of the nineteenth century) can be noted.

(1) Great Britain manifested a stratification system that was based on the layering of "orders," "ranks," and "classes." The system was in part hereditary; even the "openness" of the aristocracy tended to be a two-generational matter (i.e., the acquisition of fortunes in commercial or mercantile activity, then marrying into or buying land). American society in the early Republic, although stratified (planters, merchants, workmen, farmers), had, however, broken through the fixity of class lines both formally (for example, by prohibiting the use of aristocratic titles) and ideologically (with the stress of equality of opportunity and social mobility). Economically, too, the "openness" of the society to the west constituted an opportunity for individuals to "break out" of the stratification system. Several qualifications to this general characterization must be made, however. First, the caste status of the American black slaves constituted an even stricter hereditary "layering" than the British class system. Second, in certain pockets of American society quasi-aristocratic arrangements persisted, particularly in the larger eastern cities (Boston, New York, and Philadelphia) and in parts of the agricultural South (the plantation owners).

And third, the possibility of migration (mainly to North America and Australia) also constituted a means whereby some Britons could "break out" of the stratification system.

These contrasting class systems constituted fundamentally different "programs" that would shape the development of the educational systems of the respective societies. For Britain, there was a kind of taken-for-granted tendency to stratify the educational system in such a way that would reproduce the larger stratification system and would work to provide each "class" with what was "necessary" for its station. Furthermore, the primary guiding assumption would be that the education of the poor would be arranged "for" them by the higher classes, whose responsibility it was to do so. (The earliest "voluntary" activities reflected the efforts of landowners, merchants, and clergymen to provide money to establish schools "for" the poor; the child-labor legislation of 1833 called for industrialists to establish schools "for" the children who worked for them; and as late as the 1850s, the Newcastle Commission blamed the failure of education in remote agricultural areas and in urban centers on absentee landlords and irresponsible merchants and manufacturers who would not provide resources for schools "for" the poor.) This picture is complicated, of course, by considerable evidence of self-education on the part of the poor and by the persistent efforts of the middle classes to break into the exclusive public schools (which traditionally served the aristocratic classes primarily). It is further complicated later in the century when the working-class schools came to be regarded in part as vehicles for social mobility as well as mechanisms for reproducing a stable working class. The primary cultural and ideological thrust in the early American republic was to lay stress on the schools as a community (rather than a class) resource, open to all and constituting an opportunity for personal (rather than class) uplifting. Yet this dominant tendency, too, was qualified in many ways. First, in those areas with more quasi-aristocratic survivals, some efforts were made to provide schools "for" the poor, which, however, gradually gave way to egalitarian pressures to give common access to primary schools. Second, there was the more or less constant tendency for the better-off in large communities to revert to private academies and schools, a tendency that worked in the "British" direction of stratifying education according to class and reproducing class advantages. And finally, in the slave states, blacks were excluded systematically from all schools.

(2) Great Britain was slower in dismantling those political arrangements that restricted political participation by class. By the first third of the nineteenth century, the American states approached universal male suffrage, though some remaining property and racial restrictions still existed. Only in 1832 did the British middle classes gain enfranchisement; and only in 1867 did a portion of the working classes do so. The hereditary House of Lords continued to play a major political role throughout the century. The decline of patrician republicanism in the Jacksonian era and the rise of popular participation worked in the same direction.

The major differences emerging with respect to educational politics and decision making were that in Britain these politics tended to take the form of different factions within the ruling groups (aristocratic and middle class) fighting among themselves as to what kind of education was appropriate for the poor, though at the same time responding to political agitations by various class and religious groupings in the society. (Sometimes these agitations were not directed at educational issues as such, but concerned issues such as electoral reform and economic hardship, with the ruling groups attempting to deal with them in part through educational reform.) From early on in America, however, the issues of educational reform and educational decision making entered the arena of electoral politics explicitly and became partisan electoral issues. It was only after the extension of the franchise to the working classses that this kind of electoral development took place to a significant degree in Great Britain (for example, in the election of 1874, when Nonconformist outrage at arrangements established by the Education Act of 1870 helped to turn the Gladstone government out of office).

(3) The differentiation between religion and politics had been carried much further in the United States than in Great Britain. This had been accomplished mainly by the First Amendment of the Constitution and by the actions of the various states in their own constitutions in the early years of the republic. In Britain the Church of England was legally established as the national church, was highly privileged, and was actually represented as such in the House of Lords. The religious picture was complicated, however, by the presence of strong forces of Dissent, which had managed to secure toleration and maintained continuous pressure for parity with respect to one issue after another (access in institutions for higher education, marriage ceremonies, etc.). In addition, the religious picture was further complicated by the presence of some Catholics, increasing in number as Irish migration increased throughout the century. From the standpoint of education, one branch of the Church of England maintained that it possessed an exclusive monopoly on the education of the young and that the secular state should in no way be involved in the education of the people. At best, the state could channel resources through the Church, which would retain control of education. The Nonconformists, on their part, opposed any educational establishment that violated their religious scruples (in particular, the learning and recitation of the catechism) and resisted paying rates to support schools of the Established Church.

With respect to education, the resulting burdens of proof – and the attendant conflicts – were different. In the United States the political authorities were free (indeed, constrained) to take initiative with respect to education without resorting to or going through religious bodies; the shape of the conflict, then, was how to keep religious bodies *out* of public education. In Great Britain the political authorities could *not* intervene in the support of education without resorting to the religious bodies; the shape of the conflict there was how to intervene without at the same time drawing the opposition of one or more of the religious bodies.

Thus in the early nineteenth century the American republic had gone far toward achieving several kinds of differentiation – the differentiation between kinship and class status, the differentiation between class and political participation, and the differentiation between religion and politics – that were underway in Britain, but much further from completion than in the United States. This meant that the political struggles over education would take place on different social and political battlegrounds, and that the results of these struggles – that is, the emerging educational arrangements – would diverge greatly in the two societies.

Notes

1. It should be remembered that early formulations of the model of structural differentiation grew from empirical study and interpretation of decision-making processes in the solution of instrumental tasks (Parsons & Bales, 1955).

2. The distinction between "instrumental" and "expressive" life has been frequently invoked in the analysis of small groups, as well as the analysis of social systems generally (Parsons & Bales, 1955). Instrumental refers to the accomplishment of system tasks, whereas expressive refers to the process of dealing with members' needs, desires, interests, and so forth within the system. The alternative model I have outlined brings the expressive – which in organized society might read as "political" – dimension into the limelight.

References

Craik, H. (1896). *The state and its relation to education*. London: Macmillan.
Cremin, L. (1980). *American education, the national experience, 1783–1876*. New York: Harper & Row.
Durkheim, E. (1956). *Education and sociology*. (S. D. Fox, Trans.). New York: Free Press.
Halsey, A. H. (1973). The sociology of education. In N. J. Smelser (Ed.), *Sociology: An introduction*. New York: John Wiley.
Homans, G. C. (1965). Bringing men back in. *American Sociological Review*, 29, 809–818.
Parliamentary Papers. (1970). Third Series (Vol. CXCIX). London: Cornelius Buck.
Parsons, T., & Bales, R. F. (1955). *Family, socialization and interaction process*. New York: Free Press.
Perkin, H. (1969). *The origins of modern English society, 1780–1880*. London: Routledge & Kegan Paul.
Ravitch, D. (1974). *The great school wars: New York City, 1905–1973: A history of the public schools as a battlefield of change*. New York: Basic Books.
Smelser, N. J. (1959). *Social change in the industrial revolution*. Chicago: University of Chicago Press.
Sturt, M. (1967). *The education of the people: A history of primary education in England and Wales in the nineteenth century*. London: Routledge & Kegan Paul.

70

Against Nostalgia: Talcott Parsons and a Sociology for the Modern World

Robert J. Holton and Bryan S. Turner

Classical European sociology, as it developed in the century or so leading up to the First World War, presented a profoundly ambivalent stance towards those processes of industrialisation, democratisation and rationalisation which constituted the modern western world. On the one hand, the erosion of traditional constraints upon economic dynamism and political freedom was celebrated as an enlargement of the capacity of human societies to realise the good life. On the other hand, the challenge to social coherence and stability posed by the decline of religious authority, village life and traditional status hierarchies was deeply unsettling. This tension between 'traditional and modern values' is, as Nisbet (1967) has pointed out, fundamental to the underlying assumptions and conceptual structure of nineteenth-century sociology. It is represented in such familiar dichotomies as community and individualism, the sacred and the secular, status and contract.

It is a quite bizarre mis-reading of this interpretation to claim, as Hawthorn (1976) has done, that the project of sociology being presented is essentially conservative. Nisbet's point is, rather, that the preoccupations of Marx, Weber, Durkheim and Simmel involve a paradoxical combination of modern values such as 'science', 'reason' and 'individual freedom', with a conceptual armoury deeply embedded in the conservative desire for order and the restoration of community. While not joining the conservative opponents of the French and Industrial Revolutions, classical sociology demanded, not release from community and tradition, but alignment with social forces seeking 'new forms of moral and social community'. In this way there remained a strong element of nostalgia in the cultural preoccupations and fundamental categories of classical sociological thought.

For Marx this took the form of alignment with the labour movement, in its struggle to build a socialist or communist alternative to the alienation of human potential within capitalist society. The central place of the labour theory of

Source: Robert J. Holton and Bryan S. Turner, *Talcott Parsons on Economy and Society*, (London: Routledge & Kegan Paul, 1986).

value, and the transcendent properties of class struggle within this framework, specify both a community-like conception of the generative forces involved in wealth-creation and a theory of exploitation and social change, which grounds the claims of producers against their oppressors in a sense of violated community. As R. H. Tawney (1960, p. 36) pointed out, the underlying moral argument behind the labour theory of value is directed against the securing of 'private gain by the exploitation of public necessities denying labour the vocation of serving the common need . . .'. In this sense it represents the true descendant of the doctrines of Aquinas, with Marx as the last of the schoolmen.

Marx's humanism has of course been interpreted as an 'early' pre-scientific stage in his thought, to be differentiated from the 'later' mature, scientific Marx, by a profound epistemological rupture (Althusser, 1969). This kind of distinction is however vulnerable to Gouldner's theory of the Two Marxisms (Gouldner, 1980). Here it is claimed that both 'scientific' and 'moral philosophical' elements are necessarily conjoined within Marx's work. The twin legacies of Marx, represented by positivistic scientism and humanistic critical philosophy, are thus equally authentic Marxisms. This argument reinforces Nisbet's notion of an intrinsic tension in nineteenth-century sociology, between modern values such as the appeal to scientific authority, and the more traditional claims of communitarian humanism.

A similar ambivalence toward 'tradition' and 'modernity' is evident in the work of Max Weber. In one sense he is quite clearly aligned with the modernising aims of German liberalism. Such aims involved conflict with German autocratic and folk traditionalism and with illiberal and despotic forces outside the German nation-state, most notably Russia. Within Weber's discussion of rational–legal authority and bureaucracy, there is a clear sense of the enhanced scope for individual freedom and authoritative efficiency that such institutions represent, compared with the traditional order. Occidental rationalism is invested with many positive values compared with the civilisations of the world beyond Europe. In another sense, however, these values are linked with a strongly nostalgic hankering for a stable past. This past is one which is specifically religious and in which the possibilities of charismatic individualism are always possible. Max Weber's concept of rationalisation, which in many ways is the key to his whole sociology (Brubaker, 1984), has a nostalgic character to it. Much of Weber's sociology is based upon a religious metaphor of the tree of knowledge, and aspects of Weber's theme of rationalisation argue that modern society has lost innocence by its exposure to scientific knowledge. We can say that much late nineteenth-century social thought was a reflection on Nietzsche and, in particular, a reflection on Nietzsche's notion of the death of God. The modern world is seen as essentially secular, but a secular reality which offers very little in terms of moral guidance. It was Weber who noted that the dominance of science would in some ways liberate us but also in certain respects enslave us. It is for this reason that Weber's concept of the iron cage was so crucial to his sociological perspective on the dilemmas of contemporary society.

For Nisbet, writing in the mid-1960s, contemporary sociology was still living 'in a late phase of the classical age of sociology' (Nisbet, 1967, p. 5). Stripped of the 'tensions' between the modern and traditional worlds as defined by writers like Marx and Weber, sociology would, he felt, be theoretically impoverished, leaving little but 'lifeless heaps of data and stray hypotheses'. There is much to be said in support of this view. Leaving aside a certain uncreative piety among late twentieth-century sociologists towards the 'founding fathers', it is quite clearly the case that the project of reconciling individualism and secularisation with community and moral order remains fundamental to sociological inquiry. While a certain amount of sociology is still written on the presumption that the working class, or the destiny of particular European nation-states, is strategically bound up with the reconciling of this tension, a number of the substantive features of the classical landscape have changed.

In the first place, the Marxist reliance on the revolutionary potential of the working class is now in a profound state of political exhaustion. Gorz' (1982) cry of 'Farewell to the Working Class' in favour of alternative non-classlike social movements (e.g. feminism, peace, ecology) represents an important step beyond one version of the politics of revolutionary nostalgia. In the second place, the privileged status of a narrow set of European nation-states, as the crucible within which the connections between 'past', 'present' and 'future' are worked out, has been superseded by a number of global trends. These include the emergence of super-politics between the USA and Russia, the economic and political mobilisation of the Third World, and the development of a new Pacific economic and political order, linking Japan, China, South East Asia, Australia and the West Coast of the USA. Within this broad context, theories of social change based exclusively upon endogenous developments within Britain, France and Germany have become outmoded.

There is, nonetheless, a sense in which such developments have not disturbed the underlying tension between traditional and modern values that constituted classical sociology. This is evident in the continuing vitality of appeals to 'community' and a unitary moral order in the midst of social science and 'progressive' politics. The enthusiasm of many western Marxists for a succession of charismatic Third World movements from Marxism to the elan of the Latin American revolutionary is testimony to the search for an alternative community building eschatological force to replace the discredited western proletariat. The spectre of Weber's iron cage of rationalisation has also been challenged, most powerfully perhaps by the claims of environmentalist movements for some kind of ecological harmony between society and nature. Here 'science' and 'reason' have been confronted by a strong communitarian sense of the 'sacred'. This has been counterposed to the anomic characteristics perceived in technocratic management. While the political symbols of community among European radicals may have shifted from 'red' to 'green' (Feher and Heller, 1984), the aim of many contemporary social movements is still some type of communitarian quest.

Within contemporary sociology there is a tension between empirical scepticism about the existence of an underlying normative order, and an underlying normative commitment to community. The depiction of modern values such as 'individualism' and 'privatisation' as in some way 'pathological' or 'anomic' relies as much on ontological assumptions about human nature as upon empirical validation. This communitarian critique of modernity is one of the main elements in the attempt by industrial and urban sociology to reconstruct the social relations of the workplace and the modern city. Within this framework greater attention and sympathy is given to workers' control than to the work ethic, and greater concern shown for public rather than private types of consumption. In general, the 'public' remains preferred at the expense of the 'private', in a manner which looks backward to the civic 'virtues' of the ancient Mediterranean world as an inspiration for a critique of modernity (MacIntyre, 1981; Sennett, 1977). On this basis the private is dismissed as 'fetishised' or 'narcissistic' when judged against the collective ethics of community.

For all these continuities between contemporary and classical sociology, there remain some striking contrasts. The foremost of these is the abandonment of confident nineteenth-century expectations as to the inevitability of 'progress'. There is now a far more pessimistic tone to twentieth-century sociological nostalgia. This is especially evident in the so-called critical theory of Frankfurt School writers, such as Horkheimer, Adorno and Habermas. If nineteenth-century social theory was shaped by the aftermath of the French Revolution and then the industrial transformation of Europe, twentieth-century social thought, particularly in the case of the Frankfurt School, has been shaped by global warfare and by the social consequences of fascism. The problem for German social theory was that, given its grounding in the German rational tradition, it was difficult to see how the irrationality of German Nazi society could be explained. What haunted the imagination of the Frankfurt School theorists was the horror of the concentration camps. It was Adorno after all who said that to write poetry after Auschwitz is barbaric. This expression in many ways captures the sense of bitterness which lies at the centre of critical theory and at the heart of its rejection of the claims of instrumental rationality. Twentieth-century social theory appears, therefore, to be shaped by catastrophic global changes, and in particular, those changes associated with mass warfare, nuclear armaments and the systematic extermination of minority groups, such as the Jews in Europe or the aboriginal peoples of the Third World.

There are strong associations between Weber's notion of a rationally ordered society, Adorno's notion of the administered society and Foucault's concept of the panoptic system. These pessimistic views of bureaucracy tend to imply the moral value of a pre-bureaucratic society, characterised by immediacy, spontaneity and affectual social relations. In other words, bureaucratic society stands in direct opposition to the notion of community, where community is based upon shared common values, interpersonal direct relationships and a notion of historic continuity with the past. The critique of society implicit in the work of Weber, Adorno and Foucault suggests a reluctance, or even an incapacity, to come to terms with a society based upon *Gesellschaft* relations. Modern society, based upon such a notion of *Gesellschaft*, is the very embodiment of that instrumental rationality which these theorists saw as incompatible with human existence, at least a human existence based upon a meaningful notion of life.

By criticising mass society, writers like Adorno often appeared highly elitist and withdrawn from contemporary politics. It is also well known that Marcuse assumed that working-class politics were no longer possible in the modern world, and Marcuse sought alternative outlets for a revolutionary and radical activity. In some respects, therefore, Marcuse shared a cultural elitism with writers like Adorno and Horkheimer.

Cultural pessimism and melancholic elitism are perhaps two indicators of the increasing incoherence of the classical nineteenth-century project, insofar as this involved the rejection of key modern western values like individualism and pluralism. Another such indicator is the fate of the concept of 'community' itself. It is particularly striking that the unit-idea regarded by Nisbet as 'unquestionably the most distinctive development in nineteenth century social thought' should have become so refractory to agreed definition in twentieth-century discourse (Bell and Newby, 1974, p. x(iii)). While still part of the rhetoric of moral philosophy and democratic politics, the notion of community increasingly appears as a residual melange of spatial, structural, cultural and emotional components. This is symptomatic of the value-pluralism of modern western society wherein the nostalgia of nineteenth-century sociology appears increasingly redundant.

The confrontation of modern value-pluralism and individualism, with notions of *Gemeinschaft*, however, presents two intellectual options. On the one side lies the re-affirmation of community founded on deep emotional and moral bonds between human actors conceived in terms of what is called 'wholes'. The primary justification for this stance is the moral disorder and imprecision diagnosed in value-pluralism and individual sovereignty in moral choices. Alasdair MacIntyre (1981), in a powerful and courageous statement of this position, reverses as it were the charges made against the sociological coherence of the notion of community. For him it is 'value-pluralism' that constitutes an 'unharmonious melange of ill-assorted fragments', shored up by 'surface rhetoric'. Community, on the other hand, can be re-discovered as an authentic moral standpoint only by rejecting the Enlightenment, and returning to the classical conception of communal virtues and human teleology systematised by Aristotle. In the confrontation between value-pluralism and community MacIntyre turns his face steadfastly against the Enlightenment rationalism, which claims that there can be no rational basis for morality. MacIntyre is against modernity and its 'moral philosopher', Nietzsche, and for nostalgia.

The confrontation of value-pluralism and *Gemeinschaft* need not, however, be resolved through appeals to a backward-looking moral philosophy. The pursuit of nostalgia is not the only option available by which to face the apparently pessimistic or amoral implications of rationalisation and disenchantment. An alternative option is to consider the possibility that *Gesellschaft* permits authentic expressions of values, rather than the 'false', or 'fetishised' forms of consciousness as diagnosed by exponents of the Frankfurt School. In addition, value-pluralism under *Gesellschaft* need be considered neither as a series of private narcissistic worlds, in retreat from the public domain, nor as an irreducible battle of Nietzschian wills. Rather it can be conceived as generating a normative basis for the orderly resolution of pluralism and diversity. The underlying thesis of this study is that the sociology of Talcott Parsons represents a decisive step, both beyond classical sociology, and beyond the 'Aristotle' and 'Nietzsche' options in moral philosophy, in his elaboration of this essentially modern social order.

Compared with the sociologists of the classical period, Parsons is far less ambivalent about the modern world. The evaluative yardstick of 'community' does not appear in a strong form – whether as utopia or social ontology – as a moral foil to such modern developments as instrumental rationality, or individual achievement-orientation. Parsons is neither equivocal with respect to the operation of the market economy, political democracy and the rule of law, nor tortured by pessimistic doubts as to the possibility of a future world based on humanitarian values.

For some critics, Parsons is thereby dismissed as a commentator on the modern world. This is both for his apparent insensitivity to the casualties of capitalism and for his complacency in the face of the nuclear arms race and ecological crisis. At best Parsons seems complacent, at worst morally blind.

Such impressions are, however, largely misplaced. In the first place, Parsons' twentieth-century optimism reflects a profoundly moral and political identification with liberal democratic values, such as equality of opportunity and personal autonomy. Since a number of his critics seem incapable of distinguishing between 'liberalism' and 'conservatism', it is important to emphasise that Parsons cannot be regarded as a spokesman for the 'New Right'. The political implications of Parsons' liberalism include identification with the New Deal, the championing of negro rights (Parsons and Clark, 1966), and hostility to McCarthyism and religious fundamentalism.

Some of Parsons' optimism about the future of liberal-democratic politics seems faded and even anachronistic in the face of unease about the military and ecological consequences of superpower conflict. It is nonetheless very striking how far modern social movements for peace, environmental protection and women's rights have drawn, however unwittingly, upon the liberal-democratic legacy. This includes the emphasis on popular sovereignty in decision-making and on the establishment of social conditions which will maximise the personal autonomy of the individual (Feher and Heller, 1984).

A second element in Parsons' sociology is his rejection of the dubious sociological assumptions that lie behind political romanticism. For Parsons the emergent features of modern society, including value pluralism and political democracy, lend no credence to the eschatological view that social problems can be solved through some decisive redemptive structural change, able to release some essential communitarian quality in human nature. For Parsons the critique of existing institutions in terms of some absolutist Utopian morality is founded on some version of the doctrine of an underlying harmony of interests. This flies in the face of the heterogeneous individualism characteristic of modern society. Within Parsons' framework, there is neither room for the patrician assumption that 'non-transcendent' social practices are the work of cultural dupes, nor any place for such elitist categories as 'false consciousness'. In this sense Parsons' normative commitment to modernity is both democratic and plebeian.

Thirdly, Parsons is not an apologist for that kind of crass economic individualism that is often taken to underlie the capitalist economy. Rather, in developing Durkheim's insights into the non-contractual basis of contract, he seeks to elaborate much further the value inputs and normative rules that regulate economic life and prevent the unilateral operation of a utilitarian social order. Such rules are not located in the nostalgic communitarian civic rituals or guild-like occupational corporations that Durkheim emphasised. Instead they are given an individualistic, yet morally-informed, construction within such institutions as the work ethic and the extension of 'trust' in relations between savers, investors and producers. Such normative relations are seen to underlie the impersonality and instrumental character of economic relations.

The point here is not that the modern western economy is presented as a conflict-free mechanism always tending to benign equilibrium. It is rather that the inter-penetration of economic and moral individualism in relations between economy and society renders inadmissible any exclusively instrumental or coercive picture of modern economic life. Power relations are seen as fundamental to such relations, as are political collectivities, wherein goals are promoted and resources made available. Yet power is seen as enabling, rather than as an unchecked coercive force emanating from a single location.

In this way Parsons seeks to deny both the utilitarian Utopia of Robinson Crusoe and the negative critique of capitalist alienation from the viewpoint of the community of free producers that underlies the labour theory of value. In opposition to such nostalgic Utopias he presents the emergent structure of the modern economy, more especially the differentiation between producers and consumers, savers and investors, or employers and workers, as functional both to the normatively regulated achievement of a plurality of projects and to social integration. The increasing socialisation of production and consumption, characteristic of the modern economy, renders notions of the pre-social individual or the holistic free producer equally obsolete as romantic fictions. Parsons emerges from most confrontations with his critics as both morally engaged and politically committed, not as an apologist for capitalism, but as an anti-elitist and anti-Utopian social theorist. This standpoint moves us beyond the ambivalence of the classical sociologists towards modernity, in that Parsons unsentimentally rejects the nostalgic foils of *Gemeinschaft* or social Utopia, on which the various classic critiques of alienated labour, rationalisation and *Gesellschaft* depended. While it is obvious that his social theory emerged through a critical commentary on his classical forebears, he does not share their preoccupation with the transitional problems involved in the emergence of capitalism, industrialism and democratisation. Parsons' sociology is much more a post-classical reflection on the problems of individualism in contemporary western society, the emergence of equal rights in societies dominated by social stratification and the question of bureaucratic efficiency in relation to individual wants and needs. While he retains a sense of the 'social community' as the foundation of normative order, this term is used in a highly pluralistic and diffuse, rather than unitary and absolutist, manner. In all these respects Parsons' social theory announces the end of the classical phase of sociological thought.

The transition from classical to post-classical sociology itself reflects a shift in the cultural and political terrain of sociological thought from Europe to America. Whereas nineteenth-century sociology was shaped by an analysis of the 'great transformation' experienced by European society in the epoch of the Industrial and French Revolutions, this pattern of change was not reproduced in American historical development. Lacking a traditionalistic and feudal background, the development of American society posed rather different questions for American sociology. The historic weakness of Marxism and the continuing vitality of liberal-democratic thought within the United States represent an intellectual context significantly different from that which has prevailed in Europe for much of the last 100 years.

For Parsons, the preoccupation of European sociological thought with questions like the fate of capitalism and the politics of class represents a concern with transitional features of the great transformation, rather than with modern society itself. While capitalism has been supplanted by the differentiation between ownership and management, the continuing emphasis on class relations looks back to the past. Parsons sees the underlying normative basis of working-class and capitalist solidarity as a perpetuation of the traditional *Gemeinschaft* orientations of the European peasantry and aristocracy respectively. American society, by contrast, has emphasised the liberation of individuals, emotionally as well as politically, from communitarian bonds founded on ascriptive and particularistic bases. At the same time a sufficiently generalised set of norms has been developed to produce social order. Parsons' theory of social change is quite unequivocal about the contemporary significance of the USA, as having taken over the role of 'leading sector' in modernisation, a role previously located in seventeenth- and eighteenth-century Europe (Parsons, 1971).

The belief that the USA rather than Europe holds the key to the future of modern society is clearly not a novel one. Nineteenth-century social theorists such as de Tocqueville appreciated the extent to which American democracy represented a qualitative extension of the principles currently underlying revolutionary changes in Europe. At the same time much European scholarship has continued to treat the USA more as a 'deviant' case of western development than as a lead sector in social change. Part of the devaluation of the United States as a developmental model has built on an elitist disdain for domestic American phenomena such as mass consumerism, and the cultivation of the individual personality and body. Although such trends have been evident in European society for many years, they still remain disprivileged within the primarily 'classical' preoccupations of contemporary sociological inquiry.

The European critique of 'Americanism' has depended in large measure on the elevation of various cultural and political traditions within Europe to the status of more universalistic and 'civilised' alternatives. For some the lack of a mass socialist movement or Labour Party in the USA has hitherto been taken as indicative of American 'deviance' from a more general model of social change in the western world. The French uprising of 1968 did more to perpetuate belief in a socialist future achieved through proletarian revolution than any event since the inter-war Depression. This vision is now increasingly discredited, even amongst some of its previous proponents. While the French uprising stands more or less alone in recent European history as a quasi-revolutionary challenge to the existing order, radical French social theorists themselves now speak of the demise of the 'culture of industrialism' and bid 'adieu' to the working class (Touraine, 1981; Gorz, 1982). While Labour governments continue to be elected from time to time, it appears they must capture much of the 'middle-ground' to do so. This involves support for the rule of law above class interest, for parliamentary democracy, a mixed economy and a recognition of the 'private' as well as 'public' interests of citizens. The British Labour Party is probably the most 'conservative' and least 'radical' among western Labour movements in espousing Marxism, at a point in time when most other movements have come to accept the incompatibility of traditional conceptions of socialism with the emergent features of modern society. In such respects Europe appears to be converging (however unevenly) with the political experience of those western societies which lack a feudal status-ridden past, such as the USA and Australia.

Another component of the European critique of Americanism has been the emphasis on certain ascribed characteristics of European national cultures, which are given elevated and privileged status. It is noteworthy that such arguments usually depend on an emotional appeal to nation and national symbols. One component of this is the resistance to what is taken to be national language debasement as a result of imported American culture, which is taken to result in an impoverishment of sensibility and civility.

Nationalism of course remains a profound political force. In this context it is somewhat ironic to find French Marxist intellectuals, such as Debray (1977, p. 41), defending an ascriptive view of the motherland, 'la patrie', as a force making in some mystical way for the liberation of all oppressed people. This contrasts, at an ideological level at least, with the rational claim of American liberal-democratic pluralism to represent a universalistic, multi-cultural, non-ascriptive basis for political freedom.

Parsons' construction of a theory of modernity and social change, based on the universalistic evolutionary advantages located in western, and more especially twentieth-century American institutions, has been criticised as an apologia for American liberalism and the sectional interests of American imperialism. There are several elements to this challenge.

The first is that American liberal values have been overtaken by the development of a coercive military-industrial complex. This guarantees neither real personal autonomy to the American poor and unemployed nor freedom to the Third World. In foreign policy the universalistic logic of liberal-democratic pluralism and respect for the international rule of law has not always been uppermost in relations between nation-states in Europe and elsewhere. At least part of the European critique, of 'Americanism', rests on the perceived threat to national sovereignty posed by the military and economic institutions of the super-power (Servan-Shreiber, 1968). While liberal-democratic theory has always been faced with the dilemma of how far to use illiberal measures in defence of liberalism, the charge is that American imperialism has been structurally organised on an illiberal basis. The plausibility of Parsons' case for the USA as a universalistic lead sector in an international context is therefore seen as far more problematic than he realised.

A second line of criticism is that the alleged advantages of America's universalistic institutions have not been confirmed by the expected convergence of non-Western societies to the American model. The main problem here is the stability of the USSR. While exhibiting a certain economic dynamic, Parsons' expectation was that the undemocratic Soviet political system would prove 'unstable' (Parsons, 1971). Without the capacity of democratic societies to institutionalise individual goals and hence obtain political consent and loyalty, Parsons expected social and political instability. In this situation the options for the Soviet Union were either a convergence to the western world, or continuing instability and collapse. While 'national' resistance to Soviet domination has produced massive convulsions in Eastern Europe, the instability Parsons forecast for the Soviet Union has not eventuated.

A third more general challenge to Parsons' America-centred theory of social change is its apparent perpetuation of nineteenth-century emphases on the endogenous causes of social change within nation-states (Smith, 1973). Such a focus is problematic insofar as it neglects problems of inter-state relations and the impact of exogenous forces on social development. These include war and invasion, as well as less coercive forms of cultural diffusion, all of which have played a significant part in the global politics of the twentieth century.

While it is beyond the scope of this study to evaluate these criticisms in any empirical depth, it is possible to confirm the *prima facie* plausibility of Parsons' emphasis on the USA as a 'lead sector', against most of the charges made against him.

In the first place, there are major difficulties with views which wish to assimilate the American nation-state to the worldwide hegemonic interests of a military-industrial complex. One problem with this argument is the reductionism involved in claiming America to be a unitary political economic entity. For Arato and Cohen (1982), on the other hand, there is not one but 'two Americas'. The first is 'the republican liberal-democratic core', whose commitment to the rule of law and a free public sphere (including a free press) represents a highly legitimate and sometimes effective check on tendencies towards corruption, intimidation and arbitrary power within domestic politics. This critical public sphere is, however, conjoined to American imperialism – the other America. American imperialist involvement in 'totalitarian methods of lawless administrative-military rule' are especially evident outside the United States. Whereas Marxist political economists like Mandel (1970) have analysed relations between Europe and America simply in terms of the relative power of two imperialist blocs, the theory of two 'Americas' permits a more complex analysis of internal as well as international political and cultural characteristics.

Although functionalism has often been criticised for presenting a picture of the social system as a seamless web of interconnected institutions, in his empirical essays and shorter commentaries on American society Parsons showed that he was perfectly aware of the tensions, conflicts and strains within American capitalism. These strains were often treated in a rather conventional way, as the gap between the speed of social development and the adaptive capacity of existing institutions. The problem was thus conceptualised via Durkheim as a strain between economic individualism and moral (or institutionalised) individualism. However, Parsons also drew upon T. H. Marshall to argue that there was in modern industrial society an uneasy tension between the *political* principles of egalitarian democracy and the *economic* inequality of the market place (Parsons, 1965; Parsons, 1970). Although Parsons did not develop the theme, the relative institutional separation of economic and political realms in capitalism is crucial for the development of political opposition and social critique. Parsons did not espouse a two-Americas theory, but he was, by borrowing from Marshall, aware of the contradiction between democratic universalism and economic inequality as a necessary feature of free-market economies. Similarly, Parsons did not address the problem of the impact of American economic expansion on peripheral societies within the sphere of American political influence. It may be that the growth of the core economies requires the exploitation and subordination of both external and internal colonies. A reply to critics of US foreign policy and trade is possible through, for example, Barrington Moore's concept of 'predatory democracy', developed in his sensitive and humane study *Reflections on the Causes of Human Misery* (Moore, 1970).

Within this framework Parsons' arguments about American universalism seem far stronger in relation to the 'republican liberal-democratic core', than within the international imperialist domain. US support for totalitarian regimes within the Third World cannot easily be reconciled with pluralistic conceptions of liberal-democratic norms, especially where the regimes in question show no signs of long-term liberalisation. Arato and Cohen (1982), drawing on the analysis of Arendt (1958), have nonetheless argued that the liberal-democratic legacy has, paradoxically, been an important factor in the articulation of anti-imperialist resistance in the Third World. This western legacy, according to Arendt, exerts a countervailing check on western imperialism in a way that is not possible in the far more monolithic political structures of the Soviet empire. Here the core nation is itself dominated by a totalitarianism offering no legitimation for resistance. Accordingly, the dissident movements in Eastern Europe look elsewhere, to indigenous nationalist or religious sources or to the west for alternative bases of legitimacy.

It is also important to emphasise that the logic of Parsons' system of evolutionary universals is in large measure transnational. The emergence of the nation-state distinct from particularistic religious commitments is of course seen as a major element in the universalistic thrust of the modern world. Since the basis for normative order has remained national in scope, for the most part, Parsons conducts his analysis of social change in terms of the characteristics and performance of national units. While there is no absolutist commitment to American values on the basis of ascriptive allegiance, Parsons nonetheless accords utmost significance to the universalistic institutions located within the nation-state. Beyond this, however, Parsons goes on to consider, albeit relatively briefly, the development of an international normative order and its relationship to nation-states. Here he welcomes international organisations like the United Nations, the development of a non-aligned group of nations outside the super-power blocs, and the development of a cross-cutting system of international links which presages the end of a sharply polarised international order (Parsons, 1967). In this way his commitment to America as the leading sector in modernity is not to be read as an apology for the entire course of recent American history. What is most noticeably lacking in all of this is an adequate explanation of the symbolic resilience of the ascriptive international politics of nation-states.

The problematic standing of Soviet Russia in Parsons' theory of social change also warrants further discussion. As already indicated, the confident assumption that the lack of a political democracy would generate instabilities in the Soviet system has not so far proved accurate. Against Parsons' prognoses of Soviet convergence with the west, or of retrogression, Russia has managed to deny both political pluralism and economic freedom of choice for consumers, and yet to have secured effective compliance with the massive post-war expansion of Russian global military power. Failing the collapse of this edifice, it is unclear whether the liberal-democratic pluralism of the USA represents the only road to modernity, as measured in terms of geo-political super-power status. This in turn raises a more general problem with Parsons' social change theory, namely that 'de-differentiation' may be an authentic route to those kinds of evolutionary advantage over the environment and the organisation of social order that he associates only with differentiation.

The 'success' of the Soviet Union in this respect may at one level pose even greater challenges to Marxist social theory than it does for Parsons' meta-theoretical framework. David Lane (1981), for example, has used a modified version of Parsons' four-function paradigm to analyse those features of the Russian revolutionary experience that are neglected in Marxist accounts of the Soviet Union which seek to define this system as some variant of a mode of production, e.g. state capitalism, bureaucratic workers' state, etc. These neglected features include 'culture and values, patterns of integration, and politics as effective goal-attainment'. Lane defines the system-needs of the Soviet Union, as interpreted by the Bolsheviks and subsequent Party Leaders, not only as an upgrading of the adaptive resources of society (or in Marxist terms the productive forces), through a centralised goal-attainment system (i.e. the dictatorship of the proletariat managed by the party), but also as a high level of integration and value-generalisation. The latter needs were secured by a mixture of terror and penal sanctions, together with ideological legitimation, through the translation of Marxism-Leninism into traditional Russian values.

There has been much debate in post-war Marxism over the role of dominant ideologies in western capitalist societies, where these ideologies are thought either to integrate the society, or to incorporate the working class, or to limit the range of perceived alternatives to capitalism (Abercrombie, Hill and Turner, 1980). This debate can be seen as a feature of the exchange between Daniel Bell and his critics over the relationship between culture, polity and economics in advanced capitalist societies (Bell, 1976). Bell's thesis is that the cultural system has been uncoupled from the economy and polity; the emphasis on self-gratification in modernist cultures is no longer closely related to the requirements of efficiency in economic matters. There is thus a contradiction between the disciplines of work, and the hedonism of cultural expression. By contrast, Parsons typically assumed a much closer and more systematic relationship between culture and the economic system, although there is much debate as to whether he was committed to a theory of dominant cultures, and thus presented a mirror-image to the Marxist notion of dominant ideology (Lechner, 1984). Parsons' views on American social experience become problematic in other case studies, because American pluralism was based on a relative separation of economy and polity.

Lane's conclusion is that Parsons' social theory, while more adequately multi-dimensional than Marxism, is nonetheless founded on an illegitimate extrapolation of a general theory of the reciprocal inter-change between social sub-systems and the relatively pluralistic American experience. The example of the Soviet Union suggests an alternative basis to the integration of the social system. Above all else, modern Russia lacks the differentiated inter-relation between sub-systems found in western society. In the Soviet case the goal-attainment function remains predominant and is intimately linked to the adaptive economic functions. Links between the pattern-maintenance sub-system and the goal-attainment sub-system, involving value-commitment to the 'legality of power of office' are in consequence weak. The same applies to the connection between the pattern-maintenance sub-system and the adaptive sub-system in terms of the articulation and satisfaction of consumer wants. Lane's conclusion is that Parsons' general analytical apparatus may be used to demonstrate the possibility of different solutions to the problem of reconciling social change with social order, than those which have emerged in the West. What is less clear from his argument is the relative importance of what might be called the 'American' and 'Soviet' roads in the global evolution of modern societies.

There are two ways of assessing this problem. The first is to consider whether Western trends lead elsewhere than Parsons expected. Here, as already indicated, Parsons' vision of a pluralistic liberal-democratic *Gesellschaft* tied together by inclusive universalistic citizenship rights seems more plausible than a future based on the recreation of traditional *Gemeinschaft*, whether in socialist or Communist garb. There also appears some reason to doubt that the spectre of a bureaucratic or corporatist iron cage, riven with system-crises, is inexorably present. Against this prospect may be cited the fiscal and electoral limits to state expansionism, the continuing resilience of private consumerism, and the contemporary vitality of associational politics, including the politics of resistance to militarism and bureaucratisation. There has been massive state intervention in the economy and the growing dominance of multinational corporations, but there has also been a remarkable continuity and resilience of small business. Both left- and right-wing political parties in western capitalism have been supporting small business as a sector of the economy which can innovate and reduce unemployment. It is also the case that capitalism requires an entrepreneurial function which cannot be satisfied by efficient bureaucracy and economic planning. Political leadership and economic entrepreneurship are parallel activities; the absence of effective leadership, rather than the dominance of impersonal bureaucracy, is the critical problem in western democracies (Eden, 1983). The iron cage may not be the most appropriate metaphor for the analysis of modern democracies, since there are various conditions and processes which point in the opposite direction.

The moral here is not benign optimism, since as Parsons pointed out modern society remains faced with problems of 'intense alienation' in many groups, by lack of stability in the motivational bases of social solidarity, and the threat of nuclear destruction (Parsons, 1971). It is rather the striking capacity of liberal-democratic societies to meet a multiplicity of diffuse aspirations, by relatively stable processes of inclusion or incorporation, which maximise efficiency, individual freedom, innovation and integration. In contrast to fashionable Doomsday predictions, Parsons' argument implies that problems such as stagflation or technological change can be managed without abandonment of liberal-democratic pluralism, though not without social conflict. If there is a spectre haunting Europe, it is neither Communism nor the iron cage. The best we can hope for is individual freedom and the politics of reform, but this is in itself no guarantee against nuclear war.

While Parsons' evolutionary universals remain plausible as a statement of the continuing trajectory of social change in the west, the problem of 'American' versus 'Soviet' roads to modernity is more complex when applied to the non-western world.

In the first place the shift from ascriptive and particularistic towards more universalistic liberal-democratic institutions outside Europe and the western world is at best uneven and at worst precarious. Japan is of course important as the first major case of successful modernisation in a large non-western society. While possessing certain internal developmental advantages such as an integrated political system, the dynamic for Japan's development has increasingly come to be dominated by 'borrowed' western elements, involving a shift from patrimonial bureaucratic organisation in government and business toward democratic parliamentary institutions and individual achievement-orientation. Set against Japan, however, are a range of Third World countries that have either borrowed large elements of the centralised Soviet model, such as Cuba and Vietnam, or promoted relatively dynamic processes of social change on an ascribed, relatively undifferentiated basis, as in the resurgent Islamic societies like Pakistan, Malaysia and Iran.

In the face of this complexity, the recent history of post-Maoist China offers some indication that the Soviet route to modernity may be less typical of Third World socialism than has hitherto been thought. Maoism, while hostile to capitalism, individualism and a market economy, undoubtedly deviated from orthodox Soviet development strategies in its hostility to bureaucratisation, its commitment to mass political mobilisation and its conception of revolutionary society as conflictual not harmonious. While Maoism has itself been depicted as 'market socialism', policy changes since the death of Mao and the demise of the Gang of Four have introduced a much less ambiguous shift towards western conceptions of development. These have included the differentiation of economic goals, such as productivity and efficiency, from political and ideological controls, whether these stem from Soviet-like bureaucratic sources or from the mobilised peasant *Gemeinschaft* of Maoism. These changes in planning mechanisms have been associated with a trend towards consumer privatisation and pluralism in the economy, and a commitment to the rule of law and independence of the judiciary (Gray, 1982).

It would certainly be premature on the basis of this evidence to argue for the inexorable convergence of post-Maoist China with Parsons' western 'evolutionary universals'. China still retains a high degree of centralised planning and authority outside a democratic framework. On the other hand, recent developments do lend plausibility to the argument that non-western modes of social change may not, after all, be quite so refractory to Parsons' discussion as certain of his earlier critics believed. Parsons' evolutionary universals remain a fruitful addition to the repertoire of social change theory, even when non-western developmental patterns are brought into consideration.

The most serious difficulty with Parsons' argument lies not at the level of convergent 'evolutionary universals' within leading nation-states, but at the level of inter-state relations. Parsons shares with his nineteenth-century forebears the tendency to consider change, in most cases as the product of the endogenous history of nation-states, supplemented only residually by diffusionist connections between one national unit and another. The neglect of exogenous influences that this approach entails (Smith, 1973) may be seen as a serious deficiency in the light of international economic and political relationships that transcend national limits. The recent development of Wallerstein's 'world system' theory (Wallerstein, 1974, 1980) and the revival of interest in international geo-politics (Mann, 1984) are in large measure post-Parsonian responses to the inadequacies of endogenous nation-state analysis. While the nation-state and nationalist allegiance remain extremely resilient, phenomena such as international capital movements by multinational companies, or the concentration of international political domination within two inter-locking super-powers, both suggest that the fate of most national units is determined to a large extent exogenously.

Parsons' social change theory may at first sight seem doubly disqualified from intervening in such debates. This is both because of its 'national endogenous' bias, and its tendency to look for a reciprocal basis to inter-changes between different elements within a social system. This logic is somewhat easier to locate in domestic intra-state relations, where 'social order' is deemed functionally necessary, than in international relations between economic or political collectivities, operating outside any 'societal community, yet which possess large measures of coercive power'.

There is of course no logical reason why Parsons' social system framework need be restricted to the internal operation of nation-states. While this may be testimony to the robustness of the formal specifications of the general theory of action and social systems, whatever the setting, it is clear that the problem of international relations and international order is very much 'residual' to the main thrust of his theory of change. However we should also note that a number of sociologists are concerned to develop Parsonian sociology towards a theory of international systems which would focus on the emergence of various forms of inter-societal culture. For example, there is some evidence of a certain 'globalisation' of culture above the system of nation-states (Nettl and Robertson, 1968; Robertson, 1982). The issue here is to construct a sociological model of global culture which would be analogous to the Wallersteinian concept of 'world-system'. Although Parsonian sociology was initially focussed on the nation-state as a social system, Parsons' sociology can be developed at a more general level as a perspective on modernisation as a supra-national process.

The revival of neo-evolutionary optimism among Parsons and his American colleagues occurred at that somewhat fleeting and atypical historical moment in the late 1950s and early 1960s when the epoch of world war, fascism and capitalist collapse seemed past, and contemporary preoccupations such as the threat of nuclear war, ecological disaster and Third World famine were yet to be widely thematised. In addition, the first round of challenges to Parsonian evolutionary optimism tended to focus on domestic instabilities and conflicts connected with student radicalism and racial violence in the USA, that is on 'internal war', more than upon international disorder. In spite of events like the Cuban missile crisis of 1962, such domestic preoccupations have only subsequently become subsumed in questions of world politics.

While international relations do not feature in his key article 'Evolutionary universals' (Parsons, 1964), they are addressed at more length in the paper 'Polarisation of the world and international order' (Parsons, 1967) and more fleetingly in 'On the concept of political power' (Parsons, 1963) and in 'The system of modern societies' (Parsons, 1971). Here an attempt is made to cut through the fatalistic assumptions underlying much contemporary comment on world politics by adducing rational arguments in support of the emergent possibility of an international normative order. The problem here is couched in terms of the transcendence of the national territorial boundaries wherein commitments to normative order are generally contained. Having recognised that recourse to coercion has 'almost from time immemorial' been an 'endemic feature of relations between organised political systems', Parsons enumerates a number of possible indicators of an emergent, if rather vulnerable, international normative order. These include the ideological dimension of super-power conflict which presupposes a common frame of reference wherein differences make sense, the relative success of procedural norms for conflict resolution in international trade and international law with respect to persons, and the creation during the twentieth century of institutions like the United Nations for the first time in history. The further extension of these developments is incorporated within his discussion of evolutionary universals, by emphasis on the pluralistic rather than absolutist basis of political values, and on compromise rather than rigid commitment to final goals. While referring to the positive potential of non-aligned or neutral nations in undermining political absolutism, Parsons conceives of change very largely in terms of the triumph of western pluralism over the Soviet monolith. However, he does concede the importance of minimising the self-righteous implication that only we are true to these values, while our opponents are not!

It is not clear from this analysis how often and for what reasons the west might not have been true to its own values. Parsons evades the paradox at the heart of liberal-democratic theory whereby 'illiberal' measures are justified as means of protecting liberalism from its illiberal opponents. The possibility that the illiberal defence of liberalism may become an apologetic myth for illiberalism itself is not discussed. For all this, Parsons' specification of the social preconditions for international order is symptomatic of what has been seen as the characteristically twentieth-century commitment to simultaneous support for the 'freedom' and continuing 'life' of the human species (Feher and Heller, 1984). Since his death, the development of mass peace movements can be interpreted as manifestations of a new ultimate value of novel historical significance. For Roth (1984), support for 'peace' as the precondition for the survival of the human species and society, transcends both the salvation concerns of religious virtuosi and the political Utopias of revolutionaries. Peace movements may thereby be seen acting, in Parsonian terms, as 'steps in value-generalisation'. They presage a pluralistic international order free from the ascriptive politics of nationalism.

Although the lack of a sociology of the international order represents a major absence in Parsons' social change theory, it is arguable that Parsonian neo-evolutionary optimism represents a decisive advance beyond the two faces of classical sociology. Its modern character is to be seen both in the challenge to the Utopian mode of nineteenth-century evolutionary optimism, seeking to regenerate community around some version of the myth of *Gemeinschaft*, and to twentieth-century cultural pessimism in the face of privatised individualistic *Gesellschaft*. In contrast to Marx' eschatalogical stance towards the Communist future, Weber's stoic resignation in the face of the iron cage, and the Frankfurt School's despair at consumer society, Parsons accepts what he takes to be the universalistic thrust of modern society. This notion of universalism is grounded as much in a normative commitment to liberal-democratic pluralism, as in empirical analysis, but such normative elements are a crucial feature of all theories of social change. Pre-suppositionless, normatively irrelevant sociology is neither possible nor worth having.

Parsons' project does not involve subsuming the individual and private life under communitarian virtues akin to those of the ancient city-states, peasant village-life, or medieval guilds. Nor does Parsons expect the withering away of private property, bureaucratic administration or social conflict. Rather his evolutionism accepts the functional significance and integrity of modern social institutions. Here he follows the spirit of Durkheim's axiom that 'No persistent social practice can rest upon a lie'. What such institutions as the market, the rule of law, bureaucracy and political democracy have in common is their attempt to balance public equality of opportunity and reciprocity in exchange with diverse individual and associational 'ends'.

This is not to resurrect those rather crass versions of convergence theory in which free market capitalism is seen as the universal future for humankind. Parsons, in his critique of utilitarian economics, denies that an unregulated free market system devoid of extra-economic normative constraints could produce a stable social order. There is in other words no evolutionary advantage to social systems constructed on the basis of the unilateral domination of the free market. To think in these terms is to sacrifice social integration and distributive justice to productive efficiency. From this viewpoint Parsonian sociology might be utilised as the basis of a critique of the New Right programme of monetarism and the pursuit of welfare through the reconstitution of the traditional family. Parsons' 'evolutionary universals' are more consistent with Keynesian macro-economic planning within a mixed economy and positive legislative programmes to combat ascriptive inequalities, than with Chicago School economics and fundamentalist attempts to privatise welfare and de-secularise education. In this respect his prognoses for the American 'lead sector' in modernisation underestimated the possibility of the emergence of movements like the New Right.

Parsons' evolutionary optimism is muted, in the sense that he offers no utopian projection of social equilibrium in which social strains and conflict can ever be overcome. In this sense he is a more thorough-going conflict theorist than Marx. Although Parsons sometimes writes as if modernity were an endpoint which had actually been reached in the universalistic institutions of the western world, the formal characteristics of his differentiation-reintegration model of change point rather to modernity as an open-ended process of ever-enlarged evolutionary capacity. It should also be emphasised that this model is not unilinear in the sense that there is no expectation that all societies must inevitably follow one sequence of change. The presence of a functional advantage within a social institution gives no guarantee that the institution will always be preferred.

Parsons' sociology is therefore against nostalgia, for the modern world, and unambiguously post-classical. Unlike Weber, he did not believe that questions of value and morality would remain totally refractory to solution, given the value-conflict basic to secular society. Instead he developed a form of liberal secular Protestantism geared especially to the needs of American culture. It was his confidence in the possibility of moral debate which prevented a premature pessimistic conclusion to his thought. Parsons' legacy is therefore one which avoids on the one hand the dilemmas of pessimistic relativism and on the other avoids the problem of a purely scientific view of reality, that is a scientific view grounded in a simple positivism. Parsons provides us with a comprehensive and general theory of social action and modernity which has coherence, plausibility and relevance to moral and political choices and activism. Parsons' sociology picks out for us a range of critical issues in such fields as economic sociology, education, sociology of knowledge, modernisation, professions, medical sociology and social change which need further elaboration and investigation. He also offers a general framework within which all of this can be conceptualised. Our evaluation of Parsons provides ample basis for abandoning the attitude of critical aloofness which has so often characterised approaches to his social thought. It also invites sociologists to move beyond exegesis towards the further extension and critique of the Parsonian research programme. Parsons' legacy is rich and immensely stimulating. It is a legacy worth embracing.

References

Abercrombie, N., Hill, S. and Turner, B. S. (1980), *The Dominant Ideology Thesis*, London: Allen & Unwin.
Althusser, L. (1969), *For Marx*, Harmondsworth: Penguin Books.
Arato, A. and Cohen, J. (1982), 'The Peace Movement and Western European Sovereignty', *Telos*, vol. 51, pp. 158–71.
Arendt, H. (1958), *The Origins of Totalitarianism*, London: Allen & Unwin.
Bell, C. and Newby, H. (eds) (1974), *The Sociology of Community*, London: Cass.
Bell, D. (1976), *The Cultural Contradictions of Capitalism*, London: Heinemann.
Brubaker, R. (1984), *The Limits of Rationality*, London: Allen & Unwin.
Debray, R. (1977), 'Marxism and the Nation', *New Left Review*, vol. 105, pp. 25–41.
Eden, R. (1983), *Political Leadership and Nihilism, A Study of Weber and Nietzsche*, Tampa: University of Florida Press.
Feher, F. and Heller, A. (1984), 'From Red to Green', *Telos*, vol. 59, pp. 35–44.
Gorz, A. (1982), *Farewell to the Working Class*, London: Pluto.
Gouldner, A. W. (1980), *The Two Marxisms*, New York: Seabury Press.
Gray, J. (1982), 'Introduction' and 'Conclusion', in J. Gray and G. White (eds), *China's New Development Strategy*, New York: Academic Press.
Hawthorn, G. (1976), *Enlightenment and Despair*, Cambridge: Cambridge University Press.
Lane, D. (1981), *Leninism: A Sociological Interpretation*, Cambridge: Cambridge University Press.
Lechner (1984), 'Parsons and the Common Culture Thesis', *Theory, Culture and Society*, vol. 2, pp. 71–84.
MacIntyre, A. (1981), *After Virtue. A Study in Moral Theory*, London: Duckworth.
Mandel, E. (1970), *Europe versus America? Contradictions of Imperialism*, London: New Left Books.
Mann, M. (1984), 'Capitalism and Militarism', in M. Shaw (ed.), *War, State and Society*, London: Macmillan, pp. 25–46.
Moore, B. (1970), *Reflections on the Causes of Human Misery and Upon Certain Proposals to Eliminate Them*, London: Allen Lane.
Nettl, R. and Robertson, R. (1968), *International System and the Modernization of Societies*, New York: Basic Books.
Nisbet, R. (1967), *The Sociological Tradition*, London: Heinemann.
Parsons, T. (1963), 'On the Concept of Political Power', *Proceedings of the American Philosophical Society*, vol. 107 (no. 3), pp. 232–62. Reprinted in *Sociological Theory and Modern Society* (1967). Translated into Italian as 'Il concetto di potere politico', I. *Il Politico* (University of Pavia), vol. 28 (no. 3), pp. 614–36. 'Il concetto di potere politico', II. Ibid. (no. 4), pp. 830–955.
Parsons, T. (1964), 'Evolutionary Universals in Society', *American Sociological Review*, vol. 29 (no. 3), pp. 339–57. Translated into German as 'Evolutionare Universalien der Gesellschaft'. Reprinted in *Essays on Modernization of Underdeveloped Societies*, in A. R. Desai (ed.), Bombay, Thacker, pp. 560–88.
Parsons, T. (1965), 'Full Citizenship for the American Negro?', *Daedalus* (November). Reprinted in Parsons, T. and Clark, K. (eds) (1966), *The American Negro*, Boston: Houghton Mifflin.
Parsons, T. (1967), *Sociological Theory and Modern Society*, New York: Free Press.

Parsons, T. (1970), 'Equality and Inequality in Modern Society, or Social Stratification Revisited', *Sociological Inquiry*, vol. 40 (Spring), pp. 13–72..

Parsons, T. (1971), *The System of Modern Societies*, Englewood Cliffs: Prentice-Hall. Companion volume to *Societies: Evolutionary and Comparative Perspectives* (1966).

Parsons, T. and Clark, K. (eds) (1966), *The Negro American*, Boston: Houghton Mifflin.

Robertson, R. (1982), 'Parsons on the Evolutionary Significance of American Religion', *Sociological Analysis*, vol. 43, pp. 307–26.

Sennett, R. (1977), *The Fall of Public Man*, Cambridge: Cambridge University Press.

Roth, G. (1984), 'Max Weber's Ethics and the Peace Movement Today', *Theory and Society*, vol. 13, pp. 491–511.

Servan-Shreiber, J. J. (1968), *The American Challenge*, London: Hamilton.

Smith, A. D. (1973), *The Concept of Social Change*, London: Routledge & Kegan Paul.

Tawney, R. H. (1960), *Religion and the Rise of Capitalism*, London: Murray.

Touraine, A. (1981), *The Voice and the Eye: An Analysis of Social Movements*, Cambridge: Cambridge University Press.

Wallerstein, I. (1974, 1980), *The Modern World System*, 2 vols, New York: Academic Press.